CW00749758

BRITISH
TIN TOYS

Frontispiece: A collection of British-made biscuit tins by various manufacturers, 1910–1930s

Burnett Express Delivery van, c.1936 (right)

BRITISH TIN TOYS

Including an A–Z of British metal toy makers

Marguerite Fawdry

New Cavendish Books
London

To my grandson, Felix Fawdry

Acknowledgements

This book is based substantially on the records of Pollock's Toy Museum. My primary debt is therefore to the Museum's staff, and especially to Deborah Brown and Gay Warden, for their part in maintaining and developing those records.

In addition, I have had valuable help from individual toy enthusiasts, and from representatives of several toy manufacturing firms, museums and public libraries. Among these I would particularly like to thank the following: Mr and Mrs Colin Baddiell, Mrs Jeanne Burley, Mr Neil Adams, Mr Ian Layne, Mr Peter McAskie, Mr David Pressland, Mr Jeffrey Levitt and Mr Ian Logan, collectors; Mr H Black of Black Ltd, Mr Derek Howard of CMT Ltd, Mr and Mrs H L Kerby of Wells-Brimtoy Ltd, Mr Roger Swinburne-Johnson of Chad Valley Ltd, Mr Marcel Van Cleemput formerly of Mettoy Ltd, and Mr J H Whiston of Metal Box Co. Ltd; Mr Roger Colori of the Vestry House Museum, Walthamstow, and Mrs J Lamara of the Manchester Central Library.

Finally, my gratitude goes to the Museum's accountant, Mary Little, for cheerfully accepting the job of temporary typist.

First edition published in Great Britain by New Cavendish Books – 1990

Design and artwork – Jacky Wedgwood
Editor – Narisa Chakra
Editorial direction – Allen Levy

Phototypeset by Computape (Pickering) Ltd, North Yorkshire
Printed and bound in Hong Kong, under the supervision of Mandarin Offset, London

New Cavendish Books
3 Denbigh Road, London W11 2SJ

ISBN 0 904568 86 5

Front and back illustrations:
Wells-Brimtoy clockwork omnibus, 1936–7 and trolley bus, c.1938

Explanatory notes

Dates of formation and closure of the various firms listed are given where known. Any further information on this subject would be welcomed by the author. Where one date only is given, this indicates that the manufacturer was definitely active at that time, although he or she may have been in production before and after that date.

The symbol * together with a number in italics, indicated that an item, or items by the manufacturer is/are illustrated in colour on a separate page/pages of that number.

Captions: the manufacturer's name is usually given first, printed in bold type. In the appendices, toys are identified by their catalogue number when possible, otherwise by date. Further details about each item can be referred to in the text listings.

Contents

Preface

Several beautifully illustrated books published within the last few years have dealt nostalgically with the tin toys produced in the late 19th and 20th centuries in German, French and American factories. However, with few exceptions, British tin toys are rarely mentioned; and no one, it seems, has asked how it came about that no similar toy industry existed in Britain, although British expertise and technical inventiveness had led the world in the manufacture of tinplate.

Welsh tinplate, exported in the 19th century to the extent of 20,000 crates per year through the port of Hamburg alone, was transformed by poorly paid German workers into toys which ended up on sale in English markets and bazaars. A similar pool of cheap labour existed in England also; but it was engaged for the most part in the manufacture of other kinds of tinplate goods for which there was a more profitable, expanding market.

Yet tin toys were made in England, and it is the purpose of this book to record what is known of those who made and marketed them. This record is preceded by a brief description of the development of the tinplate industry in Britain, and is followed by four appendices which deal in greater detail with seven of the most prominent British tin toy manufacturers – Barringer, Wallis & Manners, Chad Valley, Mettoy and Wells-Brimtoy Ltd – and illustrate some early material relating to British tin toys.

Quite intentionally, the scope of this book reaches beyond the boundaries of its title to include, as so often

occurs in common parlance, metals other than tin, and, in several instances pioneer plastics manufacturers who also used metal are included. Equally, the book mentions but excludes from detailed consideration those companies which are fully covered in other books – notably in those for train and die-cast toy specialists.

One feature of the British toy industry was its reaction and indeed direct connection with the political ebb and flow of the 20th century. Thus pre-1914, the British market was largely supplied by foreign manufacturers, with the notable exception of William Britains, whose famous range of soldiers was exported throughout the world, and Meccano Ltd. The post Great War period was characterised by British manufacturers jumping on the bandwagon of anti-German sentiment, and Hornby Trains, introduced in 1920, were a good example of this reaction.

Later, the political climate in Germany in the 1930s prompted several Jewish proprietors of toy firms such as Bing and Tipp to emigrate to the UK. One of the Bing family was assisted by the family's long-standing connection with W J Bassett-Lowke in the formation of British Trix. Phillip Ullman had left his German Tipp company in 1933 and set up Mettoy in collaboration with Bassett-Lowke's associate, George Winteringham Ltd. Yet another German emigré, Max Reich founded Combex which later was to become part of Dunbee-Combex, Airfix, etc. Britain had by this time seen the creation of some of the largest toy companies in the world such as Lines Bros and Meccano, and in the post-war years, Smith and O'Dells, Lesney and Matchbox Toys.

Apart from William Britains, Corgi and Hornby Hobbies, few large scale toy producers maintain a manufacturing base in the UK, and this book is a fitting tribute to the artistry and invention applied to toys that were – Made in Britain.

Painting and lining at Bassett-Lowke's factory, 1925

INTRODUCTION

Tinplate and Tin Toys

Early uses of tin

Like the granite rocks where it is found, the ore from which tin is smelted is extremely heavy; yet tin is one of the lightest of metals, one of the most fusible and easily worked, and to early man perhaps more valuable than gold or silver. The quest for tin for use in bronze making is at the origin of some of the world's earliest trade routes; tin, like salt, was a commodity needed in many places but found in few. Modern historians may question whether the Phoenicians did in fact sail 3,000 years ago via Cadiz to the shores of Cornwall to buy cargoes of tin; but there is no doubt that tin was being exported in quantity from Cornwall to Marseilles and elsewhere in the Roman Empire before the birth of Christ. Diodorus wrote in 8 BC of the Cornish tin-makers: 'With a great deal of care and labour they dig it out of the ground, and that being rocky the metal is mixed with some veins of earth, out of which they melt the metal and then refine it, then beat it into foursquare pieces like a die. . . . The merchants transport the tin they buy from the inhabitants to France, and for 30 days they carry it in packs on horses' backs through France to the mouth of the Rhone'.

The knowledge of how to add controlled amounts of molten tin to copper so as to make the resultant bronze harder and stronger, yet at the same time easier to cast, was widespread among many cultures. It would appear however that the art of coating other metals with tin was a technique which the Romans learned from the Gauls.

Tinned Roman horse trappings and other ornaments have been found in Dorset and Yorkshire. As in later Anglo-Saxon jewellery, only the visible outsides of these objects were coated; so it would seem that the tin was applied more for its decorative than its protective effect.

It is technically more difficult to tin iron than copper, and tinned ironware is also more perishable; but tinned nails, keys, locks and other small objects dating from the Middle Ages have been found. The manufacture of tinplates – i.e. hammered sheets of iron coated with one or more layers of tin, which could be cut and shaped into all kinds of useful objects – has a more complex history.

In 1240, a Cornishman banished from his native land – perhaps a murderer – discovered in Bohemia rich

Sir Henry James's illustration of a horse carrying blocks of tin

Early mining operations

Major John Hanbury

deposits of tin ore. At some time between then and the 16th century the technique of tinplate manufacturing was mastered. By 1620, the Duke of Saxony had in his turn become privy to these trade secrets, and set up several factories in his domaine. These iron plates were transported by river to other European countries, notably to Hamburg, whence they were shipped to London.

In Crooked Lane, near London Bridge and the Fishmongers' Hall, Elizabethan and later craftsmen worked these imported tinplates into goods for domestic use: candlesticks, tinderboxes, measures, funnels, nutmeg graters, dripping pans and lanterns. Bread and food containers were also made for the Royal Navy and merchant ships. The Guild of Pewterers protested against the Crooked Lane tinmen, declaring that they were counterfeiting and deceiving His Majesty's subjects, and demanding that they be forbidden to make 'candle-sticks, pie plates, chamber pots and other dishes'. But to no avail: the use of pewter tableware gradually declined and went out of fashion, as china, japanned and tin goods gradually became less rare and costly. By 1670, the tinmen of Crooked Lane had obtained their own separate charter.

17–18th century Welsh tinplate

But why import tinplates from Hamburg when tin, iron and charcoal were plentiful in Britain? This is the question that Andrew Yarranton asked as he set about securing influential support for his scheme to start tinplate manufacture. In 1625, together with a competent interpreter and another technical expert, he set out for Leipzig and Dresden on his mission as an industrial spy.

On his return to England, Yarranton made his first attempts at manufacturing tinplate at Pontypool in Monmouthshire. His plates were tested by the Crooked Lane men, who were pleased with them; but

'Cocoanut Shies' biscuit tin for Peek, Frean & Co. 1931,
manufacturer unknown (top)

Gypsy Caravan biscuit tin, probably made by **Hudson, Scott & Sons**
for Chad Valley (bottom)

Fairy House biscuit tin for William Crawford & Sons, 1934, probably made by **Barringer, Wallis & Manners** (top)

Huntley, Boorne & Stevens tank biscuit tin for Huntley & Palmers, 1927 (left)

Racing car biscuit tin for Gray, Dunn & Co. 1928, probably made by **Barringer, Wallis & Manners** (right)

Barringer, Wallis & Manners coronation tin, 1911, and two penny toys, c.1900 (bottom)

Yarranton failed to get the necessary Royal Patent, which was granted at the last moment to an imposter, Edmund Hemming, who let the whole project collapse.

Yarranton's experiments at Pontypool had taken place in the ironworks on the property of the Hanbury family; and in 1720 – the year of the South Sea Bubble – Major John Hanbury decided to make a second attempt at the manufacture of tinplates. A lawyer by training, he was a rich, resourceful and enterprising man. His forges and ironworks were soon producing good quality tinplates.

By 1728, John Hanbury had perfected a new technique which was to revolutionize the whole industry. Instead of hammering the iron sheets to the required thickness and size, his mills at Pontypool rolled them between cylinders, giving them a uniform thickness, a greater pliability, and a better colour than anything produced up till then. Production soared: by 1750, there were four other tinplate works in operation, and by 1800, there were eleven – not all in South Wales.

Tin for food canning

A plaque let into the wall of the Aylwin School for Girls in Southwark Park Road, London, commemorating the name of Bryan Donkin, marks the next revolutionary step in the story of English tinplate. It is also one of the great landmarks in the liberation of women from some of the tedium and anxiety involved in preparing even the simplest meal.

Le Livre de Tous les Ménages, ou L'Art de Conserver Pendant Plusieurs Années les Substances Animales et Végétales, published in Paris in 1810 by Nicholas Appert, a confectioner, described how food could be preserved and sterilised in glass jars. The method was perhaps not exactly new, but the Maison Appert put the whole operation on a successful commercial footing, and it proved most useful in catering for Napoleon's armies. In England, John Hall and Bryan Donkin seized on the idea and took out a patent for preserving food in tinplate canisters. In 1812, in Blue Anchor Lane, Bermondsey, the world's first tin-canned food factory opened. Its success was immediate, and prompted two other Englishmen, William Underwood and Thomas Kensett, to cross the Atlantic and set up two separate food-preserving factories – forerunners of the great American canning industry which fed the troops on both sides during the Civil War, and without which the great expansion westward would have been that much more difficult.

The tinplate needed for new or expanding industries – sardine canning in France, for example, or toymaking in Germany – was made in South Wales and exported throughout the world. In the USA the growing oil industry added yet another market for tinplate containers; but the Tariff Act of 1890, imposed to protect the rival tinplate industries of Pittsburgh and elsewhere, brought a temporary halt to exports from Britain; one American tinplate company adopted as its trademark a soaring American eagle carrying away in its talons a rather disconsolate British lion. The lion did not stay depressed for long however: the export of the tinplate itself was succeeded by two other exports – the machines for making the tinplate, and the Welshmen skilled in working them.

Printing on tinplate

On the home market, too, there were new outlets for tinplate. In 1846, for instance, a complete new consumer industry had been established in Reading, where a small Quaker shop, by installing continuously running machinery for making fancy biscuits, had taken the first step towards becoming, within 50 years, the largest biscuit enterprise in the world. This shop, in London Road, was run by Thomas Huntley and his near relative George Palmer. Opposite it, in 1831, Thomas's brother Joseph had opened a general ironmongers; and as Thomas's biscuit business expanded, Joseph started making tin-lined wooden boxes, and later tin biscuit boxes, to pack the biscuits in. The labels, designed by Thomas de la Rue, were printed on paper and stuck on the tins.

By 1860, however, the Neath Tinplate Decorating Company was printing simple designs directly on to tinplate, by pressing them down on to the inked surface of litho stones prepared in such a way that the pattern to be printed stood out in relief. There were limits to the possibilities of this method, and other tin box makers decorated their tins by means of paper transfers. The real breakthrough in technique came in 1875, when Huntley, Boorne and Stevens acquired from the firm of matchmakers Bryant and May the licence to print tinplate by the offset litho process. This technique, which used rubber composition rollers, had been recently invented in France and patented in England, where the patent was bought up by Bryant and May.

Only simple shapes could be printed by the direct method: anything more complicated involved handwork and cost substantially more to produce. The offset litho

Tinsmith's workshop

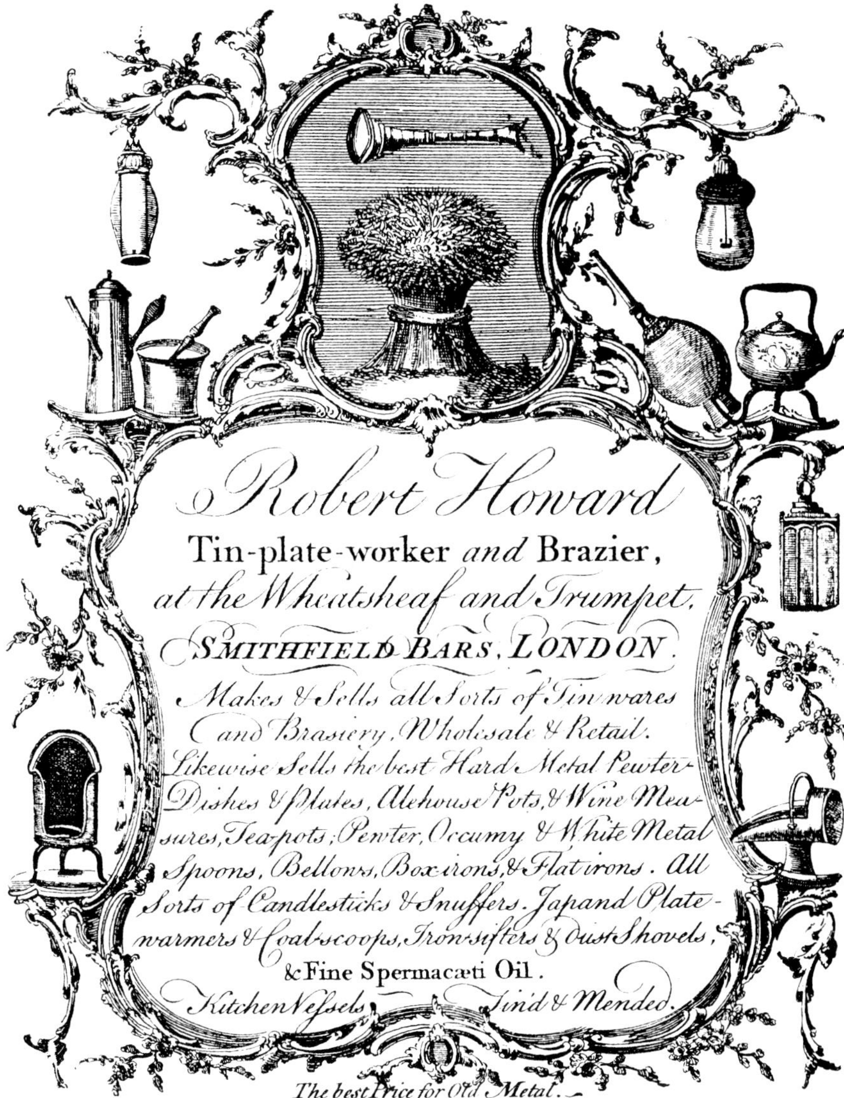

18th century tradesman's card

process allowed elaborate embossing and shaping at very little extra cost. So began the great era of beautifully decorated fancy biscuit tins – to stay until modern paper and plastic packaging took over.

English 19th century tin toy makers

The factories making tin canisters for the food trade, or simple domestic hardware such as dustpans and kitchen utensils, generally employed women or boys, all working at piece rates. The descendants of the Crooked Lane tinmen were still around however – no longer working near the Fishmongers' Hall but down in the docks, fitting out ships with lanterns and ventilators. Some of them travelled around the coast during the fish canning seasons, or stayed put in small workshops manufacturing necessities such as baths, trunks and milkchurns. Others worked in tiny garrets with one or two apprentices, or at home with their families, making small, cheap items such as oilcans, scoops, waterpots and toys, which they sold to local shops or hawked in the street markets. In order to make ends meet, many of them had to seek employment as lamplighters, in addition to making and mending lanterns.

In the *Morning Chronicle* of 28 February 1850, Henry Mayhew recorded his interview with a toy gun maker, whom he visited at work, his wife assisting him: 'I was born to the business of toy gun and pistol, as well as of tin toys which consist of mugs and trumpets; but the foreigners have got all the trumpet trade now – what we got 30s a gross for we only get 7s now. The other tin toys – such as horses and carts, got up by machinery for a penny – are made in Birmingham. None are made in that way in London; they're but slop toys. The tin toy trade at Birmingham is the factory system with children. Think of children working hard at toys – poor little things, to whom a toy is a horror!

'A gun is made in this manner. The wooden part, the stock, is made ready for the gunmaker's use by any carpenter: it is of pine. The next process is the making of the wire spring, then the barrel (tin). These different parts are then put to the stock; the lock is made by ourselves; they are of solder, and cast. The spring is placed inside the barrel, a ring is placed at the end by which it is drawn out, fastened to the pin (like the nipple of one of your deadly guns), and the weapon is ready for discharge.

'I make the week through three gross, which is 22,464. There is one other toy gunmaker in London, and he may make as many as I do, which will be 44,928 made in London. Reckon a third retailed to the public at

Britains 'Automatic Foot Race', 1885 (top)
Britains 'Automatic Horse Race', 1890 (middle left)
Britains 'Equestrienne', 1895 (bottom left)
Britains 'Tightrope Walker', 1890 (bottom right)

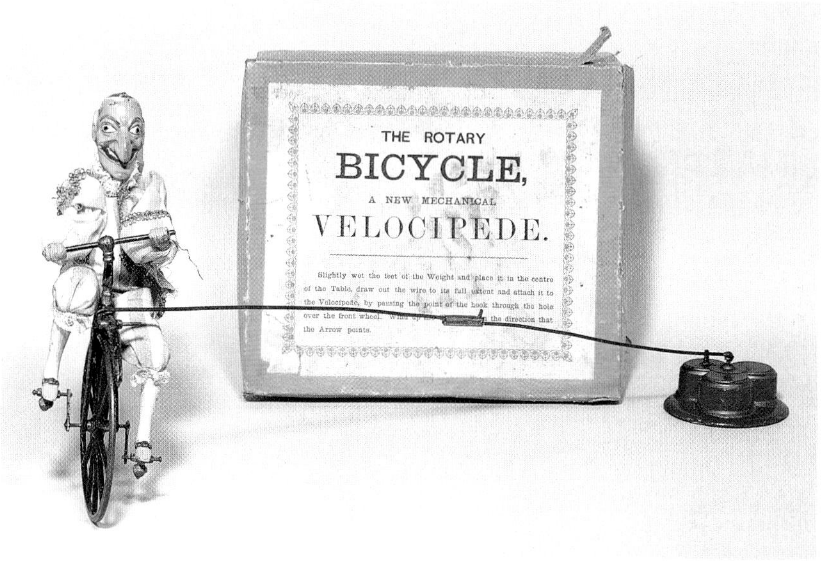

Britains rotary cyclist, c.1870 (top)
Britains Punch on velocipede, 1885 (middle)
Britains Automaton tea drinker, 1885 (bottom)
Britains penny cyclist, 1885 (left)

Engraving from *Forgotten Children's Books*

4d (called pistols), and reckon those retailed at 6d in the proportion of 6 to 4 in number with those retailed at 1s, and you have the sum of £1,238 4s.

'In war time, bless you, that was the time for my business – there was a demand for guns then, I can tell you! I sold eight then to one that I sell now, though the population's increased so. These pistols, which I get 1s 6d a dozen for now, I had 3s 6d a dozen for then. The grand thing for the toy trade was the constant report that Bonaparte was coming – there was to be an invasion, and then every child was a soldier. Guns did go off briskly at that period – anything in the shape of a gun found a customer in those days. Working people could then buy plenty of toys for their children, and did buy them too.'

In the same article Mayhew gives us this account of his work by a toy drum and tambourine maker: 'The first process in making a tin drum is to cut the tin the size required, solder the ends together, and colour the body. We then paint the Royal Arms on it, or a crown and VR. The hoops are then cut (they are beech) and coloured, and then what we call the "twig" is cut, and the parchment for the top of the drum being sewn to it, the twig is fitted to the tin body, and attached to it by the strings, which are tightened or slackened by leather braces, for the weather affects the drum. A best toy drum goes thirty-five times through our hands before it is finished, as time must be given in the working for the parts to dry and set. I don't make the sticks – the toy turners do them. I and my four boys could make a gross of small wooden drums in a day, but only a dozen of the best large tin drums, highly ornamented.

'Tambourines are made after the same fashion, but have only a limited sale. I only make about three dozen a week. I have heard an uncle whom I succeeded say – and he employed eleven men where I have four boys at apprentices' wages – that the war time was the time for the toy drum trade.'

In a previous article, published a week earlier and entitled *Science and Art in Toymaking*, Mayhew mentions clockwork mice, and gives a list of articles made by the tinman: 'tin swords and shields, peashooters and carts, money boxes and miniature candlesticks'.

At the 1851, Great Exhibition in Hyde Park, there were only twenty-one British exhibitors in the toy section, the reason being (according to the organisers) that the majority of toymakers in England were too poor: 'they were chamber masters, who seldom manufacture goods to order, but make a small number and then hawk them from shop to shop or from street to street'. The three British prizewinners were A Bouchet of Baker Street, who made a model of the Great Exhibition with moving figures; E C Spurrin of New Bond Street, who showed two mechanical models, one a farmyard, the other depicting Gulliver in Lilliput; and thirdly Madame Montanari, the maker of beautiful wax dolls.

It is more difficult to know just what the mechanical toys were like which a 'fancy toymaker' talked about when interviewed by Mayhew: 'Fancy toys are mechanical and moving toys. To describe the whole would tire you. I invent them, all that I make. My toys, though well known in the trade for their ingenuity, are not of great cost, but are chiefly within reach of the middle classes. They include animals of all descriptions – donkeys, horses, cows, cats, elephants, lions, tigers (I could make giraffes, but they're not in demand), dogs and pigs. Here is a toy of my own invention. This boy is flying a kite, and you see how, by the cranks and wires, the boy appears to advance and the kite takes the air. Here is a boat. These model men fix on here. By movements which I have contrived, they row the boat.

'My trade is a sort of individual thing: a man finds he has a turn for it, and so he takes a turn at it. There are no women in the trade that I'm aware of, except a young woman known as "the mechanic" for her remarkable taste and ingenuity.

'The introduction of French toys at a lower rate of duty (in 1842 I think it was) affected my trade. I had far fewer orders after that, and prices fell. I should say it has made 50 per cent difference to me generally. Many of the inventions or patterns that I have originated have been copied in Germany. Sometimes I get a hint from them, in return for all that they borrow, so to call it, from me. They rob me; and I take from them.'

Mayhew's fancy toy maker had many descendants contriving ingenious, hand-made novelties out of all kinds of scraps and oddments. Writing in the *New Illustrated Magazine* in November 1899, Mr George Wade says: 'The chief penny toy now most in demand is something of a mechanical kind, either in the shape of a working model or puzzle. The old kind of toy with no movement, but which was simply made to be looked at, is of no use today. People want moving engines, horses, steamers etc – and they want it for the "nimble penny".'

But not all mechanical toys produced in England were flimsy hawker's wares. In his family home at 26 Lamberton Road, Hornsey, William Britain was already, in 1845, inventing new metal mechanical toys which were clever, strong and well-made, many being set in motion by spinning flywheels. Britain had come to London from Birmingham, where he had no doubt received his training; for it was in and around Birmingham that were

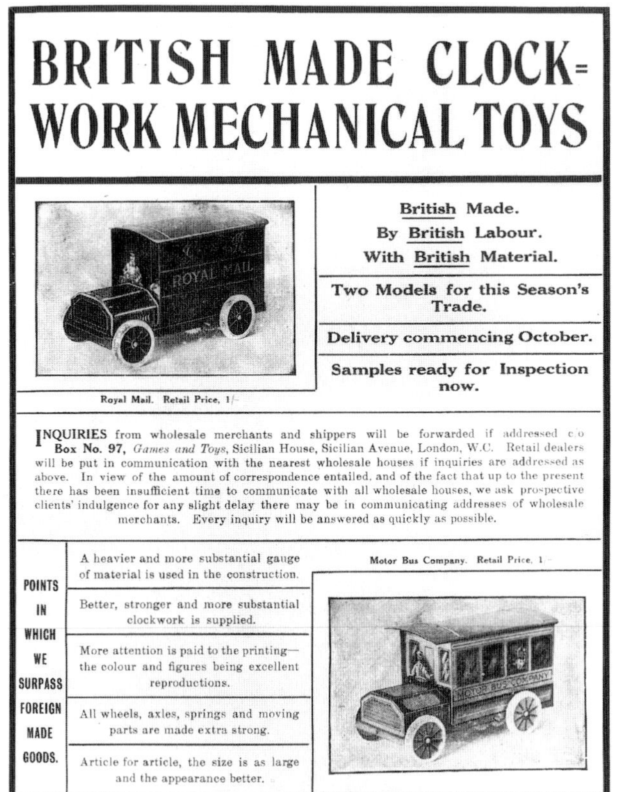

Advertisements from *Games and Toys*, October 1914

to be found the small engineering firms which turned out factory-made, non-mechanical tin toys in vast numbers: money boxes, seaside buckets and spades, cheap tin knick-knacks for Christmas crackers and Victorian dolls' houses.

World War I developments

The more elaborate clockwork tin toys that later graced the pages of Gamages' catalogues or the showrooms of such wholesalers as Hyman A Abrahams and Whyte Risdale & Co. of Houndsditch were imported from France and Germany until the autumn of 1914. The war put a stop to all imports from Germany and reduced the flow of toys from France and the USA to a tiny trickle. By October 1914 the trade journal *Games and Toys* was announcing British made clockwork mechanical toys: 'Two models for this season's trade – British-made, by British labour and with British material – which surpass foreign-made goods as they are made of a heavier gauge material, the clockwork is stronger and the printing excellent'. No manufacturer's name is given: those interested were invited to write to Box 97, c/o The Editor. In the following month, November 1914, the wholesale agents Hyman A Abrahams were advertising the same two cars. A similar advertisement two years later gave these details: A Parcels Express, an open motor car, an armoured car, an autobus and a Fire Brigade car – all obtainable at 9s per dozen; and a larger Fire Brigade car at 20s per dozen'.

It seems probable that these first English clockwork toys were made by one of the metal box makers, Barringer, Wallis and Manners, who as soon as war broke out adapted some of their tins shaped like cars or trucks to be used not only as containers but also as toys. Hudson Scott & Sons of Carlisle, who made biscuit tins for Macfarlane Lang & Co., also opened a special factory at Workington to produce practically nothing else but tins as toys.

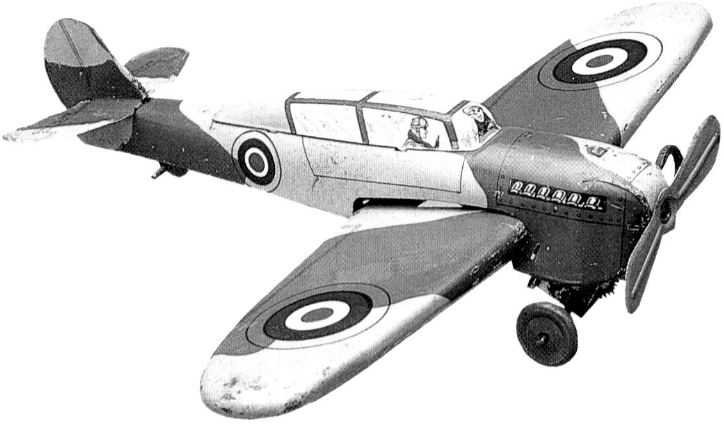

Mettoy camouflaged bomber, 1940 (top)
Wells RAF fighter, 1940 (middle)
Astra searchlight and AA gun, 1940 (left)

Britains 2 fighter aeroplanes, 1947 (top right)

Britains Monoplane flying boat, 1937 (top left)

Meccano camouflaged Tiger Moth, 1940 (middle)

Meccano seaplane, 1935 (bottom right)

A–Z of British-Made Metal Toys

This section details all known British metal toy manufacturers.

The products of the most important firms – Chad Valley, Britains, Mettoy, Wells-Brimtoy – are easy to identify, since the toys have survived as well as manufacturers' catalogues. However, a close study of the trade journals *Games and Toys* and *The Toy and Fancy Goods Trader* from 1910 onwards brings to light a host of smaller firms. Some of these only lasted for a year or so, others were briefly referred to in the caption of an illustration, often in terms so vague that it is impossible to tell whether they actually made the toys in question, or were merely agents or stockists.

As with all pioneer works, further information will no doubt surface – but at least this is a long overdue beginning.

A

Abbey Sports Co. Ltd
1921–the present day
125 Borough High Street, London
This firm is still in existence as Abbey-Corinthian Games Co. Their output consists mainly of indoor games such as chess, draughts and bagatelle boards. In 1928, they were selling 'Tock-Tock', a candle-powered racing boat driven by hot air – no boiler, nothing to explode.

"TOCK TOCK" THE NEW RACING CRAFT
DRIVEN BY HOT AIR
NO BOILER
NOTHING TO EXPLODE
Fun for all!
A MOST REALISTIC TOY
Runs any time up to 15 minutes and emits the well known "Tock Tock," "Tock Tock." Can be heard for over 50 yards.
RACES FOR THE SPORTY

Abbey Sports Co. candle-powered 'Tock-Tock' boat

Abrahams, Hyman A & Sons
1855–1926
30 St Bride Street, Ludgate Circus, London and also from 1916,
Rue de l'Echiquier Paris
Very soon after the outbreak of war in 1914, this long established firm of wholesalers made a point of advertising that they sold only British-made goods, perhaps because one of the sons had been killed in France. They also, in 1919, campaigned in newspaper letters against the importation of metal toys from Germany.

In October 1914, the trade journal *Games and Toys* carried a full page advertisement for a clockwork motor bus and a Royal Mail van, both British made. Further details were available via the editor and a box number. In the same issue the Editor of *Games and Toys* Mr Richard Simmonds wrote: 'What we want in this country are mechanical toys. One firm in the Midlands have already entered the field, and have now on the market some models . . . the firm in question have been inundated with orders'.

Nearly seventy years after, it seems safe to presume that the Midlands firm referred to was F Burnett Ltd of Birmingham who had just registered a new company and that the toys were being made for them by the tin box firm of Barringer, Wallis & Manners and sold through the wholesalers Hyman A Abrahams in London.

The following year Hyman A Abrahams were offering a clockwork tram, an open motor, a parcels express van, an armoured car, an autobus, and two sizes of fire brigade cars (all British-made). They also had a tin money box shaped like a shell, another like a gas stove and a gas fire made for John Wright & Co. of Aston, Birmingham, by Barringer, Wallis & Manners.

In 1926, Whyte Risdale & Co. Ltd, another large wholesalers, bought up their entire stock.

Abrahams motor bus, *Games and Toys*, October 1914

Acme Toy Co.
1915–1958
27 St John Street, Longsight, Manchester
Manufacturers of toys, tin boxes and hardware. The firm changed its name in

1920 to The Acme Tin Stamping Co.; and by 1958, when it was acquired first by Hall and Lane and then by Chad Valley, it was known as the Acme Stopper & Box Co. Ltd.
See Chad Valley Ltd

Aeroplanes
Experiments in making airships and aeroplanes were carried on throughout the 19th century, and there were interesting flying toys worked by spin motion or by elastic drive. The Wright brothers of America made the first powered flight in 1903.

Toy planes were marketed from about 1908 and were often very accurate in their modelling. The use of aeroplanes in World War I was responsible for many improvements in design, and for the special interest in this type of toy.

The early flying toy aeroplanes were made of bamboo, spruce, wire and oiled silk; balsa wood was not used until just before World War II. The first reasonably scaled flying planes were made by Appleby in 1932, to be followed by the F R O G planes sold by Lines Brothers. Reliable toy petrol engines came into use after World War II; and by the 1960s, with the use of expensive transistor radio control, flying planes were no longer children's playthings but adult hobbies.

The same trend has been evident in the field of static, non-flying models. The first, metal 'Joey' planes, produced by R Joseph & Co. during World War I were quite simple toys. These were then taken over by Burnett Ltd. The metal aeroplanes made by Lines Brothers, Meccano, Mettoy, Wells-Brimtoy and other manufacturers all reflect different stages in the development of aircraft and, later, space travel. During World War II special kits were produced for use in the training of RAF aircraft spotters. Today, aeroplane model kits are produced primarily for a sophisticated adult market, as are the more specialised gliders, sailplanes, soarers, towliners. Only cheap plastic toys and the various 'Wizzas', 'flying propellers' and other variations on the original 1787 'Alouette' have remained within pocket-money range.
**pp. 18–19, 58, 70, 90, 99*

Burnett 'Joey' aeroplane, 1925

Allied Tin Box Makers Ltd
1921
This company represented the amalgamation of three large tinprinting companies, Barclay & Fry Ltd, Barringer, Wallis & Manners Ltd, and Hudson Scott & Sons. Shortly afterwards renamed Metal Box Co.
*See Printing on Tinplate *pp. 10–11*

Anthony, W & Co.
1923–1936
45 Kenyon Street and 26 Regent Place, Birmingham
Tin toy makers, they advertised bells, novelties and, in 1928, viewographs and 'wonder' cameras, which took real photographs.
See Optical Toys

Arthur & Ralph
1923–27
170 St John Street, Clerkenwell, London
Toy paint box manufacturers. (Hogarth series.)

Assael Gabriel Ltd
1920
Byron House, 2 Finsbury Street, London
This firm later became Assael's United Agencies, and agents for Timpo toys. The 'Gaby' humming top they advertised in 1920 was 'British made'.
See Tops

Astra Pharos Ltd
1940
Landor Works, Askew Road, Shepherds Bush, London
Manufacturers of working models of guns, searchlights etc. 'as used by our home and overseas forces'.
*See Guns *p. 18*

Atomic
1949
Atomic jet gun made by Crescent Toy Company.
See Guns

Austin Motor Co. Ltd
1949
Subsidiary factory in Wales to manufacture an expensive toy pedal car to the standard of a full scale car with bumpers, handbrake, dummy engine with sparking plugs, pneumatic tyres, electric headlamps. Larger than ordinary toy cars. The idea came from Mr L P Lord, Chairman and Managing Director of the Austin Co., who for a number of years had been interested in the 'Development Areas'. The firm was a non-profitmaking undertaking.
See Pedal Cars

Avon Tin Printers Ltd
1936–the present day
Station Road, Kingswood, Bristol
Some fifty years ago the grandfather of Mr David Morgan, the present Managing Director of Avon Tin Printers, left the Caldicot Printing Works to set up a new firm in Bristol. He took with him many of the dies and press tools which had been in use in his old firm. Among these tools were those which had been used to make large toy milk churns for the wooden milk floats made by Lines Brothers in the 1930s. These little milk churns are still produced by Avon, but now they are decorated with pretty floral designs and used as containers for sweets or novelties.

Another speciality of Avon Tin Printers are small tins shaped like houses, and Stately Home tins designed by Ian Logan. The tooling for many of these tins are based on money-boxes produced in the 1920s. Avon Tin Printers still make money boxes, and at one time also made a tinplate replica of a jet aircraft, the Bristol 188, possibly for Louis Marx.
See Printing on Tinplate

B

Bailey, William Ltd
1905–1968
Victoria Works, 215 Brearly Street, Birmingham
Presstool makers, die-sinkers and brass founders. William Bailey was the inventor and manufacturer of two tin constructional toys which enjoyed much popularity.

The first, called 'Kliptiko', consisted of different lengths of narrow tin tubes, opened out at each end in a kind of flat open jaw which gripped other plain lengths of rolled tin. 'Kliptiko' went into production just before World War I and was patented in 1915 (No. 0628/13). In the same year 'Wenebrik' (Patent No. 382/15) was put on the market. This consisted of various small tin shapes painted red and green, which slid together to make houses, cottages and other buildings.

In 1930, William Bailey Ltd merged their sales force with that of the soft toy company, J K Farnell. By 1935, however, William Bailey Ltd gave up toy making, to concentrate solely on the brass foundry

'Betal' **Glasman** trolley bus 1938 (top left)

Burnett open tourer and saloon c.1934 (top right)

'Betal' **Glasman** trolley bus (right) and **Wells-Brimtoy** trolley bus (left) 1938

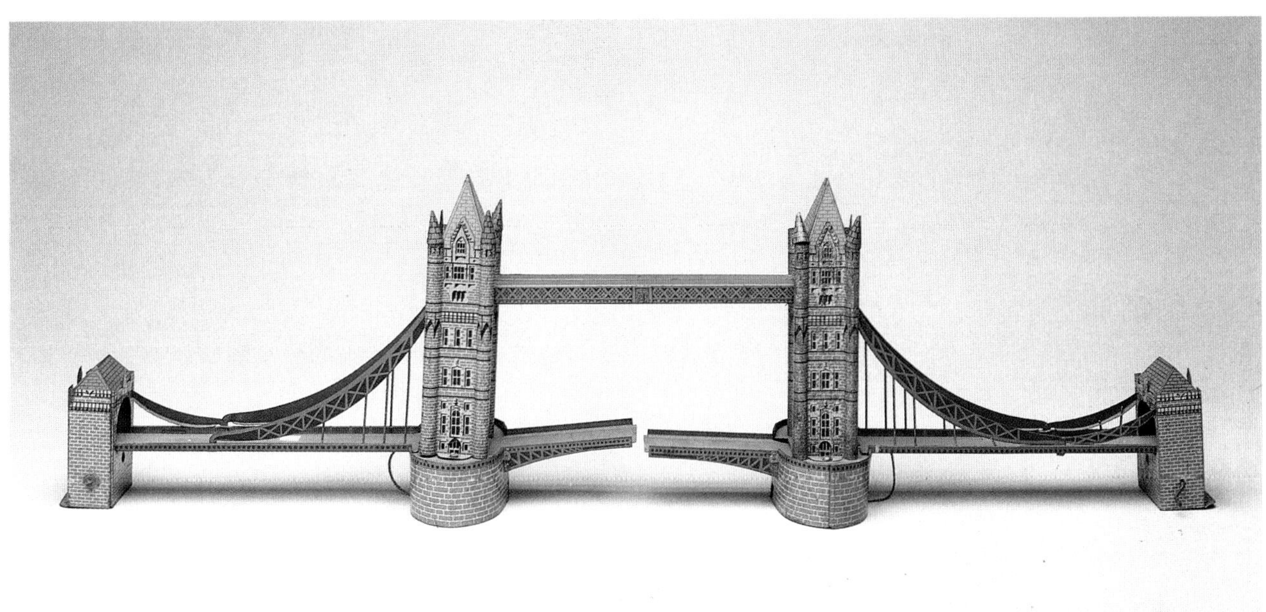

Burnett general bus, c.1920 (top left)
Burnett 'GR' Royal Mail Van, 1925 (top right)
Burnett Tower Bridge, c.1925

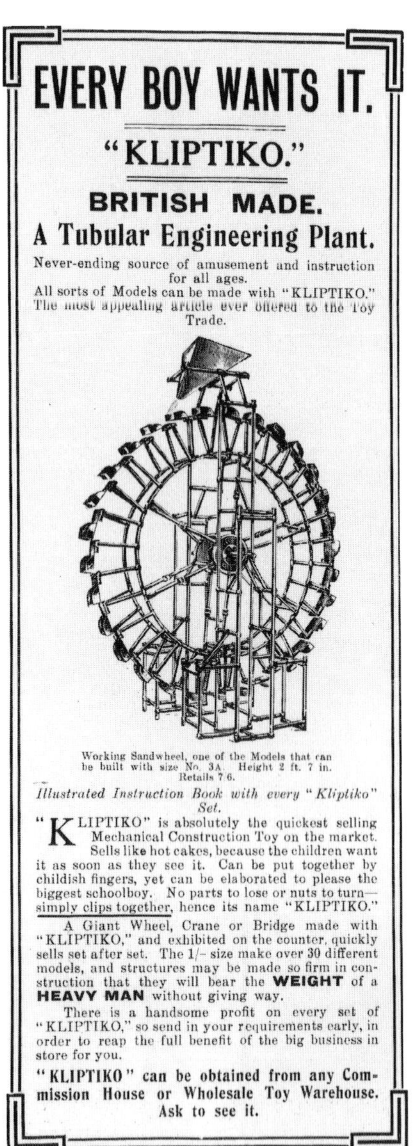

William Bailey 'Kliptiko' construction set, 1914

side of their business.
See Appendix VII

Bairntoys
See Foster, Blackett & Wilson Ltd

Barclay & Fry Ltd
1855–1921
City of London and Southwark
This company was founded in 1855 by Robert Barclay and his brother-in-law John Fry. Its principal business was printing banknotes for Barclay's Bank. In 1875, Barclay & Fry took out a patent for the application of offset printing to tinplate printing, but they did not pursue the matter and in 1877 sold the patent to Bryant & May, who in turn licensed the patent to Huntley, Boorne & Stevens. The patent expired in 1889 and it would seem Barclay & Fry then took up tinplate printing. A biscuit tin in the shape of a toy lighthouse was made for Dunmore Ltd. In 1921 Barclay & Fry joined the Association of Allied Tin Box Makers, which was renamed Metal Box Ltd.
See Printing on Tinplate

Baker, William Harding
1859–1957
168 Bethnal Green Road and 98 Gosset Street, Bethnal Green, London
The earlier trade directories list this firm under the heading Toymaker, with particular mention of drums, tambourines and drum battledores. By 1920, however, they are listed as manufacturers and dealers and the toys they handled or made included skipping ropes, lawn tennis racquets, toy rackets, shaped horses and carts, wood engines, folding dolls' chairs, express wagons, racers, toy golf clubs and banjos.

Balancing Toys and Aelian Figures
Balancing toys of a man riding horseback, or balancing on a point whilst holding a weighted bar in the manner of a tightrope walker, seem to have been popular in Europe from an early period. That they were principally for amusement seems obvious, but it has also been reported that they were used in taverns at closing time: the landlord, setting one in action, would announce that he meant to close doors when the toy was still. As the horse rears up for a few minutes this seems quite a possible explanation.

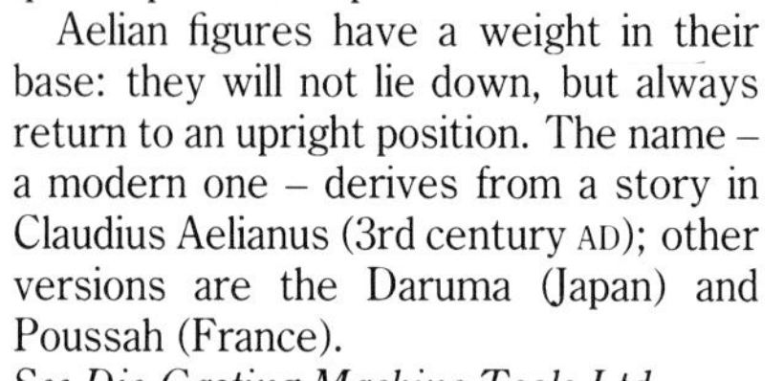

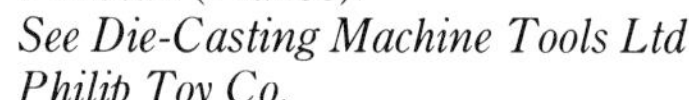

Aelian figures have a weight in their base: they will not lie down, but always return to an upright position. The name – a modern one – derives from a story in Claudius Aelianus (3rd century AD); other versions are the Daruma (Japan) and Poussah (France).
See Die-Casting Machine Tools Ltd
Philip Toy Co.

Bar-Knight steam locomotive, sold by A Bell in 1920

Bar-Knight Model Engineering Co.
1924
Minibanks Works, Alexandra Parade, Glasgow
Manufacturers of clockwork, electric and steam locomotives.
See Trains, Steam Toys

Barlow E C & Sons Ltd
1869–1929
Shoreditch, Hackney and Palmers Green
In 1869, Edward Barlow (1846–1937) was running a hand to mouth business in a shed, making paint and meat tins. The Boer War brought prosperity to this small

Balancing toy in Hampshire Country Museum's Service

enterprise as they gained valuable contracts making ration tins, then tobacco tins. In 1907, Ernest's younger son Robert Barlow (1891–1976) took over his father's business, introduced tinplate printing and greatly expanded the business. In 1929, Robert Barlow joined forces with Metal Box and became its Managing Director and ultimately its forceful Chairman.
See Printing on Tinplate

Barrett, A & Co.
See Taylor & Barrett

Barringer, Wallis & Manners & Co. Ltd
1839–1939
Mansfield, Staffordshire
The original firm of Barringer & Co. started in 1830. They were millers and producers of mustard packed in tins. By 1870 they were making their own tins. In 1889, they became Barringer, Wallis & Manners and by 1892, they were printing and making tins for themselves and for other firms.

In 1914, they started to make clockwork and other toys. They produced clockwork aeroplanes, train sets with button wheels, lorries, buses, racing cars and clockwork walking toys as well as pillar boxes, cash boxes and stage coaches.

They made toys for Burnett Ltd, notably the 'Ubilda' series. The work of tying the different parts on to perforated cardboard was done by deaf and dumb girls.

In 1939, Barringer, Wallis & Manners were taken over by The Metal Box Co. At the end of World War II they entered into an agreement with Chad Valley to manufacture tinplate toys for them, Burnett Ltd having ceased trading. The tools for making Burnett's toys were taken over and new designs added – most of the toys listed in Barringer, Wallis & Manners archives appear in Chad Valley's Export Catalogues for 1946 to 1949.
*See Appendix 1, Burnett Ltd, Chad Valley, Dunn & Taylor, Money-boxes, Penny Toys *pp. 11, 46*

Burnett 'Ubilda' saloon made by Barringer Wallis & Manners, 1934

Bassett-Lowke catalogue 1930s

Barronia Metals Ltd
See True to Type Products

Bassett-Lowke Ltd
1899–the present day
Northampton
Wenman Joseph Bassett-Lowke founded his original model business in 1899 together with Henry Franklin. In 1910, the business was incorporated into a company which survives today through one of its associate companies, Bassett-Lowke (SM) Ltd. In the early part of the century, the firm employed Henry Greenly who was instrumental in the rise of scale model railways in the UK.

Much of the company's early offerings were by German manufacturers such as Georges Carette, Gebruder Bing and, to a lesser extent, Schoenner and Marklin. As the firm developed other divisions were formed for ship-building and industrial models. However, the firm is chiefly remembered for its model railway products sold through shops in London, Manchester and Edinburgh. Bassett-Lowke catalogues and WJ Bassett-Lowke's *Model Railway Handbook* were key items of literature in the growth of the model railway hobby.

In the early 1930s, the firm was closely involved with the rise of HO electric model railways through its collaboration with Trix, which was started in Germany by, among others, Franz Bing. Bassett-Lowke commenced the serious mass-production of tinplate model railway equipment in 1930 and this continued until the late 1950s, after which time the

Biscuit tin coach for William Crawford & Sons c. 1934, manufacturer unknown (top)

Hudson Scott & Sons houseboat for W & R Jacobs 1923 (bottom)

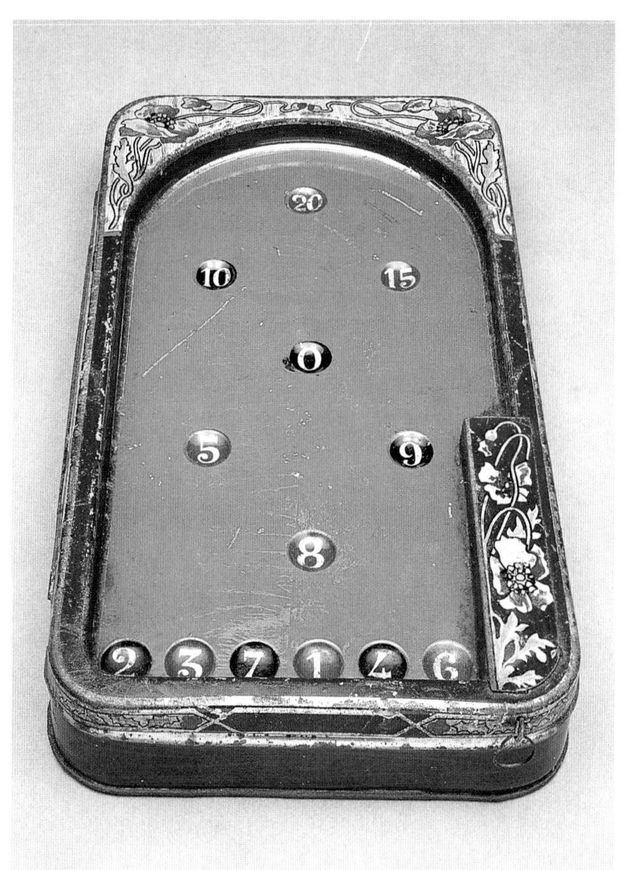

Henry Bayerthall 'Bagatelle' biscuit tin for W & R Jacob, c. 1905 (top left)

Huntley, Boorne & Stevens cabinette biscuit tin for Huntley & Palmers c. 1911 (top right)

Huntley, Boorne & Stevens kitchen range biscuit tin for Huntley & Palmers c. 1926

Huntley, Boorne & Stevens farmhouse biscuit tin for Huntley & Palmers 1931 (bottom left)

company supplied mainly small run products built for them by outside makers. In 1966, the company was taken over by a Mr Derry and Mr Riley and in 1968, Bassett-Lowke (Railways) Ltd was licensed to revive the model railway line in association with Steam Age. This revival petered out after a few years.

The rump of the company now operates from a modern factory outside Northampton and has recently been acquired by Nigel Turner, a local Northampton business man. **pp. 122–23*

Further reading: *The Bassett-Lowke Story*, R. Fuller

Bayko Construction Sets
1938–1962
Precision-moulded construction sets in coloured bakelite, patent No. 422,645, manufactured by Plimpton Engineering Co. and sold by Berwick Toy Company. In 1959, Plimpton's entire share capital was acquired by Meccano Ltd, who in 1962 completely redesigned the construction sets.
See Plastics

Bedington Liddiatt & Co. Ltd
1911–1933
Established 1911 at 4–7 Chiswell Street, 2 New Zealand Avenue, Barbican, London; 1913 at 22–3 Hamsell Street, Jewin Street, London; 1919 at 16–18 Bayer Street, Golden Lane, London.
Originally manufacturers and merchants of games, dolls and toys and agents for American and Japanese dolls and toys. Firm used trademarks 'Tessted Toys' and 'Walkabout' for mechanical soft toy animals. In 1919, they were selling a clockwork tank and British-made gyroscopic tops. Other lines included metal soldiers; 'Pin-Tung' wooden construction sets; 'Jolly Jim' puppet; 'The Rainbow Cup', a scientific toy invented by Professor C V Boys; 'The Little Clockmaker', an alarm clock construction set; 'Meta Loxo', a construction set.

The firm ceased business in April 1933.

Becklin Ltd
1948
131 West Green Road, Tottenham, London
Manufacturers of the 'Becklin Bridge' a 24-gauge steel bridge construction kit for use with model railways, lorries, cars etc. Could be used as pontoon bridge. Size: 15½″ span, 2′ 8″ overall length with 4½″ wide track.
See Constructional Toys

Betal Toys
See J H Glasman Ltd

Benbros (London) Ltd
1951–1965
145 Gosport Road, Walthamstow, London
Manufacturers of die-cast toys, in particular the 'TV series' and 'Mighty Midgets', which were similar to and designed to compete with Matchbox.

Trademarks were 'Qualitoy' and later 'Zebra Toys'

Bicycles
Various two-wheeled machines were invented early in the 19th century. The introduction circa 1889 of the chain drive and of rubber pneumatic tyres increased the use of the bicycle and tricycle. Small-scale versions for children were produced by a number of firms, one of the most famous lightweight models being the Lines Brothers Fairy Cycle of 1921.

Principal manufacturers

Aberdare Cycle Co. Ltd, London
1933 'Rodney' cycle, 'Daisy' and 'Scoota-bike'

B & T (Essex) Ltd, London
1960 Scooters and tricycles

Bomford & Co. Ltd, Birmingham
1926 Cycles and tricycles

British Lion Manufacturing, Letchworth, Hertfordshire
1915 Skate cycle

Cartwright, F A & Co., Birmingham
1896 FAC scooters, 'Cullum' tricycle

Cartwright & Watkins, Birmingham
1913 Tricycles

Cartwright, W H & Co.
1920 Cycles and tricycles

Comrade Cycle Co.
1938 'Wonder' and 'Wondersuper' cycle plus tricycles and cyclettes

Farris & Co., London
1926 Farris cycle

Field's Cycle & Chassis Works, Reading
1926 'Aeroette' cycles

Introducers Ltd, Birmingham
1914 'Watsonian Glider', 'Runabout'

James Cycle Co. Ltd, Birmingham
1913 Midget tricycle

Lines Bros, London
1922 Fairy Cycle

New Auto Scooter Co., Stockport
1923 Spring frame cycle

Norton & Barker, Birmingham
1925 'Wonder' and 'Nib' tricycles

Perry A & T Cycle Co., Birmingham
1930 'Auto bike' – small petrol driven motor cycle

Peter Pan Cycle Works, Wolverhampton
1921 Cycles, tricycles and scooters

Radnall, E A & Co., Birmingham
1926 'Dandy' folding cycles and scooters

Raleigh, Nottingham
1888 Fairy Cycle

Rees, Leon, London
1931 Tricycle

Richards, Son & Allwin, Birmingham
1924 Scooters and cycles

Robson Ltd, Birmingham
1926 'Robsonia' folding scooters, cyclettes and tricycles

SS Manufacturing Co., Stockport
1923 'Daintebike' cycles and 'Toledo' scooter

Stonehouse Works, Birmingham
1926 'Nipper' cycles

Tan-Sad Ltd, Tipton, Staffs
1920 Cycles and scooters

Theaker Bros, Sheffield
1926 Eldon cycles and tricycles

Twigg, Charles & Co., Birmingham
1949 Cycles and tricycles

Unique & Unity Cycle Co., Birmingham
1921 Cycles

Bedington Liddiatt tank locomotive from 1919 *Games and Toys*

Wearwell Cycle Co. Ltd, Wolverhampton
1946 Cycles, tricycles and scooters

Winburg Co., Birmingham
1928 Cycles

Three-wheeled vehicles

Excelsior Motor Co. Ltd, Birmingham
1936 'Ski-kar', also made 'Bluebird' cycles and tricycles

Gamages Catalogue
1919 The 'Nipper' Handsmobile (manufacturer not known)

Leonard & Francis, Birmingham
1922 'Elite' Runabout

D Sebel & Co. Ltd, Erith, Kent
1965 'Trackmaster' Go-Kart

Bilbax Toys
Post World War II
Makers of 'Silver King' mechanical sports cars, 6½″ long, made from silver coloured aluminium-like metal with bakelite wheels, wooden axles and rear wheel drive.

Bilbax Toys 'The Silver King', c. 1947

Birmingham: 'The Toy Shop of Europe'
Since Elizabethan times, the town of Redditch, not far from Birmingham, has been the centre of the English needle trade. Redditch's official guide states: 'The origin of the needle industry in Redditch is obscure. It has been suggested that the art was understood by the monks of nearby Bordesley Abbey and that at the Dissolution they passed on their knowledge to local laymen. By the 18th century, over 2,000 people of the district were employed in making steel needles by hand in their cottages.' Gradually factories were established which carried out mechanically the preliminary cutting, straightening and pointing. But as late as 1882, Sophia F Caufield and Blanche Saward, in their *Dictionary of Needlework*, reported that in the course of its manufacture, every needle had to pass through 126 hands before it was ready for sale. All the most delicate operations, such as punching the eye, were done by hand.

The beginning of the 18th century also saw the rise of many new trades in Birmingham, owing to the introduction of machinery and more economical methods of production. Steel chains and collars were made for the slave trade, cattle bells for American cowboys and axes for clearing the backwoods of America. Birmingham also became known for the

Lines Bros catalogue, 1939

SKI - KAR FULLY PATENTED

The NEW Sport!

In the "SKI-KAR" we provide a new sport—a new game—a new toy—giving healthy exercise combined with unequalled pleasure. The "SKI-KAR" is balanced in the same way as a bicycle but the centre of gravity is very low, permitting sharp turns in narrow circles. Spills hold no terrors since the fall is not from any height.

Excelsior Motor Co, advertisement in 1936 *Games and Toys*

Piot 'put-put' boat, 1895 marketed by J Robinson (top left)

Clyde Model Dockyard metal-hulled yacht, c.1905 (top right)

Sutcliffe 'Merlin' speed boat, c.1978 (middle left)

Dubilier 'Duco' submarine, 1919 (bottom)

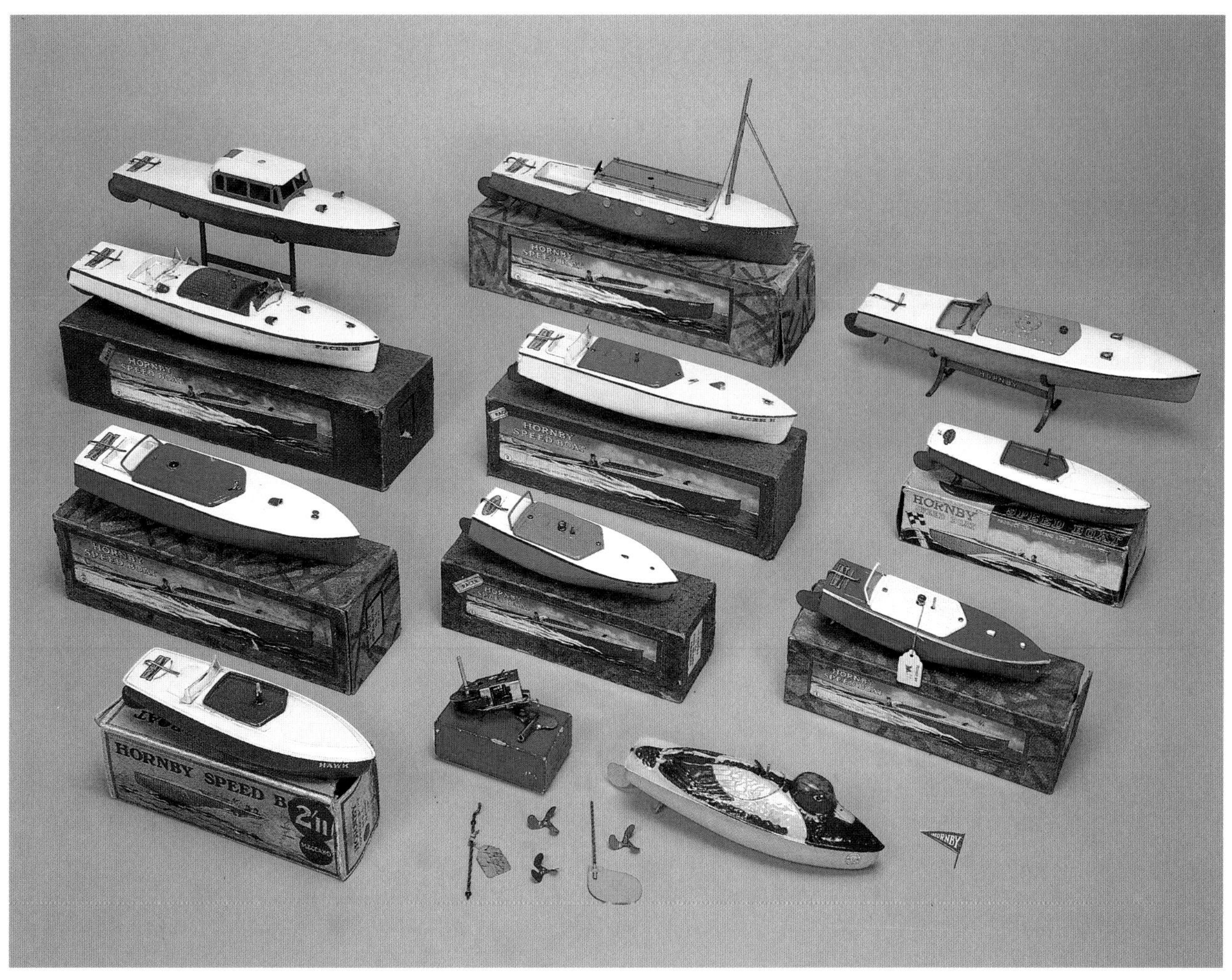

A selection from the **Hornby** range, including speed boats, sail boat and duck, 1930s

manufacture of steel 'toys' – that is to say – not children's playthings, but various pretty trifles such as buckles, bracelets and buttons. Edmund Burke, the 18th-century statesman, described Birmingham as the 'The Toy Shop of Europe'.

Children's toys, however, were made in Birmingham at the end of the 19th century and the 1914–1918 war gave considerable impetus to the home based toy trade. In 1923, for example, when there was a craze for the gambling game called 'Put and Take', Birmingham workshops turned out over two million per week, one firm alone using half a ton of metal per day. It was also only a short step to pass from the manufacture of pins and needles to that of wire spokes for bicycle and other wheeled vehicles. In 1928, the trade journal *Games and Toys* published a special 'Birmingham Who's Who', listing 53 firms engaged in the toy industry.

Anthony, W and Co., 26 Regents Place. Toy cameras, toy scales and stampings
Arbanz, Ad., 32–33 Ludgate Hill. Air guns and rifles
Aerial Pram Wheel Works Ltd Court Road, Balsall Heath. Wheels
Ashby, F and Sons, Ltd, Charlotte Road, Stirchley. Roller skates
Bailey, Wm (Birmingham) Ltd, Victoria Works, Weaman Street. 'Wenebrik' and 'Kliptico' constructional toys
Bomford and Co. Ltd, Lower Essex Street. Bomton juvenile cycles and tricycles
Bowden Brake Co. Ltd, Tyseley. 'Pied Piper' cyclettes
Bridgwater, Norman H, 55 Frederick Street. Toy watches and gilt jewellery
Brilliant Balloon and Novelty Co. Toy balloons
Butcher, J H, and Co., Ltd, 506 Moseley Road. Transfers
Cartwright, A S, Ltd, 75 Ford Street, Hockley. Toy bells, conductor sets, chimes, toy reins
Cartwright and Co., F A, Tame Road, Witton. Juvenile tricycles, cycles, wheels and rubber tyres
Chad Valley Co. Ltd, Harborne Games, dolls and soft toys
Cohen, Alec and Randall, 684 Stratford Road. Many agents, exclusive lines in general toys
Crighton, G F, Ltd, 28 Spencer Street. 'Goggly Goggles', a hawker's line
Dale, Forty and Co., Ltd, Cox Street West, Balsall Heath. 'The Scootaskate' and stampings and piercings for the toy and sports trades. Metal fittings of every description. Tennis clamps
Darlington, J T, Birches Green Works, Erdington. 'Spade of Spades', seaside spades, garden tools, flags on sticks, wood dowels
Dawes Cycles Ltd, Hall Green Works. 'Ponycycle' cyclettes
Dunn and Taylor, 61 Burbury Street Toy cash boxes
Dyson, J B and Sons, Ltd, 184 Great Hampton Row. Indoor games
Frankby Mfg. Co., London Works, Tyburn Road, Erdington. Juvenile cycles, scooters, folding baby cars
Gaiety Toy Co., Silver Works, Goodman Street. 'Gaiety Biffabout'
Goldberg, Louis, Ltd, 57 Livery Street. Toys of every description, both imported and of their own manufacture
Hall and Lane, Leopold Street Buckets, spades, watering cans
Hatton, Geo. and Co., Albion Works, Heath Street South. 'Diana' aluminium tea sets, musical skipping ropes
Hawkes, O C, Ltd, Globe Works, Bromsgrove Street. Nickel-plated mirrors, shaving sets and fancy goods
Hitchon, Robert, Ltd. Milford House, 117 Hurst Street. Buckets, spades, watering cans

Cartwright advertisement, 1929

Hughes, Geo. H, St Stephen's Wheel Works. Pram wheels
Hunt, W and Sons, 109, Gerrard Street, Lozells. Tin toys and filling novelties
Izon, T, 57–58 Inge Street. Tool sets
James Cycle Co. Ltd. Toy cycles
Lee, A. Moss and Co., Ltd, 171 Moseley Road, Highgate. Juvenile golf sets, seaside spades and garden seats
Lombard Co., The, 83–85 Lombard Street. Manufacturers of toy tricycles and juvenile cycles
Lowe, M. 10 South Road, Handsworth. Dolls' clothing
Luckett, T and Sons, Mark Lane. Toy prams
Ludlow Bros, Palmer Street. Galvanized buckets
McClelland Bros, Cambridge Street. Seaside buckets and spades
Montil Mfg. Co. Ltd, Britannia Works, Morville Street. Juvenile tricycles and motor cars
Morris, W E and Co., Ltd, Triumph Works, Ernest Street. Toy buckets, seaside spades
New Austin Tangent Wheels Ltd 250 Herbert Road, Small Heath. Wheels
Norris, J, 51 Sherbourne Road. Tin toys, filling novelties
Park, J, Ltd, 30 Frederick Street. Toy cameras
Perry and Co. Ltd, Tyseley. Component parts for toy motors and scooters
Plater, John J and Sons, 261–264 Bradford Street. Baskets, shopping bags
Radnall, E A and Co., Ltd, Vauxhall Works, Dartmouth Street. Bicycles and scooters
Richards, Son and Allwin, Ltd, Sidway Works, Granville Street. Toy motor-cars, juvenile cycles, dolls' prams, wheels
Robson, Stanley T. Ltd, 275–283 Coventry Road. Juvenile cycles and tricycles
Rothschild and Baker, 70 Summer Row. Wheel toys
Standard Cycle Co. Ltd, 40, Barn Street. 'K' cyclettes
Tan-Sad Ltd, Albert Street, Wheel toys, dolls' prams, motor-cars, scooters
Unique and Unity Cycle Co. Ltd, St Stephen's Street. Juvenile cycles and dolls' prams

In October 1956, *Games and Toys* published a long article entitled 'Spotlight on Birmingham' in which they give details of the following firms not included in their 1928 'Who's Who'.

Acme Toys. Printed tin containers and seaside buckets, tin trumpets, money-boxes and tamborines.
Artistic Plastics Co. Ltd. Trade mouldings for toy manufacturers and inflatable toys for Plastic & Erinoid Wares Ltd.
Birmingham Associated Chain Co. Ltd. Tiny metal chains for the toy trade.
Boxfoldia Ltd. Boxes and cartons.
Brookes & Adams Ltd. Carpet bowls and toy plastic cups and saucers.
Churchfield Springs Co. Ltd. Springs and small components for the toy trade.
Creswell R W Ltd. Toy bells & other tin & brass press work.
Dunn & Sutton Ltd. Play suits, Christmas crackers & carnival hats.
Giltoy Products Ltd. Traffic signs and other die cast parts for the toy trade.
Hawkins, T P & Son Ltd. Bent wire articles, buckles, axles, cranks, hooks for the toy trade.

Helix (Universal) Co. Ltd. Wooden rulers, school & other handicraft sets.
Kirby Beard & Co. Ltd. Pin manufactures since 1743, who in 1956 were making children's work boxes for the toy trade.
Malins (Engineers) Ltd. Steam engines.
Millum Ltd. Toy clothes pegs.
Munster, F J & Co. Ltd. Tartan goods and dolls in national dresses.
Payne F & Co. Strip steel pressings and tubular fabrications for the toy trade.
Phillips, J A & Co. Ltd. Bicycle fitments and roller skates.
Speedwell Gear Case Co. Ltd. Sheet-metal parts for the toy trade.
Tucker Eyelet Co. Ltd. Eyelets and small metal pressings.
Wilkes Berger Engineering Co. Ltd. Wheels and metal work for the toys and games industry.

Birmingham Model Eng. Co.
1906
45, 47, 49 Northwood Street,
Birmingham
Owned by J Bedington & Son, the company produced model steam engines and accessories under the trade mark of 'Tessted'. **p. 127*

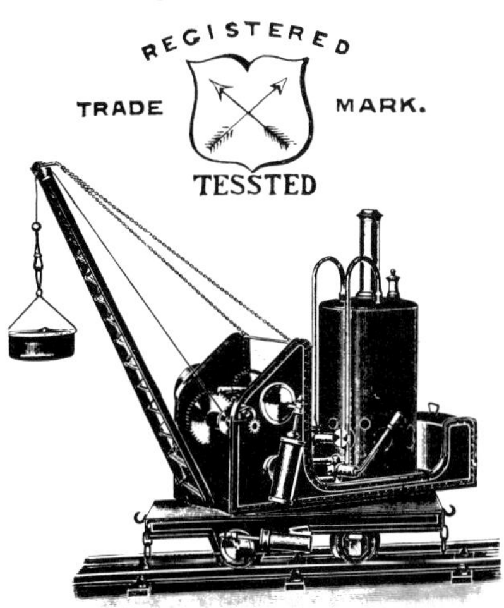

'Tessted' model steam crane from 1906 **Birmingham Model Eng. Co.** catalogue

Biscuit Tins as toys
See Barringer Wallis & Manners, Hudson Scott & Sons, Huntley Boorne & Stevens, Metal Box, Windsor Novelties **pp. 10, 11, 26, 27*

Further reading: *British Biscuit Tins*, Michael Franklin
The Golden Age of Printed Tin Packaging, David Griffiths

Bissell
See Markt & Co.

Blacks Ltd
1900–1983
6 Tin Works, 68 Litherland Road,
Bootle, Merseyside
These extracts from a letter from Mr H Black give details of the firm's history:

Brimtoy clockwork liner from 1926 *Games and Toys*

'My father, David Alexander Berger Black, was born in 1882 in Liverpool. I have reason to believe he came of Austrian Jewish stock, refugees here from the pogroms of the late nineteenth century.

'Blacks Ltd was started by father and two cousins in a cellar in Graftern Street, off Bridgewater Street, Liverpool, where they produced parrot cages. (Father met mother as her father had a pet shop in Islington, Liverpool.) From parrot cages in a cellar they progressed to making toffee trays for Williams Toffees Ltd, Liverpool. As Williams progressed so did Blacks Ltd. Whilst other customers were obviously acquired, up to the Second World War, Williams were always a favoured customer.

'I have a feeling that it was pressure from Williams that started Blacks Ltd in tinprinting, I think during the first World War. From an early age I can remember printed tins round the house and we each had a tin toy drum as a money box, which father had put a small slot in to take our pennies. There was a great ceremony the morning of going on holiday, when father attacked each drum with a tin-opener to see how much each of us had saved! These early drums were printed on tinplate and had a lacquer background with soldiers marching round the middle. They were also supplied to the toffee trade

Black Ltd Jazzband set, 1950

with one end detachable to fill with sweets for Christmas.

'During the twenties, Blacks Ltd ran mostly on orders from the toffee trade. However, the Yo-Yo boom of the early thirties showed them the possibilities in the toy trade.

'I think that the basic idea for the Tin Toy Jazz Drum came from Germany; however, as this was before my time I am not sure. Towards the end of the thirties, a new Design Drum was introduced (to compete with Hall & Lane), which had no gold lacquer on it. This enabled us to use 'Silvite', a type of blackplate on steel sheet which was not tinned but was printable. I have always favoured the earlier design myself as the gold lacquer background made it a much brighter toy. From the early thirties to the war, we supplied F W Woolworth with many thousands of Jazz Band sets and 8" drums until the early fifties, when the F W Woolworth trade petered out.

'In the sixties, we concentrated more on 'General Line' tins, printed and plain. In 1968 father (by then twice married and Mayor of Bootle 1951/52) died, leaving most of the day to day running to my brother Dave (7 years older than I) and yours truly. My brother died in 1974 and I seriously had to weigh up the position if I wanted to retire. An opportunity presented itself in 1979 and at 63 years I bowed out. It was a rather ticklish situation as one or two family interests had to be satisfied and it is remarkable how wise some people are after the event! However Blacks Ltd seems to be still prospering.' *See Appendix 1*

Blondin, Lady
See Philip Toy Co.

Boats
Principal manufacturers
Bassett-Lowke Ltd
Bowman Ltd
Brighton Manufacturing Co., 1912
Cartwright & Watkins Ltd, 1913
Dubilier Condenser Co. Ltd, 1920
Meccano Ltd, 1932/39

Britains dancers, 1890 (top left)

Britains Scotsman (middle)

Britains Little Red Riding Hood, 1935 (top right)

Britains 'Miniature London Road Roller', 1910 (bottom)

page 35

Britains two seater sports car, 1937

Britains light goods van, 1954

RUBBER TYRED
MINIATURE
MOTOR
CARS
SPORTS MODEL
OPEN TWO-SEATER
FULL SCALE MODEL
MANUFACTURED BY

BRITAINS MOTOR AND ROAD SERIES
BRITAINS LTD
LIGHT GOODS VAN
With Driver
RUBBER TYRES, CAB AND
REAR DOORS OPEN
OIL THE WORKING PARTS OCCASIONALLY
Copyright Models
MANUFACTURED BY
W Britain
IN LONDON, ENGLAND
TRADE
MARK.
BRITAINS LTD

Sebel & Co. Ltd, 1956
Sutcliffe Pressings Ltd, 1885–1982
Treforest Mouldings Ltd, 1935
Victory Industries Ltd, 1945
Wells-Brimtoy Ltd, 1932/41
**pp. 30, 31, 98*

Further reading: *Toy Boats*, Basil Harley

Bonds o' Euston Road
1895–the present day
254 Euston Road, London NW1
Manufactured a wide range of railway equipment; also boats, engines, motors and tools; distributors of many other lines. Bonds still trades in Midhurst, West Sussex.

Bowler, David, & Co.
1945–the present day
Hardley Industrial Estate, Hythe, Southampton
Among the tin toys marketed by this firm are money-boxes, drums, spring tops and Bagatelle tables. It became a limited company in 1967.

Bowman
1932
Dereham, Norfolk
Manufacturers of model steam trains, steam boats and stationary engines.

Brass and Copper Novelties
See George Whitehouse

Bremner Products (London) Ltd
1947
81b Felsham Road, Putney, London
Engineers and makers of models and high-grade mechanical toys. Trademark 'Brem Toys'. Made a Junior Engineer Constructor Crane Set and a Mechanical Crane with detachable 'Rota-Mota'. Advertisements in *Games and Toys*, May 1947, state that Brem products were made to scale and brightly coloured.

Brenco
See Brenner J G & Co.

Brennel Engineering Co. Ltd
1946
Manufacturers of 'distinctive tin toys'. Selling agent W H Cornelius.

Brenner, J G & Co. Ltd
1914–1923
Brenco Works, City Road and 59 Jackson Street, Manchester
Trade name 'Brenco'.

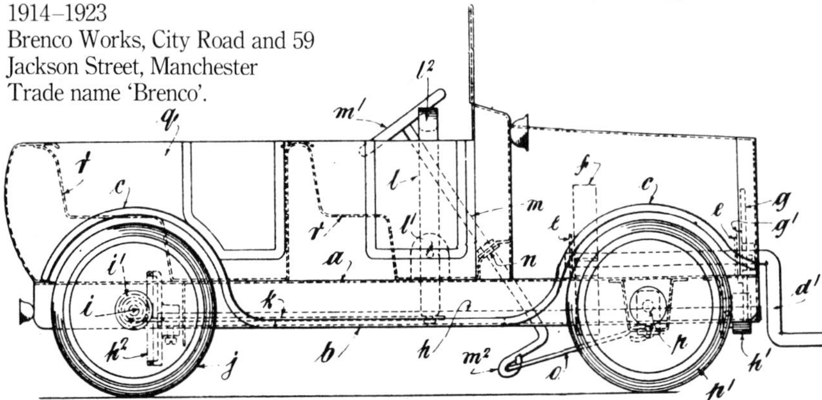

Drawing by John George Brenner, inventor. Specification No.148005, 3 November 1919

J G Brenner car and garage, 1920

This firm made a clockwork motorcar widely advertised in 1920 as the 'Rolls-Royce' of motorcars. It was sold complete with a printed tin garage. The winding key of the car did not stick on at the side, but hung down in front of the car like the starting handle of a real car.

In addition to this best-selling car, J G Brenner & Co. produced other tin toys, toy scales and cranes, a model telephone and folding dolls' beds. During the war years the metal spinning top they made had been a great success; but with the return of peace, sales declined rapidly as their usual agent refused to stock them, saying 'My customers now only want German novelties'. In the end he agreed to take 10,000 of them at a savagely cut-down price, provided all the 'British Made' labels were removed. Toy buyers who had refused to pay 65 shillings per gross for 'Brenco' tops then happily paid 72 shillings per gross, in the deluded belief they were buying a new German toy.

Brighton Manufacturing Co. Ltd
1912
12 Upper Bedford Street, Brighton
Sole agents for 'Sons of the Sea', a series of World's Warships in miniature, all correct to scale. They were advertised as 'British Toys for British Boys'.

Brimtoy
1914–1932
See Wells-Brimtoy and Appendix IV

Britains Ltd
1845 – the present day
Founded by William B Britain, a young engineer who left Birmingham in 1845 and set up a home-based factory at 28 Lambton Road, Hornsey, London, where he made mechanical toys, helped eventually by his large family of boys and girls.

Britain had five sons: William junior, the eldest, Alfred, Fred, Edward and Frank. William junior was the mechanical genius of the family and it was he who was

W Britain Senior, 1826–1906

reponsible for the invention of the small-scale hollow-cast model soldiers, animals etc. for which the firm is principally known. Before the soldiers, patents were registered for some clever mechanical toys: in 1884, a patent for a clockwork Chinaman drinking tea and a Scotsman drinking whisky. About the same time a mechanical money-box in the form of a sailor was produced, as well as a Smoking Khedive, an Indian Juggler, a Mikado with fan, and walking animals. The toys were nicely dressed and worked by strong springs.

Patents taken out in 1886 and 1888 were based on spinning principles (rod and wheel) and inertia flywheel. From these were developed racing games with epicyclic gearing: horses racing, men walking or cycling round a central hub.

THE EQUESTRIENNE.

This, as the name implies, consists of a horse galloping round a ring, as at a circus. Standing upon the back of the horse is a fairy, who, as the horse passes under the bar, stoops and then jumps, clearing the bar in a most clever manner, alighting upon the horse's back and stands, balancing herself until the horse reaches the bar, when she again jumps, continuing to ride and jump until the horse stops.

Post free, 1/3.

Britains 'Equestrienne' from 1910 catalogue

The heavy spun flywheel which by friction set other wheels in motion was capable of many variations, and was especially popular with a little road roller and a little equestrienne doing a circus act.

William Britain junior did the modelling for the soldiers, and they were successful because he insisted on their being accurate. They were painted by hand for detail. Number 1, Life Guards, was produced about 1893, and was followed by Number 2, Royal Horse Guards (The Blues), Number 3, The 5th Dragoon Guards and Numbers 4 & 5, The 1st Life Guards.

The models became steadily more ambitious. There was an issue of the full band of the Coldstream Guards in 1894 (number 37) and the Royal Horse Artillery. Moveable arms were introduced about 1896, so that the arm holding a rifle or binoculars could swing at the shoulder. Soon models of foreign troops were added: Zulus with sandbags and tent equipment; regiments of the Indian Army about the time of the Diamond Jubilee in 1897; then South African Mounted Infantry (Boer War) and South Australian Lancers. By 1899, set number 100 was reached and the boxes bore a copyright trademark with the signature of W Britain (Patent No. 459993).

In 1907, the firm was incorporated as Britains Ltd, with the five sons as directors. Up to 1912, the date of the introduction of a model appears on the box lid.

Britains 'The General' fly-wheel drive toy, c.1895

Britains farm, 1922. One of the first 'peace' toys

During the 1914–18 war, Britains continued a limited output of soldiers and cannons, besides munitions; and the period between the wars was one of great prosperity. One long-lasting success was the Howitzer gun (Patent No. 641319) which fired matchsticks with deadly accuracy. At the end of the First World War, anti-war feelings encouraged the introduction of 'peace toys', such as farm-yard sets, zoos and menageries, circus sets, football teams, US cowboys and Indians, pots and pans for dolls' houses, and even garden gnomes and hunting series.

William Britain junior, who was born on 14 December 1860, died on 24 November 1933. He had been one of the first men to invent a man-carrying aeroplane and he designed beautiful model planes. He was succeeded by his son, Denis, who had entered the firm at the age of 19 and who in World War II served as an RAF navigator and was awarded the DFC. He also received the OBE for his services to industry. In 1953, the Coronation year of Queen Elizabeth II, a beautifully designed Coronation Coach with outriders was produced – one of the last major sets.

In 1967, Denis retired as Managing Director but remained as Chairman. Gradually production was given over to plastic models, but in 1971 scale-model motor cycles were introduced and also American Civil War characters with metal bases, anticipating the American Independence Bicentenary.

In 1987, Britains Ltd became part of the Dobson Industries Group and the name of the firm was changed to Britains Petite, stressing its links with Byron International Ltd, the makers of Petite Typewriters.

See Byron Jardine Ltd, Cadbury Ltd, Racing Cars, Ronald Cameron, *Soldiers*
**pp. 14, 15, 19, 34, 35, 38, 39, 111*

Advertisement from 1945 *Games and Toys*

Further reading: *Toy Soldiers,* James Opie
The Art of the Toy Soldier, Henry Kurtz and Burtt Ehrlich

Britains football game, 1938 (top)

Britains Salesman Sample, Jockey Series, 1954 (bottom)

Britains Tourer and coupé, 1937 (top)
Britains barrage balloons, 1940 (bottom)

British Can Co.
1929–1931
This short-lived company started out as a British subsidiary of the huge American Can Company. It was formed from two older firms, E H Taylor of Liverpool, founded in 1900, and E T Gee & Co. also of Liverpool. British Can Company was soon absorbed into the Metal Box empire. At their Aintree factory, British Can Company printed the Hornby sheets for the M3 series of tank locomotives.

British Games
1932–1980
Clerkenwell Close, Gray's Inn Road, London
Manufacturers and dealers in indoor and outdoor games. In 1934, they were selling BG Midget pedal cars. In 1946, the firm, together with its parent company, Toga Ltd, was acquired by Anglo-Centrop Ltd. A new factory was opened at Warren Works, Berkshire.

British Lion Manufacturing Co.
1915
Letchworth, Hertfordshire
Produced metal parts for manufacturers' tools for toy makers. Also produced toys and novelties for sale to the toy trade, including the British Lion Skate Cycle.
See Bicycles

British Metal & Toy Manufacturers Ltd
See Wells-Brimtoy and Appendix IV

British Match Cannon Co.
See Guns

British Metal (Kingston) Ltd
An engineering firm founded in 1887 which began toy making in 1919. The firm specialised in large metal toys and used the trademark 'Kinco' with a picture of a smiling King Kinco, which was meant to promote the 'Kinco' smile. Lines included Plasto Map, Electric Fishing Game, and in 1920 the Kinco 'loom', on which children could weave on a 'model of the real thing'. 1921 saw the Garden Swing-Sway, a steel type of safety see-saw with enclosed seats.
See Constructional Toys

British Mouthorgans Ltd
See D G Todd & Co. Ltd, Musical Toys

British United Toy Co.
1908–15
Morley Works, St Peter's Road, Kingsland, London
The company, together with James Renvoise, were inventors and makers of English mechanical toys including derricks, flip flaps and gyro tops.

Briton Ferry Cannister Co. Ltd
1923
The Briton Ferry, South Wales
Listed as manufacturers of metal toys in the *Toy and Fancy Goods Trader*, 1923.

Bryant & May Ltd
1852–the present day
Fairfield Row, Bow, London
This old established match making firm opened its factory in 1861. In 1875, they bought from Barclay & Fry the patent covering the use of offset lithograph for printing on tinplate. They had hoped to use the process in making metal matchbox holders, but lost interest and licenced the process to the biscuit tin makers, Huntley Boorne & Stevens.

To promote the sale of headless matches for use in model making, Bryant & May published between 1913 and 1914 a short-lived magazine. After World War II, they encouraged the use of blank match splints by offering them to HM Prisons and other model making organisations in lots of 22,000 matches, rolled up in large 'cheeses'. In 1977, they launched the 'Woodcraft' range, a smaller kit which the firm hoped would attract the toy market, as well as card and other games. In 1980, the firm moved to High Wycombe.

Burbank Toys Ltd
1972–1980
Rixon Road, Wellingborough, Northamptonshire
A British subsidiary of the American firm Mattel, founded in 1972, but soon absorbed into the Dunbee Combex Marx group. Manufacturers of soft toys (talking and non-talking), fairytale and nursery rhyme characters filled with beans, Rupert, Pooh, Buzby, Teddy Bears, Wombles and Walt Disney characters, steel and die-cast nursery toys.

Burnett Ltd
1914–1939
11 Grosvenor Buildings, Steelhouse Lane, Birmingham
London Office: first 52 Aldersgate Street, later, in 1934, 21 Chiswell Street, London
The company was registered on 3 October 1914 as manufacturers of mechanical and automatic toys and novelties, the directors being F Burnett and E Satchwell, merchants. In March 1915, at the Toy Fair and Market held at the Royal Agricultural Hall in London, they were listed as 'manufacturers of metal and soft toys'. After the Second World War, the tools for the Burnett range of clockwork and other metal toys were taken over by Chad Valley & Co. Ltd.

Burbank Jack-in-the-Box music box, 1972

It would seem probable that the first British-made clockwork toys to be advertised in *Games and Toys* in October and November 1914, were in fact made by Barringer, Wallis & Manners for Burnett – but there is as yet no documented proof that this assumption is correct. The following list is, however, based on toys exhibited at successive British Industries Fairs, and on advertisements in relevant trade journals:

1916–1919 Motor cars, motor omnibuses, delivery vans, fire engines, indoor games made with decorated metal boxes and tin money-boxes.

Burnett van advertising 'Ubilda' series, 1930s

1925 'Joey' aeroplanes, taken over from R Joseph & Co. with no change except for paper 'RAF' discs stuck on to wings.

1928 Mechanical motor cars, omnibuses, engines, toy cannons, revolvers, money-boxes, constructional toys (possibly the first 'Ubilda'), and cash boxes and paint boxes (probably made by Dunn & Taylor).

1932 First advertisements of the 'Ubilda' series.

1933 'Ta-Ta', a walking toy of a woman pushing a pram (in red and brown).

1934 'Ubilda' series consisting of kits for making:
Locomotive, Saloon with clockwork, Coupé with clockwork, Racing car with clockwork, Fire Engine, Fort, Tower Bridge, Crane, Airliner, Aeroplane.

1935 Locomotive 'Royal Scot' in authentic colours, money-boxes, cash boxes (taken over from Dunn & Taylor).

1940 Last mention of Burnett Ltd in *Games and Toys.*

1946–1947 Tools for Burnett mechanical and non-mechanical toys at Barringer, Wallis & Manners taken over by Chad Valley & Co. Ltd.
**pp. 22, 23*

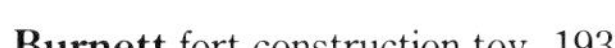

Burnett fort construction toy, 1934

Butcher, W & Sons Ltd
1915
Camera House, Farringdon Avenue, London
Manufacturers of wood and metal construction sets rather like Meccano using the name Primus Engineering. Also one of the largest camera and magic lantern manufacturers. **p. 126*

Byron Jardine Ltd
1918–the present day
Chelsea Street, Nottingham
An old established firm who after World

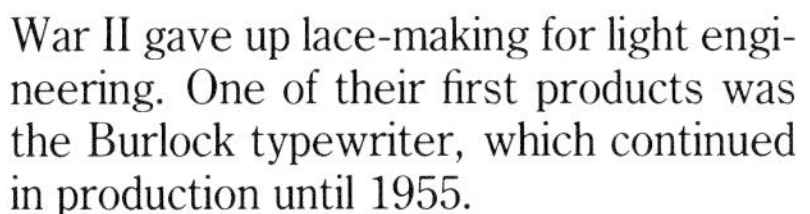

War II gave up lace-making for light engineering. One of their first products was the Burlock typewriter, which continued in production until 1955.

In 1957, they produced the 'Petite' typewriter for children, designed by E V Byers. Many of the techniques used were way ahead of those used by conventional typewriter manufacturers.

In 1960, the Mettoy Company became the sole selling agents. By 1980, different keyboards had been added to their range, an 'office activity centre', consisting of a toy-sized telephone, office stationery and a typewriter, packed in a small brief case. They also make an electronic toy cash register and a functional lockstitch sewing machine. Although the factory is still at the same Nottingham address as in 1918, the firm is now called Byron International Limited.
See Britains Ltd, Typewriters

C

CMT Wells Kelo Ltd
See Appendix IV

Cadbury Bros Ltd
1935
Well-known English chocolate manufacturers. In March 1935, vouchers from Bourneville cocoa tins could be exchanged for toys, and in October of the same year metal toys called 'Cococubs' were given away. 'Cococubs' were also strip cartoon characters who appeared in a popular newspaper of the time and in a magazine published by Cadbury Brothers Ltd. These toys were manufactured for Cadbury's by Britains Ltd.
See Britains Ltd

Caldicot Printing Works
1920–1984
Caldicot, Gwent
A firm of tinplate 'trade' printers who carried out a lot of work for Meccano Ltd, A Wells & Co. and David Bowler & Sons.

In 1984, Caldicot Printing Works were taken over by the Lin-Pac Packaging Group, at the same time as they acquired Huntley, Boorne & Stevens to form the Linpac Metal Decoration Co.
See Printing on Tinplate

Cam, Joseph & Son
1807–1934
Boston Street, Sheffield
Manufacturers of 'Boys' Favourite' tool sets.

Cambrian Can & Drum Co. Ltd
1939
Port Talbot, South Wales
Manufacturers, producers and dealers in metal and metalware of all kinds, including drums, boxes and containers. They also made mechanical toys, cars and lorries, humming tops, scales and novelties. Their products were sold by the wholesale firm Strowe & Co. They registered the trademark 'Camtoy'.

Cameron, Ronald
1960s–the present day
A freelance artist sculptor who has created many prototypes for a great number of firms. He was responsible for several new and sophisticated techniques, adopted by Britains, in producing coloured model soldiers by building up layers of different coloured plastic material and so eliminating the need for hand colouring.

In addition to working for Britains, Ronald Cameron has also worked for such major British toy manufacturers as Airfix, Charbens, Graham Bros, Hornby, Lone Star, Matchbox and Mettoy.

Cartwright, A S Ltd
1880–1950
A firm of press tool makers who also undertook all kinds of small tinplate stampings and piercings for the trade. In 1890, A S Cartwright registered the trademark 'Holdfast' for his invention of a safety fastening for the teats on babies' and dolls' feeding bottles. The firm also made little bells, babies' reins and rattles.

In 1905, this small factory, employing about twenty people, was taken over by J Kingsnorth Hussey. Within a few years he introduced many new lines: tin and later aluminium dolls' teasets, kitchen stoves, toy telephones, carpet

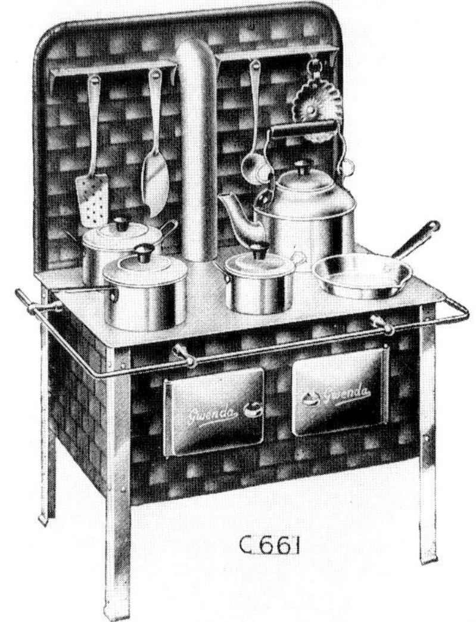

A S Cartwright 'Gwenda' cooking stove C.661, 1940

Cascelloid lid of 'Palitoy' electric train set (above) and contents (below) c. 1968

Crescent 'Knights Crusade', 1953 (top)

Charbens orchestra, c. 1960

Dear Gwenda.
So sorry I had to miss you again at Xmas.
Yours Lovingly Santa Claus.

A. S. CARTWRIGHT LTD.
WESTERN ROAD, BIRMINGHAM 18

'Gwenda' herself from January 1944 *Games and Toys*

sweepers, lawnmowers. To cover these he registered a second trademark 'Gwenda', and used a picture of his little daughter of the same name to publicise them. In 1929, a third trademark, 'Conductor', was used on toy bus conductor sets, with ticket punches that rang somewhat like the real thing.

J K Hussey had been a founder member of the British Toy Manufacturers Association and played a leading part in its activities over the years. He died in 1946 and the firm was acquired by Chad Valley, who continued the manufacture of many of the Cartwright lines for another ten to fifteen years.

Cartwright Metal Toy Co.
1922
6 Prospect Street, Union Road, Rotherhithe, London
Manufacturers of a football game played to FA rules, called 'Socker'; the automatic metal footballers had moving feet.

Cartwright & Watkins
1913
10 Bissell Street, Birmingham
Manufacturers of juvenile tricycles, tricycle horses, chain-driven cars. In 1914, manufactured metal battleships and cruisers.
See Bicycles

Cascelloid Ltd
1919–1985
Britannia Works, Cobden Street, Leicester
The firm was founded in 1919 by A E Pallett in a small workroom in Britannia Street, Leicester, where he produced penny windmills and rattles, using an early plastic material made from casein and celluloid, which two substances gave the firm its name.

The firm moved to new premises in Cobden Street, increased production, and in 1937 became a subsidiary of British Xylonite Limited with a new factory at Abbey Lane, Leicester (Britannia Works) and another at Coalville for the manufacture of Palitoy dolls. A new safety material Bexoid was used, an unbreakable and non-flammable plastic. Novelties were made including Mickey Mouse figures and other Walt Disney characters; and a football pool game 'Ace' was produced in 1936 when Pools promotion first became popular. In 1939, the company secured the rights of Novelty Games Ltd, who made knitting and embroidery sets for girls and a miniature set of Bob Snooker which had most features of the adult game.

In 1943, A E Pallett was succeeded as Managing Director by Henry Senior. Senior was a chartered accountant with experience of worsted mills and of American management methods. He reorganized the factory and introduced many new games and toys at the end of the war. The brand name Durite was registered in 1948 for a variety of sports goods and in 1955 Vogue Playthings Ltd, a subsidiary company, was producing metal construction sets and soft toys.

Caricature of A E Pallett, 1932

In 1968, General Mills of America acquired Palitoy (the company's new name), and produced popular dolls in the modern style, such as 'Tressy' and 'Action Man'. In 1978, the old established firm of Chad Valley was taken over by Palitoy. The modern factory of Palitoy Limited, Owen Street, Coalville, Leicester, produced games, trains, dolls, play-doh and a variety of construction sets. The firm was eventually acquired by Kenner Parker and in 1985 the name of Palitoy was dropped.
**p. 42*

Advertisement from 1948 *Games and Toys*

Cast Iron Toys

English foundry toys were generally simple versions of kitchen and domestic ware. A few money-boxes were also made, but toy mangles and cooking stoves were the most popular items. Many 19th century small doll's house toys and teasets were made of 'Britannia' ware (tin and antimony) or else a pewter-like metal.

See Money-boxes, Sydenham & McOustra, Wallworks Ltd

The Celt Toy and Engineering Co.

1919

Crown Works, 236 Morning Lane, Hackney, London

A branch of TEC Engineering Co., Stoke Newington. Manufacturers of cheap lines of hollow-cast lead soldiers.

See Soldiers

Chad Valley Co. Ltd

1823–1980

The firm was founded by Antony Bunn Johnson as a small bookbinding and printing firm in Lichfield Street, Birmingham. In 1860, Johnson's two sons established works in George Street, Birmingham (Johnson Brothers Ltd) where besides general printing, various stationers' sundries were manufactured. When the business was moved to the village of Harborne near Birmingham in 1897, the new factory was sited by a stream called the Chad and eventually in 1919 the name Chad Valley was adopted as a trade name for games and printed books. The business was managed by Johnson's sons and grandsons.

The Great War and the ban on German goods led to further expansion, and by 1920, their three factories were merged into one firm under the title Chad Valley Company. They specialised in promotional toys, subjects already popularised commercially in film cartoons, newspaper strips or book characters.

During World War II, their factories switched to government work, though they produced some games for the Forces and home market. After the war full scale toy production was renewed, and by 1946 their Waterloo Works concentrated solely on the mass production of rubber toys and dolls. The company also continued to acquire other long established English firms. Chad Valley did not produce any tinplate toys until the end of the Second World War. Mr Roger Swinburn Johnson explains how this came about:

'During the last war Chad Valley was doing government work, under the management of F R B Whitehouse. In 1944–45, he was in touch with John Ryan of Metal Box (later Deputy Chairman) and arranged for them to produce exclusively for Chad Valley a range of metal toys, clockwise and otherwise. Before the war, Metal Box had taken over Barringer, Wallis & Manners and Hudson, Scott & Sons. Both these companies had the tools and printing plates for a range of printed metal toys made to act as biscuit tins. Also Metal Box had available substantial stocks of tinplate and blackplate, which was in very short supply and on allocation.

'In late 1945, Metal Box started production of these models, all printed with the Chad Valley name and logo. The Ubilda Series were included. The old firm of Burnett had been acquired by Barringer, Wallis & Manners so that range also became available to Chad Valley from late 1945 onwards.

'At the same time as the production and selling started, the staffs of Chad Valley and Metal Box got together regularly to develop additional patterns, which included Humming Tops, Money-Boxes, Seaside Pails, Train Sets and a Remote Control Car. I became closely associated with this on my return to the company from the Eighth Army. By 1948, a very substantial business in metal toys had been developed and Chad Valley decided they must start some production for themselves.

'The first acquisition was the old established Birmingham firm of A S Cartwright, who made a big range of pressed aluminium teasets and cooking sets etc., together with a number of printed tinplate items – also a range of Seaside Spades, to go with the Seaside Pails ex Metal Box. At the same time Chad Valley bought the tool and gauge business of Winfield Ltd and set up a plant at Oldhill in Staffs to make clockwork mechanisms. In 1954, they also acquired 'Glevum Toys'.

'In late 1950, Chad Valley bought a Birmingham firm of tin box makers, Hall & Lane Ltd, which gave them a substantial measure of independence from Metal Box, so the output bought in was gradually reduced.' By 1960, the export trade had expanded and they had several factories employing over 1000 people. In 1972, Chad Valley became part of the Barclay Toy Group. In 1978, it was acquired by Palitoy, a subsidiary of the American firm General Mills UK Ltd. In 1987, the trade name Chad Valley was bought by the United Overseas Group, who in 1989 re-sold it to Woolworth's.

*See Appendix II, *pp. 46–7, 50–1, 122*

Principal firms taken over by Chad Valley

Isaacs & Co. 1922
'Isa' soft toy animals

Warrilows Ltd and H S Hooper Ltd 1925
Boxed games

Pinit Ltd 1926
Wooden constructional toys

Peacock Ltd 1931
Jigsaws and ABC blocks

Skaymo Ltd 1933
Constructional building bricks

A S Cartwright Ltd 1946
'Holdfast', 'Gwenda' and 'Conductor' domestic toys

Barronia Metals Ltd and True to Type Products Ltd 1946
'Knight's Head' precision engineering models

Winfield Ltd 1946
Tool, gauge, and clockwork plant

Ridingburgh Metal Toys Ltd 1949
Strong metal 'Rob' toys

Hall & Lane Ltd 1951
Metal box and toy makers
Cambridge Metal Stamping Co. (a subsidiary of Hall & Lane) domestic hardware

Robert Bros (Gloucester) Ltd 1954
'Glevum' games and toys

Acme Stamping & Box Co. 1956
Metal boxmakers (another subsidiary of Hall & Lane)

H G Stone & Co. and L Rees & Co. 1967
Chiltern range of soft toys

Chad Valley merged with Barclay Toy Group Ltd 1972

Chad Valley acquired by Palitoy, a subsidiary of General Mills (UK) Ltd 1978

Chad Valley Greenline bus No.10005 and car No.10060, 1940s

Chad Valley Midland bus, 1946 (top)

Chad Valley biscuit tin bus manufactured by Barringer, Wallis & Manners for Carr's, 1950s (middle)

Chad Valley GR Royal Mail van, originally Tipp pressings? c.1950 (bottom)

Chad Valley Road Transport van previously issued by Burnett, 1940s (top)

Chad Valley Greenline buses – single decker, Burnett pre-war version, double decker c.1949 (middle)

Chad Valley delivery van, 1946 (bottom)

Advertisement from 1950 *Games and Toys*

Charbens & Co. Ltd
1929–1980
Andover Yard, Hornsey Road, London
Firm founded by Ben and Charles Reid, hence 'Charbens'. Manufacturers of metal farm models, soldiers, metal and electro-plate novelties.

In 1960, the 'Old Crock' series of die-cast cars was produced.

In 1976, the firm became Charbens Toys Ltd, with premises at Orchard Works, St Neots, Cambridgeshire. Lines included plastic solid models of Batman, Superman, foreign costume doll series and Disney figures.
See Taylor & Barrett. **p. 43*

Cherlilea Products
1956–1973
Marton, Blackpool
Manufacturers of unbreakable hollow-cast metal figures, including British soldiers in regimental dress and cowboys and Indians. In 1973, the firm was taken over by Sharna Ware Ltd.
See Soldiers

Cheerio Toy Manufacturing Co.
1920
8 Cirencester Street, Harrow Road, London
Specialists in metal casting.
Produced boxed sets of toy soldiers, camel corps, cavalry regiments, horses for games. Possibly succeeded by Cheerio Toys & Games (England) Ltd in 1947.
See Soldiers

Childs & Smith
1956
'Nulli Secundus' Works, Atherstone, Warwickshire
Manufacturers of all-metal electric remote-controlled aircraft. Trademark 'Nulli Secundus' (second to none).

Chromolithography
Printing from stone or lithography was invented by a German printer, Aloys Senefelder in 1796. The first patent for a steam driven lithographic machine was taken out in 1863. Improvements in rotary presses followed. Colour printing, or chromolithography, was first patented in 1837. The process involved 12 or more different colour separations, from which the image was built up. This method was not used commercially until the 1870s and was eventually superseded in the late 1920s by photolithography, entailing only three or four basic colour separations.
See Printing on Tinplate

Cinema Toys
The first regular cinema shows in England were presented at the Empire, Leicester Square, London, in March 1896. The pictures jumped owing to irregular perforations in the fragile, celluloid film, which was also highly inflammable. In every High Street 'Bioscopes', 'People's Picture Parlours', 'Electric Palaces' and 'Bijou Kinemas' soon opened their doors. After the 1914–18 war, going to the 'Movies' was the great popular entertainment. Innumerable toy versions of cinema machinery were also put on the market, as well as toys cashing in on the success of Hollywood stars like Charlie Chaplin and cartoon characters like Felix the Cat and Mickey Mouse.

Joseph Isidore cinema projector, *Games and Toys* 1919

Principal manufacturers

Bailey's Agencies, London
1947 Pocket Cinema. Tube with slots for film

Beck Novelty Co., London
1922 Wonder Pocket Camera

Chad Valley
Toy Strip Projector

Cinemaker Co., Northampton
1949 Astor Cine-viser. Animated pictures in television style, light source cycle lamp battery

Construments Ltd, London
1934 Projector construction kit

Day Reflectograph Co. Ltd, London
1922 Cinematograph. No screen, no darkened room, no artificial light, operated by turning handle

Electro Pocket Cinema Ltd, Lowestoft, Suffolk
1925 Electro Pocket Camera

G. Greiner & Co., London
1948 'Alpha Kine' 16 mm projector operated from standard long life battery

Guiterman & Co., London
1937 Auto Magic Picture Pistol

Indcol Ltd, London
1930 Bicycle lamp operated projector

Joseph, Isidore, London
1919 Projector

Rees, Leon, London
1939–1948 Bingoscope Cinema. 9.5 mm complete with four Mickey Mouse films (made three models B1, D2 and C4)

Turner & Broom, Wigan, Lancashire
1948 'Rewint' pocket camera and film with 50 pictures

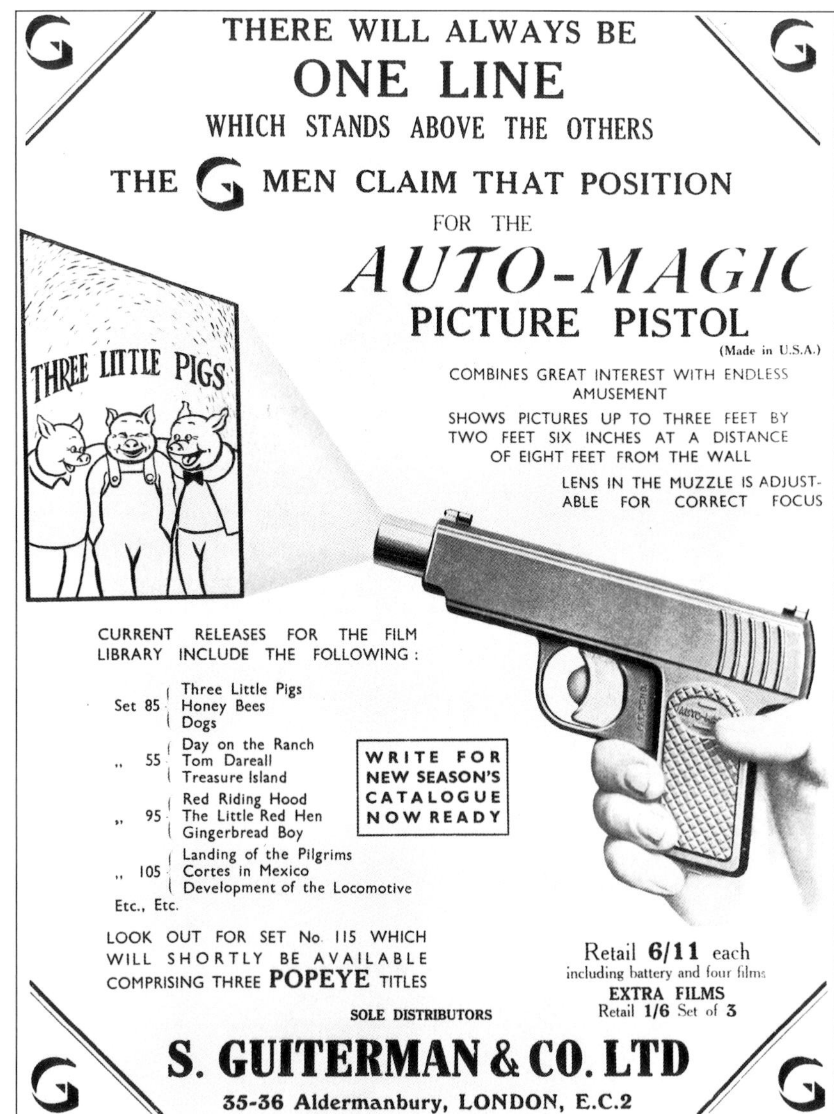

Advertisement from 1937 *Games and Toys*

Cleveland Toy Factoring Co.
1949
102 Cleveland Street, London
Advertised in May 1949 – 'Teeny Model Cars' 2″ long, the smallest clockwork cars made. Also clockwork Lord Mayor's Coach, 6″ long.

It would seem from the illustration that these toys were made of metal, but there is no indication that they were made in England.

Clyde Model Dockyard
1879–1914
Glasgow
Manufacturers of steam locomotives and accessories; 'Simpull' track; the 'Structator' constructional plane; imported various German toys. **p. 30*

Clydon Products
1948
Made Prestacon Model Engineering Kits, sold by L Rees & Co. Ltd. The kit comprised a small press for making metal toys (it could cut and bend metal), together with a guillotine, guide bars, punches for piercing dies, special spanner, screwdriver; plus strips and plates of metal, axles, pulley wheels, nuts and bolts.

Advertisement from 1947 *Games and Toys*

Kit No. 14 contained the necessary material for making a 2-seater sports car.
Kit No. 24 – Coach 21½″ long
Kit No. 34 – Double decker bus 24″ long
Kit No. 44 – Four wheel lorry 17″ long
Kit No. 55 – Six wheel lorry 26″ long
Kit No. 66 – Eight wheel lorry 29″ long
Kit No. 88 – Jeep 15½″ long

See Constructional Toys, Appendix VII

Cococubs
See Cadbury Brothers Ltd

Codeg
See Cowan de Groot

Cohen, Alex (later Alec Cohen & Randall)
1928
684 Stratford Road, Birmingham
This firm of agents dealt mainly in toys imported from Belgium and Germany.

SALOON CAR
(MECHANICAL)
MADE IN ENGLAND

Chad Valley 'Ubilda' coupé, 1946 (top)
Chad Valley saloon car and box, 1946 (bottom)

Chad Valley 'Sing a Song of Sixpence' top, 1946 (top left)
Chad Valley sand bucket, 1946, with early English sand toy and bathing hut (right)
Chad Valley pull-along, 'Tiger Tim and the Bruin Boys', 1950s (middle)
Chad Valley clockwork remote control car, 1948 (bottom)

Alec Cohen seaside bucket, *Games and Toys* 1926

They always stressed that the penny seaside tin pails they dealt in were made to their own special designs. Later Mr J Randall set up Merit Toys.
See J Randall Ltd

Constructional Toys
One of the earliest and most famous construction sets was Meccano, patented by Frank Hornby, its inventor, in 1901. Later it was copied by A C Gilbert and the similar metal set Erector was brought out in 1913. Hornby took proceedings and won his case, but Erector was altered so that it resembled but did not infringe on the Meccano design. Many other firms produced variations of the basic Meccano principle. Some of the most successful are listed here, as well as two do-it-yourself kits – which contained all the necessary tools for you to build your own metal toys.

Bailey, William, Birmingham
1914 'Kliptiko' – metal tubular sections which could slide together to build houses, cottages and 'garden cities'
'Wenebrik' – metal pieces simulating bricks and window frames etc.

Bay Manufacturing Co., Woburn, Buckinghamshire
1948 'Lynx' steel model building outfits, Meccano-like

Becklin Ltd, London
1948 Becklin Bridge – 24 gauge steel bridge construction kit for use with model railways, lorries, cars etc.

Bedington Liddiatt & Co., London
1914 Meta Loxo, a 'Tessted Toy' – flimsy aluminium and bamboo construction set

British Metal Ltd, (Kinco Engineering) London
1920 Meccano-like toy

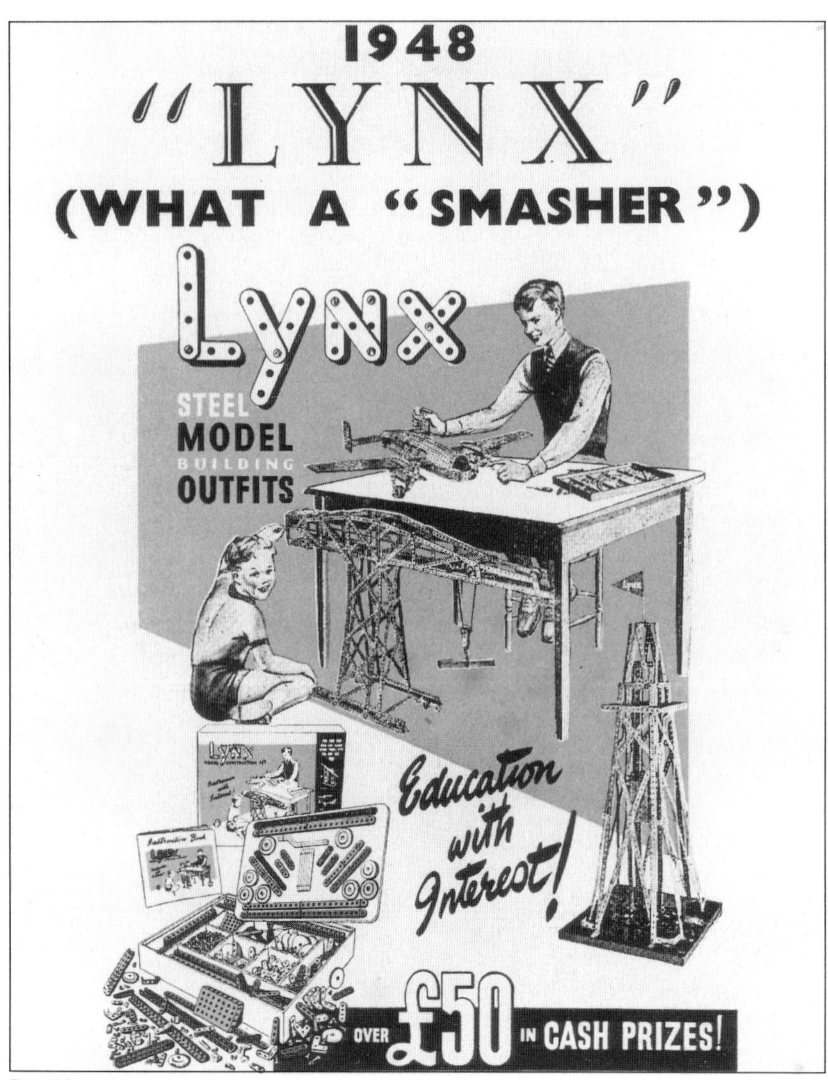

Bay Manufacturing Co. advertisement from *Games and Toys* 1948

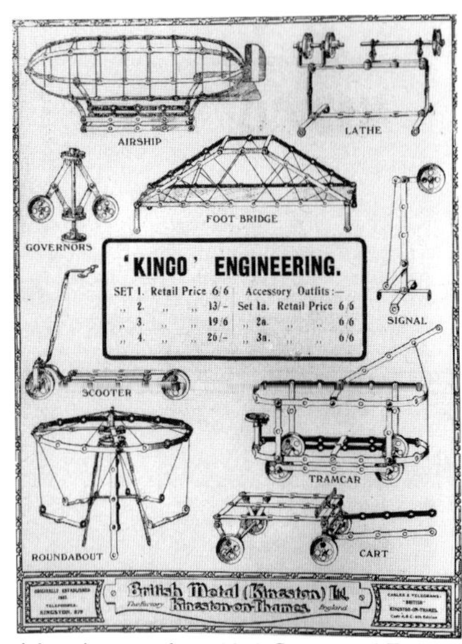

Advertisement from 1920 *Games and Toys*

Brunton & Trier Ltd, London
1931 'Manufax' – patented true-to-scale model engineering kit, high grade steel and special tools. No nuts, bolts, screws or rivets

Butcher W & Sons Ltd, (Primus Engineering)
1915 Wood and metal set with resemblance to Meccano

Chad Valley Ltd, Birmingham
1934 'Tuba' – tubular set, no screws or nuts. Motor runs on pocket battery

Clydon Ltd
1948 Prestacon Model Engineering Kits for making cars, lorries etc.

Cornelius, W H, London
1933 'Mex Makes More' – a kind of composite Meccano originally made in Japan

Construments Ltd, London
1937 Sets marketed by Leon Rees

Goodtoy Products Ltd, London
1947 Metal magnetic construction set for building houses

Gray & Nicholls, Liverpool
1919 'Framus' construction kit consisting of joints, brackets and hinged pieces made out of strips of metal

Juneero Engineering
Junior Engineering Kits

Kay Sports Ltd, London
1930 Electrical construction outfit

Kleiner, J, London
1922 'Structator' – Meccano-like toy

Meccano Ltd
1901 Construction sets

Mettamake Ltd, Liverpool
1929 'Mettabuild' – coloured metal kit with tin angles, girders and plates

N-G Neero
Engineering kits

Paton Calvert Ltd, Liverpool
1915 'Happynak' – tubular construction toy with no nuts or bolts

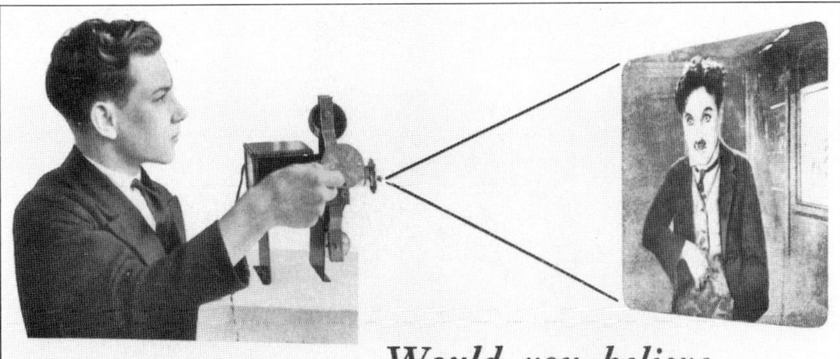

Would you believe—
A BOY CAN MAKE IT!

The NEW
CONSTRUMENTS
"200" OUTFIT
makes
3 DIFFERENT TYPES
OF HOME CINEMA

(Each Cinema will take either 9.5 mm. or 16 mm. films)

"Construments" has jumped to a leading place among constructional toys in the short space of only two years. Because—it's science—not just a toy. Makes real working instruments. Each "Construments" Set contains parts to make dozens of instruments—**Magic Lanterns—Microscopes—Cameras—Electric Torches—Morse Lamps—Home Cinemas, etc., etc.**

Yet another step forward by "Construments!" The New "200" Outfit contains parts to make three different kinds of cinemas:—

1—ORDINARY PROJECTION CINEMA
2—DAYLIGHT CINEMA
3—REVERSING CINEMA

as well as all the models which can be made by the existing "100" Outfit. We are also introducing "Construments 100 Plus," which, when added to the existing "100" Outfit, makes the equivalent of the New "200."

"Construments 200" would sell like wild-fire on the three Cinemas alone—quite apart from the dozens of other instruments you can make from it.

Retail Prices are

"CONSTRUMENTS 10" -	10/-
"CONSTRUMENTS 20" -	18/6
"CONSTRUMENTS 100" -	37/6
"CONSTRUMENTS 100 PLUS"	12/6
"CONSTRUMENTS 200"	47/6

Full particulars of the New "Construments 200" Set and of all other "Construments" Outfits from:—

L. REES & CO. LTD., 12 New Union St., LONDON, E.C.2

Advertisement from 1934 *Games and Toys*

Pioneer Models

Trix Ltd, London
1932 Trix metal bar and bolt kit

Turner, E, London
1931 'Stabil' – Meccano-like set

Further reading: *Meccano Super Models*, G Wright. *The Meccano System and Special Purpose Sets*, J Gamble and B Love
See Appendix VII

Construments Ltd
1933
18 Grays Inn Road, London
Manufacturers of scientific and optical instruments and construction kits. Lines included 'Constral' accessory set – printed photos on any material, paper, wood etc., plus fixing salts, sensitising solution and instructions. Also 'Ray Safety Cinema' with 1s range of Charlie Chaplin and Harold Lloyd films. In 1935, a Microscope 'hobby' outfit was introduced. Products were marketed by Leon Rees Ltd.
See Optical Toys

Cooper Bond Ltd
1916–1928
Minerva Works, Raymouth Street, Bermondsey, London
Tin box makers. They also made mechanical and non-mechanical toys, Royal Mail vans, motor cars, vans, caravans, trams, aeroplanes; and two games, bagatelle and a football game. For a short time they made a folding tin mould for sand castles, but in 1925 they sold the rights to Robert Brothers, makers of 'Glevum' toys.

It would seem probable that toys marked 'Minerva' were made by Cooper Bond Ltd.

Cooper Bond Ltd caravan

Cooper, H & Sons
1912
62 Wellington Road, London
Manufacturers of iron hoops, horse irons for rocking horses and trolley irons.

Corgi Toys
*See Mettoy Co. Ltd *pp. 54–5*

Further reading: *The Great Book of Corgi*, M van Cleemput

Cornelius, W H
1920–1960
23 Paper Street, London
Lines included children's transfers. In 1931, when the speed limit was introduced, a 'Speed Cop' police motorcycle combination was marketed. In 1946, manufactured wood and tin toys; 1955, foam rubber bending toys. Agents for Mettoy during early years.

'Speed Cop' with detachable sidecar, sold by W H Cornelius in 1931

Cowan de Groot Ltd
1919–the present day
Head Office since 1977 – Wakefield House, Chart Street, London
The company was founded by S D Cowan and A de Groot, and continued by their sons, Ernest de Groot and Derrick Cowan.

Cowan de Groot 'Codeg' boxers, c.1945

They were formerly large importers of toys from Germany and Japan. They used the trade names 'Codeg' and 'Codegetto' or 'Edco'. For ten years or so after World War II they did, however, have some metal toys made for them by specialist British firms – notably the 'Merry Builders', an automatic sand toy, a pair of sparring boxers and a cash register; and they also produced the John Bull printing outfits which they took over from W E Christie Ltd.

Corgi Citroen cars, 1950s and 1960s (top)

Corgi saloon cars of the late 1950s and 1960s (bottom)

Corgi Mercedes-Benz, Riley and Jaguar, 1960s (top)
Corgi early Formula 1 cars, 1960s (bottom)

Today the company not only supplies toys, fancy goods and camping equipment to chain stores, supermarkets and mail order firms, but also runs a large wholesale electrical division and owns the Russian Shop in London and the Agency for Soviet Handicrafts. *p. 102

Crackers or Cosaques

Many Victorian and Edwardian dolls' house furnishings started life inside a Christmas cracker. Most of these little metal items were made by firms in or around Birmingham. Catalogues from the old-established firm of Tom Smith, between 1877 and 1900, list over 8000 entries describing boxes of contents.

In more recent times, Barringer, Wallis & Manners made thousands of Penny Novelties for sweet manufacturers, for the Christmas stocking and Christmas cracker trade. The Welnut Engineering Co., subsidiary of Wells-Brimtoy, in addition to making all kinds of nuts, produced a variety of little tin goods as did Chad Valley Ltd.
See Penny Toys

Further reading: *Family Dolls' Houses*, Vivien Green

Crescent Toy Co. Ltd
1922–1980
67 De Beauvoir Crescent, Kingsland Road, London

The firm was founded by Henry G Eagles and Arthur A Schneider in a workshop 30 feet square at the rear of a private house. They manufactured model soldiers, cowboys, kitchen sets etc. from lead alloy. These were hand-painted hollow castings packed 1 dozen in a box and sold to wholesalers at 6s per dozen boxes. The partnership was formed into a limited company, registered in January 1925.

In World War II, production was switched to munitions and millions of components for shell fuses etc. were made. Henry Eagles died in 1942, but after the end of the war his two sons, Harry and Ernest, resumed production of metal toys including models from die-cast zinc alloy.

In 1949, the firm opened a modern factory on a $4\frac{1}{4}$ acre site at Cwmcarn, a Welsh mining village near Newport, Monmouthshire (now Gwent) and two years later transferred all production there, maintaining only an office in London. At the Welsh factory hollow-casting in lead alloy was discontinued, and the models of soldiers, cowboys etc. were made in plastic. A small range of wheeled toys, dolls' prams etc. were also introduced.

For a number of years Crescent Toys undertook the marketing of toys manufactured by Die-Cast Machine Tools Ltd.
See Die-Cast Machine Tools Ltd *p. 43

Crescent Toys Royal Horse Artillery set, 1935

Critchley Hardware Co.
1920
King Street, Stroud, Gloucestershire
Toy and hardware manufacturers. 1920 lines included dolls' prams, cradles, scooters, wheelbarrows, skipping ropes, skittles and iron hoops. By 1954, the firm was known as Critchley Brothers Ltd with premises at Brinscombe, Stroud. Lines included sewing sets, embroidery sets, wooden toys.

D

Dale Forty & Co. Ltd
1920–1936
Darwin Works, Darwin Street, Birmingham
Stamp brassfounders. The first products of this firm, made in premises which were little more than a garden shed, were metal plugs which could be used to mend holes in kettles and saucepans. Next came metal bottle caps, patented under the name of 'E-zee-on'. Then, under the energetic direction of the firm's founder, F W Wilkes, new outlets were found for these small blank tinplate discs. They were sold to clockwork toy manufacturers for making cogs and gears, and to soft toy firms for washers in teddy bears and other animal joints. Other firms used them for dolls' tea sets. Dale Forty & Co. also used them for producing a large range of ready-made wheels for the toy trade.

Defiance Manufacturing Co.
See Musical Toys

De Leef Bros Ltd
1905
Baltic Wharf, Kingsland Basin, London
Metal merchants who used some of the scrap tin they collected for making money-boxes, seaside pails, bull's eye lanterns and other small cheap toys.

Die-Casting Machine Tools Ltd
1940–the present day
The firm was founded by A R Mills and S H Ambridge at Palmers Green, London, after having previously been in partnership as Mills & Ambridge. The company was the first to produce a fully automatic zinc alloy die-casting machine, which it sold to toy manufacturers.

From 1944, the company also manufactured a range of toys which they marketed under the names Lone Star Products and Slikka Playthings. One of the Slikka toys was a model of Harry Hayseed performing on his penny-farthing bike on the high wire.

Between 1953 and 1970, toy soldiers in die-cast metal and plastic were manufactured and marketed under the name of Lone Star Die-Casting Tools Ltd. In addition to their own products the firm also manufactured accurate die-cast metal components for outside firms.

For a number of years the marketing of Die-Cast Machine Tool toys was undertaken by Crescent Toys. In 1980, Die-Cast Machine Tools bought up Crescent Toys but ran into financial difficulties and in November 1983 a receiver was appointed. The company was reformed and relaunched under the title Lone Star Toys Ltd and is still in existence.
See Crescent Toys

Dibro Ltd
1954
8/10 Lily Road, Liverpool
Manufactured small metal clockwork toys and toy watches.

Dingo
See Sale Tilney & Co. Ltd

Dinky Toys
1933–the present day
By 1930, Meccano Ltd was world-renowned for its Meccano System and Hornby Gauge 0 model railways. In 1931, a set of station staff and a lineside accessory, namely a Halls Distemper lineside advertisment was released under the label 'Modelled Miniatures'. This led to the issue in Christmas 1933 of a series of vehicles known as Meccano Miniatures and a year later these were to be christened Dinky Toys.

This range of small vehicles and accessories was to expand to over 1,000 items before production was ended at the company's Binns Road factory in Liverpool late in 1979. Dinky Toys were the first British toys utilizing advanced die-casting techniques and just as Hornby Trains were a response to German manufacturers, so Dinky Toys were a direct challenge to the American Tootsie Toy range. After the receivership in

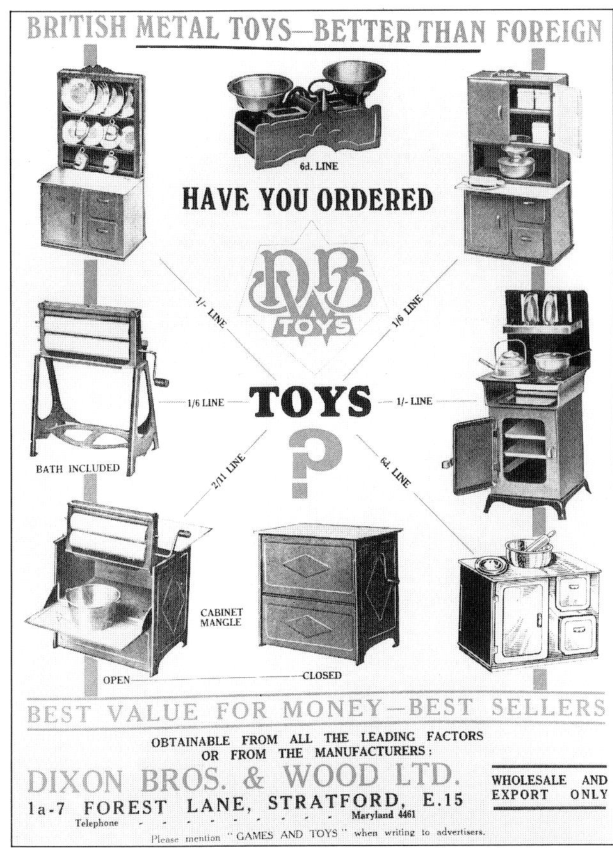

Advertisement from 1934 *Games and Toys*

Advertisement from 1919 *Games and Toys*

1979, the Dinky Toy copyrights were purchased by Airfix Ltd. In 1981, that group went into liquidation and were bought by General Mills toy group, USA. Recently the Dinky name was purchased by the Hong Kong based owner of the former Lesney range. A small series of vehicles under the Dinky label were issued in 1988. **pp. 58–59*

Further reading: Dinky Toys and Modelled Miniatures, Mike and Sue Richardson (Hornby Companion Series)
The Dinky Toy Compendium, Patrick Trench

Dixon Bros (later Dixon Bros & Wood Ltd)
1916–1937
Forest Lane, Stratford, London
A sheet metal working firm that made railway signals, tunnels and tin dolls' house furniture, toy scales, builders' and window cleaners' push carts. In 1936, they produced 'Dickery Dock', a 6d tin toy which could be used to illustrate a nursery rhyme or as a counting board, a clock or an ABC.

Dubilier Condenser Co. Ltd
1919
Ducon Works, Railway Approach, Goldhawk Road, London
A short-lived firm making clockwork submarines, cranes, fire engines and machine guns under the trademark 'Duco'. Their publicity in 1920 stated that the toys were made by 'All British Material and Labour', that they were highly finished, as cheap as similar goods of German manufacture, and were packed in strong boxes with full instructions in English and French.
**p. 30*

Dunbee Ltd
1946–80
10 Union Court, Wormwood Street, London
The firm was founded in 1946 by Richard Beecham and Basil Feldman in order to begin business in the plastics industry, a new growth industry at that time. By the late 1950s, the company had developed considerably and the founders sought to move into the toy industry. In 1960, they purchased the firm Combex from Max Reich, thus forming the Dunbee-Combex Group. The group's expansion was rapid and in 1962 it went public. In 1964, they acquired the Leon Rees group of companies and also Green Monk Products Ltd. In 1967, they purchased the UK interests of Louis Marx, thereby creating Dunbee-Combex-Marx Ltd, and in 1972, Rovex Ltd was purchased from the liquidator of Lines Brothers. Various other companies were subsequently formed within the group, including Burbank Toys Ltd, Novo Toys Ltd and Jean Sorelle Ltd. By 1979, it had grown to be one of the largest toy concerns in the world.

Unfortunately the American subsidiaries, Louis Marx & Company Incorporated and Aurora, instead of bringing in profits, proved such a financial drain that by the end of February 1980 a receiver had been appointed to sell off all the profitable assets of the Dunbee-Combex-Marx empire, such as Martlet, the do-it-yourself division, as well as Rovex division which included Pedigree, Hornby and Scalextric.
See Louis Marx

Dunn, Ralph & Co.
1906
61 Barbican, London
A London based firm who had tin toys made for them by Hudson Scott & Sons of Carlisle. They registered a game called 'Dolly's Post', and in 1912 were advertising the 'Young Gardener's' boxed sets of little gardening tools, water pistols, rattles and dolls' beds.

Dunn & Taylor
1908–1950
61 Burbury Street, Birmingham
Tinplate workers and makers of lamps and cash boxes. Their various lines of toy cash boxes were taken over by Burnett Ltd in 1935 and after World War II by Chad Valley & Co. Ltd.
See Money-boxes

Durrands Ltd
1920
52–54 Carter Lane, London
Metal toy manufacturers. Lines included trumpets, whistles, skittles, tops, rattles, mouth organs etc. Some of their products were turned in wood and bone.
See Musical Toys

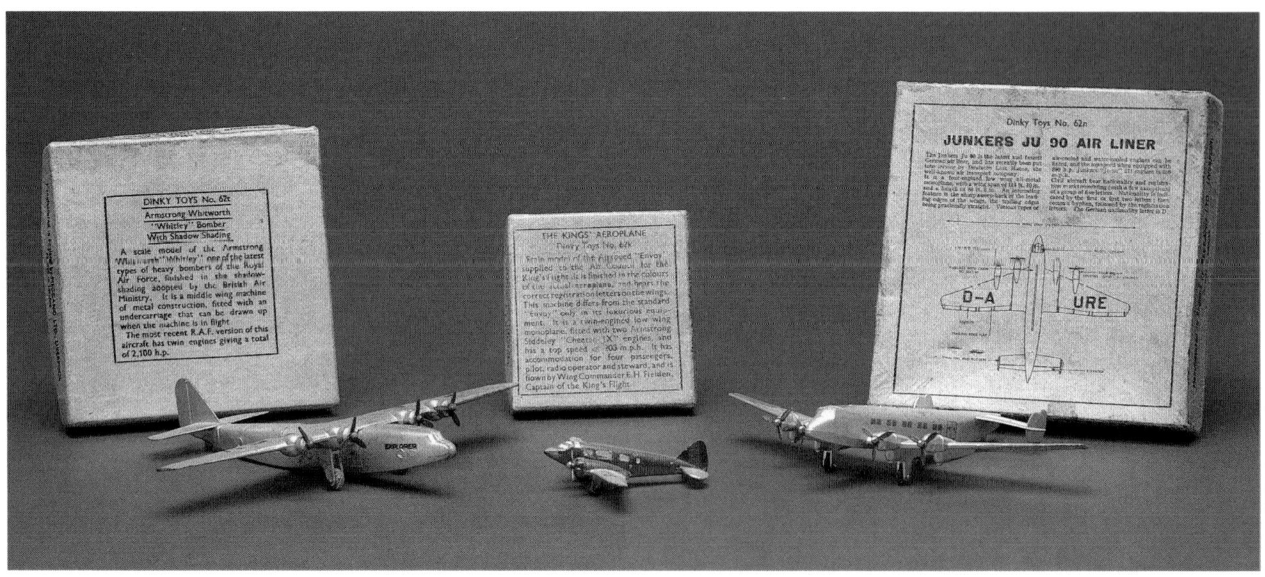

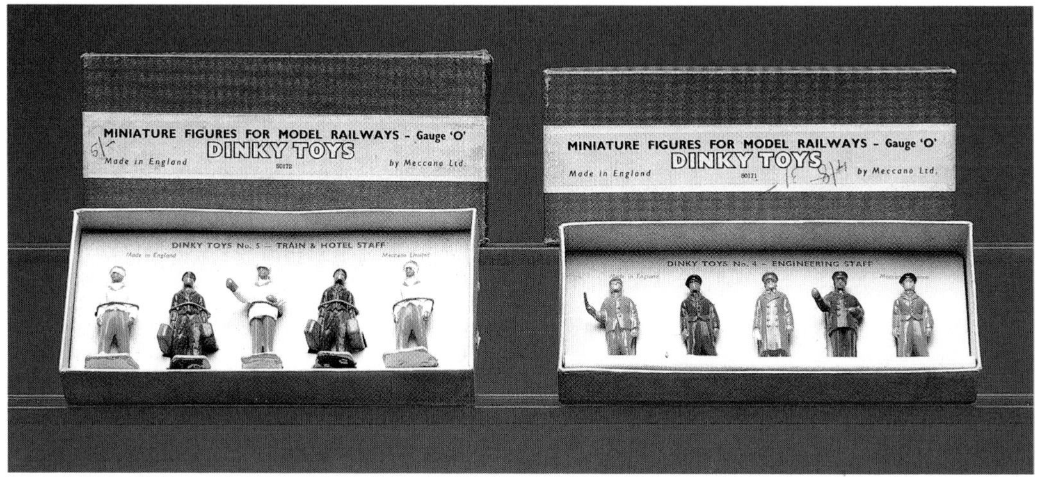

Dinky aeroplanes – Imperial Airways 'Ensign' (wrong box!), The King's aeroplane, Junker Ju 90 Airliner, 1937 (top)

Dinky Mechanised Army set, 1939–40 (middle)

Dinky hotel and engineering staff sets for model railways, post-war (bottom)

Dinky 356A Porsche, Alfa Romeo and AC Aceca 1958/61 (top left)
Dinky Lincoln, Oldsmobile and Packard, post-war re-issues of 1939 models (top right)
Dinky Meccano Passenger train and Silver Jubilee train set, c.1938 (middle)
A collection of post-war **Dinky** toys and pre-war tractor (bottom)

E

Eeles, Walker & Co. Ltd
1886–1950
118 Pitsford Street, Birmingham
The firm was founded by William Eeles for the manufacture of paper boxes, and cards for showcases or patterns. In 1908, they became Eeles Walker & Co. Ltd. By 1922, they had moved to Forward Works Crescent, Cambridge Street, Birmingham, and are listed as manufacturers of composite containers for chemicals, druggists and grocers, of leather goods and also of 'Elswal' all-British toys, which included Chinese puzzles, drums, post office money-boxes, jazz rollers and tambourines. They continued to make tin canisters until 1950.

Eeles Walker & Co 'Elswal' canisters and scales, 1922

Elite
See Leonard & Francis Ltd

Ellarco
See Rees, Leon

Emu Series
See Oppenheimer, S, Ltd

Erecto Toy Co. Ltd
1915
Gourley Street, Tottenham, London
Manufacturers of lead soldiers: territorial, cavalry, guards with sword and lance, infantry from colonial and allied armies, Red Cross nurses, wounded men. Also machine guns, motor cyclists and boxes of barbed wire entanglements and trees. The firm's publicity stressed that their designs were copyright.
See Soldiers

Euston, H R
1917
114 Fore Street, London
A firm of wholesalers who in 1919 were advertising tin aerobus money-boxes

H R Euston Aerobus money-box 1919

possibly made by R Joseph & Co., the manufacturers of the 'Joey' aeroplane.
See Money-boxes

Ever Ready Company (GB) Ltd
1952, London
Battery manufacturers. In order to promote their battery sales, the firm manufactured a battery-operated train London underground set, battery-operated speedboats and the 'Dustette', a miniature Hoover-type cleaner. In 1955 they produced night lights in the shape of cats, dogs, rabbits and motor cars.

F

Fairylite
See Graham Brothers

Fancy Tin Toy Co.
1894–1909
Cheapside and Lower Trinity Street, Deritend, Birmingham
Made money-boxes, seaside buckets and spades.
See Money-boxes

Feaver, John, Ltd
1899–1920s
Tower Bridge Road, London
In 1899, this London firm was making ration tins for the Army. In the 1920s they were printing most of the tinplate sheets used by A Wells & Co.

Finbat
See Richardson, Ernest

Foster, Blackett & Wilson Ltd
1919
121 Cheapside, London, and Northern Toy Factor, Hebburn-upon-Tyne, Northumberland
Early in 1920 introduced a Charlie Chaplin mechanical toy, possibly imported.

Framus
See Gray & Nicholls

Fraser & Glass
1920
Middle Lane, Hornsey, London
Manufacturers of metal wheels for the toy trade. Also made clockwork mechanisms.

Fry A Ltd (Fry Metal Foundry)
1916
25–36 Holland Street, Blackfriars, London
The firm manufactured metal soldiers using a mixture of lead, tin and antimony. lead was predominant, but the other materials gave added strength. The firm also produced small metal parts and wheels for toy making.
See Soldiers

G

Garnett, G E, & Sons
See Whiteley, Tansley & Co. Ltd

Glamtoys Ltd
1935–1953
Port, South Wales
Manufactured cheap small racing cars, trains, clicking frogs and animals for Woolworths. **p. 63*

Glasman, J H, Ltd
1948
'Betal Works', Plaistow Road, London
Manufacturers of die-cast toys including trains, carded tool sets, indoor games, metal toys some of which were marketed by J H Glasman under the trademark 'Betal Toys'. Others were produced for the firm of A S Cartwright (acquired by Chad Valley in 1946) under the trademark 'Gwenda'.
**p. 22*

Goldberg, I A
1912
Trumpet Works, Graham Street, Birmingham
A firm established at the end of the 19th century specialising in 'Penny Packets' and fillings for Christmas crackers and stockings. They manufactured tin kitchen

Foster Blackett & Wilson clockwork Charlie Chaplin, 1921

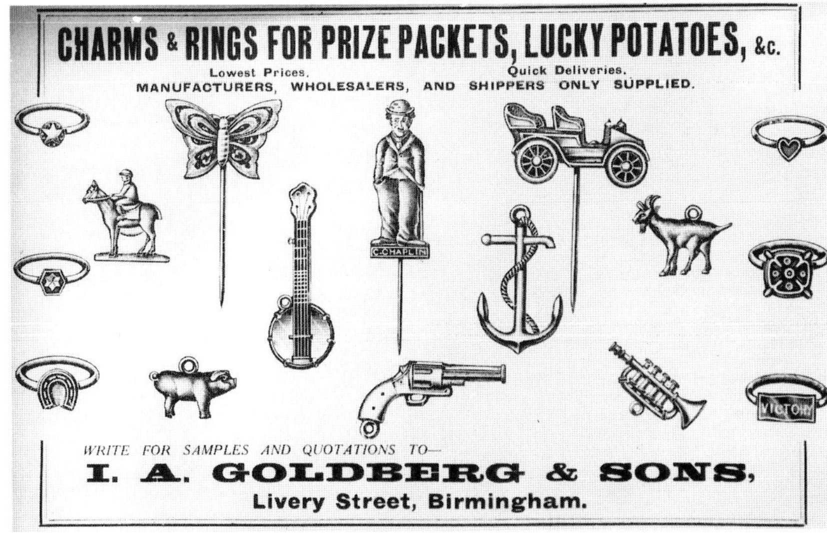

Advertisement from 1920 *Games and Toys*

utensils for dolls' houses, oilcans, tin tea sets, post office money-boxes, toy scales, aeroplanes, whistles, guns, potato guns and peashooters. In 1933, the firm moved to new premises at Livery Street, Birmingham, where they produced assorted penny and twopenny tin toys.
See Penny Toys

Graham Bros
1887
Red Cross Street, London
A firm of wholesalers who dealt mainly in imports from the Far East. They registered the trademark 'Fairylite'.

Gramophone
After the invention of the phonograph or talking machine by Edison in 1876, the gramophone with flat disc records was introduced by A Berliner of Washington in 1887. Various improvements to both these types of equipment were made, and after World War I there were toy gramophones with miniature records and toys which worked on the revolving disc of a gramophone.

Principal manufacturers

Bainbridge & White, London
1923 Race-a-home. A game to attach to the gramophone

Chad Valley
1956 Clockwork gramophone, printed tin

Edison Phonograph
1964 Model kit with bust of Edison and wax cylinder

Goodall, A H, Beccles, Suffolk
1922 Waltzing figures to work on gramophone turntable. Patent No. 183287

Gwinnett, W
1922 Toys for use with gramophone Patent No. 25132

Hastings, H A & Smith, C V, London
1921 Mechanical figures made to dance on a record by means of a magnetised spindle. Patent No. 160951

Jackson, P T, London
1922 Platform with articulated figures. Patent No. 181783

Matthews, T, Leicester
1920 Gramophone figures

Pettifer & Humphreys, Birmingham
1923 'Fairy' gramophone. A miniature gramophone with double sided record and packet of needles

'Granic'
See Gray & Nicholls

Gray & Nicholls Ltd
1915–50
17 St Anne Street, Liverpool
This firm produced 'Granic' toys and ABC blocks, as well as a construction set 'Framus' consisting of joints, brackets and hinged pieces made out of strips of metal, guillotined off scrap tinplate from a local tobacco factory, Wills & Sons, who made their own tin containers.

W H Nicholls, 1920

Greenly, A J
See Guns

Green Monk Products
1945
School Street, Darfield, near Barnsley, Yorkshire
Toy manufacturers. The firm was founded by Arthur Greenwood in 1945 in a garden shed. In 1964, the firm was taken over by Dunbee-Combex. In 1969, 100 full time workers were employed. Lines included musical metal toys, xylophones, roller chimes, drums, wheeled pull-alongs and kaleidoscopes.
See Dunbee Ltd

Guns
In the 17th century toy guns were considered to be as necessary for small boys as toy horses, whether they were small miniature guns capable of firing (for the aristocracy) or model 'mock' guns for those who played at soldiers. By the 19th century, toy guns were made in great quantities; Mayhew's interview in 1850 with a toy gun manufacturer has already been quoted in Chapter 1.

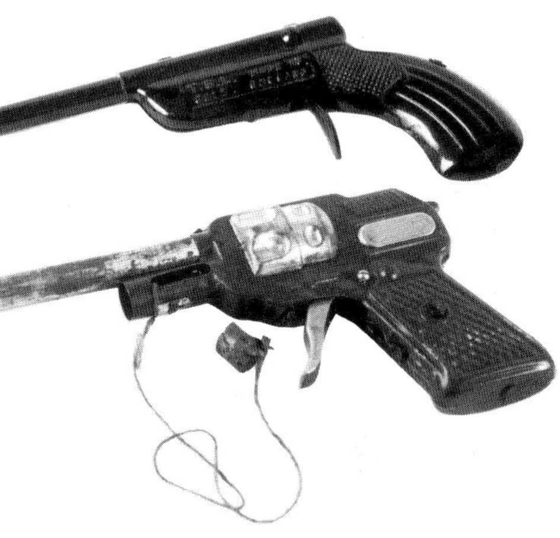

'Tan-sad gun and 'Flashmatic' pop gun, c. 1935

The claim for inventing the percussion cap goes to the famous English gunmaker, Joseph Egg in 1815. By the mid-century, toy 'cap' pistols were being made for children. Caps, 'amorces' were made of paper with a small amount of gunpowder within.

The air-rifle was produced for young people in America, first made of wood and then of metal. In England up to World War I, guns were mostly imported. War always promoted war toys, and in the 20th century there were many home-based toy gunmakers including the firm of Britains Ltd who in 1907 patented a toy machine gun: 'A capital toy for a boy as with this weapon can be put to rout brigade after brigade of soldiers'. The gun was capable of firing 200 shots a minute, since the cup of the barrel was filled with peas and the handle turned rapidly to discharge them.

After World War I, an attempt was made to ban the manufacture of toy

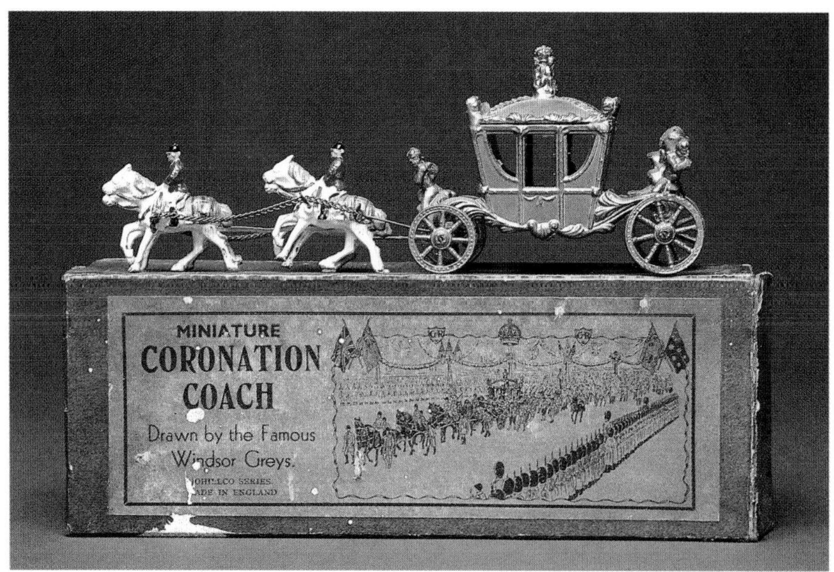

John Hill & Co. 'Johillco' miniature coronation coach with Windsor Greys, 1953 (top)
John Hill & Co. 'Johillco' Queen Elizabeth II Coronation set, 1953 (middle)
John Hill & Co. 'Johillco' fire engine, 1939 (bottom)

Glamtoys clip frog novelty toys, 1950s (top)

Glamtoys Coronation panorama, 1953 (middle)

Hudson, Scott & Co. saloon, 1920

ARE THE BEST ON THE MARKET.
NEW IMPROVED PATTERNS FOR 1914.

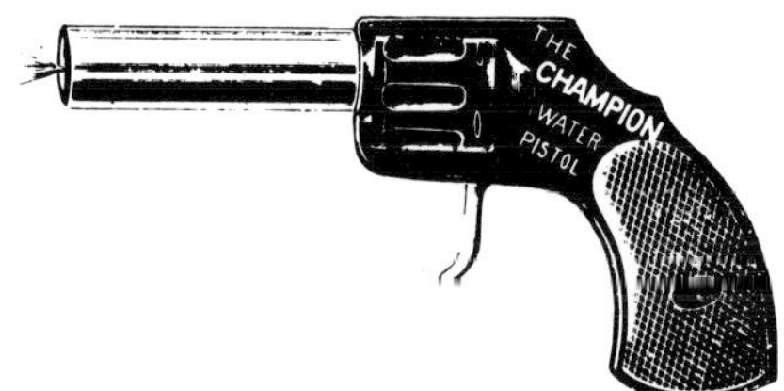

The "IMPROVED BRITISH" Retails at 6½d.

The "CHAMPION" Retails at 1/-

ENTIRELY BRITISH MADE.
TO BE OBTAINED THROUGH ALL THE WHOLESALE WAREHOUSES.
MANUFACTURED BY LEWIS WILD, 12-14, BARBICAN, LONDON, E.C.

Advertisement from *Toy and Fancy Goods Trader* 1914

pistols but to no avail; water pistols, pop guns, spud guns, cap guns, ray guns, atomic guns, fast shooters of all kinds have been produced. The following list is far from complete.

Principal manufacturers

Astra Pharos Ltd, London
1940 Working model guns and searchlights

Atomic, London
1949 Jet gun and die-cast metal machine gun

Britains, William, London
1900 Various types including 'Howitzer' gun

British Match Cannon Co., Southport, Lancashire
4.7 Naval gun, 60 pounder field gun

Bullock Toys, Bournemouth, Hampshire
1948 Various guns

Centuple Manufacturing Co., London
1915 'Hun Gun'

Eaton & Munby Ltd, Burley, Hampshire
1934 Spring-operated guns

Greenly, A J, Watford
1915 Forts and guns, 'Topping Toys'.

Halsall, David, Blackpool, Lancashire
1964/78 Various guns

Hely & Bartlett, London
1923 'Hanwell' toy cannon

Holladay, A J, London
1917 Battleships with swivel guns

Johnson, C H Ltd, Leeds
1921 'Blackcat' shooting game with guns

Lone Star Products, London
1963 Cowboy guns etc

Manufacturers Accessories Co., London
1923 Airguns

Mettoy, Northampton
1956 'Burp Gun' automatic machine gun

Metz, Paul, Birmingham
1914 Pop guns and toy pistols

Midland Gun Co., Birmingham
1914 'British Gem' air rifle

Millard Bros Ltd, London
1945 'Diana' airguns

Nottingham Die-Casting Co., Nottingham
1919 Breechloading guns

Oliver Harper & Co., London
1915 'Unity' toy series of guns

Pedley, W R & Co. Ltd, Willenhall, Staffordshire
1940 Pistols and pop guns

Pocock Bros, London
1922 Air rifles and pop guns

Regent Manufacturing Co., Willenhall, Staffordshire
1897–1913 Various pistols

SP Manufacturing Co., London
1914 Tin plate field and anti-aircraft guns

Wild, Lewis
1921–48 A variety of guns, including water pistols

Gwenda
See A S Cartwright Ltd and J H Glasman Ltd

Gyro Manufacturers
1912, Leicester
Gyro toy makers. Lines included 'Mono rail', 'Happy Dancer', 'Aerial Spiral'.
See Gyroscope

Gyroscope
The French astronomer and physicist, Jean Bernard Foucault (1819–1868), in 1850 constructed a model which he called a gyroscope, to explain the behaviour of celestial bodies and the movement of the earth. The principle of gyroscopic motion had been established sometime earlier by the English scientist, Edward Sang. Gyroscopes have played an important part in many technological developments, and have been used notably as stabilizers and navigational aids; but as early as 1859, the gyroscope was being developed as what was termed a 'philosophical toy'. Perhaps the best-known English toys based on gyroscopic principles are the gyro-cycle and the gyro-tricycle made by Lines Bros in 1939. The gyroscopic

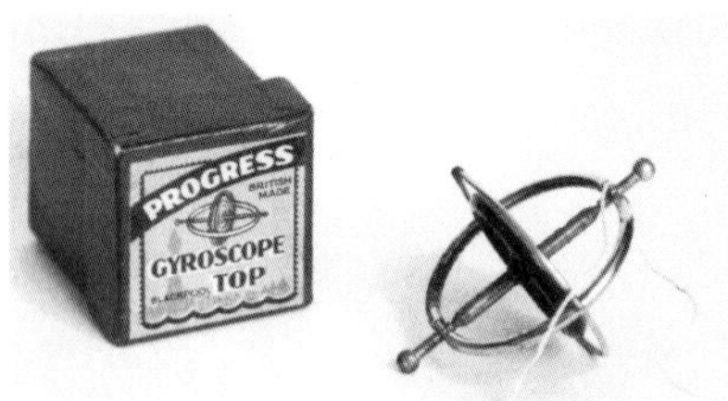

Progress Toy Co. gyroscope, c.1930

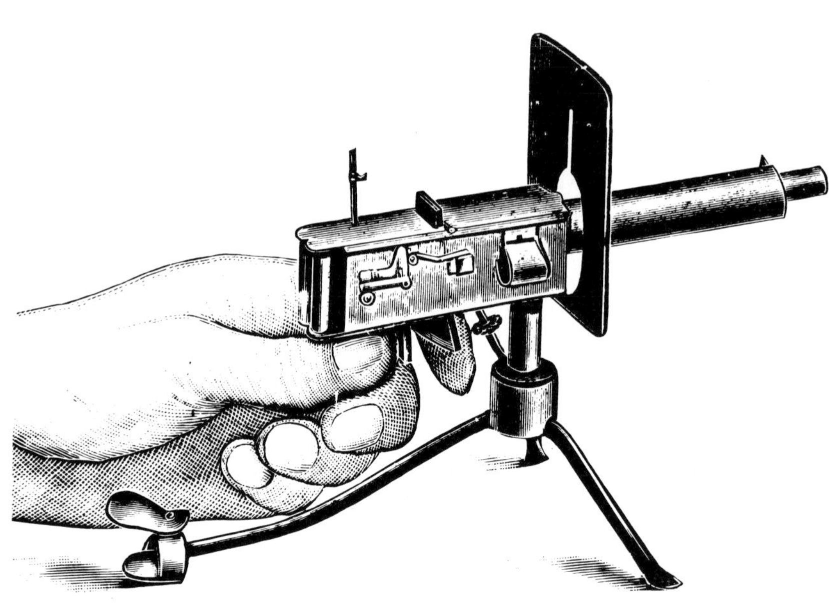

Oliver Harper & Co. machine gun, 1918

parts in all probability were made by the old-established Blackpool firm Progress Toy Co. **p. 74*
See Gyro Manufacturers of Leicester, Progress Toy Co., British United Toy Co.

Further reading: *The Top*, D W Gould *Gyroscopes et Projectiles*, H Bouasse

John Hill & Co. Coronation coach, 1953

Hall & Lane Ltd
1895–1951
Darwin Works, Leopold Street, Birmingham
Manufacturers of tin boxes, toys and hardware, tin and celluloid window tickets, showcards. In 1939, when the firm was registered as a limited company, the Director, Mr F C Hall, was also listed as 'Ironmaster, Toolmaker, Founder', and together with H F Hall, as Joint Directors of the Cambridge Metal Stamping Co., Robert Hitchon Ltd and Watkins & Carter Ltd.

The toys they produced during and after World War I included pop guns and air guns, seaside buckets, money-boxes. The firm was acquired by Chad Valley in 1951, and the son of its founder, Mr A F Hall, become Chairman of the Chad Valley Group in 1960.

Happynak
See Paton Calvert & Co. Ltd

Hare Bros
1921, Birmingham
Manufacturers of 'Harbro' tin toys. Trick money-boxes with a small drawer which received money in a novel manner; humming tops with spring wire causing tops to 'dance'.

Hill, John & Co.
1906–1956
Britannia Row, Essex Road, London
Manufacturers of cast metal toys. The firm was established in 1906 by F H Wood, an ex-employee of William Britain. Wood imitated nearly all of Britains' lines and some of his copies are indistinguishable from Britains' originals. 1934 lines included speed cops, despatch riders, tanks and motor cars, all with rubber tyres and moving wheels. By 1956, the firm's factory was in Parliament Street, Burnley, and was producing plastic figures. The firm's trademark was 'Johillco'.
*See Soldiers *p. 62*

Hitchon, Robert Ltd
1930
117 Hurst Street, Birmingham
Trademark 'Reliable'

See Hall & Lane

Holdfast
See Cartwright, A S

Holland & Blair Ltd
1940–1970s
Bensham Grove, Thornton Heath, Surrey
Engineering firm which in 1955 manufactured the Lilliput typewriter. The machine was a precision-made toy designed for children and made from steel. In 1961, the firm opened an additional factory in Gillingham, Kent. The 1972 Lilliput model carried a 2-year guarantee.
See Typewriters

Hopkins Bros
1880
Victoria Tin Works, Credon Road, Upton Park, London
One of London's oldest manufacturers of tin toys. They made brightly painted tin pull-along cruisers and steamers, motor cars, engines and carriages, steam waggons and trailers, fire engines and all kinds of dolls' house equipment.

Hornby, Frank
See Meccano

Hornby Trains
See Meccano

Hudson, J & Co.
1916
Metropolitan Whistle Works, Barr Street, Hockley, Birmingham
Manufacturers of Acme whistles, signalling and shunting horns, birdcalls, bosun, referee, policeman and scout whistles.

Hudson Scott & Sons
1799–1939
Now Metal Box Co., Carlisle
A firm of lithographic printers who in 1876 started transfer printing on to tinplate and making biscuit tins for Carr & Co. of Carlisle and Peak Frean's in London. They were one of the first to use offset lithographic tin printing.

From 1910, they were manufacturing a range of tins shaped like toys – drums, grenadiers, sentry boxes, dolls' houses, hobby horses, locomotives, railway carriages, luggage trucks, taxicabs, motor cars, seaside pails, Noah's arks and money-boxes. In 1914, they opened a special factory at Workington, near Carlisle, for the manufacture of these toys.

They produced tin toys for Ralph Dunn & Co., Lines Bros, Mettoy and Meccano. They also made seaside pails for Sharp's Toffee. When Hudson Scott & Sons were absorbed by the Metal Box Co., the tools for these pails were transferred to Barringer, Wallis & Manners, whose factory at Mansfield was also, by that time, part of the Metal Box Group.
**pp. 10, 26, 63*

Hunt, William & Sons
1903–1950
109 Gerrard Street, Birmingham
Tinware manufacturers, press-tool makers and wire-workers. This firm made tools for other manufacturers, as well as tin tubes and metal parts made up to their customers' own specifications.

In addition they made bird calls, tin flutes and whistles, 'jazzophones', peashooters, spring guns and daggers, toy candlesticks, frying pans, scales and all kinds of novelties for bazaars.

Paton Calvert elastic driven speedboat c.1934

MECCANO LTD
LIVERPOOL.
PRINCESS ELIZABETH
6201
L M S

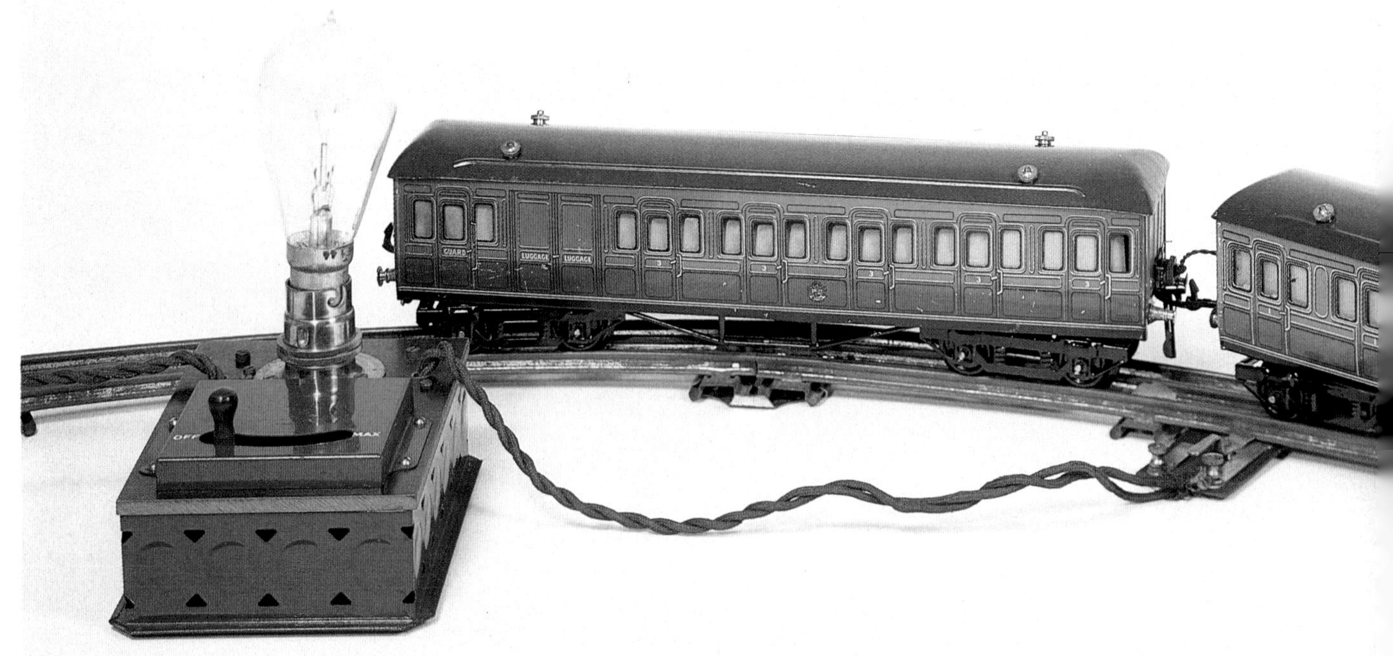

HORNBY
234
PULLMAN
ARCADIA

Hornby 'Princess Elizabeth' gauge 0, 1937 (left)
Hornby Metropolitan set gauge 0, 1927 (large picture)
Hornby SR and GWR 4-4-2 tanks gauge 0, 1930 (top right)
Hornby Yorkshire 4-4-0, 1929 (inset)

Huntley, Boorne & Stevens
1831–1918
Reading, Berkshire
Mr Michael Franklin, in his book *British Biscuit Tins*, summarises the history of Huntley, Boorne & Stevens as follows:

'The name of Huntley, Boorne & Stevens of Reading has been closely connected with the firm of biscuit makers, Huntley & Palmers, for many years. Started in 1831 by Joseph Huntley as a general ironmongers in Reading, its premises were in London Street, just opposite the baker's shop owned by his brother, Thomas Huntley. From 1837 onwards, it appears from records of the firm that they were involved in making some metal boxes, but mostly tin-lined wooden boxes for Thomas Huntley to fill with his ever-increasingly popular biscuits.

'In 1864, Joseph Huntley took into the business a partner by the name of James Boorne and the firm became known as Huntley & Boorne. Samuel Stevens, who joined the firm as a boy apprentice in 1847, was made a partner in 1872. As Huntley & Palmers' (George Palmer became a partner in 1841) biscuit making prospered, so did the tin box firm across the street. In the main, the boxes they made were decorated with pasted-on paper covers of labels, until in 1868 it is known that they covered a tin with a transfer designed by Owen Jones; the method used was a process patented by Benjamin George. Account books survive recording the purchase of transfer work from George in London. There is also evidence that in the early 1870s a few tins were made using the direct method of tin printing. However, the process that put Huntley, Boorne & Stevens in the forefront of decorated tin printers and metal box makers in Great Britain, was the acquisition from Bryant & May of the exclusive right to operate the Offset Lithographic Barclay patented process of 1875; and they were legally the only firm empowered to use that process from May of 1877 until 1889.

'Huntley, Boorne & Stevens were a separate company from Huntley & Palmers until February 1918 when the two companies were merged. Today it is a part of the light engineering and packaging division for the whole Associated Biscuit Manufacturing Ltd group.'
pp. 11, 27

Further reading: *British Biscuit Tins*, Michael Franklin

Huntley, Boorne & Stevens London bus No. 11E, 1929

Huntley, Boorne & Stevens windmill biscuit tin, c.1930

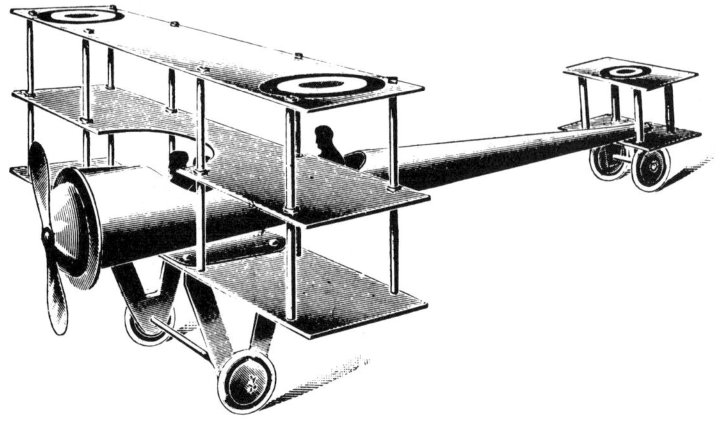
R Joseph & Co. 'Joey' tri-plane, 1919

I

Izon, Thomas
1870
57–58 Inge Street, Birmingham
Toy manufacturer specialising in seaside buckets and pails and garden tools for children. In 1922, he marketed 'The Great International Game of Football', an indoor board game played with counters and dice on a board marked like a football pitch. Izon referred to his workshop as 'The Birmingham Toy Manufactory'.

J

Jetex
See Wilmot, Mansour & Co. Ltd

Johillco
See Hill, John & Co. and Soldiers
**p. 62*

Joseph, R & Co. Ltd
1919–1925
Langton Road, Brixton, London
Manufacturers of tinplate toys and household goods. Lines included toy monoplanes and triplanes in all sizes and the 'Joey' aeroplane, made of tin and painted with aluminium paint. The 'Joey' was fixed together with nuts and bolts, so that it could be dismantled and reassembled – it was not designed to fly. The 'Joey' was also made in polished brass and aluminium as a motor-cycle mascot.

In 1925, the Langton Road tinplate works were taken over by Metalwares Ltd. It would seem that Burnett Ltd bought up the stock of 'Joey' aeroplanes, as some aeroplanes have Burnett labels stuck on to the wings, over the RAF circles. They also produced the 'José' sand mould which packed flat, but with which one could build sandcastle towers, lighthouses, windmills.
See Aeroplanes and Burnett Ltd

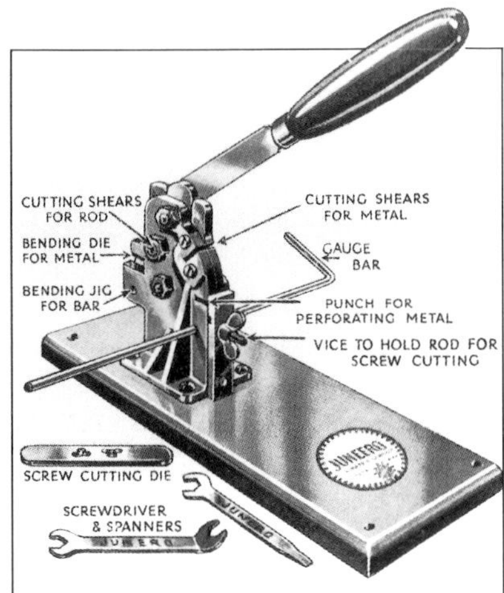

Juneero Ltd engineering construction kit, 1940

Juneero Ltd
1939
25 White Street, Moorfields, London
Manufacturers of a kit comprising a press for bending, cutting and perforating small sheets of metal. The kit also included metal rods, nuts and bolts and spanners with which to build Meccano-like toys.
See Constructional Toys, Appendix VII

K

Kaleidoscope
This optical toy, invented by Sir David Brewster in 1816, was a metal tube with two (or sometimes three) strips of glass mounted down its length. Some scraps of coloured glass or metal in the base, when viewed through the eyepiece at one end, formed symmetrical patterns through their reflections; and these constantly changed as a small handle was wound altering the arrangement of the glass. Some large and commercially designed kaleidoscopes supplied the inspiration for carpet and textile designs. The toy has remained popular and is usually made up in a tube which just needs to be shaken or twisted.

A more elaborate version called a Designoscope was produced in 1924 by the Ro-gat Tool & Stamping Co. and sold by the Twencen Manufacturing Co. It consisted of a kaleidoscope mounted on a stand. In 1943, an educational kaleidoscope called a Mirrorscope (Reg. Des. 838/617) and another called a Picturescope were put on the market, and in more recent years Ray Bradley has made and sold 'Teledoscope', using lenses and mirrors.

Kay (Sports and Games) Ltd
1935–37
Carlisle Road, The Hyde, London NW9
Owned by the Kempner family of Polish extraction. Manufactured electrical, chemistry and tool sets; a wide variety of games; and also lead miniatures.

Kelo Toys
See Appendix IV

Kew, F & Co.
1926
Endell Works, Brockley, London
Manufacturers of miniature models in cast metal including soldiers, villages, farms, railway station characters. Also Tiger Tim and the Bruin Boys; Christopher Robin and his friends (nine characters by permission of A A Milne and E H Shepard) and Oval Cricketers, a board game with miniature cricketers. Goods were sold by direct postal service as well as through the trade.
Trademarks 'Kuzu' and 'Metalad'

Kinco Toys
See British Metal (Kingston) Ltd

Kliptiko
See Bailey, William and Appendix VII

Knight's Head
See True-to-Type Products

Kohnstam, M. & Co.
1867–the present day
Fürth, Bavaria and 24 Milton Street, London
A doll and toy manufacturing firm run by Moses Kohnstam, a German toy manufacturer. The firm specialised in metal musical instruments, but also produced stuffed toys and dolls. In 1900 the firm registered the trademark 'Moko' in England, and in 1904 the trademark 'Sunny Jim' was registered for a mascot figure used in advertising the breakfast cereal 'Force'.

Moses Kohnstam died in 1912 and was succeeded by Julius Kohnstam, a naturalised British subject. In 1936, the firm registered the trademark 'Mackenry' for dolls and toys and re-registered the trademark 'Moko'. In 1947, the firm assisted in putting the Lesney Products firm on a practical footing by marketing and publicity. In the early fifties, Lesney Products acquired the firm and used the 'Moko' trademark, which they dropped in 1959.

A nephew of Julius Kohnstam, Richard Kohnstam, was managing director of R Kohnstam Ltd, a toy importing firm with premises in Hemel Hempstead, Herts.

L

Lamplugh Radio Ltd
1934
Silver Ghost Works, Coventry, Warwickshire
Manufacturers of large toys. Trademark 'Silver Ghost'.

Land Speed Record Cars
See Racing Cars

Leonard & Francis Ltd
1922
Brownsfield Mills, Ancoats Street, Manchester
London Office: 122–123 Moorgate
Manufacturers of 'Elite' steel toys.

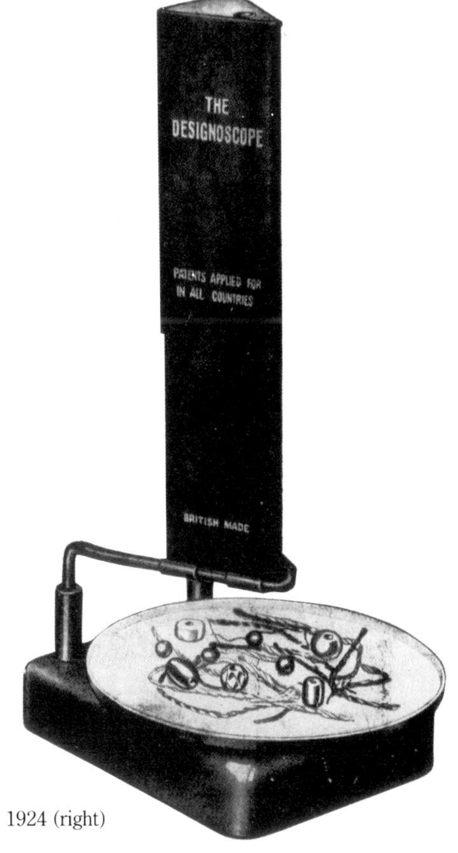

Chad Valley 'Acme' kaleidescope (above)
Twencen Manufacturing Co. 'Designoscope', 1924 (right)

International Model Aircraft 'Frog' Puss Moth, aeroplane, 1934 (top)

Lines Bros 'Tri-ang' pressed steel open truck with boxes 1947 (middle left)

Detail showing label of truck (middle left)

Lines Bros Tri-ang Sentinel steam wagon, 1933 (bottom)

Lines Bros two 'Minic' garages, 1937 and 1950s

Lesney Products Ltd
See Matchbox

Levy, F & Co.
1899
Ropemaker Street, London; from 1942 at Winchmore Hill, London
The firm was established by Jack and Fred Levy and became one of the most important wholesalers dealing in toys and fancy goods. During World War I they sold 'all-British Mechanical Motors', possibly made by Barringer, Wallis & Manners. In 1933, they put on the market a series of 'high power' mechanical motors, with simplified modern shapes. In 1948, they advertised the 'Clifford' series of tin toys, boxed games and table tennis.

Lilliput Typewriter
See Holland & Blair Ltd and Typewriters

Registered trademark Thistle Brand, 1910

Lines Bros Ltd
1919–1983
G and J Lines, the family business of the two Lines brothers, George (born 1841) and Joseph (born 1848) was established in the 1870s primarily to produce rocking horses and other wooden toys. The firm had its office in the Caledonian Road in the King's Cross area.

By the turn of the century, George Lines had retired and his brother Joseph, with the help of his sons, increased the firm's range. Its trademark, registered in 1910, was a thistle stamped on to a thin metal disc, and was attached not only to horses, velocipedes and other equestrian toys, but also to mailcarts, dolls' houses, perambulators and other large wooden toys. The five scattered and rather ramshackle workshops occupied by the firm were replaced by one large factory, purpose-built on four and a half acres of land in Tottenham, North London. It opened just a few months before War was declared in 1914 and the sons left to serve in the trenches. On their return to civilian life, George Lines, the elder brother, elected to stay on and work for his father. The three younger sons, however, decided in 1919 to set up on their own. They adopted as their trademark, a punning three lines triangle and the name Triangtois. The factory they acquired in South London, Hatcham Works, Ormside Street, backed onto the Surrey Canal. It was an old sawmill, next to a timber wharf. They produced virtually the same range of products as their father's firm; dapple grey rocking horses, pedal cars,

G and J Lines advertisement from *Toy and Fancy Goods Trader* 1914

Joseph Lines, 1848–1931

'Fairy' cycles and scooters, wooden engines and dolls' houses.

In 1923, they helped build Queen Mary's Dolls' House, working to Sir Edwin Lutyen's designs, and inventing specially delicate tools to make the elaborate, minute furniture and fittings. By then, however, Walter Lines had realized that the future lay in mass production and the use of metal sheets which could be stamped and shaped at speed. 'Cheap production', he said in 1923, 'is not obtained by cutting wages. The secret is to enable labour to produce more'.

A new factory was acquired in the Old Kent Road, trade boomed, and more space was needed. They bought up forty-seven acres of ground at Merton, near Wimbledon – farmland which had once belonged to Lord Nelson and which he left in his will to Lady Hamilton. By 1925, the largest and, at the time, the most up-to-date toy factory in the world had been erected on the site.

The combined talents and personalities of the three brothers united to form a powerful driving force which led them from success to success. Walter Lines, the eldest, swept like a whirlwind through his factories, bursting with new and creative ideas, irascible, working with tireless energy until he got every minute detail absolutely correct. William, the dynamic salesman and outgoing public relations man, kept sales soaring. Arthur, the youngest with all his family's charm and diplomatic skills, soothed ruffled feathers and ran the labour force and the factories with quiet efficiency. Year by year their empire grew.

In 1930, they obtained the concession to sell the FROG (Flies Right Off Ground) aeroplanes, made by the Birmingham firm, International Model Aircraft, and in 1932 took over the firm itself. Then Pedigree Soft Toys, another subsidiary, was founded; and plans were laid for

Walter Lines, 1922

producing a range of small pocket-money clockwork cars, the Minic series, which children could collect like postage stamps. In 1935, a range of bicycles and scooters was extended and a new factory was built for them at Handsworth.

The following year, Mr Joseph Lines died at the age of 85, working until the very last. The Tottenham factory was absorbed; George Lines joined his brothers at Merton, and they also acquired one of London's oldest and best-known toy shops, Hamley's of Regent Street. As a small boy Walter Lines had often begged a lift into London on the front seat of one of his father's horse-drawn delivery vans – not only for the ride, but also to negotiate with Mr Hamley himself some private and personal transaction concerning items of dolls' house furniture which he made in his school holidays; and in 1931, Walter Lines acquired a majority holding in Hamley's.

Lines Bros Ltd continued to expand, becoming more and more self-sufficient, as they produced more and more of the basic materials needed for the manufacture of toys. At the outbreak of war, some 2,000 people were employed at the Merton Factory and by 1945 there were over 7,000 on the payroll. The range of war material produced by Lines Bros was staggering. Rocket-propelled gliders, apparatus for laying land mines and smoke screens, gas masks, cartridge bags, ammunition boxes, scale models of tanks for army training, a top secret scale model of the D-Day landing coast, and above all millions of Tommy Guns. Walter Lines's experience of trench warfare in World War I had made him resolute in opposing any production in his factories of war toys for children; yet by an ironic twist it was his gift for inventing simple mass production methods that led to the creation of the 'Sten' gun, a deadly toylike weapon, so simple that anyone could be taught to handle it with only a few hours training, so cheap that it could be turned out by the thousand, as a virtual throwaway.

In 1946, a further factory was taken over on the site of the old Cyfarthfa Iron Works at Merthyr Tydfil, to help a very depressed area; and another, dealing with soft toys, was opened in Belfast. In 1951, Rovex Plastics Ltd of Richmond was acquired and organised for the production of electric train sets; this was followed by a brand new factory at Margate for Rovex, opened in 1953, the Richmond factory being switched to musical toys, Minic clockwork and Ballerina brand prams. The old-established firm of Simpson Fawcett at Plymouth was bought and moved to Merthyr Tydfil for Pedigree prams.

1920 trademark No.391682

The successful post-war years led to expansion abroad – a factory in New Zealand at Tamaki near Auckland; in Canada at Montreal (1947); another in Australia, seven miles from Sydney (1951); and one in South Africa near Durban (1952).

In 1964, the shareholders of Meccano

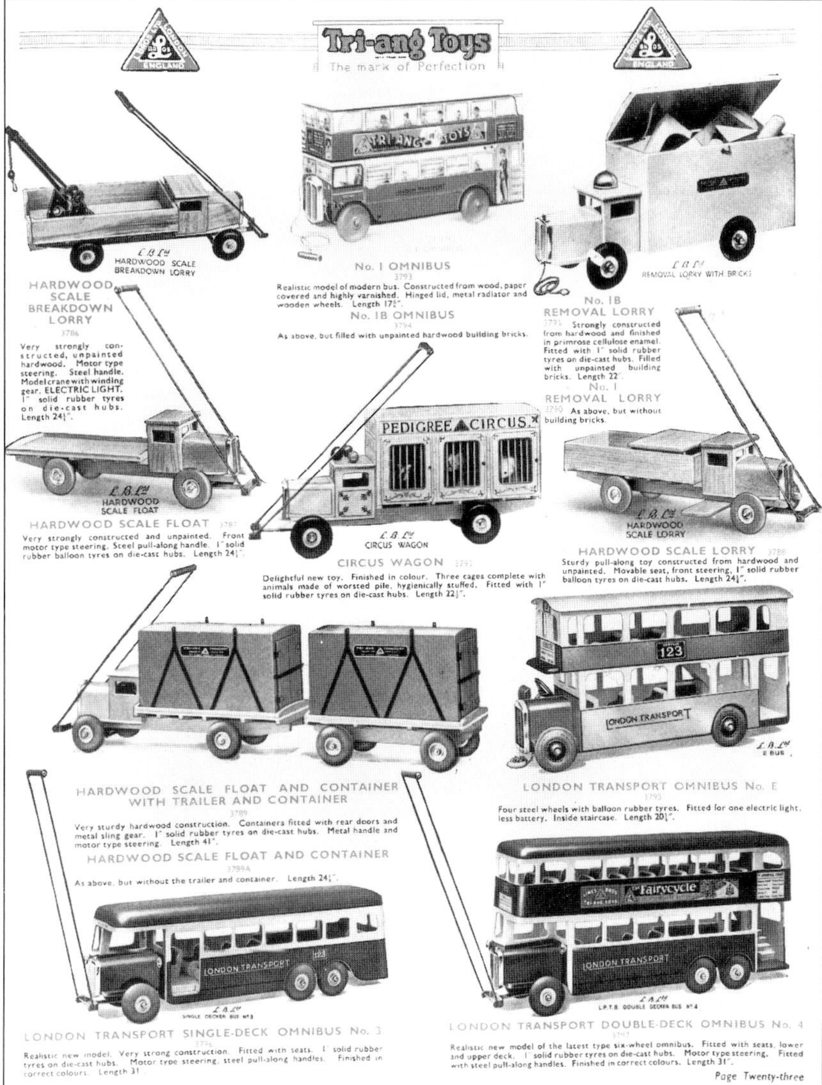

Lines Bros Tri-ang Toys catalogue, 1939

Lines Bros 'Tri-ang' Gyro Cycle, 1939 (top left)
Lines Bros 'Tri-ang' pressed steel crane, 1930s onwards (top right)
Lines Bros 'Tri-ang' refuse truck, 1935 (bottom)

Lines Bros 'Tri-ang' Royal Mail van, wood and metal, 1934 (top)

Lines Bros 'Tri-ang' Royal Mail van, 1935 (inset)

Lines Bros 'Tri-ang' Bullnose Morris, wood and metal, c.1929 (bottom left)

Lines Bros Minic van and Puff-Puff locomotive, c. 1954

Ltd were advised to accept the offer of the Lines Group of Companies; and the Hornby name was gradually phased out, to be replaced by Meccano-Tri-ang, the tools for the Hornby Dublo range going to a Lines subsidiary, G & R Wrenn Ltd.

Walter Lines retired in 1961 from the company he had helped found some 40 years previously. He was nearly 80 years old but peaceful old age had no attractions for him. He set about creating yet another enterprise. He bought and rebuilt an old furniture factory at Lavant, near Chichester in Sussex, and set about producing 'Goodwood' toys, which he had originally designed for his own grandchildren – lorries and wagons, playshops and little 'Fit-bits' and sturdy wooden toys in the tradition of those made by his father a hundred years before. 'Toy making as we know it', Walter Lines had said as a young man in 1923, 'was our own creation, it's part of our being, we love it', and he continued to enjoy it right up to his death in 1972 aged 90. He had continued, too, to take an active interest in all aspects of the toy trade and above all in the work of the Toy Manufacturers' Association, which he had helped to found and whose President he had been for many years.

By then, however, no personal, creative spirit existed at the heart of the vast Lines Group of Companies, which was only held together by a tenuous web of complicated bank loans. A few months of poor trading and the whole edifice collapsed – to reform and reappear as parts of new enterprises, or assets to rival empires. The Morden Road Factory was closed; Hamley's was bought by Debenhams; Meccano Ltd sold to Airfix Industries; Rovex, Hornby and Tri-ang Trains to Dunbee-Combex; while the factories in France were snapped up by General Mills of America. In 1983, a Manchester firm Sharnaware Ltd, bought the Tri-ang trade name and are manufacturing toys under the label Sharna Tri-ang. *pp. 70–1, 74–5, 106–107*

Further reading: Tri-ang Toys 1937/38, Golden Era Catalogue, FROG Model Aircraft, Richard Lines and Leif Hellström, *The Minic Book*, Peter Bartok

Lord Roberts Memorial Workships poster, 1915

Lledo (London) Ltd
See Matchbox

Lone Star Products
See Die-Casting Machine Tools Ltd

F W Long train set, 1939

Long, F W Ltd
1920
Market Street, Smithfield, Birmingham and Wormwood Street, London
Agents for five large British manufacturers. Lines included seaside buckets and spades, tin drums, tambours, teasets and the 'Lanco' series of train sets.

Lord Roberts Memorial Workshops
1915–the present day
Headquarters at Britannis Road, Fulham, London
A doll and toy manufacturing organisation established after the outbreak of World War I to provide work for disabled soldiers and sailors, and using money subscribed as a memorial for Lord Roberts, British Commander-in-Chief during the Boer War.

Various existing factories were taken over, including the Novelty Construction Co. Ltd, Fulham, which was enlarged.

During the following years workshop branches were opened up all over the British Isles – in Brighton, Birmingham, Colchester, Belfast, Bradford, Liverpool, Edinburgh, Leeds, Southampton, Plymouth and Cardiff. Ex-servicemen were taught the trade of toy making, especially metal work, to professional standards. By the middle of 1916, other industries had been added to the toy making – wooden household articles, cabinet making and leather work.

Circa 1921, the head office was at 122 Brompton Road, London, SW3, where it still exists.

Lowe, Keith Ltd
1949
Manufacturers of tubular steel toys including rocking horses, scooters and Pogo sticks. They also produced a sewing machine called 'Little Lady' advertised as being 'just like mother's'. Trademark 'Kelo'. Taken over by Wells-Brimtoy.
See Appendix IV

Lütticke, George Frederick & Lütticke, Amy Emily
1876–1897
Roseville, Gipsy Hill, London
Took out various patents for very clever mechanical toys: acrobat No. 3888, in October 1876; clockwork figures of boxers etc. No. 16198, in October 1889; dancing figures No. 30870, in December 1897.

Lynwood Toy Co.
1918
36 Camomile Street, London
Manufacturers of toy soldiers and miniature models including sailors, nurses and Charlie Chaplin. The toys were made up from a hard composition material as metal was rationed at that time.
See Soldiers

M

Machines for toy manufacture
Also dies used in the manufacture of sheet metal toys.
See Rhodes, Joseph & Sons Ltd

Made in England
A number of toys are simply marked 'Made in England', 'British Made' or 'Made in Great Britain'. It is difficult to attribute them to a specific manufacturer. The relevant information was perhaps only printed on the original box in which the toy was packed.

Magic Lanterns
There is an account of a Magic Lantern demonstration in Pepys' Diary for 1665, but it was not until the middle of the 19th century, with the invention of oxy-hydrogen limelight, that exhibitions of lantern slides to large audiences became possible. The lanterns used for these shows were beautifully made from brass and mahogany by expert craftsmen. Much cheaper and smaller japanned tin versions were, however, available for use at home, some being little more than a bicycle lamp with a space to insert small glass slides.

'Spectre' magic lantern, 19th century

Principal manufacturers

Archer & Sons
Lord Street, Liverpool
19th century

R R Beard
10 Trafalgar Road, London
19th century

W Butchers & Son
Camera House, Farringdon Avenue, London
19th and 20th century

L Casella
23 Hatton Gardens, 147 Holborn Bar, London
19th century

T H Doublet
4 City Road, London
19th century

W C Hughes
Brewster House, Mortimer Road, Kingsland, London
19th century

Newton & Co.
3 Fleet Street, London
1850s

Perken, Son & Co. Ltd
99 Hatton Garden, London
Late 19th century

Riley Bros Ltd
Goodwin Street, Bradford, Yorkshire
1890s

J H Steward
406 Strand, London
19th century

Walter Tyler, London

W Watson & Sons
313 High Holborn, London
19th century

Wrench (Bijou Toy Lanterns)
London
Established 1916

Malins Engineers Ltd
1934–1980
Price Street, Birmingham;
later at Thorns Road, Birmingham
A firm founded by a Birmingham engineer, Geoffrey Harry Malins. Born in 1892, he was apprenticed to the Austin Motor Company, served in the Royal Navy during World War I, and was afterwards in charge of the private electricity

Malins 'Mamod' tractor, 1963

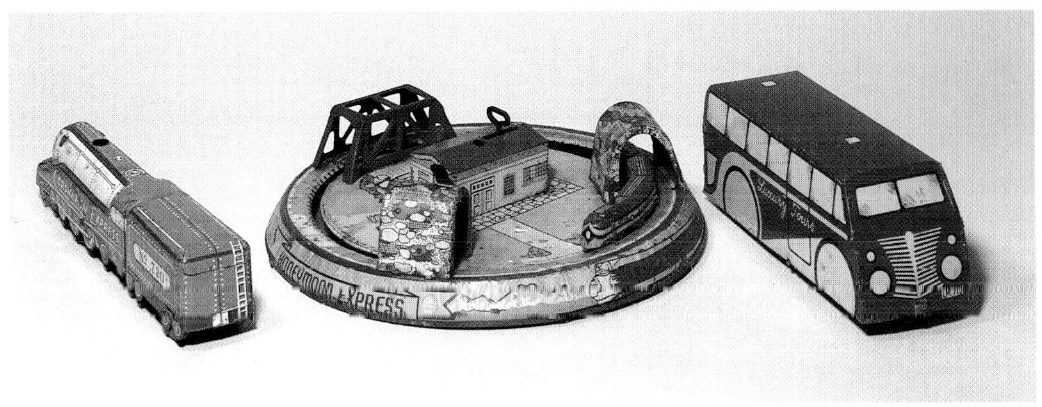

Marx floor train, 'Honeymoon Express', 1930s and coach, 1950s (top

Marx saloon 1949, racing car 1930s and army lorry 1940s (middle)

Marx Smokey Joe, 1930s (bottom left)

Marx 'Streamline Speedway' set, 1930s (bottom right)

Marx streamlined LNER clockwork train, 1930s (top)
Marx 'Sparking Warship', 1950s and tanks, 1930s (middle)
Marx clockwork carts and animals, 1940s and 1950s (bottom)

generating station at Dunlop Rubber Works, Fort Dunlop. In 1934, he set up on his own as GM Patents Company at 26 New Buildings, Price Street, Birmingham, making components for mechanical toys to be used with the models made by Meccano and by Hobbies of Dereham. He also introduced a simple marine steam plant with stern tube and propellor for home-made boats. Hobbies of Dereham was also the first outlet for his model steam engines (1936–1937); thereafter Malins registered the brand name 'Mamod' and issued his own catalogue.

During World War II, the Price Street workshop was given over to war work. In 1948, his son Eric joined Malins and they expanded and modernised the firm, moving to larger premises in Camden Street, Birmingham. In 1961, the firm introduced a very successful steam roller, and during the 1960s it continued to expand, moving in 1962 to larger premises in Thorns Road, Brierley Hill and being joined in 1968 by Eric's son Stephen. Further extensions were made in 1975, the year when the firm's founder, Geoffrey Malins, died.

Stephen Malins, a racing car enthusiast, designed a 1930s style steam motor car, which enjoyed considerable success; but the financial strains of producing in 1979 a new steam locomotive, the first to be mass-produced since World War II, proved too great and in 1980 the firm was sold to C C Cooper Holdings Ltd, whose Chairman, C C Cooper, was a well-known Midlands steel industrialist. However, two years the firm was sold again and 'Mamod' steam engines are now available from Mamod Ltd, Ascot.

Further reading: *Toyshop Steam*, Basil Harley

Mamod
See Steam Toys and Malins Ltd

Mann, George & Co. Ltd
1900–21
Gray's Inn Road, London and also at Prospect Works, Otley, Yorkshire and Leeds
At their works in Leeds and Otley, George Mann & Co. Ltd specialized in tin printing machines, transfer presses, varnishing machines etc. used in the manufacture of tin toys.
See Printing

Mar Toys
1948
Toy and game trademark Patent No. 657620 registered by Louis Marx & Co.

Marden, Illingworth
c. 1850s–the present day
Coxmoor Road, Sutton in Ashfield, Nottinghamshire
Marden, Son and Hall of Bristol were a firm of printers founded in the middle of the last century who are known for their involvement in the printing of cigarette cards for the tobacco firm Wills. They are now part of Lawson-Marden Group and make novelty tins for Hunkydory Designs Ltd and tins in the shape of houses and cars for Ian Logan Ltd.

Markt & Co. (London) Ltd
1925–1931
98/100 Clerkenwell Road, London
Manufacturers of 'Bissel' model toy carpet sweepers, including 'Little Gem'. Advertisements incorporated the following rhyme: 'The children enjoy this Bissel toy for the dear babies like to play ladies'. By 1931, the firm had premises in Portpool Lane, London, and the carpet sweeper range included 'Little Helper', 'Little Jewel' and 'Junior'.

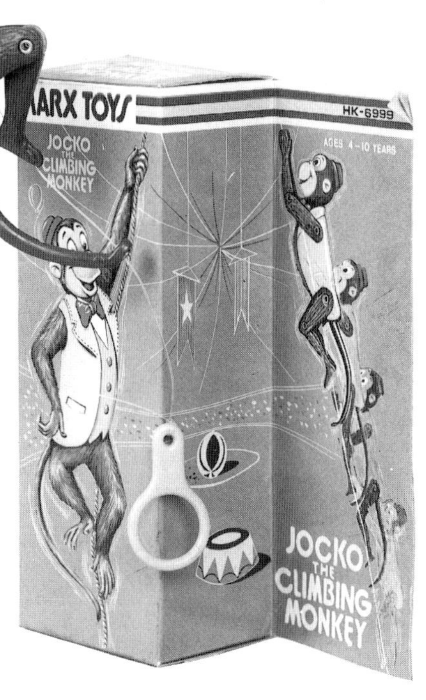

Marx 'Jocko, the climbing monkey', 1950s

Marlborough Manufacturing Co.
1918
338 Clapham Road, Stockwell, London
Manufacturers of composition models including soldiers, sailors, admirals, Charlie Chaplin, Red Cross nurses. All their soldiers are stamped with the letters MMC.
See Soldiers

Marx, Louis, & Co. Ltd
1932–1967
An American firm, which ran a subsidiary company in England from 1932 to 1967. Louis Marx was born in New York in 1896, and was one of the outstanding toy men of the 20th century. At age 16, when his father lost the family tailoring shop, he was apprenticed to Ferdinand Strauss, who produced cheap mechanical toys. Five years later he fell out with Strauss and set up on his own account in New York. With a brother he founded Louis Marx & Co. and by 1921, they had a small metal toy factory.

When Strauss died in 1922, Marx purchased his dies of the climbing monkey toy and the Alabama Coon dancers, and sold millions of these through the 6d stores. In 1932, he extended his operation to England, buying a factory in the Midlands – Waddans Pool Works, Dudley, Worcestershire. From 1948, he worked from Fforestfach Trading Estate, Swansea, Glamorganshire, making die-cast toys in plastic, and electric train sets.

In 1967, Marx's UK interests were acquired by Dunbee-Combex.
**pp. 78–9*

Matchbox Toys
1947–1982
Rifleman Pub, Shacklewell Lane, Edmonton, Middlesex (1947) and Lee Conservancy Road, London (1964)
Part of Lesney Products, the history of Matchbox Toys begins before World War II, when Rodney and Leslie Smith, unrelated 12 year-olds at the Central School, Enfield, decided that when they left school they would set up an engineering firm together. Leslie then worked for seven years with J Raymond Wilson, a die-casting firm, and Rodney in general engineering. Both served in the Royal Navy and on demobilisation with a £600 war gratuity they set up a small factory in a disused pub. Jack Odell, an expert in die-casting, joined them, and in 1947 the firm was registered as Lesney Products (the name derived from an amalgamation of the first and last parts of their first names).

Their first products were metal string cutters made with razor blades; then, besides doing a variety of industrial die-casting work, they planned to make metal

Matchbox toys, 1950s

Leslie Smith and Jack Odell, directors of **Lesney Products Ltd**, 1961

"MATCHBOX"®

toys. Their first model was a large Aveling Barford Diesel Road Roller. Late in 1950, they produced, for the Festival of Britain, a 15″ scale model of the gold state coach, with King George VI and Queen Elizabeth; but it was not very popular, and output was small because the Korean War limited supplies of zinc.

Rodney Smith now left the firm, selling his shares to his partner. Leslie found it necessary to combine with the Kohnstam firm, who could undertake marketing, so the trademark 'Moko' was added to the product (*See Kohnstam, M, & Company*). Lesney Products scored their first big success with a small-scale coach for the coronation of Queen Elizabeth II in 1953. Priced at 1s 6d, it was packed in a 'Matchbox' style box, rather like the novelties sold in Victorian times, when tiny German kitchens etc. were made up in actual matchboxes. The boxes were produced by Boxes Limited, Dace Road, London.

Further miniature models were now planned. The first three were scaled down from earlier, larger models – road roller, dumper truck and hand cement mixer; the fourth, the famous No. 5 London Bus, was designed as a miniature. During 1959–1960, the series was expanded to 75 models; in 1960 the company went public, bought out the Kohnstam agency and deleted the Moko mark from their goods. In 1964, a huge new factory was opened in Hackney Wick, and in 1966 the firm's success was crowned by the Queen's Award to Industry.

When competitive 'Hot Wheels' and racing cars were introduced by rival firms, such as Mattel, Matchbox brought out a racing track with electric battery (1969), and 'Helter Skelter', with a plastic track (1973). The growing collector's market was served by the introduction of the very accurate 'Yesteryear' models.

However, after thirty years of unbroken success the firm was suddenly beset with financial and other problems. In 1980, Jack Odell came out of retirement in an attempt to put the engineering side of the firm in order. He said, 'It was like being put in as Captain of the Titanic ten minutes before she sank'. In June 1982 the receiver was appointed. Three months later, Mr David Yeh of Universal International, Hong Kong, bought Lesney Products Ltd. Mr Yeh had gained his first experience in die-cast toy manufacturing with the Hong Kong Branch of Louis Marx.

Meanwhile, Mr Odell had been busy and by January 1983 had set up a new company, Lledo, to manufacture die-cast toys, beginning with a series of veteran horse-drawn vehicles.

Further reading: *Collecting Matchbox Diecast Toys*, K McGimpsey and S Orr

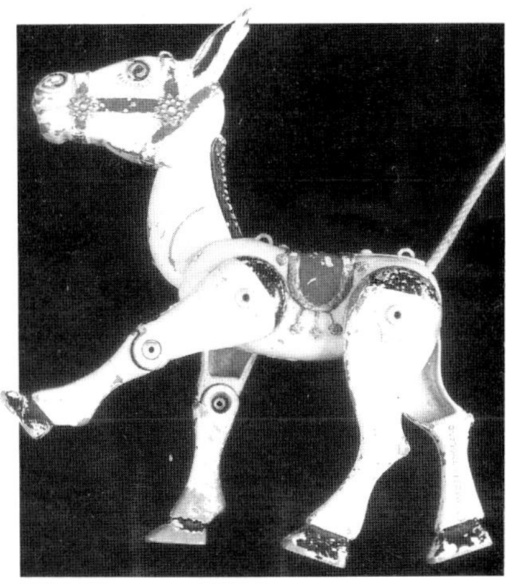

Lesney Products 'Muffin the Mule', c.1951

Meccano 'Mechanics Made Easy', 1901–08

Meccano 'nickel period' items including No.2 storage cabinet, 1908–26 (top)

Early **Meccano** accessories including a butterchurn, 1912 and a steam engine, 1914 (bottom)

Mazak

Mazak is an alloy containing 3–4% aluminium, 1–2% copper and 92–96% zinc with a trace of magnesium. Minute impurities can cause intergranular corrosion known to model collectors as fatigue. This material was used extensively by all the major diecast toy manufacturers including Dinky, Corgi, Lesney, Timpo, etc.

Meccano Ltd

1901–the present day
Binns Road, Liverpool

As a clerk in Liverpool in the late 1890s, Frank Hornby was influenced by the Victorian savant, Samuel Smiles, in his principal pastime, namely as an amateur engineer and inventor. Among other inventions was his attempt to devise a machine to solve the problem of perpetual motion. He designed for his two sons, Roland and Douglas, a model crane using parts which could be bolted together and later dismantled. For his prototype he used copper sheeting cut with shears, wheels cast at a foundry, rods obtained from a clock-maker and nuts and bolts made by his own hand. The metal strips measured 2½″, 5½″ and 12½″ and were all ½″ wide. Once the crane was built, he realised that these metal parts had potential as a construction toy for a variety of models.

Hornby took out patents for 'Mechanics Made Easy', as he called it (Patent No.587, 9 January 1901). Working at home and in a small workroom at 12 Duke Street, Liverpool (under the name Elliott and Hornby), boxed sets were packed and despatched. The trade name of Meccano was registered on 7 September 1907 and Meccano Ltd formed as a company in 1908. As the toy grew in popularity larger premises were opened, first at 274 West Derby Road and then, in 1914, at a fine new factory in Binns Road, where production seems to have continued without interruption throughout World War I. In 1916, the first edition of *Meccano Magazine* appeared; it included a competition for the best models built by boys.

FRANK HORNBY
1863–1936

A series of lawsuits were commenced in the USA in 1912 for patent infringement, culminating several years later with a case against several American companies including A C Gilbert.

In 1920, 0 gauge Hornby Trains were introduced. Lithographic tin printing was undertaken by the Metal Box Company; and in 1921 a factory was opened outside Paris to manufacture French Hornby, Meccano etc. The 1930s saw an extension of the range of Hornby toys, including car and aeroplane constructor sets. In addition, Meccano introduced small diecast toys originally launched as Modelled Miniatures, but soon re-named Dinky Toys.

Originally, Meccano parts were of plain metal, unpainted, but lacquered to prevent tarnishing; but in 1926, when Meccano was 25 years old, the first sets in colour were produced, the strips being painted green and the panels red.

Frank Hornby died in 1936 and his sons, Roland and Douglas, were left as directors. Meanwhile the Meccano Guild had united boys in a fellowship throughout the world – one of Hornby's dreams – and a Hornby Railway Club was formed to match the Guild. Meccano was regarded very seriously by scientists, who used it in designing more complicated models; it was also widely used in schools, including those for the blind.

By 1935, the Hornby factory was making speed boats, Elektron electric set, Kemex chemistry sets and Dolly Varden dolls' houses, as well as train sets and accessories, Dinky Toys and Meccano. In 1938, the Hornby Dublo range was introduced and was to prove equally successful. In World War II, the factory was turned over to government work; and when full toy production was allowed again in 1947, Meccano had difficulties owing to metal shortages.

By the end of the 1950s, Meccano Ltd's Hornby Dublo Trains faced overwhelming competition from Tri-ang, with their two-rail 00 gauge system. In 1960, Meccano took over Bayko from Plimpton Engineering, but were unsuccessful against the newly launched Lego sets. Moreover there was a world-wide recession in the market for train sets.

Finally, in 1964, Lines Group bought the company. The tools for the Hornby Dublo train range passed to G & R Wrenn Ltd, and the company name was changed to Meccano–Tri-ang Ltd. When the Lines Group in turn was forced into liquidation in 1971, all assets were transferred to a new company called Maoford Ltd. Renamed Meccano Ltd, the company was then sold on to Airfix Industries Ltd. Meanwhile the name 'Hornby' was acquired by Dunbee-Combex Ltd, who continued to produce Hornby trains at their Rovex factory near Margate, Kent.

In 1981, UK production of Mecccano ceased. Meccano products are currently being manufactured in France.

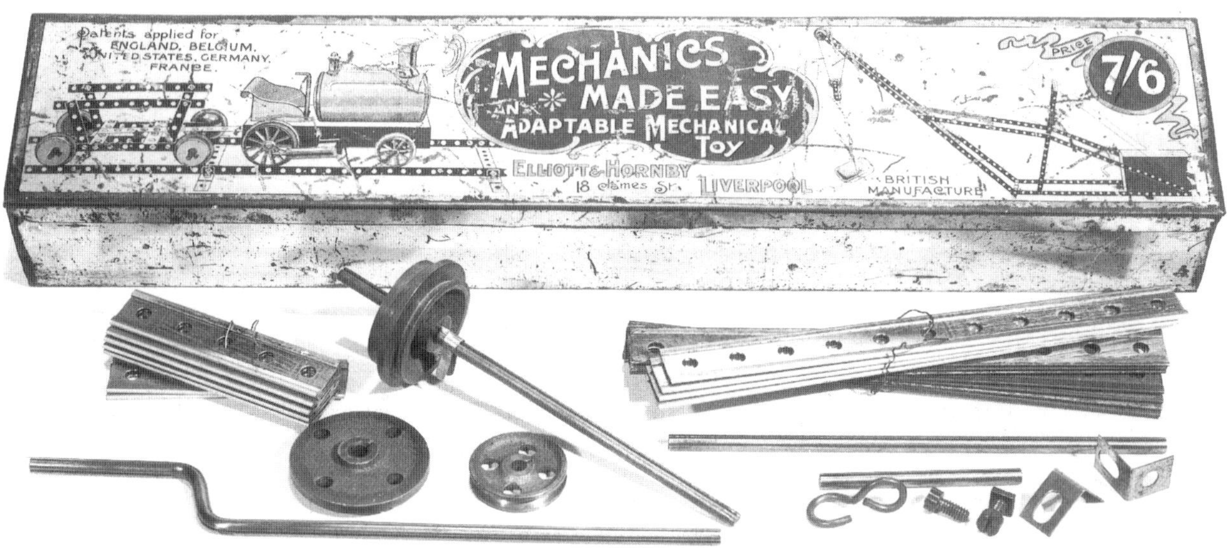

Meccano 'Mechanics Made Easy' kit, 1901

Winston Churchill and his Meccano, detail from painting, taken from screened photograph

H I F Peel, in a letter to *The Sunday Times* in April 1980, wrote as follows: 'Some years ago I attended a conference at the Institution of Mechanical Engineers to discuss ways of reducing the shortage of professional engineers. Eventually the last speaker climbed the rostrum and said; "Hands up all those who had Meccano when they were young!" Everyone in that packed lecture hall raised his hand and a great cheer went up.

'If the children of this country had been given free Meccano instead of free milk, then the British manufacturing industry would now be the finest in the world.'

In Cape Town, South Africa, a Meccano museum has been founded by Peter Matthews. In England, M W Models in Henley-on-Thames, is a mecca for all Meccano enthusiasts and collectors.

**pp. 19, 31, 66–7, 82–3, 86–7, 90–1, 122–123*

Further reading:
The Life Story of Meccano, Frank Hornby
The Hornby Companion Series Vols 1–8.
Vol 1, The Products of Binns Road, Peter Randall
Vol 2, The Meccano Super Models, Geoff Wright
Vol 3, Hornby Dublo Trains 1938–64, Michael Foster
Vol 3a, Hornby Dublo Compendium, Allen F. Ellis
Vol 4, Dinky Toys and Modelled Miniatures, Mike and Sue Richardson
Vol 4a, Dinky Toy Compendium, Patrick Trench
Vol 5, The Hornby Gauge 'O' System, Chris and Julie Graebe
Vol 5a, Gauge 'O' Compendium, Chris and Julie Graebe
Vol 6, The Meccano System and the Special Purpose Meccano Sets, Bert Love and Jim Gamble
Vol 6a, The Meccano System Compendium, Bert Love and Jim Gamble
Vol 7, The Meccano Magazine 1916–1981, Joseph Manduca
Vol 8, The Hornby Companion, Roger Beardsley
The Boy who made a Million Dollars with a Toy, M P Gould
Along Hornby Lines, Bernard Huntington

Mechanex Ltd
30 Bridge Row, London
Manufacturers of small $3\frac{1}{2}''$ aluminium boats (Patent No. 585.015) which were operated by a few drops of unlighted methylated spirit. Very similar boats working on small chunks of camphor, or even baking powder, were made by other obscure firms. Slightly larger metal boats were made by Meta Products, burning the same kind of solid methylated blocks as were used in camping stoves.

Merit Toys
See Alex Cohen and Randall, J

Meta Products
See Mechanex Ltd

Metal Box Ltd
1921
Initially known as Allied Tin Box Makers Ltd, the company was founded in 1921. It was formed from three tin printing firms, Barclay & Fry Ltd (London), Barringer, Wallis & Manners Ltd (Mansfield) and Hudson, Scott & Sons (Carlisle). All had been 19th century pioneers in printing on metal. It was in the James Street factory at Carlisle that the tinplate sheets for Hornby trains were printed.

In 1945, Chad Valley entered into close co-operation with the Mansfield branch producing toys printed with the Chad Valley name and logo. These included humming and spinning tops, globes of the world, 'pile-ups' (stackable cans which fitted one inside the other) and the Chad Valley clockwork lorry, based on Barringer's own lorry which ran until 1954.

In 1969, production of tin toys ceased in the Mansfield factory, and the toolsets were sent to Hall and Lane in Birmingham by then part of the Chad Valley Group.
See Barclay & Fry Ltd and *Hudson, Scott Ltd*

Further reading: Articles by Ian Layne in *HRCA Journals* for 1985
Metal Box – A History, W J Reader

Metal Crafts Training Institute
1920
1B Mountgrove Road, Highbury, London
The proprietors are listed as the Iron and Steel Strip Syndicate and the company was founded to give training and employment to disabled men of HM Forces.

The director of the adjoining British Metal & Toy Manufacturing Co., Sidney Stowe, was actively engaged in this project and it is possible that 'Brimtoy' clockwork parts were also used for the French Whippet Tanks made by the Institute. The Institute's main products, however, were vertical and horizontal steam engines.
See Appendix IV

Metal Toys
See Tops

Mettoy Co. Ltd
1933–1983
Northampton and Swansea
The company was founded in 1933 when Phillipp Ullmann of Bechmann & Ullmann, one of the premier tin toy manufacturers of Nuremberg, arrived in England with his second-in-command, Arthur Katz, as a refugee from Nazi Germany. His first premises were at 14 Harlestone Road, Northampton, where he manufactured tin toys with lithograph tin plate supplied by Winteringham Limited, a firm well-known for their contract work for Bassett Lowke. In the mid-1930s, Mettoy made clockwork lorries and aircraft, many of them for Marks & Spencer's stores. Eventually Mettoy took over Winteringham Ltd and, expanding, acquired a new factory on the Fforestfach Trading Estate near Swansea.

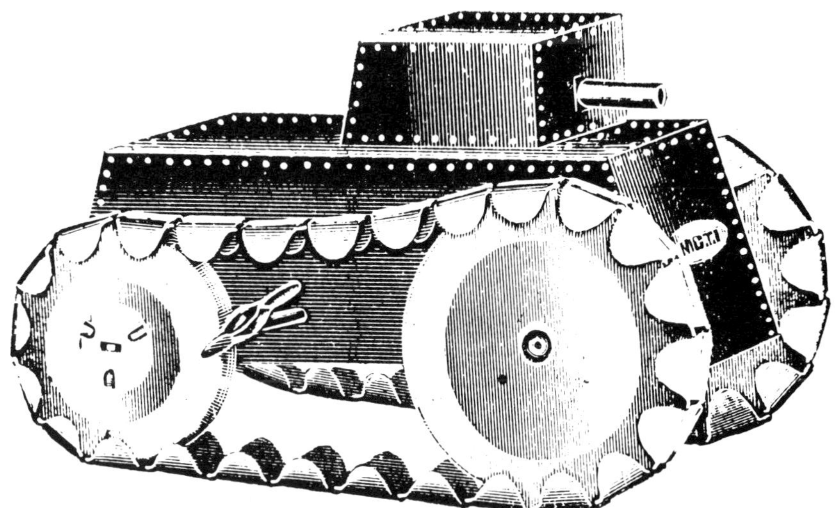
Metal Crafts Training Institute tank, 1920

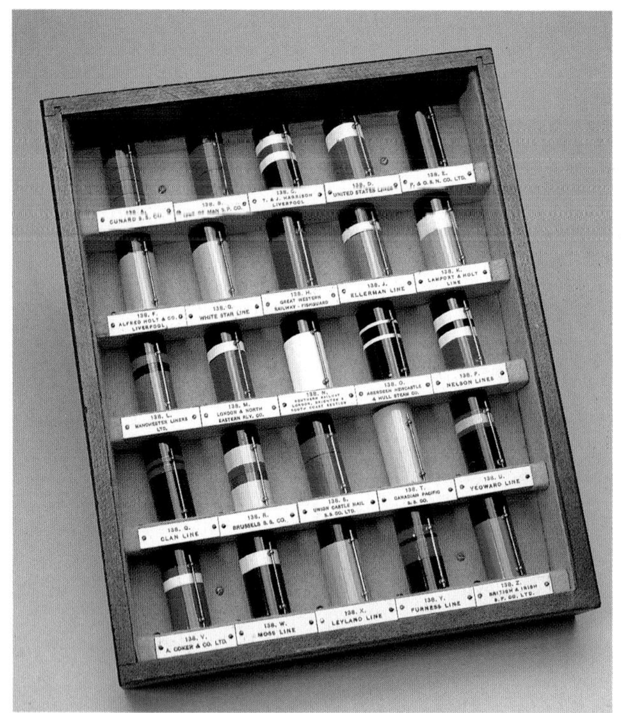

Meccano funnels for boats, 1930s (top)

Meccano No.8 set and instructions for 6, 7 & 8, 1938 (bottom)

Meccano Elektron sets, 1930s (top)

Meccano sets Nos. 0, 1, 4 and Ea 1934–41 (bottom)

During World War II, the factory went over to war production, reverting to toys seven years later. In 1946, they produced a metal kitchen stove which really worked, and also enjoyed an immense success with their Petite typewriter, manufactured by Byron Jardine but marketed by Mettoy.

In 1948, Henry Ullmann, son of the founder, brought back from the USA new methods for producing plastic toys, and expensive machinery was installed. The first plastic toys included a sewing machine, a cash register and a washing machine; then, from designs supplied by Howard Fairburn, they started a line of mass-produced miniature car models made with zinc alloy die-cast. The first group of 'Corgi' toys were cars with windows, treaded tyres and realistic detail. The brand name Corgi was suggested by the Queen's predilection for that dog breed and the Welsh manufacturing connection.

In 1954, Mettoy bought Playcraft Toys Ltd and the name of the firm became Mettoy/Playcraft. In spite of diversifying into the field of computers, by 1982 Mettoy was beset by financial trouble and in November 1983 the receiver was appointed. The Wembley and Playcraft trade names were bought by Guinness Brothers plc of Hockley, Essex.

In 1984, with support from the Electra Investment Trust, several former employees of Mettoy started a new company, Corgi Sales Ltd, to make a range of up-to-date die-cast models.
*See Appendix III *pp. 18, 94–5, 98–9, 102–03*

Further reading: *The Great Book of Corgi – 1956 to 1983,* Marcel van Cleemput

Advertisement from 1946 *Games and Toys*

Mills Bros Ltd
1919–1930s
Traded under the name of 'Milbro' and produced a range of railway equipment with metal locomotives and wooden rolling stock.

Minic Cars
See Lines Brothers Ltd

Minimodels Ltd
1945–the present day
New Lane, Havant, Hampshire and Tennyson Road, London
In the 1940s, the firm introduced small miniatures worked by clockwork, including a car which reversed each time it hit an obstacle. After the keywind cars came the 'Scalex' model range, driven by a keyless clockwork mechanism which was automatically wound by pulling the car back. The models had all-steel bodies and rubber wheels. In 1955, the 'Startex' range of scale models was introduced; these were fitted with 'no-key clockwork mechanisms: just pull the self starter'.

In 1958, 'Scalextric' racecourses were introduced in four different sized kits, with electric motor and clip-together

Mettoy racing car No.3093, 1949

track. In 1969, came the 'Jump Jockey' electrical steeplechase game, operated by remote control.

Fred Francis was the inventive genius behind Minimodels. *p. 110

Further reading: *The Complete History of Scalextric*, Steve de Havilland

MIP
See Multum in Parvo Co. Ltd

Mirrorscope
1943
A triangular variation on the Kaleidoscope. Registered designs were numbers 836/617 and 638 663/34. A 'Stymit' product, sold in 1943 by Style Toys Ltd, London, made in two sizes, 8″ and 12″.
See Kaleidoscope

Mobo
See Sebel, D & Co. Ltd

Model Toys
1953–1979
Shotts, Lanarkshire, Scotland
The firm was originally founded in 1941 under the name Toy Importers Ltd and in 1942 began the manufacture of toys under the registered trademark of 'Timpo'. In 1953 the firm's name was changed to Model Toys.

Die-cast manufacture was dropped in the mid-1950s in favour of plastic toys. The method they introduced eliminated hand-painting and used moulded colours all governed by machinery, plastic injection-moulding being faster and cheaper. They handled a big export business (67% of output) and won the Queen's Award to Industry in 1972. In 1975 they produced a battery-operated Prairie Rocket Wild West Train, based on 1850s American railway equipment.

The firm was liquidated in 1979.
See Toy Importers Ltd

Moko
See Kohnstam, M & Co. and Matchbox Toys

Money-boxes

Metal: A former Director of Chubb & Sons Lock and Safe Co., Mr Leonard W Dunham has formed a large collection of English money-boxes. From the huge range it is only possible to mention a few of the main manufacturers of metal money-boxes:

H R Euston, 1917
Fancy Tin Toy Co., 1894–1904
Hare Bros., 1921
Hat Trick Money-Box Co., 1928

Cast iron: Mr Robert Starkie after World War I set up a small foundry in Burnley to manufacture a mechanical 'Moneybank Sonny Boy' who ate pennies placed in his hand, rolled his eyes and wiggled his ears. These banks were then made by the foundry Moorhouse Ltd. From 1950,

Ashworth 'Sonny Boy' money bank, 1954

Barringer, Wallis & Manners money-boxes – gas fire 1916, pillarboxes 1950s

when Mr Starkie retired, Thomas Ashworth & Co. of Burnley made them in aluminium and they were on sale until 1960. Sydenham & McOustra made cast iron still banks, notably one of Blackpool Tower. Another manufacturer was Chamberlaine Hill.

Brass and tin:
George Whitehouse made brass and copper money-boxes. Barringer, Wallis & Manners from 1914 made cash boxes and tin pillarbox banks for a number of firms, notably Burnett, Chad Valley and Dunn & Taylor.

Further reading: *Penny Wise*, published by Hove Museum

Moorhouse Ltd
1921
Padiham, Burnley, Lancashire
Advertised mechanical toys including 'Nigger Money Bank' with moving eyes, ears and hand, 'Charlie Chaplin Bank', 'Tank Bank' with or without gun and 'My Dolly's Wringer'.
See Money-boxes

Morestone
See Morris and Stone (London) Ltd

Morris & Stone (London) Ltd
1954
95 Church Street, Stoke Newington, London
Manufacturers of 'Morestone' quality die-cast scale model toys including stage coach complete with galloping horses and cowboys; hansom cabs with driver, lamps and reins; snack bar complete with bartender, horse and equipment.

Sam Morris, on leaving the army, started a toy wholesale business, but as he could not obtain sufficient stock he began producing his own die-cast models.

Morris, Wm, E & Co.
1904–1950
Triumph Works, Ernest Street, Birmingham
Manufacturers of metal seaside buckets and spades and garden sets.

Multum in Parvo Co. Ltd
1884
Clerkenwell Green, London
Produced the Lamplough patented table cricket game with little tin figures and a spring-driven ball. One of the tin colour-printed figures represented the well-known cricketer, W G Grace. The game was invented by Harry Lamplough c.1900. The firm used the trademark MIP.

Musical Tops
See Tops

Musical Toys
Mozart's father, Leopold, composed a charming little symphony using toys bought at a local fair. Other 18th century composers such as Andreus Romberg wrote similar entertainments using toy drums, tin trumpets, rattles and bird calls. All these instruments were available until plastic took over, but the toy orchestra was augmented by new instruments which reflected the changes of fashion in popular music. At the time of Minstrel Shows, there were toy banjos, swanee whistles and mouth organs. With the rise of the big dance bands, in the 1920s, toy jazzband sets appeared in Woolworth's and other chain stores.

Meccano aeroplanes, 1931–41

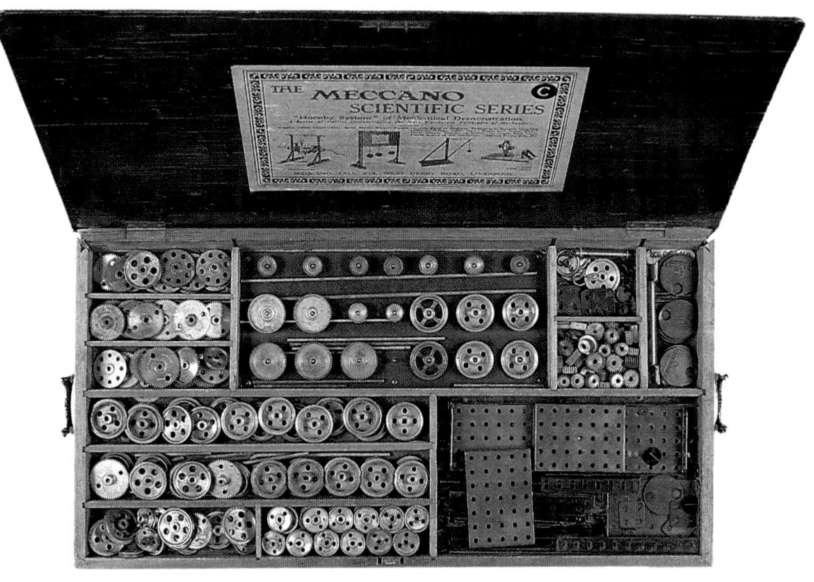

Meccano mechanised army outfit No.A, 1939–41 (top)
Meccano traction engine, 1950 (middle left)
Meccano motorcycles and cars, 1930s (middle right)
Meccano Scientific Series instruction set, 1909 (bottom)

Principal manufacturers

Barnes & Mullins, Rathbone Place, London
1925 'Swanee' whistles, banjos, and mandolines

Black Ltd, Liverpool
1920 Jazzband drums

British Mouth Organs Ltd, Southport, Lancashire
1955 'Play Boy' and 'Band Boy' harmonicas and 'Bing Boy' mouth organs

Clarke Tin Whistle Co., Manchester
1910 Whistles

John E Dallas, London
1925 One Man Jazzband

Defiance Manufacturing Co., London
1917 Tin whistles, flutes, musical submarines and Victory trumpets

Durrands Ltd, London
1920 Trumpets, whistles, mouth organs

Eeles, Walker & Co. Ltd, Birmingham
1922 Trademark 'Elswal'. Drums, jazz rollers, tambourines

Fyfe Douglas Co., Glasgow
1922 Toy pianos, 'musically correct, mechanically perfect'

Green Monk Products, Barnsley, Yorkshire
1945 Musical metal toys, drums, xylophones etc.

Howard, G, London
1870 Toy drums

Hull Toy Works
1914 Pianos

Keim Metal & Stamping Co. & E J E Tools & Components Ltd, Feltham, Middlesex
1949 Trademark 'Keimola'. Trumpets, music boxes, musical rollers.

Lewis, L M Ltd, London
1926 'Kazooz', 'Hum' drummer jazz outfits

Marsh, B, London
1947 Distributor of 'Planetone' miniature baby grand piano and plastic harmonicas

Marshall & Wegh Ltd
1949 'Hill Billy Tremolo' harmonica

Moon Workshops, London
1947 'Pixiano' toy pianos

Charles Orme & Co. Ltd, London
1918 'Alley Warbler'

Pattison, Donald, Sunderland
1952 'Whizz Wheels', mouth organs, trumpets and other musical toys

Pomeranz, M. Ltd, London
1948 Conductor mouth organ, four-note clarinet

Selcol Products Ltd, London
1963 Swing music set called 'Acker Bilk's Jazz Band'

Simons, E, London
1919 'Drum-o-phone' – a drum with cymbal attachment which could be played with piano or gramophone

Green Monk Products 'Sooty' Xylophone, 1954
Advertisement from 1963 *Games and Toys*

Simons Ltd
'Drumophone', 1915

E H Napier 'Napro' carpet locomotive, 1948

N

Napier, E H Ltd
1945
Minerva House, 76 Hatton Garden, London and after 1949 at Kingsland Road, Dalston, London
Toy wholesaler and distributors. Used trade name 'Napro'. Advertised in 1948 a metal carpet locomotive, and 'Welkut' models. In 1949, advertised 'Twenty Questions', based on the BBC radio game, which included 200 collated questions plus an electrical applause indicator.

New Milton Sheet Metal Works Ltd
1948
Old Milton Road, New Milton, Hampshire
Manufacturers of metal toys for other firms. They went into voluntary liquidation in August 1948.

Newton, William E & Fred
1850–1890s
Fleet Street, London
Opticians dealing in lanterns and lantern slides, including moving astronomical diagrams, stereoscopic slides and viewers. They also sold steam locomotives.
*See Magic Lanterns *p. 126*

Normansell, R
1909
Deritend Works, Birmingham
One of the oldest firms manufacturing seaside buckets and spades. Possible successor to Fancy Tin Toy Co. Ltd.

Norris, James
1852–1950
51 Sherbourne Road, Birmingham
This long-established firm made tin stampings and piercings for the trade. They specialised in novelties for filling Christmas crackers and stockings, and also made spring guns, peashooters, seaside spades, dolls' kitchen equipment, stoves and scales. They advertised the 'Sherbourne' series and in 1927, a banjo whistler and other whistles.

Norristoy
1948
C W Norris Ltd, Toy Division, Farnworth, Bolton, Lancashire
Produced a metal articulated lorry set, van, hay truck and petrol tanker.

Nottingham Die-Casting Co.
1920
Queen's Bridge Road, Nottingham
Toy manufacturers. 1922 lines included 'Topping' racing game.

O

Oliver, Harper & Company
1915
252 Goswell Road, London
Toy manufacturers. Firm was founded by T A Grimes, Oliver and Burbey to fill the gap caused by the lack of imported toys during the First World War. They produced the 'Unity' toy series which included a French 75 mm gun, an anti-aircraft gun, a naval gun, a mountain gun, an exploding mine, a bomb-thrower and a searchlight. They were designed by Burbey, a practising engineer, who also supervised the construction of the models.

After the war the firm produced wooden toys including toy mangles, dolls' cots, cranes and seaside spades, and were one of the first firms to introduce British-made metal toys.

By 1923, the firm had premises in Church Lane, Beddington, near Croydon, Surrey. Lines included 'Simpull' train sets, but the firm largely specialised in the manufacture of baby carriages and toy prams.

Oliver Harper French field gun, 1915

Oppenheimer, S, Ltd
1946
Otley Works, Otley, Yorkshire also at 17 Wilson Street, London
Dealers and wholesalers in fancy goods, games and toys. 1947 lines included paintboxes, pencil cases etc.
Trademark 'Emu' Series

Oppenheimer Ltd
Peter and Pat see-saw, 1946

MADE IN ENGLAND

FRUIT & VEGETABLES

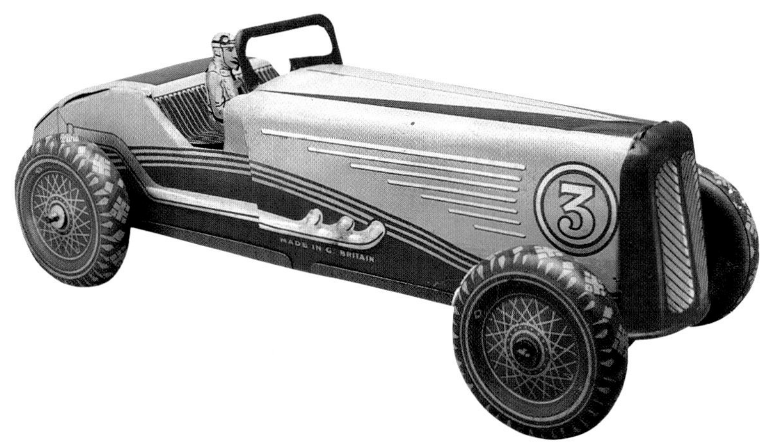

First and second series **Mettoy** open lorries, 1936 and 1939 (page 94 top left)
Two **Mettoy** clockwork racing cars, 1936 and 1941 (page 94 top right)
Mettoy lorry, c.1939 (page 94 middle)
Mettoy fruit and vegetable lorry, 1951 (page 94 bottom left)
Mettoy racing car, 1948 (page 95 top)
Mettoy saloon and box, 1936 (page 95 bottom)

Optical Toys
The experience of watching the landscape through the spoked wheels of a farm cart as it trundled down the lane may have been the first clue that led eventually to the vast 20th century industry of moving pictures. It was, however, in 1825 that Dr Roget first showed why separate drawings passing quickly before the eyes of a viewer appear to form one moving picture. During the ensuing 160 years this phenomenon, persistence of vision, has been developed and used in a vast number of devices and machines, whose inventors gave them learned Greek or Latin names.

The 1876 catalogue of the Oxford Street toy shop, A N Myers & Co., devotes six pages to optical toys. It can be consulted at the Tolson Memorial Museum in Huddersfield.
See Cinema, Kaleidoscope, Thaumotrope, Zeotrope

Further reading:
Movement in Two Dimensions, Olive Cook
Victorian Kinetic Toys, Philip and Caroline Sayer
Making Scientific Toys, Carson T H Ritchie

Optimus
See Perken, Son & Rayment

P

Palitoy
See Cascelloid

Paton, Calvert & Co. Ltd
1887–1940
Binns Rd, Old Swan, Liverpool
Manufacturers of 'Happynak' metal toys. In 1915, they launched a very simple constructional toy assembled without nuts and bolts, followed in 1920 by metal kitchen, dinner and teasets, seaside pails, drums, money-boxes, acrobatic clowns and skittle sets. In 1935 these same toys were printed with Mickey and Minnie Mouse designs.

A short book, entitled *The First Fifty Years of My Adventures in Commerce* edited by P Nodin and published as the firm's Silver Jubilee Souvenir, gives details of Sir James Wallace Paton's career. His father was captain of the *Leviathan* and later of one of Brunel's famous transatlantic steamers, the *Great Eastern.* His son, James Wallace, was born on board ship. As a boy he had set his heart on following his father to sea, but cancelled his indenture when his eldest brother lost his life trying to save a shipmate off Cape Horn.

In 1887, with five employees he set up in business at 34 Moorfield, Liverpool, to sell 'Paton's Cleanall Powder', a mixture he had invented for cleaning ship's paint. This was a success and by 1891 he had

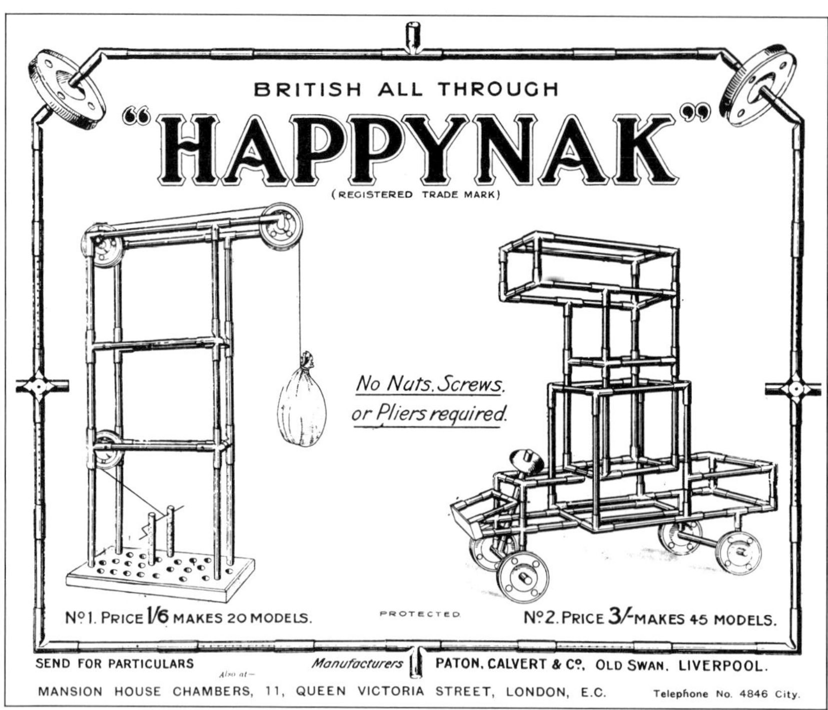

Advertisement for 'Happynak' toys, 1914

moved to larger premises and was also marketing a 'matchless metal polish'. He had launched this with considerable publicity and by a widespread distribution of tiny free samples put up in small round chip boxes – a selling technique quite new at the time. He had married Miss Kate Calvert in 1891, and in this same year his father-in-law, Harry Calvert, joined him as a partner and they established the firm as Paton, Calvert & Co.

In 1901, Paton invented the 'Deep Gap' stamping press, which revolutionised the manufacture of small tins and led to another expansion of the business. By now the staff numbered some four hundred people. The firm also changed its trading name to The Matchless Metal Polish Co.. To mark the end of the South African War they added commemorative medals to their range of products; and further medals were struck for the Coronation of Edward VII and for that of George V.

In 1908, new factory and office premises covering five acres was acquired in Binns Road, Old Swan, opposite Frank Hornby's Meccano factory. In addition to many successful business activities, James Wallace Paton accepted a number of public duties. He became a councillor, then Mayor of Southport, and also served as a JP for Lancaster County.

During World War I, the Binns Road factory turned to the manufacture of food containers, and of metal valves and eye pieces for gas masks. They also supplied the army and the navy with all the polishes they needed to blacken boots and shine brass buttons. The firm was also responsible for a new patent design for a fuse case which saved the government thousands of pounds. At the end of the war, James Wallace Paton received a knighthood for these services.

In 1919, the firm reverted to its old name of Paton, Calvert & Co. and set about revitalising its peacetime activities. New tin stamping and printing machinery was installed. The cardboard and paper printing side was modernised, photographic and art studios were created. In addition to the box making, the manufacture of cleaning materials and the 'Komo' line of household equipment, the output of the metal 'Happynak' toys was also expanded. Factory space was increased in 1932, and again in 1934 and 1935, but by the outbreak of World War II toy making had completely ceased.

Further reading: *The First Fifty Years of My Adventures in Commerce,* ed. P Nodin

Paton Calvert & Co. 'Happynak' bucket, 1922

Pedal Car Manufacturers

Allwin Toys, Birmingham
1930 Allwin C T 20″

Argyle **p. 106*
1930s pedal cars

Austin Motor Co., Wales
1948 Tourer and Racing Car

Blenheim Manufacturing Co., London
1920 Blenheim Model Pedal Car

British Games Ltd, London
1934 BG Midget 1 and 2

G and J Lines, London
1909 Gordon Bennett

Lines Bros, London **pp. 106–07*
Produced many models such as the 1926 Tin Lizzie, the Airflow, Vauxhall Majestic and electric Rolls-Royce.

Patterson Edwards **p. 107*
1950s 'Leeway' Pedal Cars

Tan-Sad Ltd, Birmingham
1937 Bentley Racer, Snipe Pedal Car, Berkeley Pedal Car

Tucker, R A
1920 The Assheton Car

Charles Twigg & Co. (Prams) Ltd, Birmingham
1949 Flying Ace 100 Deluxe
102 Fire Engine Chief

Vernon Toys Ltd, Liverpool
1947 Pedal Car with RAF markings

Further reading: *Children's Cars*, Paul Pennell

Pedley, W R & Co. Ltd
1893–1940s
Dimminsdale, Willenhall, Staffordshire
Presswork specialists and toy manufacturers, successors to Regent Manufacturing Co. and Remanco Ltd. 1942 metal toy lines included upright and table mangles, handcuffs, peashooters, toy pistols, water pistols, cap guns, pop-guns, lawn mowers, dustpan and brush sets.

In addition to toy manufacturing, the firm made metal pressings and components for the toy trade.

Penny Toys and Novelties
In Volume 10 of the *Strand Magazine*, published in 1895, an article describes what is called the 'gutter-man's art'. Most of the objects seem to be English-made, including miniature clay pipes, dolls' furniture, pottery bird whistles, jumping jacks and such novelties as a doll in a walnut shell, a mouse in a matchbox, wire puzzles and miniature bibles, watches, pen knives, garden tools and wheelbarrows for the dolls' house. These would have been made by the street hawkers themselves or by poor artisans. Others would have been made by the firms which made seaside buckets, peashooters, tin whistles and other small items for bazaars, for the summer trade and for Christmas stockings and crackers. The name 'Penny Toys' was, of course, derived from the fact that they sold for a penny.

Barringer, Wallis & Manners made for the confectionery trade a number of small 'Penny Novelty' tins which could be filled with tiny sweets.
*See Appendix I, Barringer, Wallis & Manners *p. 11*

Further reading: Volume 10, *Strand Magazine*, 1895

Perken, Son & Rayment
1895
99 Hatton Garden, London
One of the most important manufacturers of magic lanterns in the second half of the 19th century. They used the trade name 'Optimus'. The lanterns, in various sizes and shapes, were made with japanned metal exteriors, or from mahogany lined with metal. They had compound condensers composed of two plano-convex lenses of four inches diameter, and front lenses giving fine definition. An oil lamp, incandescent gas burner or oxy-hydrogen limelight was used for illumination. The lanterns were especially used for educational purposes, with photographic slides of historical and geographical interest, or from the fields of natural history, geology and astronomy. For the latter, ingenious mechanical contrivances illustrated movement of the stars and planets.
See Magic Lanterns

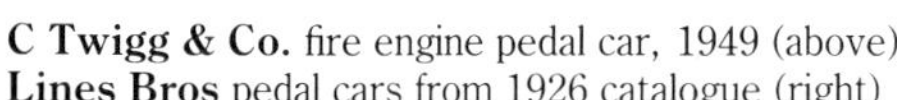
C Twigg & Co. fire engine pedal car, 1949 (above)
Lines Bros pedal cars from 1926 catalogue (right)

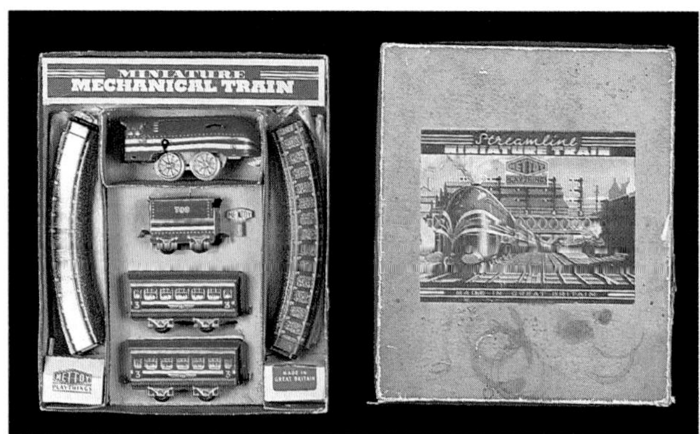

Mettoy Coronation train set, c.1938 (top)

Mettoy 'Joytown Flying Squad Station' with police car and ambulance, 1951 (middle)

Four **Mettoy** speed boats, one unidentified speed boat and a 'Tri-ang' rowing boat, c.1950s (bottom)

Mettoy monoplane, c.1936 (top)
Two **Mettoy** clockwork road rollers, 1951 (middle right)
Mettoy 'Blackbird Pie' money-box, 1958 (middle left)
Mettoy printed tin dolls' house, 1955 (bottom)

Petite Typewriters
See Byron Jardine Ltd and Typewriter Manufacturers

Philip Toy Co.
1920
6 Philip Lane, Wood Street, London
Manufacturers, dealers, importers and exporters of toys, dolls, games, balls and books, including toy bears and rabbits, wooden and mechanical toys and the 'Lady Blondin' automatic toy which 'walks on string or wire suspended in mid-air. Creates sensation whenever seen'.

Phoenix Toy Works
1919–1930
29 White Post Lane, Victoria Park, Hackney Wick, London
First listed as scrap iron merchants. In 1921 they were making metal parts for other toy manufacturers and producing peashooters, aerial flyers such as 'Goldfish in a bowl' and other tin toys and novelties under the direction of Robert Emmett.
See Thaumatrope

Pioneer Models
1926
London and Birmingham
Manufacturers of a Meccano look-alike system.
See Appendix VII

Piot, Désiré Thomas
1891
10 Buckingham Street, London
Engineer who patented a small steam generator which was particularly applicable to toy boats.
*See Appendix VI *p. 30*

Plastics and Other Compositions
In the interests of economy, or at times when certain metals were in short supply, toy manufacturers have had recourse to substitute alloys and various compounds; examples include zamark and stenolite, lead alloys used respectively by Meccano and Treforest Mouldings; or mazak and timpoline, compositions of chalk, plaster of Paris and glues, which were used to make 'Timpo Toys' during World War II.

The search for a man-made, easily moulded material had been undertaken by a number of 19th century scientists. One of the first of these early plastics was 'parkesine', made by Alexander Parkes in 1862 from cotton waste treated with castor oil and nitric and sulphuric acids. The quantities produced were very small, until five years later Parkes's associate, Daniel Spill, put on the market 'xylonite', which was developed by The British Xylonite Company.

In 1870, using camphor instead of castor oil, John Wesley Hyatt produced in America a very similar cellulose-based plastic, which he called 'celluloid'. It was possible to add colour to the blocks or sheets of this new material, which was used for small household items. In England the first celluloid toys – babies' rattles and little coloured balls – were made c. 1895 by blowing hot air or steam between sheets of celluloid, enabling them to be moulded into shape.

Until World War I, France and Germany were the main manufacturers of celluloid toys. During the war years, Japanese and Japanese-American businessmen stepped in to fill the gap caused by the collapse of the German toy trade, and began the production of cheap celluloid toys copied from German originals. At the end of hostilities, in 1919, two British firms were set up with the same objective: The Ivorine Manufacturing Co. and Cascelloid Ltd.

According to Mr A E Pallett, the founder of the last-named firm, 'cascelloid' was a new form of non-flammable celluloid using gelatin and casein. In 1935, cascelloid was replaced by a still safer material, 'bexoid', and in 1937 by 'plastex', made from chemically-heated rabbit glues. By this time the firm had changed its name to Palitoy Ltd and continued to expand, making a wide variety of toys and dolls, until in 1968 it was acquired by the giant General Mills Corporation of America. Celluloid and its various aliases had one great drawback – they would burn up in a flash and in 1967 celluloid was banned by new regulations on toy safety.

We owe the discovery of another early plastic, so it is said, to a scientist's cat, which knocked a bottle of formaldehyde into its saucer of milk. The resultant mess, when examined by the cat's master, A Spitten, set him on the path of developing, with his collaborator, W Krische, a plastic material 'casein' made from dried milk curds, pulverised and then chemically treated. As the end product broke rather easily, however, it was not much used in the toy trade.

Cellulose and casein plastics are only partly synthetic; quite early on in the 19th century several scientists had produced in their laboratories small quantities of materials such as polyvinyl chloride and polystyrene. The first entirely synthetic plastic to be made on a commercial basis was 'bakelite', named after its inventor, the Belgian scientist, L H Baekland, who patented it in the USA in 1909. It is heavy

W R Pedley & Co. advertisement in 1940 *Games & Toys*

The 'Circus', one of the first plastic toys sold by Woolworth's in 1947

and hard, and was widely used in the electrical industry; but as its natural colour is dark brown or black, its use in the toy trade was restricted to counters and pieces in games sets, parts of strong 'scientific' toys, and construction toys such as 'Bayko'.

In 1931, a Yorkshire firm was advertising a series of clockwork toys, including notably Malcolm Campbell's record-breaking racing car 'Bluebird', made from 'ranlite', a new lightweight, unbreakable material. A few years later Hilary Page, a talented toy designer, was getting large audiences for his BBC radio talks in which he stressed the importance of play during the first five years of a child's life. He was a strong advocate of good quality plastic toys for young children, and set up his own firm, Kiddicraft, to market toys made out of 'bri-plax', a strong non-flammable and fast-coloured plastic which he patented in 1940.

During the war years many advances were made in the techniques of large-scale production of nylon fibres – polystyrene, PVC and polythene – but it was only after 1950 that these plastics were increasingly employed in the toy trade.
See Bayko and Cascelloid Ltd

Playcraft Toys Ltd
1955
120 Moorgate, London
Subsidiary of Mettoy Co. Ltd. In 1956, the firm introduced 'Corgi' toys (realistic scale models) and in 1963, the Petite Typewriter, a working miniature.
See Mettoy and Typewriter Manufacturers

Plimpton, J C & Co. Ltd
1914–1959
116 Old Hall, Liverpool
By 1939, the firm was called Plimpton Engineering Co. with premises at 15 Gibralter Row, Liverpool. 1938 lines included 'Bayko' constructional sets in light, washable bakelite. In 1959, Meccano Ltd acquired the company.
See Bayko Construction and Meccano Ltd

Presswork Products Ltd
1932–1939
Great West Trading Estate, Acton, London
This firm had two main lines – musical tops, and nursery clocks. The tops were marked 'Presstone' and came in five sizes – the largest were 7 inches, 8 inches and 9$\frac{1}{4}$ inches and each had 4 reeds. The clocks had either a fairytale scene or a picture of boy scouts on the clockface. All the parts and all the tools for stamping out the parts were made on the firm's premises.

Prestacon Model Engineering Kits
See Clydon Products, Appendix VII

Prestyn Toys Ltd
1949
Lanfranc Road, Bow, London
Manufacturers of metal toys. Lines included clockwork aerotower, 'Sulman Special Racing Car' with steering wheel, hub caps and bonnet strap with No. 8 stamped on the side.

Primus Engineering
*See Butcher & Sons Ltd and Constructional Toys *p. 126*

Advertisement in 1934 *Games and Toys*

Mettoy clown motorbike, 1951 (top)

Acrobatic clown motorbike, probably **Cowan de Groot** 'Codeg', c.1945 (bottom)

Mettoy Red Indian motorbike, 1949 (top)
Mettoy black faced clown motorbike, 1949 (middle)
Mettoy police patrol motorbike, 1949 (bottom)

Black Ltd flat printed box lid, 1950

Printing on Tinplate

There are three different ways in which a design can be printed onto thin sheets of tinplate; these methods do not differ greatly from those used to print onto paper or textiles.

The simplest process used from the middle of the last century was somewhat akin to printing from woodblocks. By using acid to eat away the unwanted parts, the design to be printed was first produced in relief on a special slab of stone, then inked and pressed onto the sheet of metal previously coated with a background colour. A patent for this method was assigned to the Neath Tinplate Decorating Company in 1868.

The second method is very similar to that used for decorating porcelain, glass or papier maché. Special transfers were printed on paper. The sheets of metal to be printed were then covered with a coat of varnish, and the paper transfers were stuck down and left to dry. The paper backing was soaked off with warm water, leaving the design on the surface of the tin. Finally, another coat of varnish was applied and the sheet of tinplate was then baked in an oven.

A printed biscuit tin sentry box, 1914

Between 1860 and 1873, Benjamin & Fry who were specialists in banknote printing took out a patent covering the use of offset lithograph to printing on tinplate. They soon lost interest and two years later sold the patent to Bryant & May, the matchstick makers, who thought they might use it to make tin holders for matchboxes, before they in turn found it more convenient to licence the process to the biscuit tin makers, Huntley, Boorne & Stevens of Reading.

In offset lithography, the design to be printed is transferred from the stone to the specially prepared surface of a rubber backed blanket, which is then wrapped round a roller of the printing press. Photo-lithography was first introduced in the late 1920s by Barringer, Wallis & Manners and Hudson Scott.

Until 1939, the sheets of tinplate used generally measured 28″×20″, a size convenient for one man to pick up and carry to the printing press. Each colour printed required one pass through the printing press, plus twenty minutes in the stove oven. The colours were built up in a fixed sequence. First one or two coatings of a white background, then the parts of the design which were coloured in pale shades, fawn, yellow, pink, light blue, followed by the darker colours red, dark blue, brown, black, plus finally clear lacquers and sometimes bands or touches of gold gilding. Most sheets were handled at least a dozen times before being interleaved with tissue paper and packed in boxes.

Until the end of the 19th century all lithography onto tinplate was done on flatbed presses. In 1903, Barringer, Wallis & Manners installed Rotary Presses, which had been patented in 1892 and which were made for them by George Mann of Leeds. The printing of tinplate in long continuous strips was not introduced until 1939 in Ebbw Vale.

*See Avon Tin Printers, Barclay & Fry, Barringer, Wallis & Manners, Barlow Ltd, Black Ltd, British Can Co., Bryant & May, Caldicot Printing Works, Cambrian Can & Drum Co., Fever Ltd, Hudson Scott, Huntley, Boorne & Stevens, Marden Illingworth, Metal Box Ltd, Tin Plate Decorating Co. *pp. 10, 11*

Further reading: *Towards a History of Tinplate-Printing,* Alec Davis; *British Biscuit Tins,* M J Franklin; *Metal Box – A History,* W J Reader

Progress Toy Co. Ltd

1920–1980
Kirby Road, Blackpool, Lancashire
In 1980, shortly before it closed down this firm was one of the last three firms in the world making gyroscopic toys. The other two were in the USA and Japan.

In 1969, the Shipman family who had run the Progress Toy Co., sold out to Mr Crabtree and his son, who then changed the name to The Progress Gyroscope Co. They only made one product – a gyroscopic top in two sizes, sold by Randall's Ltd. Before World War II, the firm's output was more varied. They made gyroscopic parts for other manufacturers, notably Lines Bros. They also made toys which spun round a five foot circle of steel strip. The Progress Toy Co. Ltd appears to have been connected with the firm 'Gyro-manufacturers' of Leicester, who in 1912 advertised 'Mono Rail', 'Happy Dancer' and 'Aerial Spiral Gyro Toys'.

Lewis Wild who in 1916 advertised 'Mono Rail' with the 'Gyro Loco', was a toy wholesaler not a manufacturer.
See Gyroscope

R

Racing Cars and Land Speed Cars

Toy racing cars were produced by all the major tin toy manufacturers. Later, various die-cast manufacturers such as Dinky and Corgi produced ranges of racing cars. Chad Valley, Mettoy, Prestyn and Wells-Brimtoy all made racing cars which varied in size and colour and which were marked with different numbers. However, the basic torpedo shape did not change very much over the years.

In addition to ordinary racing cars, the major toy makers produced a very attractive selection of Land Speed Record Breakers. At Easter 1928, at Bonneville Flats, Salt Lake City, Captain Malcolm Campbell broke the world speed record. His 'Bluebird' car reached 206 miles an hour. This feat caught the imagination of many small boys, and by May the agents Bedington, Liddiatt & Co. were announcing that they had the sole rights for Great Britain and the colonies of a British-made, exact reproduction of the famous car. Wells-Brimtoy also modified one of the standard racing cars and christened it 'Bluebird'. The following year in March, at Daytona Beach, Sir Henry Seagrave reached 231 m.p.h. His car, 'The Golden Arrow', was produced by Ranlite Toys, in a new plastic bakelite material (1931). Various clockwork models of foreign manufacture such as 'The Golden Arrow' and Kaye Don's 'Silver Bullet' were distributed in the UK (see opposite). The 'Silver Bullet' was made in three sizes plus a miniature model.

In 1931, Sir Malcolm Campbell had won back the World Speed Record – now 246 m.p.h. – and toy versions of 'Bluebird II' were in production even before the record was broken. Other toys such as fairy cycles and pedal cars were

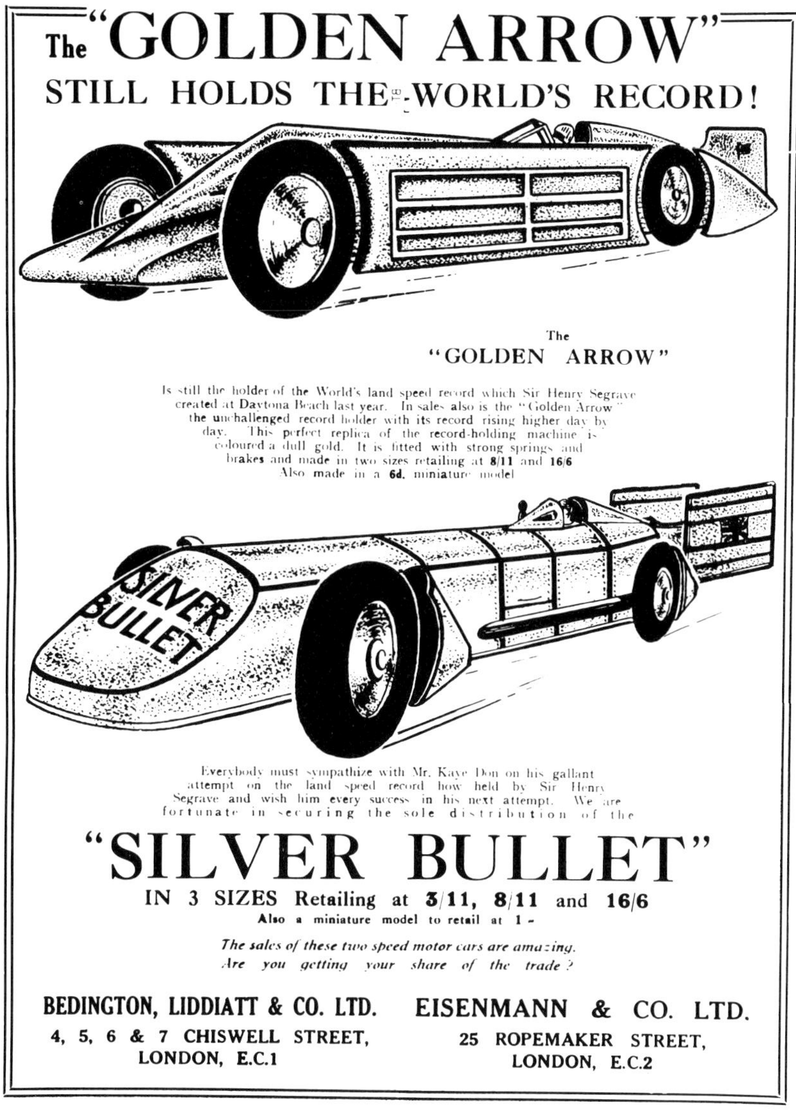

Advertisement in 1930 *Games and Toys*

christened 'Bluebird' that year; and there were also 'Bluebird' aeroplanes, based on the plane used by the Hon. Mrs Victor Bruce in her record solo flight round the world.

The next much-publicised battle took place at Bonneville Flats, at Easter 1938. First John Cobb in a Napier Railton Special broke the record; then next day Captain Eyston in 'Thunderbolt' reached $357\frac{1}{2}$ m.p.h.

In 1947, John Cobb broke the record again in another Napier Railton.

Britains Ltd produced a $6\frac{5}{8}$" ingenious model of this car. The body could lift off to show the car's layout. A $10\frac{1}{2}$" silver metal clockwork model was also produced (and sold by Eisenmann), with John Cobb's autograph on the body and American and British flags on the bonnet. **pp. 110–11*

Wells-Brimtoy racing car, 1952

Rainbow Tops
See Bedington, Liddiatt & Co. Ltd, Louis Marx and Tops

Randall, J (Toys & Games) Ltd
1940–1978
Merit House, 67 Bunhill Row, London (destroyed in the Blitz).
Merit House, Southgate Road, Potters Bar, Middlesex
J Randall resigned from Bell (Toys & Games) Ltd in March 1940 to set up his own business. He changed its name to Randall, J & L Ltd in 1943 and throughout the war produced box games, embroidery, leathercraft, needlework etc. and a very successful Juvenile Morse Signalling set.

1947 Many boxed games and metal puzzles
1954 Became British manufacturers of 'Slinky', an American invention, consisting of a fine metal spring that walked downstairs.
1955 Inflatable toys; plastic Space Saucer; construction sets.
1961 The Potters Bar factory was extended to double size (originally built 1948). Produced educational games and handicrafts.
1978 Firm bought by Letraset (Trademark 'Merit') and is now known as Merit Toys Ltd.

Ranlite Toys
1931
Tree Street, Halifax, Yorkshire
Manufacturers of a series of clockwork toys made of a very lightweight unbreakable material, bakelite. Trademark 'Ranlite'

Rees, Leon
1879–1963
Leon Rees was born in Bavaria. He emigrated to England where he joined Eisenmann & Co. and married Maud Eisenmann. After World War I, he became UK representative of Bing Werke of Germany. With H G Stone at Chesham (later Amersham Works), he started Chiltern Teddy Bear and adopted the trade name 'Elarco'.

1923 They were producing a range of wooden toys and sports goods.
1930 Dorco brand surf-riding rubber goods.
1931 Kiddies' steel trike.
1947 Prestacon model engineering set and Bingoscope toy cinema projector.

After World War II they opened a further factory at Pontypool for soft toys. They were also concessionaire for a large range of toys apart from those

Lines Bros 'Ace' pedal car, c.1928 (top)
Lines Bros Brookland No.8 racing car, c.1930 (middle)
Argyle pedal car, c.1930s (bottom)

Leeway Triumph Dolomite, c.1950 (top)
Lines Bros Magna No.8, c.1935 (middle)
Lines Bros (for Liberty's) junior pedal car, c.1934 (bottom)

manufactured by the firm. The Rees Group was finally acquired by Dunbee-Combex in 1964 and then by Chad Valley Ltd.

Regent Manufacturing Co.
See Pedley, W R & Co.

REM
See Remoline Co.

Remanco Ltd
See Pedley, W R & Co.

Remoline Co.
1919
4 Denman Street, London
Manufacturers of metal toys and fancy goods. Trademark REM. Lines included brass scales with black enamelled base, price 4½d.

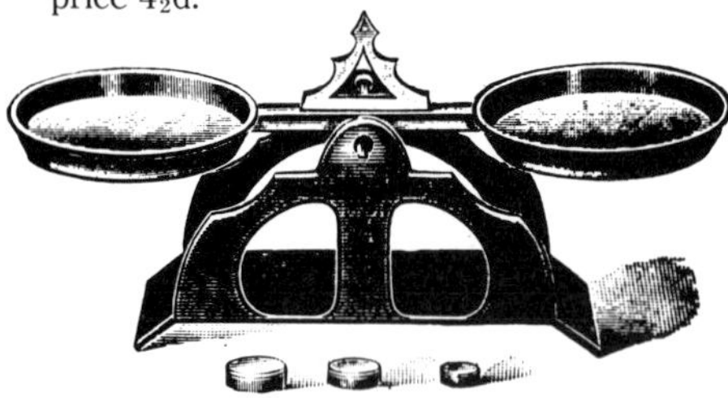

Remoline & Co. toy scales, 1919

Rhodes, Joseph & Sons Ltd
1824–the present day
Grove Ironworks, Wakefield, Yorkshire
Old-established firm which specializes in machines, cutters and dies used for stamping out sheet metal and making toys. Now known as Rhodes Interform Ltd.

Rhodes triple press, 1913 catalogue

Richards Son & Allwin
1924–1934
A firm formed in 1924 by the amalgamation of Oscar O Richards & Son with Sidway, Allwin Ltd at Sidway Works, Granville Street, Birmingham. Oscar Richards was an engineer and had been in business since 1909. His son, O L Richards, was enthusiastic about flying machines and held a pilot's licence. Under the trade name Allwin the firm made folding dolls' prams and pushchairs, scooters and juvenile bicycles.

In July 1934, Richards Son and Allwin merged with Tan-Sad to make a new company, Tan-Sad and Allwin. Oscar Richards and his son retired from the Board of Management to start a new firm, Richards and Son, for the manufacture of tools and patterns.
See Tan-Sad

Richardson, C E & Co. Ltd
1906
C E Richardson originally had a small business in John Street, Sheffield, for making small tools, glass cutters and photographic material. In 1906 he invented an unusual toy to be used with kites – a parachute or messenger which ran up the kite string, and was automatically released when it neared the kite and fell gracefully to earth. By 1908 the kites had been such a success (he was making 18 different sizes) that he moved to a new factory in Napier Street. Here he produced kites and strong wooden toys and also marketed one of the first model aeroplanes, 'Aerial Torpedo', which could fly a quarter of a mile. His next success was a landmark in toy history – the 'Skacycle' – later more popularly known as a scooter. A registered trademark for this toy 612,163 protected his rights.

In 1912, the business was made into a private company and the huge success of the Skacycles registered under his trade name of Finbat in 1913 led to further expansion and a new factory at Aizlewood Road at the beginning of 1914. However, this factory was almost immediately made over to war service with only limited toy making. In 1915, a new line recorded was a repeating toy rifle with detachable bayonet 'for drilling the boys'. When the war ended it seems many firms were quick to adapt the Richardson brainchild, and improved variations of his Skacycle appeared.
See Tan-Sad

Richardson, Ernest
1906
The brother of C E Richardson, he began life as a cutler in Sheffield making pocket knives, then worked in engineering for

ARE UNRIVALLED for THEIR WORKMANSHIP

ALLWIN COASTER

There is an enormous and ever increasing demand for our Toys. This obviously proves that the public recognise the intrinsic merit of our lines

Our lines include FOLDING BABY CARRIAGES, DOLLS' PRAMS and COTS, SCOOTERS, KIDDY CARS, COASTERS, JUVENILE CYCLES, Etc., Etc., fitted with "ALLWIN" BALLOON TYRES.

For FINE FINISH and Sturdy Construction "ALLWIN" TOYS are supreme.

May we send you our Catalogue?

RICHARDS, SON & ALLWIN, Ltd.
SIDWAY WORKS, GRANVILLE ST., BIRMINGHAM
Telegrams: Sidway. Code: Bentley's. 'Phone: Midland 217

Advertisement in 1928 *Games and Toys*

ten years and started making tools for toys. First design was for the diabolo spinning top. Subsequently he designed wooden toys, kites and model aeroplanes using the trademark 'Finbat'.

Ridingbery Metal Toys Ltd
1840–1949
Edwin Ridingbery, who died aged 84 in 1958, originally took over his father's toy-making business at Lawrence Hill, Bristol. Later he was at Bath Buildings, Bristol and in 1948 at Feeder Road, Bristol. He manufactured precision sewing machines and other toys under the trademark 'Rob'. For a short time this sewing machine was marketed by Casceloid Ltd. In 1949, the machine production was taken over by Chad Valley.

Rob Toys
See Ridingbery Metal Toys Ltd

Romside Manufacturing Co. Ltd
1948
147/9 North Street, Romford, Essex
Manufacturers of metal dolls' house fittings, windows, doors and fire surrounds etc.

Rovex Industries Ltd
1951–1972
Morden Road, Merton, London
In 1951, the Rovex Scale Model Co. of Richmond, Surrey was purchased by Lines Bros and became one of their group of companies. In 1958, Rovex took over Pedigree Dolls and Pedigree Soft Toys and production of the dolls moved to Market Way, Canterbury, Kent. By 1970, they had amalgamated with another Lines Company, Tri-ang, calling themselves Rovex-Tri-ang Ltd and continued using the old premises at Morden. In 1960, Rovex Scale Models Ltd, Westwood, Margate, Kent built Tri-ang Railways (electric trains) 00/HO gauge and various construction accessories. In 1972, Rovex Ltd and Rovex International and Hornby Hobbies were sold to Dunbee-Combex Ltd.
See Dunbee Combex Ltd

S

Sale Tilney & Co. Ltd
1939
3 Lloyds Avenue, London
Merchants and importers of clockwork metal toys, cars, lorries etc.
Trademark 'Dingo'.

Santoy Manufacturing Co.
1921
Manufacturers of collapsible metal sandcastle moulds.

Scale Models Ltd
1939
Brooklands Motor Course, Weybridge, Surrey

D Sebel & Co. 'Mobo' remote control car, 1947

Advertised model racing cars with independent suspension and interchangeable and detachable clockwork motors, price 3/6d each.

Sebel, D & Co. Ltd
1920–1972
West Street, Erith, Kent
In 1920, David Sebel founded a company for manufacturing toy wheels and motor bodies, iron railings, fire escapes etc. Later he patented wheels for truck and trolley manufacture. His son, Harry Sebel, joined the firm in 1931. During World War II, production was limited to war materials.

1947 'Jobo' toys and 'Bronco', then mechanical tortoise and Scottie. The earlier models were designed by George Moorwood RA, sculptor and artist in metal.
1955 'Mobo Swift' electric motor boat, 'Mobo Sprite' model yacht, 'Mobo' remote control racing car, toddlers tricycle, wheelbarrow, scooter and rocking chair.
1956 The firm acquired 'Jetex', the toy business of Wilmot, Mansour & Co. Ltd. Mr J N Mansour together with several 'Jetex' executives and personnel joined the Sebel organization.
1965 Gradually stopped production of toys to concentrate on garden furniture and metal chairs and tables.
1972 Taken over by Barclay Toy Group.

Sewing Machines
The first practical domestic sewing machine was patented in 1851 by Isaac M Singer of New York. He was one of the first to use mass production techniques to make, and modern advertising methods to promote, this invention. It brought about revolutionary changes in everyday life, freeing women from innumerable hours of tedious plain sewing and providing for the first time the means of large-scale manufacture of cheap, serviceable clothes.

During the latter half of the 19th century many tiny machines were made, some only five inches long and extravagantly ornamented, some with frames shaped like dolphins, cherubs or mermaids. Yet they all functioned as efficiently as larger models and were made for the adult market, not as toys for children. It was not until after World War II that toy sewing machines were produced by English firms.

Principal manufacturers
Bailey's Agencies, 'Little Betty', 'The Comet', 1956
Burbank, 1974, 'Sew Magic'
Byron Jardine, 1980, 'Lockstitch'

Bailey's Agencies 'Little Betty' sewing machine, 1956

Minimodels Goldie Gardener Land Speed Record Car, c.1950 (top)
Two **Wells** racing cars, 1930 (middle)
Minimodels Railton Land Speed Record car, c.1950 (bottom)

Britains Railton 'New Wonder Car' 1930s (top)

Bluebird by unknown British manufacturer, 1935 (middle)

Britains Bluebird, Land Speed Record Car, 1937 (bottom)

Cinemaker, 'Astor'
Clydon Products
Daniel Judson & Son Ltd, 1939, 'Tabitha'
Grain, E L, 1940, Plastic sewing machine
Rees, Leon & Co., The 'Vulcan', 1960
Ridingbury Metal Toys (marketed by Cascelloid) 1948, 'Rob' sewing machine

Sharna Ware Ltd
1958–the present day
Lumb Lane, Droylsden, Manchester
The bulk of this company's range falls into the category of big wheeled toys, pedal cars, etc. In 1983, they produced a Rolls Royce which was electric driven. The age range catered for is 1–8 years. In 1983 they purchased the factory in Wales and the name 'Tri-ang'. The company is now known as Sharna Tri-ang Ltd.
See Cherlilea Products and Lines Bros

Silver Ghost
1934
Trademark of Lamplugh Ltd
See Lamplugh Radio Ltd

Simons, E
1919
100–102 Houndsditch, London
This firm advertised the 'Drum-o-phone', a drum with cymbal attachment which could be played with piano or gramophone. It gave the continuous roll of a kettle drum at a single beat.

Slikka Playthings
See Die-Casting Machine Tools Ltd

Soldarma Ltd
1921
12 Hyde Road, Hoxton, London
Manufacturers of toy soldiers and metal novelties.
See Soldiers

Soldiers
In the King's Lynn Museum, Norfolk, is a large display of medieval pilgrims' badges. Those of St George on horseback might easily be thought to represent mounted knights; indeed, until the Reformation all kinds of religious medallions and figurines were made, either of flat lead like these pilgrims' badges, or from the more costly metals of pewter, silver and gold. As saints went out of fashion, pewterers, silversmiths and other craftsmen turned their hands to more secular subjects, and we read of kings and great noblemen having armies of silver or leaden 'soldyers'.

There are now many erudite encyclopaedias and specialist books dealing with the history of model soldiers. The aim here has been simply to list the English firms which produced toy soldiers as children's playthings from the end of the 19th century until the toy safety regulations of 1967 completely banned the use of lead in the manufacture of toys.

Britains Worcester regiment set 18, 29th and 39th regiments, c.1900

The best known are the hollow-cast soldiers made by William Britains Ltd. Their first patent dates from 1900, but the firm had been producing soldiers since 1893. In spite of temporary difficulties during the two world wars, Britains maintained their universal popularity. In 1954, they took over the plastic soldiers made by Herald, and from then on plastic gradually replaced metal. By 1962, metal soldiers were only produced for the export trade.

Before World War I, a number of small London firms and foundries produced pirated versions of Britains' models, while others created their own designs. The following list does *not* include the names of well-known makers of model soldiers such as Richard Courtenay, Russell Gamage and Frederick Ping, as their products were meant for collectors and not for children.

Principal manufacturers
Abel & Fry, London, 1910–1914, hollowcast
Armitage, London, pre-1939, hollowcast
Azco (Cards) Ltd, Birmingham, 1945, hollowcast
Barker (Charles), London, 1910–1933, 'Reka' hollowcast
Benbros (London), Ltd, London, 1951–1967, hollowcast and plastic
Benson, London, 1950, hollowcast
Berwick Toy Co., Liverpool, pre-1939, hollowcast
Betal Products (Glasman Ltd), London, 1955, hollowcast
BMC, London, 1918, hollowcast
Britains Ltd, London, 1893–the present day, hollowcast and plastic
Britya, London, 1900, hollowcast
Charbens & Co. Ltd, London, 1920–1968, hollowcast
Cheerio Toy Mfg Co., London, 1920, hollowcast
Cherilea Products Ltd, Blackpool, 1948, hollowcast and plastic
Crescent Toy Co., London, 1922–1983, hollowcast and plastic
Davies & Co., London, 1903, hollowcast. Pirated Britains
Dunham, White & Co. Ltd, London, 1929, hollowcast
EMI Ltd, London, 1950, hollowcast
Erecto Toy Co. Ltd, London, 1915, hollowcast
Fry Ltd, London, 1914, hollowcast
Fylde Mfg Co., Blackpool, 1945–1950, hollowcast. Taken over by Cherilea
Haig Toys, Edinburgh, 1918, hollowcast
Halbert Castings, London, 1950, hollowcast
Hanks Bros & Co., London, 1900–1914, hollowcast
Hill, John & Co., London, 1900–1967, 'Johillco' hollowcast. Pirated Britains
Kews Ltd, London, 1925–1958, 'Ku-Zu', hollowcast

Haig Toys soldiers, 1918

Advertisement in 1915 *Games and Toys*

Lone Star Die-casting Tools Ltd, London, 1953–1970, hollowcast and plastic
Lord Roberts Memorial Workshops, London, 1915, soldiers
Lynwood Toy Co., London, 1918, composition
Marlborough Mfg Co., London, 1919, 'MMC' composition
Mudie, David, London, 1902, hollowcast. Pirated Britains
Noble, London, 1960, hollowcast
North Park Toys, London, 1958, solid
Reka Ltd (Chas Barker), London, 1910–1933, hollowcast
Renvoise, James, London, 1900–1914, hollowcast
Russell Mfg Co. Ltd, London, 1914–1918, hollowcast
Sacul Playthings Ltd, London, 1945, hollowcast
Soldarma Ltd, London, 1921, hollowcast
Standfast Toy Mfg Co., London, 1920, hollowcast
Stoddart Ltd, London, 1921, hollowcast
Taylor & Barrett, London, 1930, hollowcast
Toy Importers Ltd, London, 1943–1979, 'Timpo' hollowcast and composition
Turnbull, Chas Edward & Co., London, 1914, hollowcast
Waterloo Toy Co., Liverpool, 1906–1914, hollowcast
Wendan Mfg Co. Ltd, Liphook, 1947, 'Wend-Al' aluminium
Wood, G W (later 'Johillco'), London, 1912, hollowcast

Further reading:
The World Encyclopaedia of Model Soldiers, John G Garratt
The Art of the Toy Soldier, Henry Kurtz
Toy Soldiers, James Opie
Old British Model Soldiers, 1893–1918, L W Richards

Spring Tops
See Tops

Standfast Toy & Manufacturing Co. Ltd
1920
76 Duncombe Road, Holloway, London
Manufacturers of high grade metal soldiers. Trademark 'Standfast'.
See Soldiers

Steam Toys
Steam power, being the prime mover for industry since the beginning of the nineteenth century, was also to provide the motive power for early toys. The development in the late nineteenth century by the German toy industry of techniques for producing double-acting cylinders made it possible to produce steam-driven toys at prices hitherto unattainable. Prior to that time, steam toys were expensively produced mainly by such French and English manufacturers as Stevens Model Dockyard, Bateman and Radiguet. In many cases the brass models they produced were subsidiary products of optical and scientific instrument makers.

Mass-produced German toys saw the demise of the earlier type of steam toy manufacture and by the beginning of the Second World War, the production of steam toys had been largely replaced by that of electrically-powered toys. Today the firm of Mamod, which has survived several reorganisations, still produces a range of solid fuel-burning vehicles.

Workshop of the **Standfast Mfg Co.**, Holloway, 1920

Principal manufacturers

Bailey's Agencies, London
1948 Twin-cylinder vertical oscillating cylinder engine with horizontal boiler

Bar-Knight Model Eng., Glasgow
1920–1925 Horizontal mill engines, vertical oscillating engines, locomotive engines

Bassett-Lowke Ltd, Northampton
1901–1950 Locomotives, stationary and marine engines

Bedington, Liddiatt & Co. vertical steam engine, 1919

Bateman, J & Co. Ltd, London
1880–1890 Dribblers and other brass engines 'The Original Model Dockyard'

Bedington, Liddiatt & Co., London
1919 Vertical engine

Birmingham Model Engineering Co.
1906 'Tessted' locomotives and steam engines

Bonds o' Euston Road Ltd
1880 Locomotives and marine engines

Bowman Models Ltd, Dereham, Norfolk
1923–1935 Stationary engines, locomotives and steam launches

British Model & Electrical Co.
1880s–1900 Brass model locomotives and other scientific models

Signalling Equipment Ltd steam engine, 1930 (top)

Meccano steam engine, 1920 (bottom)

Stereoscopic and Photographic Company and **The London Stereoscopic Company**
group of turn of the century scientific toys several operated by steam (top)

Taylor & Barrett Tower Bridge, 1930s (bottom)

Clyde Model Dockyard
1789–1970
Produced model steam engine parts. Much of their production was supplied by Radiguet & Massiot of France, despite claims that everything was 'British-made'.

Crescent Toys Ltd, Cwmcarn
1947 Brass horizontal engine

Dubilier, London
1919 'Duco' submarine

Graham Brothers, London
1948 The Fairylite PWE launch

Hobbies Ltd, Dereham, Norfolk
1923–1938 Kits for steam launches

Hobran Engineering Co., Wolverhampton
1916 Steam mechanical toys

Jubb, W H, Sheffield
1915–1922 Steam engines and scale model locos

Mamod

Malins (Engineers) Ltd, Staffordshire
(Trade name 'Mamod')
1936 Steam engines, stationary engines etc.

Meccano Ltd, Liverpool
1929 Vertical engines **p. 114*

Newton & Co., London
1860 Dribblers and brass engines

Piot, Désiré Thomas
1890s
Engineer who patented toy boat steam generator
*See Appendix VI *p. 30*

Randall Ltd, Stationary engines

Rees, L & Co.
1948 Stationary geared oscillating cylinder engines and slide valve engine

Richardson, George & Co., Liverpool
1868 Locomotives, ships and stationary engines

Signalling Equip. Ltd, London
1946–1965 Range of stationary engines and die-cast marine engines **p. 114*

Simpson, Fawcett & Co., Leeds
1919–1920 Vertical and horizontal engines

Star Manufacturing Co., London
1917 Range of engines

Statham, W E Ltd
1860 Wide range of engines

Steven's Model Dockyard, London
1843–1920 Piddlers and locomotives

Stuart Turner
Late 19th century
Manufactured pumps and small marine engines; as well as parts for stationary steam engines

"VEITCHI"
Mechanical Steam Models

"Veitchi" models were the first vertical steam engines made in Great Britain and are equal, if not superior, in every way to the German made article.

Best quality materials and first class British workmanship throughout.

Prices from **1/3** retail upwards.

A Good Selling Line.
WHOLESALERS please note that orders for Christmas trade are now being booked and will be delivered in strict rotation. To avoid disappointments order now.
Full particulars and catalogues gratis.
Special terms for large quantities.

TECHNICAL ENGINEERING CO., LTD.,
Clyde Street and Cheapside, Liverpool.

Perfectly Simple

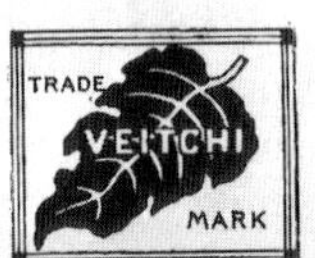

Simply Perfect

DON'T READ THIS
IF YOU ARE NOT INTERESTED IN TOYS.

Advertisement in 1959 *Games and Toys*

Sutcliffe, J W Ltd, Horsforth, Leeds
1885–the present day
Warships and launches

Technical Engin. Co., Liverpool
1914 'Veitchi' early fixed cylinder engine

Tribe & Austin Ltd, Manchester and London
1919–1921 Mobile steam toys, road wagon with gear drive, horizontal transverse boiler, tanker, roller, tractor and stationary engines

Victory Industries Ltd
1948 'Miss England' PWE launch

Whiteley, Tansley & Co., Liverpool
1920 'Whitanco' steam engines

Wild, Lewis & Co., London
1916 Vertical engines

Woods & Co., Oxford Street area, London
Late 19th century
Optical and scientific instrument makers

**pp. 30, 114, 126*

Further reading: Toyshop Steam, Basil Harley

Steven's Model Dockyard
1843–1920
Until 1912 produced brass locomotives in at least 18 designs. In 1880 the trains had mahogany tracks and elaborate construction. Also sold boat fittings and stocked clockwork submarines and other goods made by Bing.

Stoddart's Acorn Toy Co.
1921
16 Park Road, North Acton, London
Manufacturer of metal toys and soldiers, who also produced in 1949 the 'Mechanical Fisherman', the 'Umbrella Clown' and the 'Mechanical Walking Man'.

Sturditoys
1947
Made by Bournemouth Novelty Co. Stamped heavy sheet metal, electrically welded and riveted with no sharp corners. Produced water towers, coal truck, delivery truck, dump truck and steam shovel.

Style Toys Ltd
1943
See Mirrorscope

Sutcliffe Pressing Ltd
1885–1982
Atlas Works, Horsforth, Leeds
Firm founded by J William Sutcliffe, a sheet metal worker who at the age of 20 started up in business making and mending domestic pots and pans. To this he added bread tins, developing and washing tanks for the photographic trade, and finally in 1903, engineers' oil cans.

For many years these oilcans were the firm's basic output, but today it is better known for the toy boats which it started to produce after World War I. The first, a 12 inch battleship, and five other boats issued between 1920 and 1928, were driven by a patented method of propulsion by water circulation enabling them to run at slow speed for over an hour. A change was then made to clockwork. At first the motors were bought in from another manufacturer, but soon they too were all being made on the premises.

Between the two World Wars, Sutcliffe boats ranged in length from 8 inches to 2 feet, and included speedboats as well as cruisers, submarines, destroyers and battleships. In 1978, they added to the range of nine boats still in production a clockwork near-replica of the 'Valiant', the first battleship they made. Mr J William Sutcliffe's son, Mr J K Sutcliffe, ran the family firm until his retirement in 1982. **p. 30*

Stoddart Acorn Toy Co. umbrella clown, 1949

Sydenham & McOustra
1912
Beacon Foundry, Beacon Street, Walsall, Lancashire
Manufacturers of cast iron toys. Among the best-known of their mechanical cast iron banks or money-boxes were the 'Jolly Nigger', who threw a penny into his mouth, and the 'John Bull', painted in six colours, whose action consisted of a dog jumping up and throwing a penny into a barrel. Others included the 'Eiffel Tower', the 'Shilling Beehive', 'Westminster Abbey' and the 'Villa' banks. In addition they made metal animals, toy mangles, fire grates and fenders, flat irons, bedsteads, the 'Lion' cap-pistol, and a series of carded tool sets, the 'Young Carpenter', 'Young Gardener' Butcher, Bricklayer, Miner etc.. They also manufactured numerous puzzles, one of which, 'Faith, Hope and Charity', sold 50,000 in a year.

Sykes, W M & Co. Ltd
Horbury, Yorkshire
An old-established sports goods manufacturer who began to make wooden toys in 1938 ('Trojan Toys', marketed by J K Farnell Ltd); also cricket bats, outdoor games and miniature billiard tables. Purchased Dunham White & Co. Ltd of Stratford, London, manufacturers of metal toys; and in 1940, the stock, goodwill and trademarks of F H Ayres Ltd.

T

Tan-Sad Ltd
1920
Freeman Street, Birmingham, and Toll End Road, Tipton, Staffordshire
F H Headley took over a business manufacturing motor-cycle seats and also made strong prams and folding scooters. He registered the name 'Tan-Sad' as his trademark on 30 January 1922 and patented a construction set made of metal tubing.

1928 'Tupperary Tim', a pedal-driven horse with realistic galloping action.
1935 moved to Tipton factory and amalgamated with Richards, Son & Allwin Ltd, largest producers of prams, scooters etc. in the country.
1974 merger between Tan-Sad Ltd and Goodwood Playthings.

F H Headley of Truro, Cornwall, founder of Tan-Sad and a member of an old Quaker family, died in July 1930.

Tansley Brothers
See Whiteley Tansley

Taylor & Barrett
1920–1941
Schofield Road, Holloway, London, N19
Shortly after their demobilisation from the army Fred G Taylor and his brother-

Sydenham & McOustra toy mangle, 1913

in-law, A R Barrett, decided to go into the toy business. Before World War 1 Fred Taylor had been an engineer mainly concerned with the installations of lifts. He had great skill with his hands and designed and made the moulds for the new enterprise. His relations, A R and S Barrett, had both previously worked as lead casters for Britains Ltd and knew quite a bit about the toy trade.

Some of the first toys they made were a camel and an elephant with a seat on its back, which later became part of the Tiger Hunt set, a Chinaman pulling a rickshaw, Red Indians paddling their own canoe either to the left or to the right, a Zulu, a governess cart and pony. These were sold through wholesalers such as Whyte Ridsdale to other manufacturers,

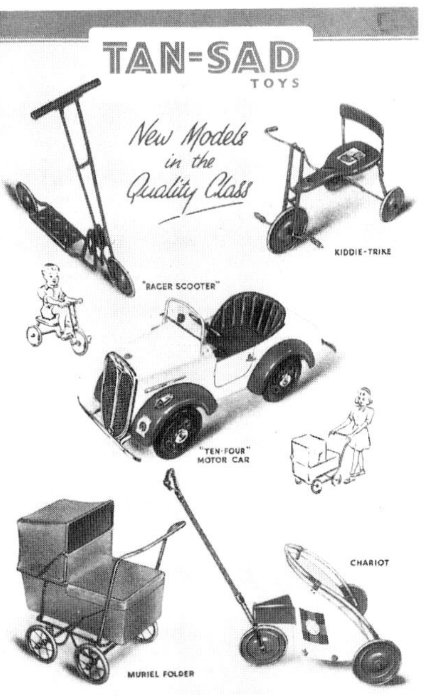

Advertisement in 1928 *Games and Toys*

Taylor & Barrett elephant ride, husky sled team and chimps' tea party, 1930s; windmill 1950s (top)

Taylor & Barrett domestic fires, telephones and iron, 1930s and 1950s (middle)

Taylor & Barrett dolls' house appliances, 1930s and 1950s (bottom)

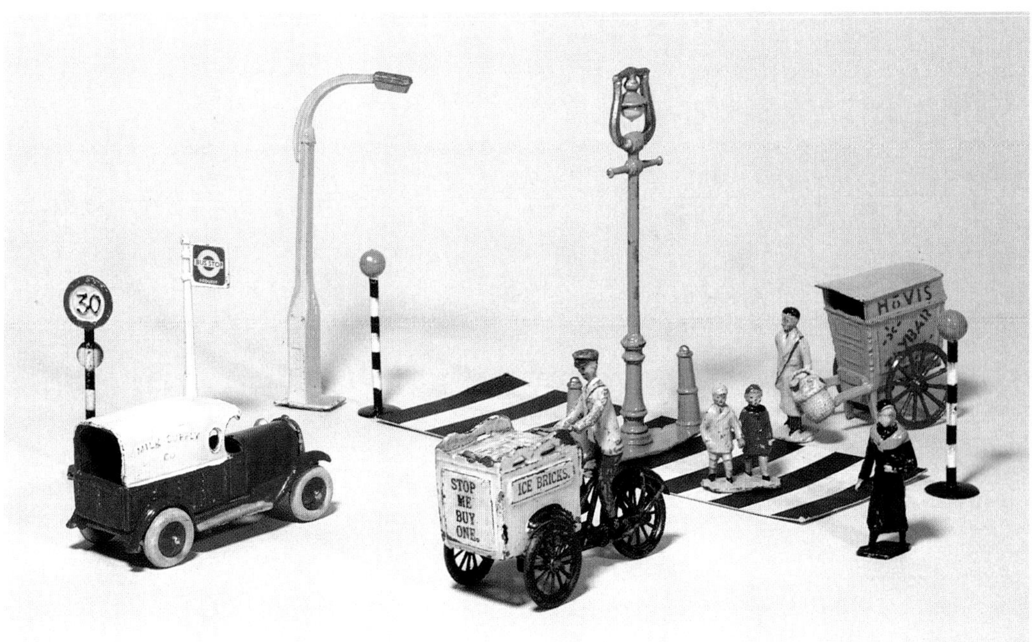

Taylor & Barrett milk van, ice cream van, Hovis van, 1930s; figures, street signs and lamps, 1930s and 1950s (top)

Taylor & Barrett bus, pumps, street sweeper and window cleaner, 1930s; mobile Animal Health Trust van and poplar tree, 1950s (middle)

Taylor & Barrett petrol pumps and aeroplanes, 1930s (bottom)

in particular Charbens, or direct to big stores like Selfridges and the Co-operative Society.

In 1929 the firm moved from its ramshackle workshop to Park Works, 125 High Street, East Finchley. Soldiers, a Roman chariot, a costermonger's barrow with plants or vegetables, a window cleaner and his equipment, zoo animals, a chimpanzees' tea party, ladies and gentlemen, postmen, cars and fire-engines with rubber tyres, as well as innumerable items for dolls' houses – telephones, Georgian 'silver' teasets, birdcages, vacuum cleaners, kitchen utensils, plates of food, cats and dogs and many other small scale models – were added to the stock list.

In 1940 the factory was destroyed in an air-raid. Larger premises were found, but had to close down almost immediately as lead was needed for bullets, not frivolous novelties. The moulds were divided between the two partners for safe keeping and everything else sold.

After the war, the partnership was not renewed. In 1945 Fred Taylor and his son-in-law Mr Squires registered a new company, F G Taylor & Sons, at 22 Hampden Road, Upper Holloway, London, N19. The firm was in existence from 1945 to 1980. Fred Taylor's own son also became a director. On the moulds which Fred Taylor had retained, T & B was struck out and replaced by F G T & Sons; they adopted as their logo **F**– or **G**–ood **T**–oys. In 1962 the firm became a limited company, by which time most of their output was made from plastic and was being sold to A Barton & Co., the dolls' house specialists.

Meanwhile A Barrett, with his two sons Alfred and Bert, had also set up a separate company, A Barrett & Sons (Toys) Ltd, at 9 Sonderberg Road, London, N7. They were in existence from 1945 to 1982. At first they only made soldiers, painted and unpainted, but gradually the range grew to include farm and zoo animals, small cars and puppets, for The London Toy Co. In 1953 they also started to make dolls' house equipment for A Barton & Co. In 1970 the firm moved to New Addington, renting factory space from Barton's and installing injection moulding machines. By 1983 Barrett's ceased its separate existence and was finally completely absorbed by A Barton & Co. *pp. 115, 118–19*

Terry, Herbert & Sons Ltd
1855
Terry Works, Redditch, Worcestershire
This firm became known world-wide for the manufacture of all sorts of springs for clockwork and also high compression springs for industry. In 1915, they produced sets of dominos made in metal and stamped with the trademark 'Terry'.

Tessted Toys
See Birmingham Model Engineering Co.

LATEST NOVELTY! WONDERFUL SELLER!

Parrot in Cage.

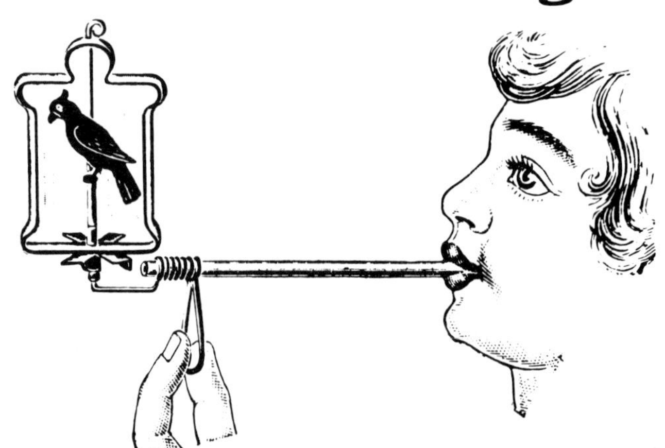

One of the most fascinating articles ever sold at One Penny. Blowing into the tube an illusion of a Parrot sitting in its cage is demonstrated.

Price **7/6** per Gross.

Sample Box of 3 dozen, 2/- Carriage Paid.

CHEAPEST HOUSE FOR JOKE ARTICLES.

SCENT Bombs, Electric Snuff, Hitching Powder, etc.

Write for List:

M. DAVIES & Co. 39, Gt. George St. LIVERPOOL.

Advertisement for thaumatrope toy, sold by M Davis & Co., 1914

Thaumatrope
If a coin is spun on its edge fast enough, both sides appear to be seen at the same time. In 1826 a Penzance doctor, John Ayrton Paris, made up boxed sets of pictures on cardboard discs which he called 'A Thaumatropical Amusement, which would demonstrate the facility of the retina of the eye to retain the impression of an object after its disappearance'. He adopted as a trademark the most popular set of two images, a bird in a cage. Metal variations of this toy were the 'Goldfish in a bowl' and the 'Parrot in a cage'. In both these toys a shiny thin metal strip bent to shape was revolved at speed round a spindle which passed through the bird or the fish.

Thistle Brand
Trademark used by G & J Lines Ltd

Timpolin
Brand name for a material invented by a Mr Gawrylowica to replace cast metal in the manufacture of aeroplanes, animals, garages etc.. He was managing director of Toy Importers from 1942, when they became manufacturers of toys instead of importers, and were also involved in munitions.
Trademark 'Timpo'.
See Toy Importers Ltd and Model Toys

Tiptree Tops
See Tops

Tin Plate Decorating Co.
1861
Melincrytham, Neath, Glamorganshire
This firm in association with the tinplate manufacturers Leach, Flower & Co. is generally credited as being one of the first to print sheets of tinplate by the direct method, as described in two patents they took out in 1864.

Tireless Spinner
1912
A metal disc with a spiral design and bright colours which spins on a pedestal. Sold by Lewis Wild.

Tock Tock
See Abbey Sports Co.

Todd, D G & Co. Ltd
1947–1974
Grosvenor Works, Tulketh Street, Southport, Lancashire and 82a Shakespear Street, Southport
Doll and toy manufacturers.
Distributor: J Cowan (Dolls) Ltd
Trademark *Rodnoid* No. 660719
Registered in September 1948 for toys and games.
1955 Firm's subsidiary companies included British Mouthorgans Ltd and Toy-Time Toys Ltd.
1969 Firm became Bluebell Dolls Ltd and in 1974 doll-making side of the business was taken over by Denys Fisher Toys.

Toledo Metal Wheel Co.
1925
145 Leander Road, Brixton Hill, London
Made toy scooters and automobiles.

Tops (Teetotems and Twirlers)
The earth and the stars spinning through space are tops. Since pre-historic times men in all parts of the world have made tops and twirlers of wood, bone, clay or stone and used them as fire-drills, weapons or pastimes. Mathematicians, physicists and anthropologists have written learned papers on the subject. Books on the history of tops enumerate peg tops, whipping tops, humming tops and the many games that can be played with them.

The physicist James Maxwell (1831–1879), in his experiments on the properties of light, used coloured discs spinning on a top. Soon after, 'Rainbow' chromatic and kaleidoscopic tops appeared on the nursery floor.

During the First World War, a number of British firms made metal spring tops and plunger-operated humming tops. The yo-yo, the diabolo, the gyroscope and the tippee top are other variations. The tippee top, invented in 1953 (Patent No. 656540), spins until it turns itself upside down in mid-career. Teetotems, with numbers or other marks on their sides, are used instead of dice in playing board and other gambling games. Around 1920, there was a craze for 'Put & Take', a mild gambling game, which used a special metal teetotem (Patent No.102,476). The Sanfarian for playing 'In and Out' was another variation.

Principal manufacturers and agents

Assael, G M, London
1920 Advertised the 'Gaby' humming top

Bedington, Liddiatt & Co., London
1911–1933 Rainbow cup, merry whirl musical top

J G Brenner & Co., Manchester
1915 Brenco top

Cambrian Can Co., Port Talbot
1948 'Camtoy' spring tops

Chad Valley, Birmingham
1946–1975 All types of tops **p. 51*

London Enterprise & Scientific Novelty Co., London
1923 Bell diaphragm and optical disc tops

Marx, Louis & Co., Swansea
1948 Rainbow colour cup tops

Menda, M, Birmingham (Trademark MMB)
1919 'Mozzle' humming top

Presswork Products Ltd, London
1934 Musical and Choral tops

Sanfarian Ltd, London
1922 Teetotum for playing 'In & Out' game

Whiteley, Tansley Ltd, Liverpool (Trademark 'Whitanco')
1922 'Top-o-tops' – the top that never stops

Windsor Novelties, London
1921 'Put & Take' teetotum

MINOR SPORTS.

GAMES WITH TOPS.

WHIP-TOP.

This is an excellent amusement. The top is easily set up by twirling it with both hands on a smooth surface, and applying the whip with gentleness at first, increasing the vigour of the blows as the top gets firm on its pointed end. There is a local variety of the whip-top, which is too singular for us to pass unnoticed. We allude to the Colchester top, of which an engraving is presented in the margin. Its construction is most simple, and, for spinning, it is said considerably to excel the tops made in the common form. The only games we have ever seen with whip-tops are "races" and "encounters;" in the former, the object is to flog the top to a certain distance first; in the latter, the tops are whipped against each other until one is knocked down. The best material for a whip, at this capital sport, is a dried eel-skin; it far surpasses cord, or leathern thongs.

17

Page from *The Boy's Own Book*, 1864

Toy Importers Ltd
1941–1953
26 Westbourne Grove, London
Makers of 'Timpo' toys. Made wide range of wooden toys including forts, aerodromes, ranches, garages. Also lead soldiers and animals.
In 1942, Mr Gawrylowicz, Managing Director, was instrumental in developing a new material, 'timpolin', as a substitute for metal. The firm also made Timpo Compo toys – practically unbreakable – in bright colours: limousine, trucks, racing cars and soldiers.
In 1949, produced a van and lorry series: 'Wall's Ice Cream', 'Smith's Potato Crisps', 'Ever Ready' trade names printed on miniature vans.
In 1953, the firm changed its name to Model Toys.
See Model Toys

G Assael Ltd 'Gaby Top', 1920

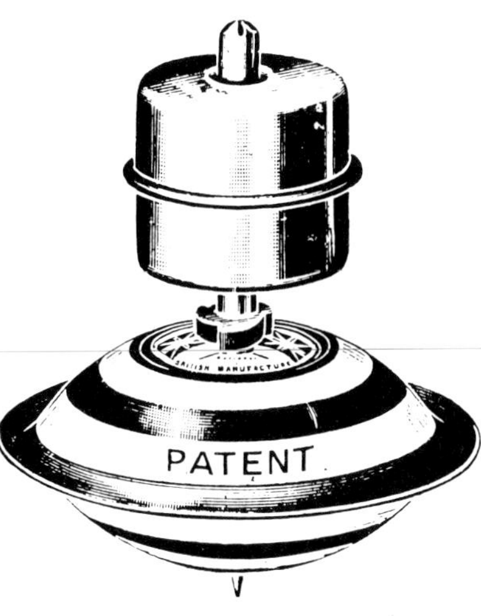

London Enterprise Scientific Novelty Co. musical top, 1932

Sanfarian Ltd 'Put and Take' teetotem, 1920

Chad Valley 'Ubilda' locomotive, 1947 (top)

Bassett-Lowke 0 gauge scale model locomotive, the 'Duchess of Montrose', c.1950 (bottom)

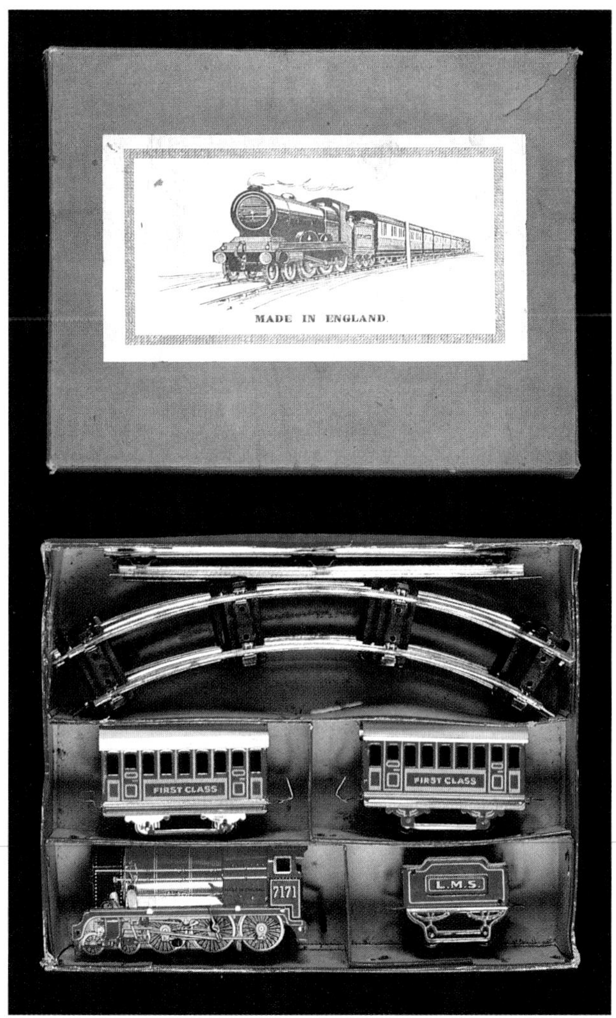

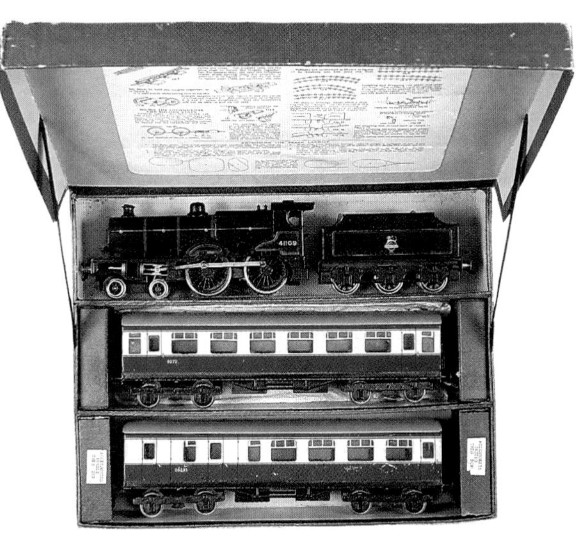

Wells-Brimtoy 0 gauge train set, 1936 (top)
Hornby 0 gauge goods set, 1921 (bottom left)
Bassett-Lowke 0 gauge train set, 1950s (bottom right)

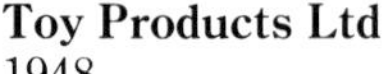

Toy Importers Ltd 'My Pet' boston terrier, 1943

Chad Valley train set, 1945–50

Toy Products Ltd
1948
Argent Works, Bolt Lane, Walsall
Manufacturers of handicraft outfits and toys. Produced streamlined metal cars in brilliant colours and toy animals on wheels.

Trains
The rise of the public railway in the mid-nineteenth century was echoed by toy and model train manufacuters from an early stage. Initially cheap tin, solid wood or brass pull-along toys were prevelant, to be superceded by mechanical toy and model trains in clockwork, steam and later electric. German manufacturers dominated the English market until the 1920s, when firms such as Hornby, Bowman, Bassett-Lowke, Leeds Model Company and others got under way. Such general toy firms as Brimtoy, Mettoy and Chad Valley produced a range of cheap tinplate toys for the juvenile market. It is interesting that in the post-Second World War period very few continental manufacturers found it worthwhile to produce British outline trains. **pp. 42, 50, 59, 66–7, 122–23, 126–27*

Principal manufacturers

Bar-Knight, Glasgow, 1924

Bassett-Lowke Ltd, London, 1899–1953 **p. 122–23*

Birmingham Model Eng. Co., 1906 trademark 'Tessted' **p. 127*

Bonds o' Euston Road, London, 1895–1930s

Bowman, 1920s–mid 1930s

Carson, Birmingham, 1905–1913 Locomotives in gauge 1 to $3\frac{1}{2}''$. Later acquired by Bassett-Lowke

Chad Valley Ltd, Birmingham, 1823–1980

Edward Exley Ltd, 1924–1980s Scale and semi-scale passenger vehicles

Ever-Ready Co. Ltd, London, 1950 Battery operated train

Graham Farrish, 1950s–the present day 00 and N gauge model railways

Felmer Distributing Co., London, 1949 'Toymatic' model railway signal

Hornby Trains, 1920 onwards **pp. 66–67, 123* Gauge 0 and later Hornby Dublo

Jubb, W H Ltd, Sheffield, 1921 Steam locos and cast metal railway station characters

Leeds Model Co, 1920s–1950s Produced a range of gauge 0 locomotives and roling stock

Lines Bros, London, 1919–1971

Marx, Louis & Co. Ltd, Swansea Electric train sets **pp. 78–9*

Mettoy, Northampton, 1930s **p. 98*

Mills Bros (Model Engineers) Ltd, Sheffield, 1919–1930s 'Milbro' scale model railways

Oliver, Harper & Co., London 1915–1923 'Simpull' train sets

Napier Ltd, London, 1948 'Napro' Carpet Locomotive (all steel)

Newton, London, 1890s brass steam locomotives **p. 126*

Primus Engineering, 1920s constructional locomotive **p. 126*

Regent Mfg. Co., Willenhall, Staffordshire, 1913

Rovex Industries Ltd, London, 1960 Built Tri-ang railways

Signalling Equip. Ltd, London, 1948

Trix Ltd, London, 1938 Electric model railways

Wallworks Ltd, 1890–1910 cast iron floor train **p. 127*

Wells-Brimtoy, London & Holyhead, 1919 **pp. 123, 142*

Whiteley, Tansley & Co. Ltd, Liverpool, 1915 'Whitanco' railway station accessories

Further reading:
The Bassett-Lowke Story, Roland Fuller & Allen Levy
A Century of Model Trains, Allen Levy
Hornby Dublo Trains, Michael Foster
The Hornby Gauge 0 System, Chris Graebe
Model Railways 1838–1939, Hamilton Ellis
Toy Trains – A History, Pierce Carlson
Toys at the London Toy Museum, Allen Levy

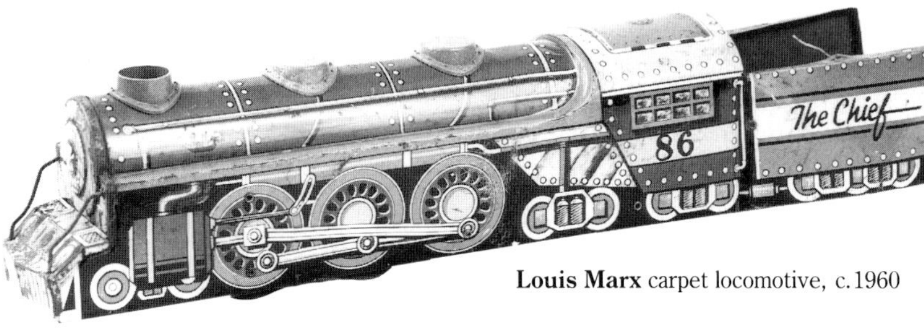

Louis Marx carpet locomotive, c.1960

Treforest Mouldings Ltd
1935–1940
Treforest Trading Estate, Cardiff
Firm founded by F Winkler with financial backing from Lord Nuffield. Manufacturers of waterline scale model ships of all nations. Also wooden toys, Stenolite animals and garden gnomes, pliable lead soldiers and 'Tremo Toy' range of pull-along, floating and educational novelties. Around 1940, the firm changed its name to Tremo Mouldings Ltd, with premises at John Street, Cardiff.
In 1941, the firm used trademarks 'Jolly Roger' and 'Little Ann'. Firm's home trade was handled by Strome & Co. of London, W1

Tri-ang
See Lines Bros Ltd

Tribe & Astin

1916–1925
97 Bridge Street, Manchester
Merchants and manufacturers of asbestos and other products. At the end of the 1914–1918 War, they had a lot of unused factory space and a large and skilled work force, but very few orders. The directors decided to try their hand at toy manufacturing on mass production lines.

The tin plate parts were stamped out into simple basic shapes then stove-enamelled and assembled to form seven types of steam driven vehicles. Some had swivel steering and geared transmission. They all looked somewhat clumsy.

Trix

1932–1958
45–47 Clerkenwell Road, London
HO trains were introduced into Britain in 1935, through a sole concession granted to Bassett-Lowke Ltd. The business was formed earlier in Germany by S Kahn and Franz Bing, but the rise to power of the Nazi party hastened their departure to Great Britain, where the business was set up in Clerkenwell. Shortly afterwards, Anglicized versions of German production were first imported and then produced in Northampton. A company known as Precision Models was formed in association with Bassett-Lowke to manufacture Trix Twin railways in the post-war period.

Production of Trix construction outfits was also started in England and the company enjoyed a decade of success. However, a need for significant re-financing arose and in 1956 the Trix company was sold to Nutraco Nominees Ltd. By 1958, substantially more capital was required for new lines and during that year the assets for the former Trix company were purchased from the official receiver by Dufay Ltd. Although some remarkably good models were produced in the ensuing period, in 1962 the company was sold once again and in 1963 became part of the Courtauld Group. The history of this company is complicated owing to the parallel development of Trix in Germany who had successfully capitalized on the N gauge market for model trains through its Mini Trix range. This pioneering company no longer has a manufacturing base in the UK.

Further reading: *The History of Trix in Britain*, Anthony Matthewman

True-To-Type Products Ltd

1946, Hereford
Barronia Metal Works, after spending the war years making sophisticated instruments for the Ministry of Defence, was taken over by Chad Valley in 1946 to reproduce precision-made toys.
Trademark 'Knight's Head'.

Mettoy – Byron Jardine 'Petite' typewriter, 1960

Tuba Engineering

See Chad Valley and Constructional Toys

Typewriter Manufacturers

Byron Jardine Ltd
1925 Barlock typewriter
1955 Petite typewriter: 27-character all-capital keyboard
1956 Petite typewriter: 54 characters

Holland & Blair
1955 Lilliput typewriter

Mettoy
1957 Petite typewriter: 81 characters, using plastic materials

Twencen Manufacturing Co. Ltd

See Kaleidoscope

Twigg, Charles & Co.

1949
Birmingham, Warwickshire
Manufacturers of tricycles, juvenile cycles and toy fire engines. These had

Advertisement in 1920 *Games and Toys*

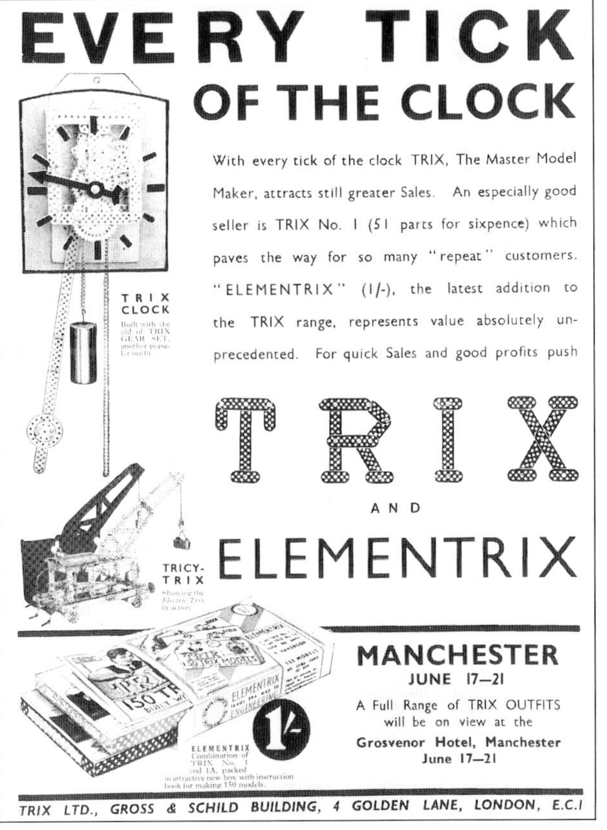

Advertisement in 1935 *Games and Toys*

Newton brass steam locomotive, 1890 (top)
Primus Engineering locomotive and coach, 1920s (middle)
British Model and Electrical Co. steam locomotive, 1900 (bottom)

Birmingham Model Eng. Co. 'Tessted' gauge 3 steam locomotive, 1906 (top)
Wallworks cast iron floor goods train, 1900 (bottom)

pressed-steel bodies, balloon disc wheels and hand brakes, and were finished in high-gloss stove enamel.
Trademark 'The Flying Ace'

U

Ubilda *See Burnett*

Unity Toy Series
See Oliver Harper & Co.

V

Van Riemsdyck
c. 1947–1950s, London
Manufacturers of toys and models including controlled clockwork mechanisms. Associated with Walker-Fenn's model railway products.

Victory Industries *See Trix*

Vietchi Steam Toys
See Steam Toys

Vortex Patent Toy Co.
1912
John's Place, Acton, London
Manufacturers of Vortex Patent Fun Wheel, also magic lanterns, colour tops and carpentry sets.

Vulcan Sewing Machines
1960
Toy machines produced by Leon Rees.
See Sewing machines

Vulcan sewing machine, 1960

W

Wallworks Ltd
1882, Manchester
Manufactured toys as a sideline to their main foundry work. Mainly produced cast iron floor trains, but the range also included a steam roller and buses for promotional purposes. **p. 127*

Waterline Models
See Treforest Moulding Ltd

Wells-Brimtoy
*See *pp. 110, 123, 130–31, 134–35, 138–39, 142, 193–221*

Welkut Models
1939
68 Carshalton Park Road, Carshalton, Surrey
Manufacturers of model boats, garden toys, toddle cars and toy railway and airport accessories.

Welnut Engineering
Manufacturers of Christmas cracker fillings etc. Subsidiary of Wells-Brimtoy.
See Wells-Brimtoy and Appendix IV

Wenebrik
See Bailey, William and Constructional Toys

Whitanco
*See Whiteley, Tansley & Co. Ltd *p. 143*

Whitehouse, George & Co. Ltd
1941
Barford Tube Works, 48 William Edward Street, Cheapside, Birmingham
Manufacturers of brass and copper novelties, money-boxes, dolls' furniture in colour-finished metal, and items for the souvenir trade.
See Money-boxes

George Whitehouse brass money-box, 1945

Whiteley, Tansley & Co. Ltd
1914–1925
Beech Street, and Lotus Works, Broadgreen Road, Old Swan, Liverpool
The brothers, Ernest and James White-

Advertisement in 1920 *Games and Toys*

Ernest Whitely, 1920

ley, were both qualified engineers. They started out as gold pen makers, but by 1915, they had switched to war-work and were making jigs and press tools. At the British Industries Fair of that year, however, they took a small stand to show the toys they had been making as a sideline – all types of cannon, artillery sets, pistols, toy watches and cash registers. They adopted the trademark 'Whitanco' and in the following year were making clockwork motor cars in addition to soldiers, horses and carts. By 1919, they could claim that they were the largest mechanical toy makers in England and in that one year they had made and delivered over a million clockwork toys and half a million non-mechanical ones.

They made tanks, 8″ long, which could climb up steps; touring cars, 8″ long painted in three colours; and Landaulettes in three sizes, 8″, 10″ and 13¾″, also painted in three colours.

In 1921, they were marketing what a trade journal called 'one of the most ingenious and educative toys which embodies engineering, clockwork and railway instructions'. The toy was a clockwork train, made up of 139 interchangeable, detachable parts.

A few months later, James Whiteley and W T Mould took out a patent for a spinning top – 'The Top-o'-tops that never stops'. The following year they were making miniature chocolate vending machines for their railway stations, a large motor car with headlamps and rubber tyres on the wheels and a clockwork 'Liverpool Bus'.

Mr Ernest Whiteley had been elected Vice-Chairman of the British Toy Manufacturers' Association, and in speeches and press interviews he stressed the difficulties facing the British toy industry: 'The factory acts and trade unions' he said 'controlled working conditions in factories. Many neutral countries during the war years have seized on the opportunity to build up their toy industries, using poorly-paid women and children, working in appalling conditions, 12 hours a day for a wage of a few pennies.' Mr Whiteley's many appeals to the government to protect and support the British toy industry had no effect – his warnings went unheeded. Foreign competition forced Whiteley, Tansley & Co. like many other firms at that time to abandon toy making and take up new and more profitable lines. In 1923, Ernest Whiteley joined forces with another old-established Liverpool engineering firm, J E Garnett & Sons Ltd, and set about adding telegraph and telephonic instruments, precision tools, to their list of products. By 1925, toy making had been abandoned, and by 1930 they were only making wireless apparatus. *p. 143*

Whyte, Ridsdale & Co. Ltd
1867–the present day
73–76 Houndsditch, London
Present address: River Way, Templefields, Harlow, Essex
The firm founded by H Whyte was a large wholesale business dealing in imported toys. During World War I, they advertised a large range of clockwork toys, train sets, tin musical cats, running snakes, 'nigger' orange sellers, touring cars – probably of French and American manufacture. The clockwork runabout car advertised in 1916, however, had 'Made in England' on its running board. It might possibly have been made by Whiteley, Tansley & Co. Ltd of Liverpool.

Wild, Lewis
1848–1921
Born in Nuremberg, Lewis Wild was apprenticed to a toy firm at age 19. In 1874, he settled in England and founded a toy warehouse dealing mainly in toys made in the United Kingdom. In 1915, used 'Harmless' tin for toy rifles and pistols which shot rubber-tipped arrows. In 1916, Lewis Wild retired from the business due to ill health and his son George ran the firm.

Wilkes Berger Engineering Co.
1948
Hillcrest Works, Moseley Road, Birmingham
Produced quality metal components for the games and sports industry.
Trademark 'Hillcrest'

Telephones – 6740 AVENUE (3 lines) Telegrams "WHYTESDALE, ALD. LONDON"

Whyte, Ridsdale & Co.

FANCY GOODS, TOYS, JEWELLERY,

72, 73, 74, 75 & 76, Houndsditch, Bishopsgate, and 35, 36 & 37, Camomile St., LONDON, E.C.

WE beg to advise our clients that we are not showing at the Board of Trade Exhibition, but at our showrooms in Houndsditch. We are exhibiting the LATEST NOVELTIES in British made Toys and Fancy Goods, in addition to a large assortment of French, American, and Japanese articles.

GUARANTEED CLOCKWORK. o PAINTED IN VARIOUS COLOURS.

BRITISH MADE

G.E.R.

ENGLISH RAILWAYS. Stout Metal Build. STANDARD 0 GAUGE RAILWAY LINES.

Price, 12 6 per doz. sets. Exact as illustration. Also supplied as above, without carriage, price 8 6 per doz. sets.

CORPORATION TRAMWAYS

PAINTED TIN TRAM CAR to pull along. Each in a box. F 8488. Price 3 per doz., or 33 per gross.

MODEL MAKER'S AEROPLANE SET
MATERIAL & INSTRUCTIONS FOR CONSTRUCTING
BI-PLANES & MONO-PLANES
PROPELLER (Aspen) WOOD
SKID MATERIAL
WAFER WOOD
SPARS

HOW TO MAKE AN AEROPLANE. Complete set of Parts, with full directions. Mounted on attractive cards. M 2221, Price 7 6 per doz. sets.

Fires a Cap and shoots a Wood Shell.
LATEST BRITISH NOVELTY!
F 8627.
Price 4 6 doz.

ENGLISH DRESSED DOLLS.
Biscuit China Heads.
L 3834. Prices 8 6, 13 6, 18 per doz.

SHIPPERS ARE ASKED TO WRITE FOR OUR ALL-BRITISH CATALOGUE.

Advertisement in 1915 *Games and Toys*

Brimtoy poster, as advertised in 1920 *Games and Toys*

Brimtoy petrol tanker, 1929 (top)
Brimtoy tip truck, 1929 (bottom)

Williams & Gray Ltd
1928–1950
30–32 St Paul's Square, Birmingham
Toy pistol manufacturers.
Trademark 'Limit'

Wilmot, Mansour & Co. Ltd
1955
Salisbury Road, Totton, Hampshire
26 Chester Road, Macclesfield, Cheshire
Sheldon Works, Sheldon Road, Cricklewood, London
Manufacturers of 'Jetex' jet-propelled toys and 'Wimco' brand toys. Lines included an RAF interceptor plane, 'flies 400 yards'; helicopter, 'ascends to over 100 feet'; an unsinkable, plastic speed-boat; space ship and launching ramp; electric police launch; and rocket-firing fighter plane.
In 1956, D Sebel & Co. Ltd acquired the 'Jetex' and toy business of the firm, and Mr J N Mansour, together with several key executives and personnel, joined the Sebel organisation.
See Sebel, D & Co. Ltd

Touring car advertised by **James Wisbey** 1919

Wimco
A trademark.
See Wilmot, Mansour & Co. Ltd

Windsor Novelties
1915
49 Churchfield Road, Acton, London
Produced practical jokes, tricks and puzzles including pretty tins of dummy chocolates.

Wisbey, James
1919
Houndsditch and Bishopsgate, London
By 1943, they were incorporated into Whyte, Ridsdale & Co. Ltd.
See Whyte, Ridsdale & Co. Ltd

Wright, John & Co.
1916
Aston, Birmingham
Agents who sold money-boxes which were shaped like a gas fire and had printed on the back 'Injector Ventilating' 'Thermox' Gas Fire. These money-boxes were made by Barringer, Wallis & Manners and could be bought in gas offices.
See Barringer, Wallis & Manners

Advertisement for **Wilmot, Mansour & Co. Ltd**, 1955

Advertisement for **Wright's** 'Gas Fire' money-box, 1916

Z

Zang, M
1906–1966
Darwin House, 48–54 Old Kent Road, London
Came to England from Poland in 1906 and worked in the furniture-making business, process engraving etc. In 1944, he entered the toy trade, manufacturing 'Tipsy Toff' and 'Toy Drum Major'. In 1946, he manufactured 'true to life' models of world-famous aircraft and airmen from many countries, moulded in

strong composition with rotatable propellers and in correct colours and national markings. In 1957, he created the first plastic miniature series, 'Herald', for Britains.

Zebra Toys
See Benbros (London) Ltd

Zimmerman, William
Bishopgate Street, London
In 1895, this firm laid claim to being the oldest toy firm in London. It was originally founded by John Zimmerman, a master toy maker, in the late 18th century. His son expanded the business by importing and by encouraging local toy makers to produce novelties like tin whistles, penny beech horses and imitation watches. William Zimmermann extended the store to include all manner of fancy goods as well as toys, and as a wholesaler shipped goods all over the world. He was of the opinion that every type of toy could be made in London without using imports.

Further reading: *Mayhew's Report on London Poor, 1850*

Zoetrope (Daedalum or Wheel of Life)
This optical toy consists of a cylindrical metal drum pierced with slots evenly spaced round the sides. Strips of drawings are placed round the rim and when the drum revolves the pictures, when seen through the slots, appear to move. The owner of Regent's Park Coliseum, W Horner, made the first Daedalum in 1834, but it was not exploited commercially until the 1860s.

In France, the same basic phenomenon of persistence of vision was used in the Praxinoscope, developed in 1877 by Emile Reynaud. Instead of looking at the pictures through the slots of a revolving drum, one saw them reflected in a moving polygon of mirrors set in the middle of the drum.
See Optical Toys

A zoetrope

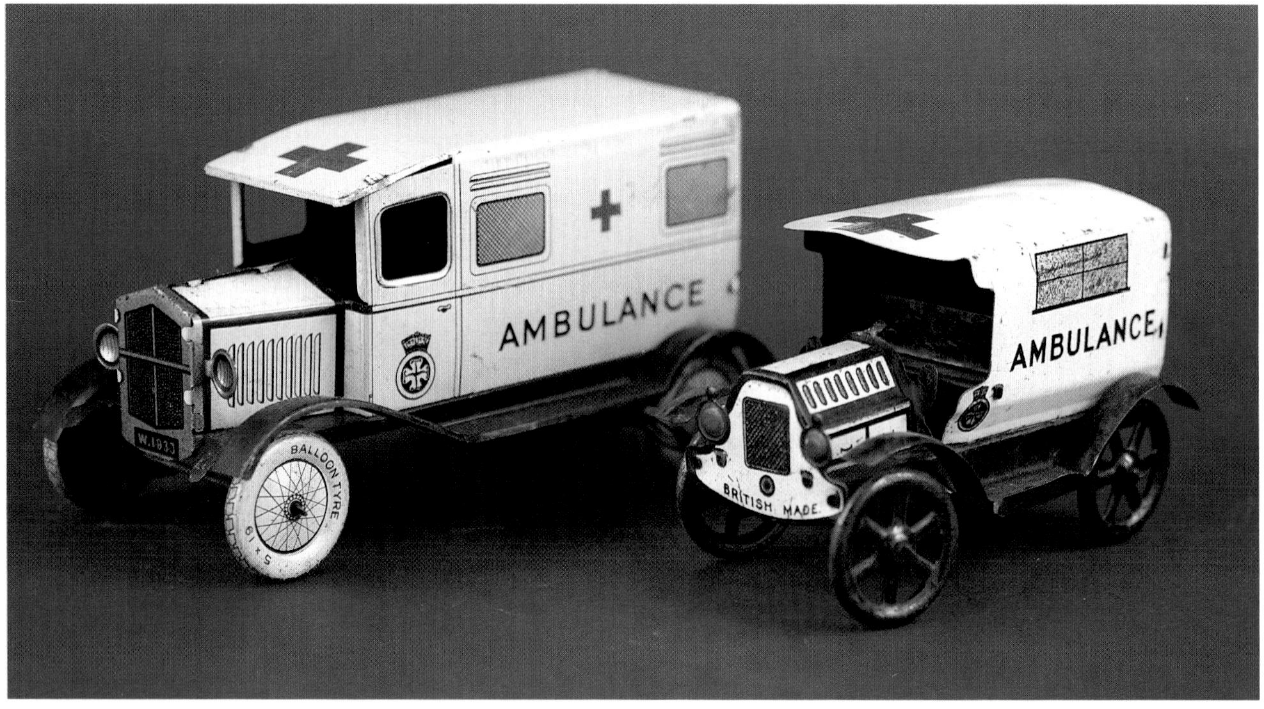

Wells-Brimtoy police van, 1937 (top)
A Wells & Co. ambulances, 1934 (left), 1927 (right)

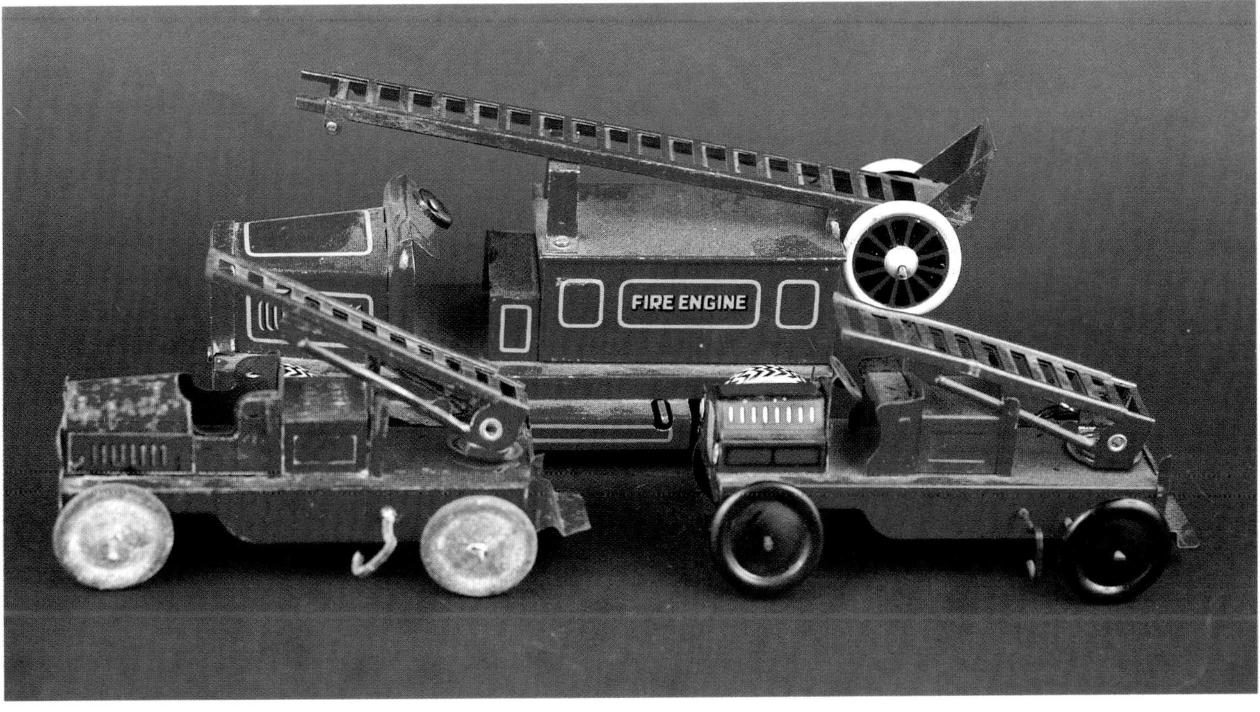

A Wells & Co. Carter Paterson Express van, c.1925

Wells-Brimtoy fire engines 1928–1936 (bottom)

APPENDIX I

Barringer, Wallis & Manners

Barringer, Wallis & Manners were absorbed into the Metal Box empire in 1939. From 1870 onwards they were making lithographed fancy tin boxes for the biscuit and confectionery trades. At the outbreak of World War I, they started making clockwork and other toys.

In 1982, Mr J A Whiston, the Branch Training Officer of Metal Box, Mansfield, interviewed several former employees, one aged 95, another who started work in 1925 at the age of fourteen. Both remember making the first remote control car, clockwork train sets with button wheels, monoplanes for a firm called Hughes, pull-along buses, lorries, stage coaches and a Royal Coach for the coronation of George VI in 1937 for the Crawford Biscuit Company, and for Burnetts, Ubilda construction sets, racing cars and money-boxes. The pensioners also said they made walking dolls, spinning and humming tops.

From old files in the company's archives Mr Whiston also extracted the two following lists. The first, from a file entitled 'Toys' and with the date 11 November 1927 on the inside front cover, gives details of the toys made for Chad Valley until 1969 when the tool sets for the last toy tops, globes and pile-ups were sent to Hall & Lane of Birmingham. The tools for some other Chad Valley toys were scrapped between 1951 and 1955. The second file marked 'Advertising Novelties', list the little sweet containers, 'penny novelties' made for Batgers Clarnico, Pascall and Rowntrees.

Saloon car for Chad Valley

FILE 1 TOYS
Dated 11 November 1927

Page 1
Racing Cars (Chad Valley)
7¾″ Racer, blue/orange with red/blue base aluminium
11½″ Racer, red and cream
red and cream (new wording and mechanism)
blue and cream
light and dark blue (aluminium)
with base red
with base green
Tools scrapped 16 March 1955

Page 2
Buses (Chad Valley)
6″ single decker 'National' red (tin)
6″ double decker 'Green Line' (tin)
10″ double decker 'Green Line' (tin)
10″ double decker 'London Bus' (tin)
12″ single decker, red and white (tin)
12″ single decker, blue and cream (tin)
12″ single decker, blue and cream (aluminium)

Page 3
Saloon Cars (Chad Valley)
6¾″ Saloon Car, red and cream
9″ Saloon Car, blue and cream (tin)
9″ Saloon Car, red (aluminium)
9″ Saloon Car, green (aluminium)

Page 4
Miscellaneous Toys (Chad Valley)
5″ Loco, green
Royal Mail Van
Removal Van
Buffet Car ('Mac's Snacks')

Page 5
0 Gauge Train Set
Coaches, red and green
Tankers
Milk Wagon (tin couplings and wheels)
Petrol Wagon (tin couplings and wheels)
Regent Spirit (new coupling and plastic wheels)
Esso (new couplings and plastic wheels)
Fresh Milk (new couplings and plastic wheels)
Railway Chassis and loose containers
Cattle Truck
Milk Van
Railway Container Lorry and loose container

Page 6
0 Gauge Train Set
Engine, red/green, passenger
Engine, red/green, goods
Tender, red/green, LMS printing
Red tender, British Railways, new style couplings
Green tender, British Railways, new style couplings
Blue tender, British Railways, new style couplings
Brake Van, tin coupling and wheels
Brake Van, new coupling and plastic wheels

Page 7
0 Gauge Train Set
Trucks red (new coupling and plastic wheels)
green (new couplings and plastic wheels)

British Railways grey (new coupling and plastic wheels)
open cast, coal, orange (new coupling and plastic wheels)
Lines, straights, curves, curve fitted with brake,
½ straights, left hand points, right hand points, acute angle crossing
Station, 'Bognor Regis' (island with building)

Page 8
0 Gauge Train Set
Signal Box, single section (like a lean-to)
Signal Box, double section (V roof)
Single Signal, home
Single Signal, distant
Double Signal, home (equal bracket)
Double Signal, distant (equal bracket)

Page 9
Number 2 Train Set
Engine blue
Tender blue
Coaches red and cream, 10141, 10139
Coaches red and cream, Master Cutler 10129

Page 10
Wills display stamping for train sets, all 1″ × 2″
'Capstan', 'Bristol' and 'Woodbine'

Page 11
Dial Scales (Chad Valley) with drawing

Dial scales for Chad Valley

Page 12
Tea Set (Chad Valley)
Alloy tea pot (supplied by Chad)
4 plates, 4⅛″ diameter
4 saucers, 3¼″ diameter
4 cups, 2⅜″ at top, 1½″ at bottom
1 cream jug, 2 9/16″ at top, 1 9/16″ at bottom
1 sugar bowl, same as cream jug
4 alloy spoons (supplied by Chad)
1 tea tray 12″ × 8⅛″
All packed in special cartons
Crown Derby design and Old English design

Page 13
Money-Boxes (Chad Valley)
Book money-boxes (aluminium)
Treasure Island Pirates design, 1948
Westward Ho design, 1949
Dick Whittington design, 1949
Happy Days design, 1949
Endeavour design, 1953

Pile-ups for Chad Valley

Page 14
Post Office Money-Box (Chad Valley)
Oval, 3⅜″ × 1¾″ × 4½″ deep
5″ × 1¾″ × 4½″ deep

Page 15
Toy Clock Face (Chad Valley)
With nursery rhymes, 6″ square

Page 16
Pile-ups
Sizes 2 5/16″, 2 9/16″, 2 15/16″, 3⅝″, 4″
Chad Valley nursery rhyme subjects (6 pieces)
(6 pieces, 7 pieces and 8 pieces)
Chad Valley, Alice in Wonderland

Page 17
Shallow Pile-ups (Chad Valley)
Months of the year design

Page 18
Building Bricks (Chad Valley)
Picture bricks, 1″ cube

Page 19
'Eagle' Gas Stove Money-Box
(J Wright & Co., Birmingham)

Page 20
Picture Frame Money-Box
Kittens, rabbits, lambs, puppy designs

Page 21
'Safe' Money-Box (Chad Valley)
Name 'Chubb' on box. Size 4¼″ × 2⅝″ × 2⅛″

Page 22
Constructional Toys (Chad Valley)
Ubilda Coupé Motor Car, mechanised
Ubilda Fort
Ubilda Fire Engine
Ubilda Loco
Ubilda Shovel
Ubilda Coupé
All these tools scrapped 31 October 1951

Page 23
Steam Roller (Chad Valley)
Non-mechanical, size 5½″ high × 7¼″ long × 4 5/16″ wide

Page 24
Magic Lantern (Chad Valley)
Sketch only

Page 25
Miscellaneous (Chad Valley)
Tambourine, 1½″ × 5½″ diameter
Bouncing Top with rod, 3 11/16″ diameter, rod 12″ (later pattern with whistle)
Humming Top, 7½″ diameter × 7¾″
6″ diameter × 7″
Designs included 'Little pigs', 'Sing-a-song-of-sixpence' and 'Little Red Riding Hood'
Scales, 6¼″ long × 2½″ wide. Blue, red, green and bunnies design (aluminium)
High Flyer (Fan) with twisted rod for spinning
Size 3¾″ diameter
Whistling Top, nursery rhyme design, 6″ diameter
Hey, diddle, diddle
Choral top
Sing-a-song-of-sixpence
There was a crooked man
Little Red Riding Hood
Noddy's
Nursery design

Page 26
Globes
Terrestrial Globe (Chad Valley)
Size 5″ diameter × 8″ high
Sphere held in position by spring clip
Originally a novelty container (W Crawford & Sons)
World Globe (Chad Valley). Similar to above but no spring clip and quadrant clipped together but not soldered
World Globe (Chad Valley), die-cast quadrant
5″ French Globe
5″ Physical Globe
5″ Globe (Henry Thorne). With centre liner and rivetted clasp on North Pole of quadrant to enable sphere to be opened and used as a container

Page 27
7″ Globe of the world

Page 28
Watering Can (Chad Valley)
Blue design

Page 29
Bucket (Chad Valley)
Bottom embossed with star fish

Page 30
Buckets
4lb bucket 5⅜″ diameter bottom
2lb bucket 4⅛″ diameter bottom
1lb bucket 3¼″ diameter bottom

Wells-Brimtoy camouflaged army truck and gun lorry, 1940 (top)
Wells-Brimtoy camouflaged army lorry with searchlight, 1940 (bottom)
Wells-Brimtoy covered army lorry, 1940

Wells-Brimtoy Distributors trolley bus, 1955 (top)

Wells-Brimtoy Distributors Routemaster double-decker bus, 1955 (middle)

Wells-Brimtoy Distributors Gyro Greenline bus, 1955, National coach, 1947 and Pocketoy Greenline bus, 1945 (from left to right, bottom)

Seaside bucket (Chad Valley)

4″ diameter

3¼″ diameter

3¼″ diameter Life on the ocean wave

5⅜″ diameter sand pail

3¼″ Hey, diddle, diddle

3⅞″ Paddling pool

4⅛″ Nursery rhymes

Page 31

Sharps Toffee Pail

8⅛″ × 7⅞″

Page 32

Irish Aluminium Co. 3¼″ diameter, bottom only. ‘Pirate’

Page 33

Drum (Chad Valley). Size 7⅛″, spun on top and bottom extra deep. Body beaded top and bottom. Fitted with cord for carrying.

Page 34

Magnetic Target (Chad Valley)

9″ diameter

Page 35

Cash Boxes (Chad Valley

3″ × 2″ × 1⅜″ deep

3⅞″ × 2½″ × 1½″ deep

6¾″ × 4″ × 2¼″ deep

Cash Boxes (Edward Sharp)

4⅞″ × 3″ × 1¾″ deep

6¾″ × 4″ × 2¼″ deep

3″ × 1⅞″ × 1⅜″ deep

5¾″ × 3½″ × 2″ deep

Cash Boxes (Chad Valley)

3⅞″ × 2½″ × 1½″ deep

6¾″ × 4″ × 2¼″ deep

5¾″ × 3½″ × 2″ deep

4¾″ × 3″ × 1¾″ deep

6¾″ × 4″ × 1¾″ deep with tray (29 April, 1957)

Cash Boxes (Central Commercial)

4¾″ × 3″ × 1¾″ deep

5¾″ × 3½″ × 2″ deep

Page 36

Old ½ lb Motor Van for CWS Crumpsall Biscuit Van and Gray Dunn’s Motor Bus Tools scrapped January 1952

Page 37

½ lb Lawn Mower (Barringer Wallis & Manners) (also for CWS)

Page 38

Crawfords Railway Carriage/CWS Crumpsall Restaurant Car

Photo shows four wheeled coach – two firsts, two thirds. 7″ long – should be 0 Gauge

Page 39

Gray Dunn’s Motor Cycle Van

Motor cycle with closed combination (chair) and driver

Page 40

Gray Dunn’s Racing Car

6″ long

Page 41

8 lb Motor Car

Made for Fryers. Illustration shows light and dark blue saloon car with passengers and white tyres.

FILE 2 ADVERTISING MATERIAL

Penny Novelties

Pascall’s penny rifle, 6″ long (drawing)

Rowntrees penny hockey stick, 5″ long (drawing)

Clarke, Nicholls & Coombes penny cigarette, 1¾″ long (drawing)

Rowntrees penny cricket bat, 4½″ long (drawing)

Batgers penny fountain pen, 5″ long (drawing)

Clarnico penny golf club, 5½″ long (drawing)

Rowntrees penny key, 4″ long (drawing)

Rowntrees penny axe, 4″ long (drawing)

Rowntrees penny banana, 3½″ long (drawing and photo)

Rowntrees penny grandfather clock 3½″ high (drawing and photo), also for Ridgeways, ‘Five o’clock tea’

Rowntrees penny golliwog 3¼″ high (drawing and photo)

Rowntrees penny novelty of HM the King/HM the Queen. Each 3″ high (drawing and photos)

Rowntrees Birdcage (photo)

Rowntrees Summerhouse (photo)

Rowntrees Lantern (photo). All 1½″ square with removable top

Rowntrees penny piano (drawing and photo) 2″ × 2″ × 1″ also for Bailey’s Agencies as a pencil sharpener holder

Rowntrees penny camera, 1½″ cubed (drawing)

Rowntrees penny meat pie, 2½″ oval (drawing and photo) also for Batgers – dish of apples

Rowntrees penny Punch and Judy show, 3″ × 1½″ × ¾″ (drawing and photo (P & J)

Batgers penny wardrobe, 3″ × 1½″ × ¾″ (drawing and photo (P & J)

Batgers penny sentry box, 3″ × 1½″ × ¾″ (drawing and photo (P & J)

Pascall’s Punch and Judy, 3″ × 1½″ × ¾″ (drawing and photo (P & J)

Pascall’s penny soldiers – 4 types, 3½″ high (drawing)

Rowntrees penny lantern, 1½″ diameter (drawing and photo)

Rowntrees penny Chinese lantern, 1½″ diameter × 2½″ (drawing and photo) also for Dells

Rowntrees penny pussy cat, 2″ high (drawing and photo)

Clarnico penny teddy bear, 2¼″ high

Rowntrees penny rugby football, 2½″ oval (drawing)

Rowntrees penny walnut, 2½″ oval (drawing)

Rowntrees penny pillar box, 1⅜″ diameter × 2″ (drawing)

Rowntrees penny association football

Rowntrees penny globe

Rowntrees penny cricket ball

Rowntrees penny Nibs toffee ball, 1¾″ diameter

Unbreakable Pencil & Chalks Co. soccer ball pencil sharpener holder, also in Coronation design

Globe also made for Chad Valley. Tartan design for Invicta Plastics

Rowntrees Threepenny Globe, 2¼″ diameter

Rowntrees penny straw hat, 3″ oval (drawing)

Rowntrees penny butterfly, 2″ × 1½″ (drawing)

Doll’s trunk 2⅜″ × 1⅞″ (drawing)

Rowntrees penny easter egg

APPENDIX II

Chad Valley 1823–1978

It was only after World War II that Chad Valley added lithographed tin toys to the variety of games, dolls, and soft toys that it produced in its own factories and in other subsidiary firms. The first toys were made by Barringer, Wallis & Manners, using tools made before the war for Burnett Ltd.

In 1946, Chad Valley took over the 'Holdfast', 'Gwenda' and 'Conductor' range of printed aluminium domestic toys made by A S Cartwright Ltd, as well as Winfield Ltd, tool and clockwork manufacturers. Three years later they acquired the 'Rob' trademark for strong metal toys made by Ridingbury Ltd and finally in 1951, Hall & Lane Ltd and its two subsidiary companies, Cambridge Metal Stamping Company and the Acme Stamping and Box Company. Gradually all the tools made by Barringer, Wallis & Manners were scrapped or passed on to these companies and by 1969 the transfer was complete.

The following list covers only part of Chad Valley's output of tin toys. In addition to the toys bearing the brand name, or of the subsidiary companies and intended for sale in the normal trade outlets at a fixed retail price, Chad Valley made a wide range of similar but unmarked toys for Woolworths or other chain stores to be sold at lower prices.

'Ubilda' touring car No. 10054

Fire engine No. 10033 (for reluctant firemen!)

Numbers given in the captions refer to the toy's catalogue number.

UBILDA CONSTRUCTION TOYS

Toys made by Barringer, Wallis & Manners, first for Burnett Ltd and then taken over by Chad Valley in 1946. Tools scrapped 1955.

UBILDA (NON-MECHANICAL) TOYS

Locomotive LMS No. 17841, Red
Locomotive LNER No. 2684, Green
Catalogue No. 10010A. Size 10″
Price 97s per dozen. 1946–49

Car, Coupé Catalogue No. 10011
Size 8″ Price 108s per dozen. 1946–48
p. 50

Fort Catalogue No. 10009
40 parts Price 143s per dozen. 1946–49

UBILDA (MECHANICAL) TOYS

Fire Engine Clockwork
Catalogue No. 10033. Size 8″
Price 118s per dozen. 1946–49

Touring Car Clockwork, blue, yellow and black
Catalogue No. 10054. Size 8″
Price 120s per dozen. 1946–49

Locomotive Clockwork
Catalogue No. 10010. Size 10″
Price 108s per dozen. 1946–49 *p. 50*

Tower of London Working model 40 separate parts. 1949–50

Jib Crane Working model
Catalogue No. 12009. 1949–50

Tip Crane Working model
Catalogue No. 12010. 1949–50

Gantry Crane Working model
Catalogue No. 12011. 1949–50

Shovel Working model. 1949–50

VEHICLES

Toy vehicles made by Barringer, Wallis & Manners first for Burnett Ltd and then taken over by Chad Valley in 1946. Tools for racing cars scrapped 1955.

Racing Car Mk I Clockwork, open base
Catalogue No. 10001. Size $7\frac{3}{4}$″
Price 38s/6d per dozen. 1946–50

Racing Car Mk II Clockwork, solid base
Catalogue No. 10001A. Size $7\frac{3}{4}$″
Price 43s per dozen. 1948–50

Racing Car Clockwork, open base
Catalogue No. 10003. Size $11\frac{1}{2}$″
Price 43s/6d per dozen. 1946–50

Racing Car Clockwork, solid base
Catalogue No. 1003A. Size $11\frac{1}{2}$″
Price 53s/6d per dozen. 1948–50

Saloon Car Red and cream. Size $6\frac{1}{2}$″.
1946–50 *p. 50*

Wells-Brimtoy Shell petrol tanker, 1934 (top left)
Wells-Brimtoy Distributors open touring car, friction drive, 1955
Wells-Brimtoy Distributors mechanical kangaroo, 1950 (top right)
Wells-Brimtoy Distributors 'Puffing Billy' train, c.1934 (middle)
Wells-Brimtoy kitchen sink, 1920 (bottom)

Whitanco limousine from ex-Carette/Bub tooling, 1920 (top)
Van Riemsdyck 0 gauge London tram, c.1948 (bottom)
Whitanco tank, c.1919 (inset)

Racing car No. 10001

Racing car No. 10003

Royal Mail van No. 10130

Delivery van No. 10032

British Rail van

Gypsy caravan biscuit tin

Saloon Car Mark I Clockwork
Catalogue No. 10004. Size 9″
Price 49s per dozen. 1946–50 **p. 50*

Saloon Car Mark II Clockwork
Catalogue No. 10004A. Size 9″
Price 51s per dozen. 1946–50

Car, Heavy Coupé Red and black. Clockwork
Catalogue No. 10022. Size 9½″
Price 116s per dozen. 1946–48

Car, Heavy Tourer Clockwork
Catalogue No. 10036. Size 9½″
Price 116s per dozen. 1946–48

Car, remote control (compressed air) solid base, blue saloon type
Catalogue No. 10046. Size 7½″. 1948 **p. 51*

Car Similar to remote control but without steering mechanism, fitted with clockwork
Catalogue No. 10060. Size 9″
Price 91s per dozen. 1948

Bus Green Line and Midland Red. Clockwork
From 1949 coloured figures at windows. Also in blue and green and made of aluminium
Catalogue No. 10005. Size 12″
Price 71s per dozen. 1946–52

Bus London double decker and Green Line. From 1948 figures at windows. Clockwork
Catalogue No. 10045. Size 10″
Price 87s per dozen. 1946–52 **p. 46*

Bus Single deck, National
Catalogue No. 10073. Size 6″. 1949–54

Bus Double deck, Green Line
Catalogue No. 10071. Size 6″. 1949–54

Royal Mail Van Clockwork. On side 'Post early in the day' and 'Say it with a Greetings Telegram' No. plate. CV 1032
Catalogue No. 10130. Size 10″ **p. 46*
1950–51

Delivery Van Clockwork
On side 'Chad Valley Co. Ltd, Harborne' No. plate. CV 10032
Catalogue No. 10032. Size 10″
Price 78s per dozen. 1946–49 **p. 46*

Removal Van Clockwork
Catalogue No. 10133. Size 5″. 1950–55

British Rail Van Clockwork
Red and cream. 5½″ long

Buffet Car On side 'Mac's Snacks'

Steam Roller Non-mechanical
Catalogue No. 10131.
Size 5½″ high × 7″½ long

The following toys were probably not made by Barringer, Wallis & Manners

Scout Car Friction sparking
Catalogue No. 12053. Size 6″. 1955

Bumper Car Clockwork
Catalogue No. 11060

Racing Car Non-mechanical
Catalogue No. M58. Size 11½″. 1958

Gypsy Caravan Possibly made by Hudson, Scott & Sons for Chad Valley. 6″ long with hinged lid. 1937

Steam roller No. 10131

'Flying Scotsman' No. 10000

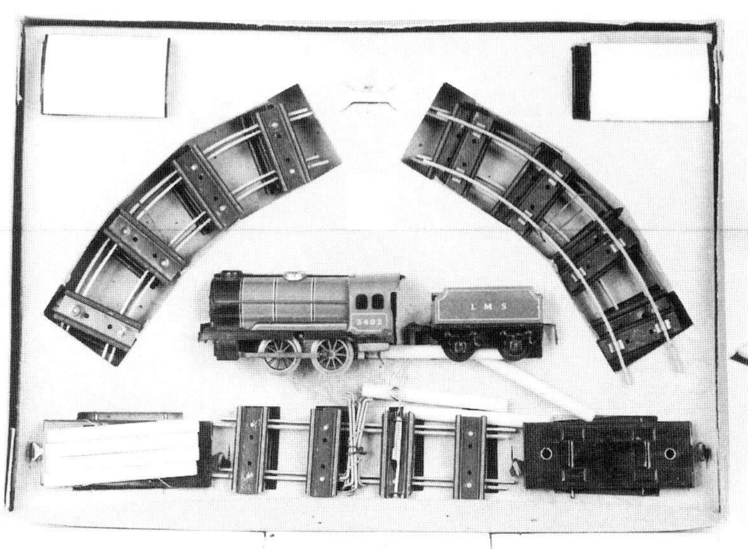

0 gauge LMS train set

RAILWAYS

Railway stock made by Barringer, Wallis & Manners for Chad Valley

Locomotive LNER Flying Scotsman
Catalogue No. 10000. Size 5″
Slightly different design 10000C
Price 33s per dozen. 1946–50

Electric Train Set
Catalogue No. 10058. 1948

Signal Boxes Single and double sections
Catalogue No. 10125. 1950

Signals Home or distant, single and double

Train Sets 0 gauge, LMS. Red, green or blue. Engines, tenders, goods and passenger coaches. Also railway track

Station 'Bognor Regis'

Signal box No. 10125

The following two toys were probably not made by Barringer, Wallis & Manners

Overhead Railway 1 coach, folding track. Clockwork
Catalogue No. 10069. Size 3″. 1949–57

Carpet Loco (Byro Flash friction)
Catalogue No. 12052. Size $7\frac{1}{2}$″×3″. 1952

Money box No. 10012

Money-box No. 12033

Money-box No. 12034

MONEY-BOXES

Originally made by Barringer, Wallis & Manners first for Dunn & Taylor, then for Burnett and finally for Chad Valley.

Red Oval Post Office
Catalogue No. 10012. Size 3″
Price 4s/6d per dozen. 1946–75

Red Oval Post Office
Catalogue No. 10013. Size 4″
Price 6s/10d per dozen. 1946–75

Red Oval Post Office Complete with opening door, lock and key
Catalogue No. 10014. Size 5″
Price 13s/6d per dozen. 1946–75

Circular, coloured Air Route design
Catalogue No. 10038. Size 5″
6s/8d per dozen. 1946–75

Book, Treasure Island design Lock and key
Catalogue No. 10025. Size 7″×4″×1″
Price 25s per dozen. 1946–75

Nest of Three Cashboxes Without trays, complete with locks and keys
Catalogue Nos. 10015/16/17
Sizes 5″, 6″ & 7″
Price 80s per dozen. 1946–75

Cashbox With tray and key
Catalogue No. 10018. Size 7″
Price 48s per dozen. 1946–75

Cashbox With tray and key
Catalogue No. 10019. Size 8″
Price 64s per dozen. 1946–75

House Money-box Catalogue No. 10082

Chubb Safe Money-box (Export) 1952
Size 4¼″×2⅜″×2⅛″. Catalogue No. 12067

Globe Money-box (Export) 1952
Catalogue Nos. 11200/1. Sizes 5″ and 7″

Telephone Money-box (Export)
Door opens
Catalogue Nos. 12034 and 12037. 1952

Bucket Money-box (Export)
Catalogue No. 12033. 1952

Picture Frame Money-box (Export) 1952

Sooty Money-box 1956
Catalogue No. 12056. Size 3″

Muffin the Mule Money-box 1956

Prudence Kitten Money-box
Catalogue No. 12057

Robin Clock Money-box 1956
Catalogue No. 12071

Clock Money-box 1959
Catalogue No. 14101

Donald Duck Money-box (clock) 1958
Catalogue No. 12099

Sambo Money-box Takes coins on his tongue and swallows them into the box
Catalogue No. 12080. 1958

Noddy Bucket Money-box 1958
Catalogue No. 12033

Calendar Money-box Drum Major, Guardsman, Soldiers
Catalogue No. 12092. Sizes 7″, 8″ & 9″

Thrift Family Money-box 1965
Catalogue No. M35. Size 9¼″×3½″×2½″

TOPS

Wide variety of tops made by Barringer, Wallis & Manners until 1975

Humming Tops 6″ and 7″
Designs: Three little pigs
Sing a song of sixpence *p. 51*
Little Red Riding Hood
Catalogue No. 10034. Price 89s per dozen

Whistling Tops 6″
Designs: Hey diddle diddle
Sing a song of sixpence
Little Red Riding Hood
There was a crooked man
Noddy
Nursery Design & Choral

High Flyer Tops with twisted rod for spinning

Bouncing Tops 3½″ Catalogue No. 10024.
Price 19s/6d per dozen

GYRO AND JET TOYS

Space Cruiser (Gyro mechanism)
Catalogue No. 12111. 1958

Airliner (Gyro mechanism)
Catalogue No. 12112. 1958

Jet Boat Driven by hot air jets
Catalogue No. 11081. Size 9″. 1953

Jet boat No. 11081

Rose Cottage dolls' house No. M67B

Suburban villa No. M67

DOMESTIC TOYS

Electric Cooker 4-volt battery
Catalogue No. 10133. 1950

Washing Machine
Catalogue No. 11082. 1956

Modern Cooking Stove
Catalogue No. 11092. 1956

Cooking Stove Catalogue No. 11067
Size $13\frac{1}{2}'' \times 10\frac{1}{2}'' \times 8\frac{1}{2}''$. 1957

Dust Pan & Brush
Catalogue No. 12114

Metal Dolls' House (2 designs) Tudor style or Rose Cottage, 4 rooms. Carpet and rugs printed on floors and decorated walls. Supplied flat. Size 17″×13″×9″. Catalaogue No. M67. 1962

Dolls' House Suburban villa. Printed inside and out Catalogue No. M67. 1963

Dolls' House Country house. Printed inside and out Catalogue No. M67
Size 14″×13″×7″ 1963

Originally made for Cartwright & Co.

Cooking Stove with 4 accessories
Catalogue No. 11011. Size $7\frac{1}{2}'' \times 8\frac{1}{2}'' \times 4\frac{1}{2}''$
Price 93s per dozen. 1946–57

Cooking Stove with 5 accessories
Catalogue No. 11012. Size $8\frac{1}{2}'' \times 11\frac{1}{8}'' \times 5\frac{1}{2}''$
Price 139s per dozen. 1946–57

Cooking Stove with 9 accessories
Catalogue No. 11013. Size $10\frac{1}{2}'' \times 14'' \times 7\frac{1}{2}''$
Price 216s per dozen. 1946–57

Electric Cooking Stove with accessories. Catalogue No. 10067. 1951 or 1954

Carpet Sweeper 1946

Iron Catalogue No. 11016. Size 3″×3″×1″
Price 117s per gross. 1946

Electric cooker No. 10067

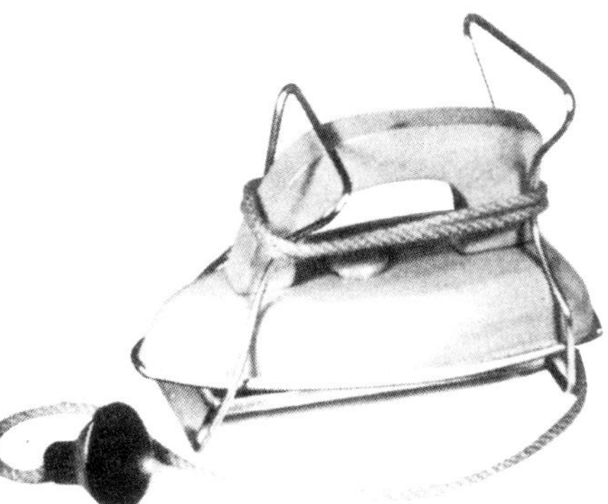

Electric iron No. 11094

Iron Catalogue No. 11017
Size $4'' \times 2\frac{1}{2}'' \times 2\frac{1}{8}''$. Price 146s per gross. 1946

Modern cooker No. 10092

MUSICAL TOYS

Drums Catalogue No. 10053. Sizes 6″, 7″, 8″, 9″. Price 52s per dozen. 1946–60

Jazz Band Set (Export)
Catalogue No. 12084. 1952
1956 – Sooty Jazz band set
1973 – Young Beats band set
1974 – Top of the Pops band set

Fun Band Set (Export)
Catalogue No. 12035. Size 9″. 1952

Tom Tom Drum Catalogue No. M49
Size 11″×$7\frac{1}{4}$ dia. 1961

Banjo Catalogue No. 12085. Size 19″
1954

Trumpet Catalogue No. 11068
Size 15″ and 10″. 1952

Ukelele Catalogue No. M53. 1958

Hurdy-Gurdy Monkey pops up and down as the music plays. Catalogue No. M91
Size 11″×9″×7″. 1961

Sooty Jazz Band No. 12034

Fun Band set No. 12035

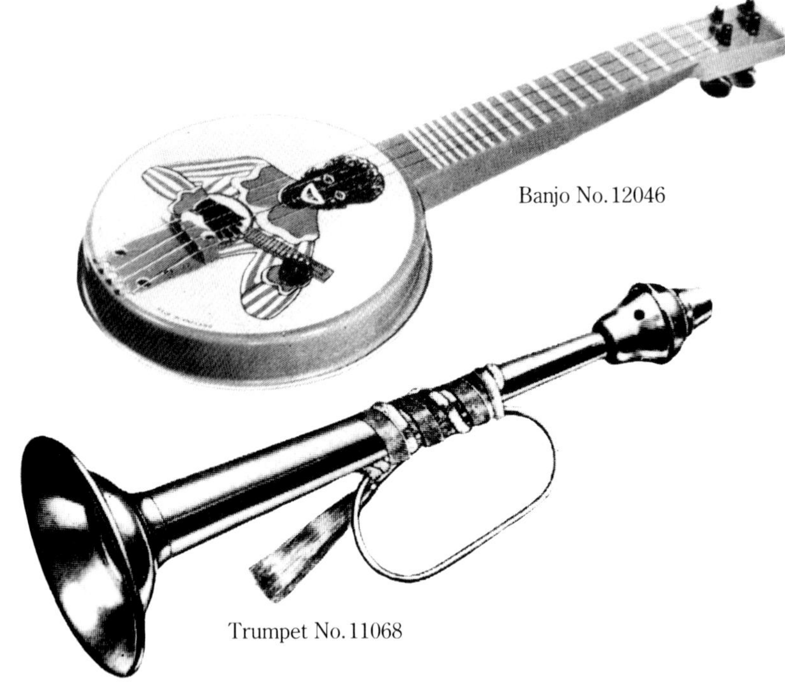
Banjo No. 12046

Trumpet No. 11068

Drums: (front) Nos. 46–49
(back) Junior and Major Cadett drums Nos. M107 and M108, Tom-Tom drum No. M116

Clockwork gramophone No. 9039

Watering can No. 12021

Jack-in-the box No. M90

Hickory Dickory clock No. 12048

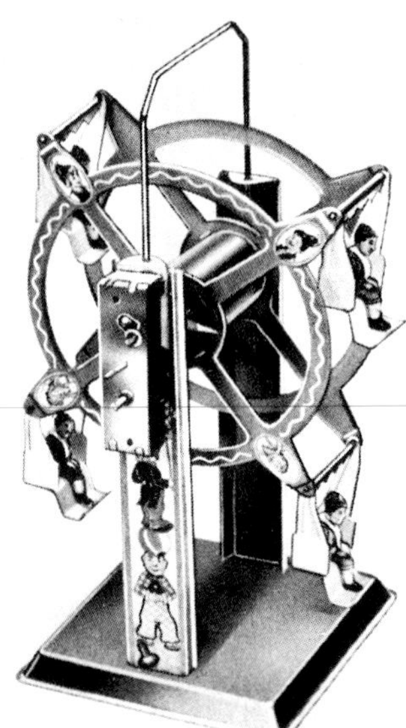

Ferris wheel No. 11080

MISCELLANEOUS

Jumping Kangaroo Clockwork
Catalogue No. 11061. 1951–54

Gambolling Ape Clockwork
Catalogue No. 11062. 1951–54

Jumping Frog Clockwork
Catalogue No. 11063. 1951–54

Jack-in-the-Box Rubber clown with bowler hat. Catalogue No. M90
Size $4\frac{1}{4}''\times3\frac{3}{4}''\times3\frac{1}{4}''$. 1961

Ladybird Clockwork
Catalogue No. 10132. 1950

Ferris Wheel Tinplate and precision clockwork. Export Catalogue No. 11080. 1953

Gramophone Clockwork-printed tin
Catalogue No. 9559. 1956

Clock, Hickory Dickory Dock
Catalogue No. 12048. 1954

Kaleidoscope Printed tin
Catalogue No. M103. Size $8\frac{1}{4}''\times2\frac{1}{4}''$. 1959

Filling Station 1955

Garage and midget cars 1954

Farmhouse inc. collapsible metal barn, 22 plastic animals, 2 tractors and farm machinery. Catalogue No. M69

Village Pump Printed in red and green on tinplate. The 'well' filled with water and could be pumped into small bucket.

The following toys were made by Barringer, Wallis & Manners

Seaside Pails Brightly printed pictures on outside
Catalogue No. 10068. Size 5″
Price 12s per dozen
Catalogue No. 10020. Size 6″
Price 21s per dozen
Catalogue No. 10021. Size 7″
1946–75 *p. 47

Terrestrial Globes Sphere held in position by spring clip. (1970 Moon globe showing Apollo landing sites).
Catalogue No. 10028. 1948–1975

World Globes 5″ and 7″

Pile-ups Circular. Set of 6, largest $4\frac{1}{2}''$ dia. height $18\frac{1}{2}''$, months of the year design. Catalogue No. 10169. 1950

Pile-ups Circular. Set of 4, largest $3\frac{1}{2}''$ dia. height $10\frac{1}{2}''$

Building Bricks $1\frac{1}{2}''$ cubes (picture bricks). Set of 12 cubes.
Catalogue No. 10202. 1953

Watering Can Detachable nose, swivel top handle. Export only.
Catalogue No. 12011
Size $7''\times4''$ or $8\frac{1}{2}''\times4\frac{1}{2}''$.
1953 Catalogue No. 12121. Nursery rhyme design.

Scales Tin with brass pans
Catalogue No. 10008. Size $6\frac{1}{2}''\times2\frac{1}{2}''\times2\frac{1}{2}''$
Price 19s/10d per dozen. 1946–59

Dial Scales Catalogue No. 10179. 1952

Tea Sets Only plates, cups and saucers, cream jug and tea tray. (Teapot and teaspoons made by another manufacturer.) Crown Derby and Old English designs, packed in special cartons.

Tambourine Catalogue No. 10026.
Size $5\frac{1}{2}''$ dia. Price 23s per dozen. 1953

Magic Lantern Fitted with adjustable lens. Export Catalogue. 1948

APPENDIX III

Mettoy 1933–1983

As its name implies, the main products of the Mettoy Company Ltd were metal toys. In the early years, these were lithographed tinplate, later strong steel and from 1956, die-cast Corgi toys. The firm did however try to diversify a little with the manufacture of the 'Wembley' range of playballs, some ingenious folding kites, the Playcraft 'Bruna' and nursery toys, and the Petite typewriter made in conjunction with Byron Jardine Limited. They also ventured into the market for Walkie-Talkie Sets, telephone sets and hi-fi record players using electronics.

In the following list only the main tinplate toys produced between 1936 and 1958 have been included, with naturally a gap for the War years when production of toys was stopped, except for a limited amount of toys made for export in 1940. Some of the large toys made of metal such as the hospitals, garages, filling station, merry go-round and other large novelty toys have also been omitted. Catalogue numbers refer to the year in which the toy made its first appearance.

Under the heading *Railways* no attempt has been made to list railway equipment such as stations, tunnels, signal boxes and signals, nor the varying contents of all the boxed train sets produced by Mettoy during its years of full production. The list given refers only to the sets produced before World War II.

Advertisement in 1942 *Games and Toys*

Limousine No.59

Racing car No.88

CARS

Limousines

With chauffeur. Catalogue No.59
Size 10¾″. Price 13s/6d per dozen
1936–37 and 1940

With chauffeur and two electric headlights
Catalogue No.59/7. Size 10¾″. Price 25s per dozen. 1936–37 and 1940

Camouflaged army officer printed on door
Catalogue No.61c. Size 10″. 1940

With reversing action. Catalogue No.63
Size 11″. 1940

With chauffeur and two electric headlights
Catalogue No.74/7. Size 14½″. 1940

Cabriolets

With sliding roof. Catalogue No.70
Size 14½″. Price 30s per dozen.
1936–37 and 1939–40 *p. 95

With sliding roof and 2 electric lights
Catalogue No.70/7. Size 14½″
Price 37s/6d per dozen. 1936–37 and 1940

With sliding roof, 2 electric lights and rubber tyres
Catalogue No.70/7R. Size 14½″
Price 51s per dozen.
1936–37 and 1940

Roadster No.25

Miniature Rolls-Royce No.505

Crazy Cop No.6350

Racing Cars
Catalogue No.88. Size 12¾″
Price 13s per dozen. 1936–37 and 1939–41 **p. 94*
With turntable electric searchlight Catalogue No.88/6. Size 12¾″ Price 21s per dozen. 1936
With sparking mechanism (Export list) Catalogue No.90/2. Size 12¾″. 1940

Sports Cars
Catalogue Nos. 25 and 26. Size 8″
Price 7s per dozen. 1936–40

Miniature Clockwork Models made 1951
Standard Vanguard. Catalogue No.502 Size 2⅞″
Rolls-Royce. Catalogue No.505. Size 3″
Police Car. Catalogue No.510. Size 2⅞″
Taxi. Catalogue No.511. Size 2⅞″
Fire Service car. Catalogue No.512 Size 2⅞″
Standard Vanguard. Catalogue No.602 Size 4″
Standard Vanguard, automatic reversing mechanism. Catalogue No.603 Size 4¼″
Rolls-Royce with automatic reversing mechanism. Catalogue No.605. Size 4½″
Rolls-Royce with automatic reversing mechanism. Catalogue No.606. Size 4½″

Scale Model Cars made 1951
Standard Vanguard. Catalogue No.702 Size 5½″
Standard Vanguard, automatic reversing mechanism. Catalogue No.703. Size 5½″
Rolls-Royce. Catalogue No.705. Size 5⅝″
Rolls-Royce with automatic reversing mechanism. Catalogue No.706. Size 5⅝″
Standard Vanguard Saloon. Clockwork forward, stop, reverse mechanism, adjustable steering. Catalogue No.902 Size 8¼″
Rolls-Royce limousine, battery operated Clockwork motor with forward stop and reverse. Catalogue No.905. Size 11″
Rolls-Royce limousine, headlights battery operated. Clockwork motor with forward stop and reverse Catalogue No.905L. Size 11″
Deluxe Streamline Limousine with clockwork motor. Catalogue No.909 Size 9½″
Car. Catalogue No.907. Size 9½″
Open four-seater Sports Car with rubber tyres, powerful clockwork motor and detachable caravan trailer with sunshine roof. Catalogue No.907T. Size 17¾″
Streamline 'Fire Chief' Speed Car with flywheel motor and siren rubber tyres Catalogue No.909/2. Size 9½″
Two-seater Sports Car, clockwork driven with adjustable windscreen and steering. Catalogue No.3019. Size 6¼″
Open Touring Car. Clockwork with spare wheel. Catalogue No.3024A. Size 8″
Car, clockwork. Detachable caravan trailer with sunshine roof and support stand Catalogue No.3023T. Size 16″
Racing Car. One piece body, clockwork, enclosed adjustable steering Catalogue No.3082/1. Size 7″
Racing Car. Clockwork, enclosed adjustable steering Catalogue No.3084. Size 9¼″
Large Racing Car, beautifully moulded driver's head. Clockwork, fully enclosed adjustable steering Catalogue No.3086/1. Size 11½″
Racing car, long bonnet high powered with adjustable front wheels Catalogue No.3088. Size 12″
Giant Heavy Racing Car with powerful clockwork motor brake and steering wheel control. Catalogue No.3093 Size 15¼″
Clockwork Limousine and detachable caravan. Catalogue No.33306T Size 11″
Shooting Brake with stock clockwork and adjustable steering Catalogue No.3312. Size 6¼″
Police Car, mechanical heavy flywheel drive and siren. Catalogue No.3320 Size 6¼″
Crazy Cop Mechanical Police Car, full of amusing antics. Catalogue No.6350

Fire Engine No. 110/6

Small 'Esso' and 'National' petrol tankers No. 113

COMMERCIAL VEHICLES

Fire Engines

With double ladder. Catalogue No. 102 Size $11\frac{3}{4}''$. Price 13s 6d per dozen 1936–37 and 1939–41

With longer double ladder and one electric light. Catalogue No. 105/6 Size $13\frac{1}{2}''$. Price 25s per dozen 1936–37

Large with double ladder Catalogue No. 110. Size $15\frac{1}{4}''$ Price 37s/6d per dozen. 1936–37 and 1939–40

Large with double ladder, light and bell Catalogue No. 110/6. Size $15\frac{1}{4}''$ Price 45s per dozen. 1936

With ladder and searchlight Catalogue No. 111. Size 15″ Price 51s per dozen. 1937 and 1940–41

With large double ladder Catalogue No. 107. Size $13\frac{1}{2}''$ 1939 and 1941

With large double ladder, turntable and electric light. Catalogue No. 107/6 Size $13\frac{1}{2}''$. 1940

With elevating ladder and moveable turntable. Catalogue No. 3102/2 Size $11\frac{1}{2}''$. 1951

Clockwork with bell and front wheel steering and adjustable extending ladder with turned edges. Catalogue No. 3110 Size 15″. 1949 and 1951

With detachable ladder, flywheel motor and siren. Catalogue No. 3321. Size $6\frac{1}{4}''$ 1951

Mechanical Fire Engine, clockwork with detachable ladder, adjustable steering Catalogue No. 3310. Size 6″. 1951

Lorries

Tip lorry. Catalogue No. 116. Size $7\frac{3}{4}''$ Price 7s per dozen. 1936–37 and 1940–41 **p. 94*

Tip lorry with trailer. Catalogue No. 118T Size $15\frac{3}{4}''$. Price 13s per dozen. 1936–37 and 1940

Tip lorry. Catalogue No. 122. Size $12\frac{1}{4}''$ Price 13s per dozen. 1936–37 and 1940

Tip lorry with trailer. Catalogue No. 122T Size 21″. Price 27s per dozen. 1936–37

Eight-wheeler lorry, removable truck Catalogue No. 128. Size $16\frac{1}{2}''$ Price 37s/6d per dozen. 1936–37 and 1939–40

Eight-wheeler, removable truck with six-wheeled trailer. Size 30″ Catalogue No. 128T. Price 60s per dozen. 1936–37 and 1940 **p. 94*

Large tip lorry. Catalogue No. 125 Size $11\frac{1}{4}''$. 1939–41

Lorry with trailer and hood Catalogue No. 118TH. Size $15\frac{3}{4}''$. 1940

Petrol lorry with pool on side Catalogue No. 114. Size 8″. 1939

Small petrol lorry with National on side Catalogue No. 113. Size 7″. 1940 With Esso on side, 1951

Eight-wheeler lorry with hood Catalogue No. 128H. Size 17″. 1939–41

Tip lorry with load, turnable and electric searchlight. Catalogue No. 124/6L Size $12\frac{1}{2}''$. 1940

Tip lorry. Catalogue No. 124. Size $12\frac{1}{2}''$ 1941

Large petrol lorry with two lights Catalogue No. 127/7. Size $10\frac{3}{4}''$. 1940

Eight-wheeler lorry with six-wheeler trailer and hoods Catalogue No. 128TH. Size $31\frac{1}{2}''$. 1940

Large low truck, two lights, heavy dipped finish. Catalogue No. 190/7. Size $13\frac{1}{2}''$ 1940

Timber lorry with load, heavy dipped finish Catalogue No. 193. Size 14″ 1940

Six-Wheeler Lorry. Catalogue No. 118 Size $9\frac{1}{2}''$. 1940

Large Petrol Lorry. Catalogue No. 127p Size 10″. 1940

Petrol Tanker, clockwork, 6-wheeler articulated. Catalogue No. 3114B Size $8\frac{1}{4}''$. 1951

Tip Lorry, clockwork fitted with strong motor. Catalogue No. 3116A. Size $7\frac{1}{2}''$ 1951 **p. 94*

Royal Mail Van, clockwork, 6-wheeler with rear door to open Catalogue No. 3123/3. Size $9\frac{3}{4}''$. 1951

Removal Van. Catalogue No. 116B Size $7\frac{1}{2}''$. 1941

Transport Carrier with 2 miniature cars Catalogue No. 119/3. Size $10\frac{1}{2}''$. 1941

Ambulance. Catalogue No. 123/2. Size 10″ 1941

Circus Van, clockwork with rear door to open. Catalogue No. 3123/4. Size $9\frac{3}{4}''$ 1951

Biscuit Van, 6 wheels with opening door at rear. Catalogue No. 3123/6. Size 10″ 1951

Petrol Tanker, clockwork, 6-wheeler with dummy feed pipe and control valve Catalogue No. 3127A. Size $10\frac{3}{4}''$. 1951

Eight-Wheel Lorry with detachable truck, fitted with stationary device Catalogue No. 3128/A. Size 17″. 1951

Delivery Van with strong clockwork and adjustable steering Catalogue No. 3314. Size $6\frac{1}{4}''$. 1951

Shoveller, 1951 (copy of toy made by Einfelt)

Tractor No.660

Road Rollers and Tractors

Tractor with clockwork mechanism and adjustable steering rubber tyred wheels. Catalogue No.660. Size $2\frac{5}{8}''$ 1951

Tractor with clockwork mechanism, detachable farm trailer, adjustable steering rubber wheels Catalogue No.661. Size $6\frac{1}{4}$. 1951

Heavy Tractor, steering wheel control Strong clockwork contained in rear driving wheel designed to pull farm implements. Catalogue No.3262 Size $7\frac{1}{2}''$. 1951

Giant Tractor, clockwork with starting handle and steering wheel control, rubber tyres on rear wheels Catalogue No.3264. Size $9\frac{1}{4}''$. 1951

Road Roller, diesel, automatic forward and backward movement. Catalogue No.181 Size $7\frac{3}{4}''$. Price 13s per dozen. 1936–37

Road Roller, large automatic forward and backward movement. Size $12\frac{1}{4}''$ Catalogue No.186. Price 37s/6d per dozen. 1936–37 and 1940

Road Roller, larger size, automatic forward and backward movement and one electric lamp. Catalogue No.186/6 Size $12\frac{1}{4}''$. Price 45s per dozen 1936–37 and 1940

Steam Roller, automatic forward or backward movement Catalogue No.182. Size 9″. 1940

Large Steam Roller, automatic backward movement. Catalogue No.187. Size 12 1940–41

Road Roller with clockwork mechanism and adjustable steering rubber tyred wheels. Catalogue No.663. Size 2″ 1951

Road Roller, automatic forward or backward action, steerable, strong clockwork mechanism. Size 8″ Catalogue No.6180/1. 1951 **p. 99*

Clockwork Steam Roller with automatic forward and backward movement adjustable steering Catalogue No.6182. Size 9″. 1951

Giant Steam Roller powerful clockwork automatic forward and reverse action, steerable. Catalogue No.6187/1 Size $11\frac{3}{4}''$. 1951

Road Roller fully detailed coloured model with mechanical to and fro action Catalogue No.8102. Size $4\frac{3}{8}''$. 1951

Shoveller, clockwork with eccentric movement, 1951

Commercial

No. 3123/6

BISCUIT VAN. 6-wheeler, with door at rear to open.

CAMION DE LIVRAISON DE BISCUITS, à 6 roues, avec ouverture facile par porte à l'arrière.

CAMION BIZCOCHES. 6 ruedas y puerta trasera que se puede abrir.

10 x $4\frac{1}{4}$ x 4 inches. 10 ozs.
255 x 105 x 100 mm. 280 gms.

No. 3123/4

BINGO'S CIRCUS. 6 wheeled, witn door at rear to open.

CIRQUE "BINGO," avec 6 roues et ayant portiere qui ouvre en arrier.

CIRCO "BINGO," con 6 rucdas y con e puerta abierta atras.

10 x $4\frac{1}{4}$ x 4 inches. 10 ozs.
255 x 105 x 100 mm. 280 gms.

BRITISH MADE

12

Page from Mettoy catalogue 1949

Military

Lorry with searchlight and 2 soldiers Catalogue No.135. Size 10″. Price 27s per dozen. 1937 and 1940

Lorry with anti-aircraft gun and 2 soldiers Catalogue No.136. Size 11″. Price 27s per dozen. 1937 and 1940

Lorry with 4 benches and 2 soldiers Catalogue No.138. Size $12\frac{1}{4}''$. Price 27s per dozen. 1937, 1940 and 1941

Lorry camouflaged with hood Catalogue No.117HC. Size $8\frac{1}{2}''$ 1930–40 **p. 94*

Six-Wheeler Lorry, camouflaged Catalogue No.119. Size $9\frac{1}{2}''$. 1939–41

Lorry with aeroplane carrier and aeroplane. Catalogue No.126A Size 16″. 1939 and 1940

Eight-Wheeler Lorry with 16 soldiers Catalogue No.128M. Size 17″. 1939 and 1941

Lorry with aeroplane and aeroplane with spark. Catalogue No.128C. Size 17″ 1939–41

Tank with sparking mechanism Catalogue No.131. Size $5\frac{1}{4}''$. 1939

Anti-Aircraft Unit with sparking gun Catalogue No.142. Size $14\frac{1}{2}''$. 1939

Army Gun Carriage with sparking gun Catalogue No.137. Size 11″. 1940

Large Army Tank with sparking mechanism. Catalogue No.132 Size $7\frac{1}{4}''$. 1940

Army Lorry with searchlight Catalogue No.140. Size $14\frac{1}{2}''$. 1940

Mechanised Carrier with 2 miniature aeroplanes. Catalogue No. 119/2 Size $10\frac{1}{2}$". 1941
Army Transport Van Catalogue No. 123/1. Size 10". 1941
Army Lorry with trailing searchlight Catalogue No. 126/1. Size 11". 1941
Army Lorry with trailing gun Catalogue No. 126/2. Size 12". 1941
Army Tank. Catalogue No. 131/1. Size $5\frac{1}{4}$" 1941
Heavy Army Tank with caterpillars, sparking gun and gun firing noise Catalogue No. 133. Size $8\frac{3}{4}$". 1941
Army Lorry with searchlight Catalogue No. 135A. Size $11\frac{1}{4}$". 1941
Army Lorry with sparking anti-aircraft gun and 2 soldiers. Catalogue No. 136A Size 12". 1941
Six-Wheel Lorry with special detachable aeroplane. Catalogue No. 3126/B Size 16". 1951
Army Motorcycle with sparking gun Catalogue No. 148. Size $5\frac{3}{4}$". 1939–40
Army Motorcycle with sidecar and sparking gun. Catalogue No. 159 Size 8". 1940
Large Army Motorcycle with sparking mechanism. Catalogue No. 158 Size $7\frac{1}{2}$". 1940
Motorcycle, camouflaged Catalogue No. 148/1. Size $5\frac{3}{4}$". 1941
Army Pillion Motorcycle, camouflaged Catalogue No. 156. Size 9". 1941
Army Gun. Catalogue No. 134. Size $6\frac{1}{2}$" 1940
Searchlight on base with morse tapper Catalogue No. 139A. Size $4\frac{1}{2}$". 1940
Anti-Aircraft Gun on base Catalogue No. 141. Size 6". 1940p
Searchlight Trailer on wheels Catalogue No. 144. Size $4\frac{1}{2}$". 1940
Army Gun, sparking. Catalogue No. 134A Size $6\frac{1}{2}$". 1939–41
Army Gun unit trailing gun Catalogue No. 137/1. Size 11". 1941
Army Lorry with 4 benches and 10 soldiers. Catalogue No. 138A. Size $12\frac{1}{4}$" 1941

MOTORCYCLES

With sidecar. Catalogue No. 153. Size 8" Price 13s per dozen. 1936–37 and 1940
With sparking mechanism Catalogue No. 151. Size $7\frac{3}{4}$". Price 13s per dozen. 1937 and 1940p
With sidecar and sparking mechanism Catalogue No. 161. Size $8\frac{3}{4}$". Price 27s per dozen. 1937
Motorcycle. Catalogue No. 149. Size $7\frac{1}{2}$" 1939 and 1941
Motorcycle. Catalogue No. 155. Size $8\frac{1}{2}$" 1939
With sidecar and pillion passenger Catalogue No. 160. Size $8\frac{3}{4}$". 1939–40
Gyro Cycle. Catalogue No. 2. Size 3" 1940
Motorcycle. Catalogue No. 150. Size $7\frac{1}{2}$" 1940
With sidecar, clockwork mechanism, AA and Clown. Catalogue No. 3022BA Size $3\frac{3}{8}$". 1951
Motorcyclist Sportsman, clockwork Catalogue No. 3149A. Size $7\frac{3}{4}$". 1951
Motorcyclist, clockwork, clown with pillion rider. Catalogue No. 3155. Size $8\frac{3}{4}$" 1951
Large Motorcycle Clown design *p. 102* Catalogue No. 3158/2. Size 7". 1951
Large Motorcycle Indian design *p. 103* Catalogue No. 3158/3. Size 7". 1951
Dirt Track Rider, fully detailed clockwork Catalogue No. 3158/4. Size $7\frac{1}{2}$". 1951

OTHER VEHICLES

Caravan only
Catalogue No. 95. Size $7\frac{1}{2}$". Price 13s per dozen. 1936

Car with caravan Catalogue No. 96 Size $17\frac{1}{2}$". Price 25s per dozen. 1936–37

Car with caravan Catalogue No. 97 Size 19". 1936 and 1940

Caravan No. 95

Motorcyclist sportsman No. 3149A

Advertisement for military vehicles, 1940 *Games and Toys*

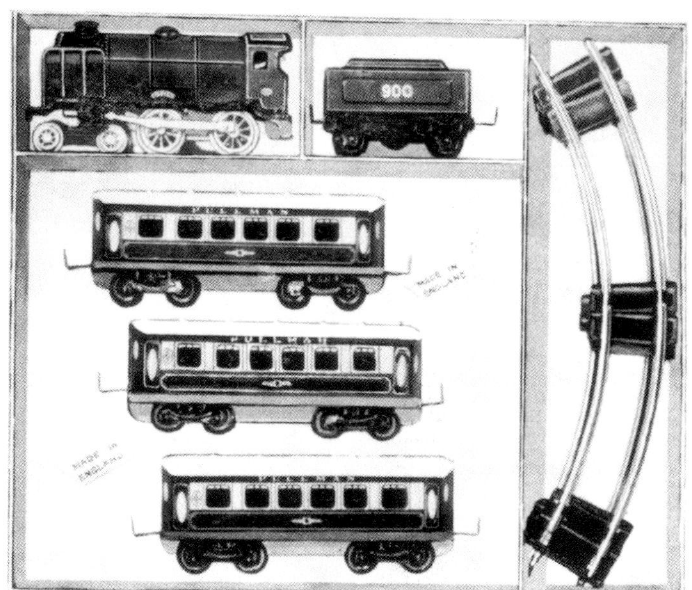

No. **453.**

. 453.	**Passenger Train Set:** Locomotive with Smoke Deflector and Piston Rod, heavy bogie, Tender, 3 Pullman Coaches, 6 heavy curved rails. **Chemin de Fer:** Locomotive avec Visière de cheminée et Tige de piston, bogie lourd, Tender, 3 Pullman Wagons, 6 rails courbes lourdes. **Ferrocarrile:** Locomotora con bogie, Visera de la chimenea y Vástago del embolo, Tender, 3 Pullman Vagónes, 6 rieles curvos sólidos.	$16\frac{3}{4} \times 14 \times 2\frac{1}{2}$ inches. 435 × 365 × 65 mm. 63 ozs. 1825 gramm.	**90/-** doz. 1 doz. per carton.

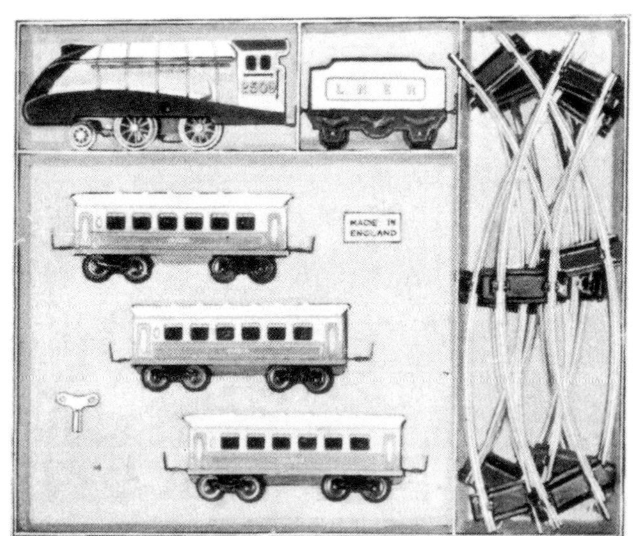

No. **463.**

463.	**Passenger Train Set:** Sparking Streamline Locomotive, Tender, 3 Pullman Coaches, 6 curved rails. **Chemin de Fer:** Locomotive Allumage Fuselé, Tender, 3 Pullman wagons, 6 rails courbes. **Ferrocarrile:** Locomotora Encendido Fusiforme, Tender, 3 Pullman Vagónes, 6 rieles curvos.	$16\frac{1}{2} \times 14 \times 2\frac{1}{2}$ inches. 430 × 365 × 65 mm. $57\frac{1}{4}$ ozs. 1660 gramm.	**108/-** doz. 1 doz. per carton.

Page from **Mettoy** catalogue, 1937

RAILWAYS

1936
Catalogue Nos. 491, 492, 493, 496, 497, 511, 512, 513, 530, 532, 535, 537, 540, 545, 602, 606, 610, 615

1937
Catalogue Nos. 341, 342, 351, 352, 353, 361, 362, 399, 402, 403, 404, 404c, 405, 431, 432, 451, 452, 453, 463, 471, 550, 552, 554, 556, 560, 561, 562, 565, 566, 567, 617, 617/6, 619, 630, 661, 662, 663, 651, 652, 653, 654, 658

1939
Catalogue Nos. 310, 337, 342, 348, 352, 353, 402, 404, 405a, 452a, 453, 456, 458, 524, 526, 529, 550, 555, 601

1940
Catalogue Nos. 311, 318, 320, 331, 332, 346, 347, 464, 457a, 702.

Locomotive and tender

AEROPLANES

Monoplanes

With detachable wing. Catalogue No. 6 Size 11″. Price 7s per dozen. 1936–37 and 1940 *p. 99*
Running and flying with detachable wing Catalogue No. 14. Size 19½″. Price 25s per dozen. 1936–37 and 1940
Running and detachable wing and one green and one red electric light Catalogue No. 14/7. Size 19½″. Price 31s per dozen. 1936–37 and 1940
With detachable wing, camouflaged Catalogue No. 9. Size 12″. 1939 and 1940
With detachable wing. Catalogue No. 10 Size 13″. 1939
Camouflaged. Catalogue No. 11C Size 12″. 1939 and 1941
Monoplane. Catalogue No. 11. Size 12″ 1940
With two engines and running propellor Catalogue No. 11A. Size 12″. 1940
With two cruising aeroplanes Catalogue No. 21. Size 12″. 1940

Monoplane (Export). Catalogue No. 10 Size 13″. 1940
With sparking mechanism (Export) Catalogue No. 12. Size 12″. 1940
Large with 2 lights (Export) Catalogue No. 16/7. Size 15½″. 1940
With detachable wing camouflaged Catalogue No. 7. Size 11″. 1941 *p. 18*
With sparking mechanism, wing folds back, camouflaged. Catalogue No. 12C Size 12″. 1941
Large Monoplane. Catalogue No. 16A Size 15½″. 1941
Running and flying with detachable wing Catalogue No. 14c. Size 19½″. 1941
With clockwork mechanism and brake Catalogue No. 2005. Size 5″. 1951
Clockwork No. 2007A. Size 11″. 1951
Clockwork with folding wings and working safety propeller. Catalogue No. 2012A Size 12¼″. 1951
Clockwork with detachable wing Catalogue No. 2010/1. Size 12½″. 1951
Clockwork, hinged wing Catalogue No. 2011. Size 11½″. 1951

Biplanes

With detachable wing and electric light Catalogue No. 6B6. Size 11″ Price 13s per dozen. 1936–37
With detachable wings Catalogue No. 10B. Size 14½″ Price 13s per dozen. 1936–37
Running and flying with detachable wings Catalogue No. 14B. Size 19½″ Price 33s per dozen. 1936–37 and 1940
Running and flying with detachable wings plus one white light in centre Catalogue No. 14B6. Size 19½″ Price 37s/6d per dozen. 1936–37
Running and flying with detachable wings plus green and red electric light Catalogue No. 14B7. Size 19½″ Price 40s per dozen. 1936
With sparking gun and running propeller camouflaged. Catalogue No. 12Bc Size 12″. 1939–41
With 2 lights, sparking gun and running propeller, camouflaged Catalogue No. 12B7c. Size 12″. 1939
Running and flying with detachable wings Catalogue No. 15B. Size 19½″. 1939–41
With sparking gun and running propeller Catalogue No. 12B. Size 12″. 1940
With single light, sparking gun and running propeller. Catalogue No. 12B6 Size 12″. 1940
With 2 lights, sparking gun and running propeller. Catalogue No. 12B7 Size 12″. 1940
With 2 lights, green and red, running and flying with detachable wings Catalogue No. 15B7. Size 19½″. 1940
Large Biplane with 2 running propellers and 3-action clockwork Catalogue No. 17B. Size 15½″. 1940
Large Biplane with 2 lights, two running propellors and 3-action clockwork Catalogue No. 17B7. Size 15½″. 1940

Monoplane No. 2005

Others

Tower with 2 cruising aeroplanes Catalogue No. 164. Size 7¾″. 1939–40
Lighthouse, 3 cruising aeroplanes and light. Catalogue No. 169. Size 11½″ 1939–40
Aerodrome with cruising aeroplane Catalogue No. 3. Size 5½″. 1940
Autogyro with running blades and propeller. Catalogue No. 19. Size 12″ 1940
Large Tower with 2 cruising aeroplanes Catalogue No. 167. Size 9½″. 1940
Airport with two aeroplanes and one miniature car, non-mechanical, folding cardboard base. Catalogue No. 162 Size 10½″. 1941
Airport with 2 cruising aeroplanes mechanical and 2 stationary aeroplanes, folding cardboard base Catalogue No. 163. Size 10½″

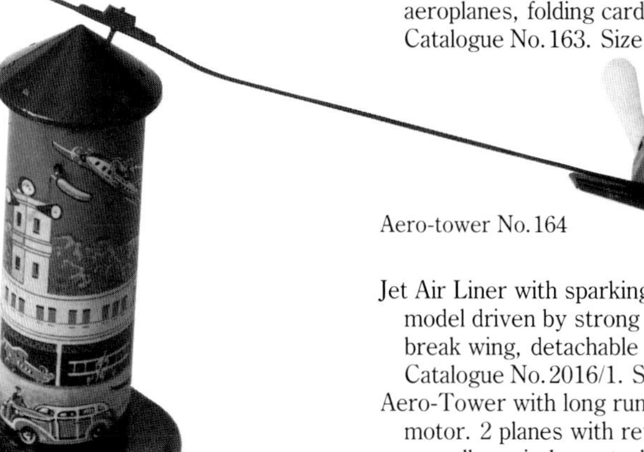
Aero-tower No. 164

Jet Air Liner with sparking engines, heavy model driven by strong clockwork with break wing, detachable Catalogue No. 2016/1. Size 15½″. 1951
Aero-Tower with long running clockwork motor. 2 planes with revolving propellers circle control tower Catalogue No. 2164/1. Size 11″. 1951

Dolls' house No.6255

DOMESTIC WARE

Brush and Pan Sets With dustpan, duster, handbrush, feather duster, long mop. Catalogue No.234. Size 22" 1931–41
With dustpan, duster, handbrush, long mop, 2 feather dusters, broom Catalogue No.236. Size $27\frac{1}{2}$". 1939–41
Brush and Pan Set. Catalogue No.230 Size $9\frac{1}{4}$". 1940
With dipped finish. Catalogue No.231 Size $9\frac{1}{4}$". 1940
With apron, duster, dustpan, handbrush, 2 feather dusters, long mop, broom Catalogue No.237. Size 25". 1940
With apron, duster, dustpan, handbrush, 2 feather dusters, long mop, broom, handmop. Catalogue No.238. Size 25" 1940
Brush and Pan Set. Catalogue No.229 Size $9\frac{1}{4}$". 1941
With dustpan, handbrush, duster, long mop, feather duster, carpet sweeper Catalogue No.239. Size $23\frac{1}{2}$". 1941
With dustpan, long mop, feather duster, handbrush, broom, duster, carpet sweeper. Catalogue No.240. Size $27\frac{1}{2}$" 1941

Carpet Sweepers Catalogue No.250 Size $5\frac{1}{4}$". 1941
Catalogue No.252. Size $6\frac{1}{4}$". 1941
Catalogue No.254. Size $7\frac{3}{4}$". 1941

Telephone Catalogue No.282. Size 9" 1939 and 1941
Catalogue No.280. Size 9". 1940

Kitchen Stoves Catalogue No.290 Size 8". 1939–41
With utensils. Catalogue No.292 Size $15\frac{1}{2}$". 1940 and 1941
Stove Utensils. Saucepan, frying pan, round dish, meat dish, two lids Catalogue No.289. Size 9". 1939–40

MISCELLANEOUS

Furnished Dolls' House with garage and car, 6 rooms, chimney and TV aerial Catalogue No.6255. Size 23". 1951–55

Filling Station Catalogue No.4 Size $9\frac{3}{4}$". 1939–41

Filling Station and Car Catalogue No.4C. Size $9\frac{3}{4}$". 1939–41
Garage with miniature car Catalogue No.3c. Size 5". 1941

Clown and Drum Catalogue No.1110 Size 9". 1941

Clown and Xylophone Catalogue No.1115. Size 9". 1941

Cat with Bell Catalogue No.1132 Size $11\frac{1}{2}$". 1941

Jumping Rabbit Catalogue No.1136 Size $11\frac{1}{4}$". 1941

Runaway Dog Catalogue No.1140 Size 10". 1941

Circus Catalogue No.1159A. Size 12" 1941

Dog and Bell Catalogue No.1214 Size 12". 1941

Billy the Fisherman No.6330

Jumbo Elephant Catalogue No.1217 Size 9". 1941

Jumbo and Roller Catalogue No.1218 Size 15". 1941

Bellroller Catalogue No.1221. Size 16" 1941

Porter and Truck with clanging bell Catalogue No.1230. Size $12\frac{1}{4}$". 1941

Jockey on Donkey with galloping movement. Catalogue No.1235. Size 9" 1941

Lifting Jack for car Catalogue No.6205. Size $3\frac{3}{4}$". 1951

Willoughby Cartooner Fascinating tracing device with pantograph movement Catalogue No.4850. Size 14". 1951

Fearless Freddie Mechanical acrobat on his flying trapeze. Catalogue No.6172 Size $11\frac{1}{2}$". 1951

Twin Tunnel Train Passenger and goods trains travel around until stopped at the station by signal brake. Aeroplane circles overhead. Clockwork, metal base Catalogue No.6166/1. Size $6\frac{1}{2}$". 1951

Joytown Service Station Garage with sliding doors and open 2-seater sports car and saloon car. Clockwork with adjustable steering. Catalogue No.6200. Size $8\frac{1}{4}$" 1951

Joytown Fire Station with sliding doors. Clockwork fire tender and fire chief. Catalogue No.6201. Size $8\frac{1}{4}$" 1951. Also **Flying Squad Station** with police and ambulance. *p. 98*

Car fitted with fly-wheel drive and siren Catalogue No.6201. Size $8\frac{1}{4}$". 1951

Bobby the Walking Policeman Clockwork. Catalogue No.6310. Size 5" 1951

Giddy the Walking Gnome Clockwork driven. Catalogue No.6311. Size 5". 1951

Billy the Fisherman Fishes for 15 minutes on one winding Catalogue No.6330. Size $4\frac{1}{4}$". 1951

Mystery Road Race Track and clockwork car, automatic direction change Catalogue No.6410. Size 20". 1951

Joytown Grand Prix Pit 2 racing cars cross over 14 curved and 2 straight track sections. Catalogue No.6417. Size 14" 1951

Happy Hayseed and his bucking tractor Powerful clockwork motor Catalogue No.6439. Size 6". 1951

High Speed Launch Strong clockwork, adjustable steering, water resisting Catalogue No.6602. Size $7\frac{3}{4}$". 1951 *p. 98*

Ocean Liner Strong clockwork, adjustable steering, water resisting Catalogue No.6603. Size $7\frac{1}{4}$". 1951

Cabin Cruiser Largest model, strong clockwork, adjustable steering Catalogue No.6607. Size $14\frac{1}{4}$". 1951

Super Speed Race Track with clockwork car. Catalogue No.6409 Size 14". 1951

Sub-Machine Gun with sparks flying from barrel and realistic repeating noise Catalogue No. 7101. Size 21". 1951

Disneyland Moviedrome 6 cartoon colour strips showing Disney characters in action. Catalogue No. 7160. Size $6\frac{1}{2}$". 1951

Disneyland Skating Rink Mickey and Donald in action. Catalogue No. 7154 Size $6\frac{1}{4}$". 1951

Pick-a-Winna Derby Party Game Catalogue No. 7070. Size $6\frac{1}{4}$". 1951

Model Drophead Sewing Machine Hand wheel operated needle bar, moving treadle and opening drawers Catalogue No. 8001/1. Size $4\frac{3}{4}$". 1951

Ducky He rolls his eyes and jabbers away as he runs around. Clockwork Catalogue No. 8006. Size 4". 1951

Blackbird Pie Catalogue No. 6176 Size 9". 1958 **p. 99*

Jack-in-the-Box A musical surprise action toy. Turn the handle and it plays the tune 'pop goes the weasel' Catalogue No. 6177. Size $6\frac{1}{4}$". 1948

Airport Metal Construction Catalogue No. 6272. Size $23\frac{1}{2}$". 1958

Service station Catalogue No. 6280 Size $24\frac{5}{8}$". 1958

'Supertype' Typewriter Provision made for storage of stationery Catalogue No. 4317. Size $11\frac{1}{4}$". 1951

Jack-in-the-box No. 6177

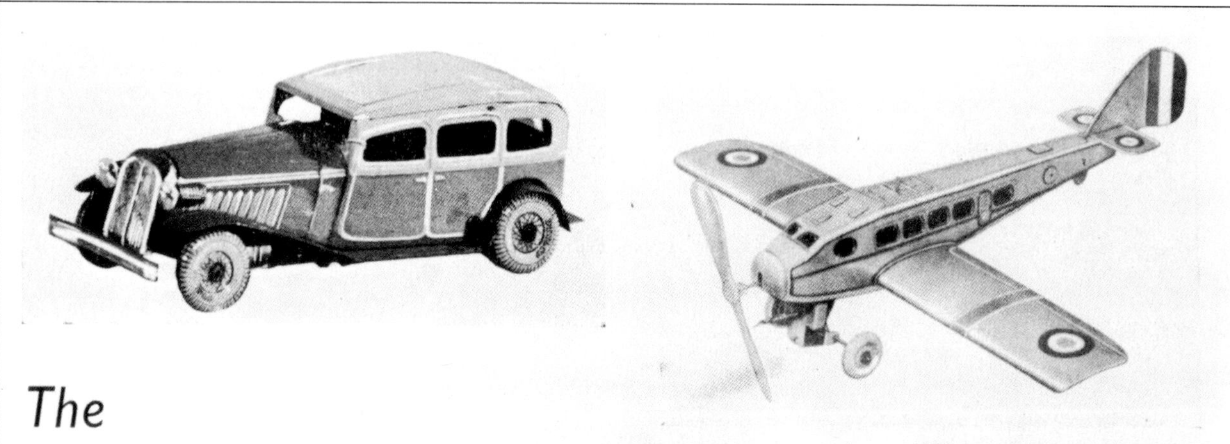

Advertisement from 1936 *Games and Toys*

Advertisement from 1940 *Games and Toys*

APPENDIX IV

Wells-Brimtoy 1914–present day

The roots of the present day firm of CMT Wells Kelo of Holyhead, North Wales stretch back to the outbreak of World War I. Certain toys such as metal spades and seaside buckets were in production from 1914 until four or five years ago. The first clockwork train set produced in England was hailed as a triumph for the British toy trade by *The Times* in 1915. Metal clockwork train set no. 980 still featured in Wells Kelo catalogues for 1986.

In view of the company's long history and its various metamorphoses, it has been decided to list the principal toys produced in the seven different stages of its existence. Once the tools for a specific toy had been made, they continued in use for many years with only minor variations and the dates given in the following list are those of its first appearance, either in the trade journal *Games and Toys*, or in the firm's catalogue for the appropriate year. The company's history may be divided into seven parts:

British Metal and Toy Manufacturers Ltd, 1914–1921

Brimtoy Ltd, 1923–1932

A Wells and Company, 1919–1932

Wells-Brimtoy Ltd, 1932–1939

Wells-Brimtoy Distributors, 1945–1965

CMT Wells Kelo Ltd, 1970–1981
(part of the Central Manufacturing and Trading firm)

1981, CMT purchased by Casparo Industries Ltd

The British Metal and Toy Manufacturers Ltd 1914–1921

The manufacturers of the clockwork cars advertised in October 1914 in the trade journal *Games and Toys* were not alone in recognising that the war with Germany would leave a void in the home market which they could hope to fill. On 12 September 1914, The British Metal and Toy Manufacturers Ltd was registered as a new company. Its financial support came from a large Welsh company, Richard Thomas & Co. Ltd, who owned the South Wales Steel and Tinplate Works at Llanelly, as well as tinplate works in Lydney and the Forest of Dean in Gloucestershire.

The new company's toymaking was based on a small foundry, The Riverside Metal Works, at 129 Highbury Quadrant, London. Its trademark, Nelson's Column encircled by the words 'Brimtoy Brand. British Made' was registered on 4 December 1914 (No. 364815). The Managing Director, Mr Sidney Stowe, had previously run on the same premises a metal manufacturing company, J Lunzer & Co. Ltd; and before the outbreak of war he had investigated the possibility of producing in

Sidney Stowe, August 1918 (above)

Clockwork assembly room, Riverside Metal Works, 1918 (right)

Clockwork train set from 1915 *Games and Toys* (above)

First tourer, 1919 (right)

Brimtoy trademark, 1915 (below)

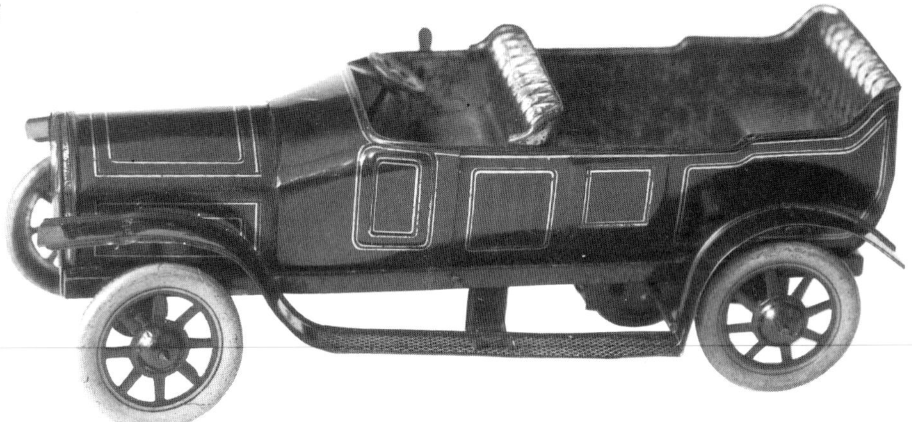

his Highbury works a metal appropriate for making clockwork. From 1914 onwards, the factory was principally engaged in a government war contract; but Stowe used scrap metal – and overtime and night shift work – on toy production, and soon the first clockwork locomotive made entirely in Great Britain was careering round Sir Solhern Holland's office at the Board of Trade.

It was 'a great achievement', said an article in *The Times* recording the event some time after. According to contemporary accounts the factory was a model of compactness, and the systematic methods of production were commented on at length. Over 8,000 tinplate sheets were printed per day; and there were 48 heavy powered presses and over 100 small hand-presses. The clockwork assembly was chiefly the work of women and girls. The machine tools and the cardboard boxes were also made on the premises.

The first products of the new company were clockwork train sets and railway accessories; then pull-along-carpet engines, little toy kitchen stoves, dolls' kitchen accessories, and tin moulds for building sandcastles. It would seem that the first Brimtoy car did not go into production until 1918, and could not possibly have been made for Brimtoy by the German firm of Bing, as has been suggested by some books on tin toys. However, we do know that Stowe had in his office a collection of German toys. Significant, too, is the fact that the British Metal Toy Manufacturers' sales manager, Oswald Benjamin, who joined the firm in May 1915, had previously worked for Bing as their London representative.

Sidney Stowe seems to have had a certain taste for public speaking and a flair for getting his firm's activities reported in the press. Soon after the outbreak of war, at an exhibition at the Victoria and Albert Museum, he was addressing a meeting of British metalworkers and toy manufacturers on the need to replace German imports by British made goods. In 1918, government officials, local dignitaries and journalists invited to the opening of the works' welfare rooms and canteens at Highbury were told that 'all the workers are given lectures on all subjects affecting the factory, and each one is made to feel that he or she is not only a unit, but a valuable cog in the machinery of production'.

Very soon afterwards, Stowe is once more addressing the public, this time on the subject of everyone's right to work, and the need and duty to provide suitable employment for our brave homecoming war heroes. The occasion was the opening of a Metal Crafts Training Institute, annexed to the factory, for the training of discharged soldiers and sailors. Stowe had hoped to get government support for this scheme, but to no avail; to no avail also was his last appeal to the public before he disappeared from view.

In March 1919, he addressed a large group of toy buyers, seeking their support for British made toys in preference to German. 'The alleged deficiency in design and quality of British made toys is caused, not by inefficiency, but by shortage of raw materials,' he

Stand H 59.—British Metal & Toy Manufacturers, Ltd., Audrey House, Ely Place, London, W.C.

The above firm have taken one of the largest spaces at the Exhibition, and there is no doubt that many buyers will attend this stall. Although only recently established, the progress that this firm is making is wonderful, and the "Brimtoy" brand of metal toys is already famous throughout the trade. The feature of this stand, in our opinion, will be their clockwork train. This compares favourably with the German. The price of this, including track, commences at 1s., and this comprises engine and tender. The other prices go up to half a guinea, and we can assure our readers that this train is one of the best British-made toys that has ever been produced. The finish is excellent. There are no sharp corners whereby a child can cut the hands. The printing is beautiful, while the circle of rails is well made and has no sharp points. This firm will also be showing a range of railway accessories, such as signal boxes, station, goods sheds, etc. These are made to sell at 1s., and we particularly call our readers' attention to the finish of these goods, which is a point the manufacturers have evidently paid much attention to.

The British Metal & Toy Manufacturers, Ltd., are making a fine range of tin teasets, for which they can guarantee immediate delivery. These are put on the market in various designs and subjects. On view at their exhibit will also be shown a fine range of kitchen sets to retail at 1s. These are manufactured in assorted colours, and are so made that they can be packed nicely in a box for export.

Advertisement from *Games and Toys*, 1915

said. The size of a tinplate is 28 by 20 inches. But it has been impossible during these war years to secure a single sheet for toymaking. Waste cuttings of all sorts, sizes and gauges have had to be used; defective and rusty metal has had to be cleaned and hammered out – thus increasing the prices. Shortages of wire and metal for making pinions were acute. No lead was available for making wheels, so tin ones had to be used. Lead was also needed in the soldering processes and above all in the printing inks – often plates had to go twice through the printing presses because of the poor quality of the wartime substitute inks.'

Nevertheless, in spite of a further cash injection by Richard Thomas & Co., Stowe's plea for cooperation from the toy buyers and wholesalers during the difficult transition from war to peace had no success; on 1 November 1921, a compulsory winding-up order was issued on the firm.

The official bankruptcy report makes chilling reading. Failure of the company during the years 1919–21 due to the importation of toys from Germany; raw materials bought at a time when prices were high, but products having to be sold below the cost of production; the company's affairs entirely controlled by one director – Mr Sidney Stowe – and according to the company secretary Mr Jones, the failure largely due to Mr Stowe's mismanagement. Considerable transactions appear to have taken place between the company and other concerns in which he was interested – the Safety Box Co. and the Metal Crafts Training Institute. 'Mr Stowe', added the secretary, 'is believed to have left the country.'

Brimtoy Ltd 1923–1932

Mr Stowe disappeared from the scene somewhat ambiguously. But Mr Jones and the other directors, free from debts and other encumbrances, soon reappeared at the helm of a new company: Brimtoy Ltd, registered on 4 August 1923 – at the same address, Riverside Works, Highbury Quadrant; with the same showrooms in Holborn; and producing during the next nine years, under the direction of Mr T H Brimfield, the same range of toys. This with the addition of more boats, different types of motor cars, a crane, tin dolly baths and a novelty engine whose driver every now and then looked out of the cabin window to see if the way was all clear.

In 1932, Brimtoy was absorbed into another North London tin toy-making firm, Wells o' London. Welsh

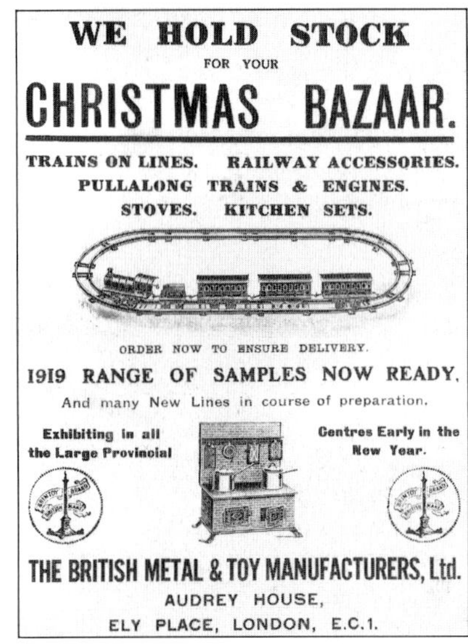

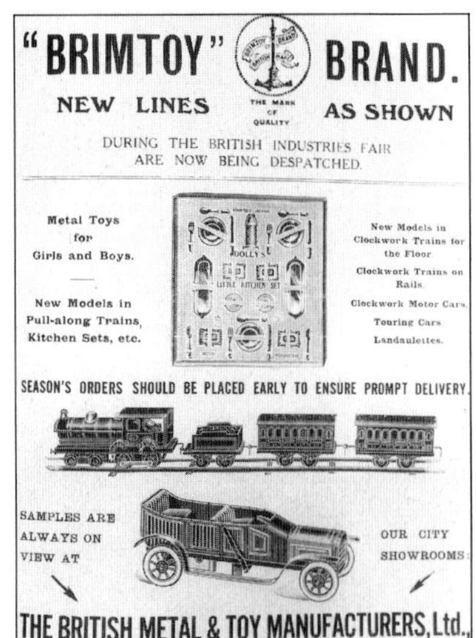

Advertisements from *Games and Toys* (left to right) 1917, 1918, 1919

W P Jones, 1918

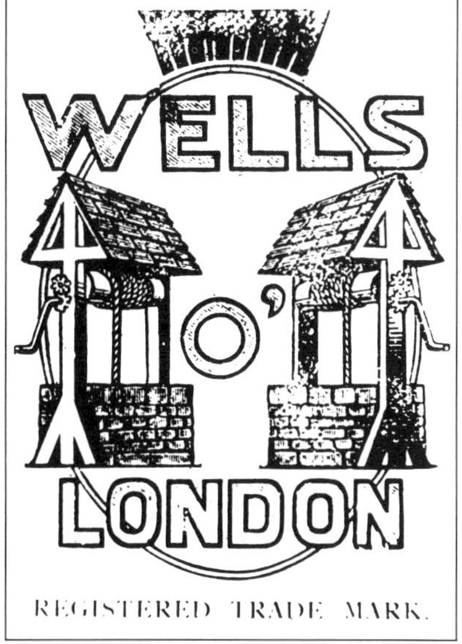

Trademark of A Wells & Co. Ltd. 1924

Alfred Wells, 1926

know-how, finance and enterprise had helped create Brimtoy Ltd – the outstanding success and phenomenal growth of Wells o' London was due to the force of character and personality of one man – Alfred W J Wells.

A Wells & Co. Ltd 1919–1932

Like the Crooked Lane tinmen or the toymakers interviewed by Mayhew in 1850, Alfred Wells had started work in one tiny basement room. The address was 28 Dame Street, Islington – the date, 1919. The products were first a metal toy crane and next a small metal tennis racquet. Wells was his own factory hand, office boy, packer and salesman, his only assistant being a younger sister; but, unlike his Elizabethan and Victorian predecessors, Alfred Wells had had a solid engineering training at Chubb's Safety Locks, and was capable of designing his own, rather unorthodox machine tools. Capable, too, of landing a large order from the chain store, Woolworth's. Thus the firm A Wells & Co. Ltd was born; larger premises were acquired, first at Shepherdess Walk, near Kings Cross, then at Somers Road, Walthamstow; and in 1924, the trademark 'Wells o' London' was registered.

Shortly after the move to Walthamstow the firm's mechanical era began, with the production of a clockwork train set with 0 gauge track, which retailed at 6d per set. Not even the Germans could equal this rock bottom price. For whereas German competitors had factories specialising in one item only, like mechanisms or wheels, it was a principle of Wells' company to make all associated parts on the premises, since Britain at that time had not yet established a toy industry and the only source of such supplies was Germany itself. In the opinion of Mr J McCarter, then technical advisor to the company, there was no doubt that this principle played a great part in its success. At all events it was during this period that the business expanded at a remarkable rate, with the company employing its own travellers and beginning to export its own products. By 1930, another factory, covering an area of 2½ acres, had been built at Walthamstow, in Stirling Road.

The Vestry House Museum in Walthamstow has made a special effort to collect toys and material

The Press room, Somers Road factory, 1926. Accidents were frequent, especially on the guillotines

Somers Road factory, 1926. Each girl assembled one toy at a time

Advertisements from Games and Toys (left to right from top) 1920, 1927, 1928, 1929

connected with the factories of Wells-Brimtoy and their next-door neighbour, W Britain Ltd. In 1974, in conjunction with an exhibition devoted to local industries, the Museum's staff recorded a number of interviews with people who remembered working at Somers Road, Stirling Road and the woodwork shop at Gosport Road.

Mr 'Alfie' Wells was described as a strict employer, 'an old-fashioned Victorian type'. One woman who had started work in the factory at the age of 15 said 'he came from the West End, and was a very tough personality. He used to swear a lot, and drink'. She left at the age of 20 to get married; but many stayed on with

The Wells-Brimtoy factory in Stirling Road occupied over one acre of land in 1935. The Wells-Brimtoy delivery van at the 1935 Olympia Trade Fair (inset)

the firm until it moved to Wales, and one recalled how Mr Wells offered to buy him a house in Holyhead and pay for a nurse to look after his elderly, invalid mother.

Others described how in 1928–9 a conveyor-belt system was installed in the Somers Road factory (possibly the first in the British Isles), and how the foreman and the manager had their offices positioned above the factory floor, where they could see everything that was going on and regulate the speed of the conveyor belt. There was no union, and no canteen facilities at the Somers Road factory.

Wells-Brimtoy Ltd 1932–39

In 1932, when Brimtoy Ltd was taken over, its factory in Highbury was kept in full production. Two years later, in 1934, Mr Wells was elected chairman of the British Toy Manufacturers' Association. A contemporary caricature shows him blazing away, repeater cap and pea pistol in hand, while his firm's sparking loco fired away at his feet. The caption: 'Mr A W J Wells creating much noise and sparkle at the Toy Fair'.

Each year some 12 to 20 new lines were tooled up. An engineer who was with the firm from 1927 till the outbreak of World War II described some of the manufacturing processes:

'One of the German machines which Mr Wells had bought in the twenties made wheels for tin toys from two long strips of tin which were fed into the machine in lengths just sufficient for one side of a wheel to be cut out; and the two halves of the hollow wheels were joined inside the machine before popping out at the other end ready to be enamelled. At this date the metal fed into the machines was not printed with the designs of the toys, and everything had to be enamelled after it was completed. Later, sheets of tin were printed with the toy designs, before being cut and pressed into shape, by a firm called Feavers in Tower Bridge Road. The Somers Road factory had a paint-spraying shop.

'These German machines were made by a firm called ALBA. Mr Wells seems to have regularly visited the Leipzig Toy Fair, and he enjoyed adapting the machines he bought to make different types of toys or to work more efficiently. He particularly favoured machines which could make complete parts for the toys, such as wheels, from continuous strips of metal, as this was more economical than having the various stages done by women workers in the factory. The women were still used for assembling the toys, however.

'Machines also made the winding handles, from wire strips. Huge rolls of wire the size of car tyres were stored at the factory, for making axles and keys. The keys were often made from square wire, as this prevented them from slipping on the cogs. One machine did the whole process of cutting the key, complete with bent loop handle. All the parts for the clockwork mechanism were also made at the factory – 10-foot rods of extruded brass were supplied by the Delta Metal Co. of Greenwich, to be sliced into the thin cogs required. Later, in the thirties, Wells were also making lead wheels, die-cast, for train sets at the Stirling Road factory, since it was necessary to give the tin trains sufficient weight to stay on the rails.

Advertisement from *Games and Toys*, 1940

'At the Stirling Road factory there were the following departments: machine shop, toolroom with five toolmakers, paintshop, and die-casting shop – all on the ground floor. Across the yard – a packing shed with a store above. Upstairs in the main factory was the assembly room, with about 100–150 girls working there.'

Thus the great majority of the workers were women, often quite young girls. In the 1930s times were hard, money was short, and many were laid off after Christmas until new orders were received. During these periods of unemployment some employees painted Britains' toy soldiers at home. For painting a gross of knights on horseback they were paid 3s 6d.

The War Years 1939–45

In World War II, two of the firm's factories were destroyed in the blitz – Somers Road and Highbury; while the main factory at Walthamstow, and new ones in Barnet and Holyhead, Anglesey, had to concentrate on war production. Upwards of 1,000 employees worked by day and night producing (among other equipment) gas masks, Sten gun magazines, and anti-vibration devices essential for protecting instrumentation in aircraft. Until 1941, a few tin toys were, however, produced for the export market; for during the early months of the 'phoney' war, tin was not really in short supply. It was aluminium that was scarce – over 1,200 tons of expensive tin, for instance, were used to make milk bottle tops, to save on aluminium foil.

The Japanese attack on Pearl Harbour in late 1941 put a stop to the use of tin for all non-essential products; and for several years after the end of the war the quotas of metal allocated by the Ministry of Supply were very small indeed.

Post-War – Wells-Brimtoy Distributors Ltd 1945–65

After the war, the company formed its own sales organisation, Wells-Brimtoy Distributors Ltd, and turned its attention to peace-time production. A new 80,000 square feet factory was financed and erected by the company at Kingsland, Holyhead and officially opened by Lady Megan Lloyd George in 1946. The London branch of the organisation was made responsible for the design and complete tooling-up for mass production of alarm clocks; and London technicians went to Holyhead to train unskilled workers in the intricate techniques of horology. Within twelve months, some 400–500 people were being employed, and an output of 15,000 clocks per week was achieved and maintained till 1952. The company was known as the Anglesey Instrument and Clock Company – the trademark for the clocks was 'Weltime'.

Meanwhile the older Holyhead factory changed over to tin toy production, including tin whistles and noise makers for what is known as the 'toy filling trade', and clockwork mechanisms to feed the Walthamstow factory. This factory meanwhile resumed the production of innumerable mechanical lithographed toys and games for its many wholesale and retail customers. By now plastic had been developed, and the Pocket Toy series of miniature clockwork toys, launched in 1949, was in metal and plastic. The company's turnover during these years was almost 1 million.

In 1955, a new trademark, 'Welsotoys', was registered and appeared on the new ranges of wooden and plastic toys which were added to the older clockwork, friction or gyro-driven vehicles. Meanwhile, however, competition from cheap Japanese imports was affecting the company adversely. The Barnet and Walthamstow factories were soon closed down and all production concentrated at the Progress Works, Kingsland, Holyhead, which were greatly expanded and modernised.

In October 1965, the company's founder, Mr A W J Wells, died at the age of 77, and the company found itself obliged to seek financial assistance from outside.

C M T Wells Kelo Ltd 1970 – the present day

The solution was found in the amalgamation of the firm with Keith Lowe, engineers and makers of large metal toys such as scooters, rocking horses and pogo sticks, sold under the brand name of 'Kelotoys'. Keith Lowe was part of the Central Manufacturing and Trading Group Ltd, so the new company's name became C M T Wells Kelo. It was very successful during the 1970s, when its wide-ranging products included, besides hardware and anti-vibration mountings, mechanical toys in plastic and metal, and children's trikes, scooters and pedal cars.

C M T Wells Kelo was acquired in its turn in 1981 by Caparo Industries Ltd, whose director Mr Swraj Paul was a friend of Mrs Indira Gandhi, Prime Minister of India, and has large family interests in several Indian steel mills. A far cry from 'Alfie' Wells's basement workshop in Dame Street, Islington.

WELLS-BRIMTOY DISTRIBUTORS LTD.
STIRLING ROAD, WALTHAMSTOW, LONDON E.17.

Post-war advertisements from *Games and Toys*

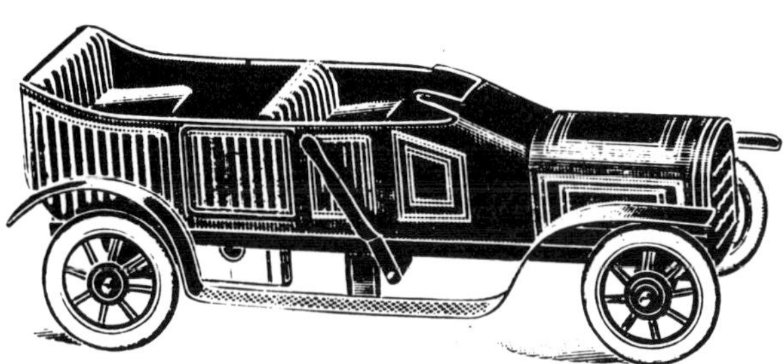

Brimtoy open tourer, 1919

Brimtoy delivery van, 1918

Brimtoy clockwork covered lorry, No.74

Brimtoy model tractor No.87

Brimtoy clockwork liner No.91 (above)
Brimtoy monster pull-along engine, 1920 (left)

The prices and numbers for the British Metal and Toy Manufacturers and Brimtoy Ltd come from the 1929 catalogue. The catalogue numbers for the early years of Wells and Company come from the 1932 catalogue, the prices 3d, 6d and 1s lines are the retail chain store prices.

The British Metal & Toy Manufacturers Ltd 1914–21

Factory: Riverside Works, 129 Highbury Quadrant, London
Showroom: Audrey House, Ely Place, Holborn, London
Company registered: 12 September 1914
Directors: S Stowe, W P Jones, C H Bond
Trademarks: Nelson's Column, Brimtoy Brand, British-Made

CARS AND OTHER VEHICLES

Open Tourer Clockwork. Size 11″. 1918

Delivery Van Clockwork. 'Brimtoy Express Delivery' on side. Size 11″. 1918

Covered Lorry Clockwork. Adjustable for straight or circular run. Size 12″. 1920
Catalogue No.74

Mail Van Clockwork. Size 11″. 1920

Tractor Clockwork, slow running
Catalogue No.87. Size 7″. 1920

RAILWAYS

Train Sets
Locomotive, tender, 1 coach and track
Clockwork. Price 1s a set. 1914
Locomotive, tender, 3 coaches and track
Clockwork. Price 10s 6d a set. 1915
(Locomotive No.265 'Lloyd George'
Railway Stations, 1915
Railway Signals, 1915
Monster pull-along engine, red and green
Size $16\frac{1}{2}$″ long×8″ high. 1920

DOMESTIC TOYS

Kitchen Range with shelf and 2 oven doors, 3 saucepans, 1 grater and 3 baking dishes. Size $7\frac{1}{2}$″. 1915

Kitchen Range with shelf and 2 oven doors, 2 saucepans, 1 grater and 3 baking dishes. Size $7\frac{1}{2}$″. 1917

Dolly's Little Kitchen Set, 1917

Dolls' Tea Sets 1917

Doll's Bath on Stand
Catalogue No.53/2. Size 6″ long×5″ high
1920

MISCELLANEOUS

Houses and Towers for shaping sandcastles, 1916

Mystery Crane When bucket is placed on hook, it descends with circular movement. The hook then rises to its original position. Catalogue No.56
Size 12″ high. 1920

Metal Guns and Swords advertised in 1915

Also agents for **Vertical Steam Engine** made by subsidiary Metalcraft Training Institute. 1918

Liners Clockwork, 2 funnels. 1919
Clockwork, 3 funnels. 1920
Catalogue No.91. Size 11″ long

Brimtoy Carter Paterson van, No.13, c.1927 (top)
Brimtoy Speedboat Nos.B6–B8 (above)
Brimtoy 'All Clear' clockwork locomotive, 1924 (left)

Brimtoy Ltd 1922–32

Factory: Riverside Metal Works, Green Lanes, Highbury, London
Office and Showrooms:
1924 133 Highbury Quadrant, London
1929–31 103 Aldersgate Street, London
Director: T H Brimfield
Trademark: Nelson's Column, Brimtoy Brand

CARS AND OTHER VEHICLES

Royal Mail Van Open cab and driver, opening rear door. Tyres Dunlop Ltd Clockwork No. Plate MS 3517
Price 12s 6d per dozen
Catalogue No.100. Size 10″. 1929
Catalogue No.100E with electric light

Express Transport Van Clockwork 1929. Variation on Royal Mail Van
Catalogue No.100. Size 10″. Price 12s 6d per dozen

Express Transport Van Clockwork 1929. Variation on Royal Mail Van
Catalogue No.100. Size 10″. Price 12s 6d per dozen. Catalogue No.101E, with electric light

Limousine with chauffeur. Clockwork 1929. Catalogue No.131. Size 14½″
Price 24s per dozen. Catalogue No.131E, with electric light. Price 30s per dozen

Open Sports Car Clockwork. 1929
Catalogue No.129. Size 11″
Price 24s per dozen. Catalogue No.129E, with electric light. Price 30s per dozen

Large Blue Line Bus Pull-along. 1929
Catalogue No.118. Size 16½″. Price 18s 6d per dozen. Catalogue No.118E, with electric light. Price 25s per dozen

Large Lorry Pull-along. 1929
Catalogue No.122. Size 16½″. Price 25s per dozen

Large Petrol Tank Lorry Pull-along 1929. Catalogue No.124. Size 11½″
Price 20s per dozen **p. 131*

Large Tip-up Truck Pull-along. 1929
Catalogue No.125. Size 16½″
Price 18s per dozen **p. 131*

London Bus 6 wheels, 1929
Catalogue No.130. Size 17½″
Catalogue No.130E, with 2 electric lights

BOATS

Racing Motor Boats with driver and dashboard. Clockwork, several colours 1929
Catalogue No.B9. Size 9″
Price 9s per dozen
Catalogue No.B10. Size 10½″

Speed Boats Clockwork. 1929
Catalogue No.B6
Small price 16s 6d per dozen
Catalogue No.B7
Medium, price 24s per dozen
Catalogue No.B8
Large, price 40s per dozen

Surf Boat Clockwork. 1929
Catalogue No.90. Price 12s per dozen

Steamers Clockwork, 2 funnels and mast, several colours. 1925
Catalogue No.B1. Size 9″
Price 9s per dozen
Catalogue No.B2. Size 10½″

Sand Boat Pull-along on 4 wheels. 1929
Catalogue No.123. Size 16½″

DOMESTIC TOYS

Kitchen Range 1 oven, 2 saucepans, 1929
Catalogue No.21A. Size 6½″×4½″×6½″
Price 6s per dozen

Kitchen Range 1 oven, saucepan and kettle, 1929
Catalogue No.21B. Price 6s 6d per dozen

Kitchen Range 2 ovens, 2 saucepans, 1929
Catalogue No.21C. Size 7½″×5″×8″
Price 7s 6d per dozen

Kitchen Range 2 ovens, saucepan and kettle, 1929
Catalogue No.21D. Price 9s per dozen

Bungalow Cooker 1931
Catalogue No.21E. Price 15s per dozen

Large Cooking Range 1931
Catalogue No.21F. Price 30s per dozen

SEASIDE AND NURSERY TOYS

Nursery Truck 1925
Catalogue No.777. Size 12″
Price 12s per dozen
Catalogue No.83. Small
Price 3s 6d per dozen

Sand Truck with detachable spade. 1929
Catalogue No.777A. Size 12″
Price 15s per dozen

Seaside Buckets Dia. 4½″, 6″ and 3¾″
Catalogue No.103

RAILWAYS

All-Clear Engine Clockwork. 1924
Driver looks out of engine window to see if way ahead is clear. No.35 on side
Made in various sizes

Monster Engine 6 wheels, connecting rod. 1929
Catalogue No.119
Price 18s 6d per dozen
Catalogue No.119E, with electric light

More train sets, stations, signals, various locomotives and railway stock were added to the original sets produced by British Metal Ltd between 1923 and 1932. In the 1931 price list they are numbered from 30A–30GS, 50–50D, 700–700B

A Wells & Co. Ltd 1919–32

Factory:
1919 Basement of 28 Dame Street, Islington, London
1921 Shepherdess Walk, London
1924 Somers Road, Walthamstow, London
Company incorporated: 1930
Director: Alfred W Wells
Trademarks: Wells o' London, Wells

CARS AND OTHER VEHICLES

Royal Mail Vans Solid gears, clockwork. Red, black and gold. 6½d line
Style No.4. Size 5″. 1927
Style No.21. Size 7″. 1928

Racing Cars (numbered 1–16), clockwork. Yellow and black or blue and black. 6½d line
Style No.10. 1927

St John's Ambulance Vans
Clockwork. White, black and red. 6½d line
Style No.13. Size 5″. 1927 *p. 134*
Style No.20. Size 7″

Carter Paterson Vans Solid gears, clockwork. Green, black, red and yellow 6½d line
Style No.17. Size 5″. 1927
Style No.22. Size 7″. 1928
(with 'A Help in Every Home' on side)

Delivery Lorry Solid gears, clockwork Red, black and white. 6½d line
Style No.6. Size 4¾″. 1926
(one version with plain sides, a second version with 'Motor BP Spirit' on side)

BP Petrol Lorry Green and yellow Clockwork
Style No.19. Size 5″. 1928

Express Delivery Van Solid gears Clockwork. Yellow and black
Style No.31. Size 5″. 1930

Coupé Car with chauffeur. Clockwork
Style No.35. Size 7½″. 1932

Saloon Car Clockwork. Yellow and black, red and black or blue and black
Style No.14. Size 6″. 1929
(Another version size 7″ with electric light in front, 1929)

Fire Engine with solid brass cut pinion gear. Clockwork. Style No.12. Size 6″ 1928

Fire Escape with extending ladder. 6d line. Clockwork. Style No.9. Size 6″. 1927 *p. 135*

Ice Cream Carriers Red, black, white and silver. Clockwork. Style No.16 Size 4½″. 1927

RAILWAYS

Locomotive to fit 0 gauge train track Red, black and gold. Clockwork. 6½d line
Style No.6. Size 5″. 1921

BP Petrol Tank Style No.19. Size 4″ 1928

Railway Carriage Style No.23. Size 4″ 1928

Cattle Truck Style No.24. Size 4″. 1928

Pullman Coach Style No.26. Size 4″ 1928

Train Sets
Engine and passenger coach
Style No.5/1. 1928
Engine, tender and goods truck
Style No.5/2. 1928
Engine, tender and petrol tank
Style No.5/3. 1928
(Box size of 1928 sets. Size 3½″×11½″)
Engine, tender, 1 carriage and oval track
Style No.L/1. 1929
Engine, tender, 1 carriage and oval track
Style No.L/2. 1929
Engine, tender, 2 carriages with oblong track
Style No.L/3. 1929
(Box size of 1929 sets 12″×10″)

Railway Signals Style No.8. Size 9½″ 1932

AW Model Crane to fit 0 gauge track, ratchet revolving platform. Style No.7 Size 6½″ long. 1920

MISCELLANEOUS

Boats Pull-along boat. 1s line
Floating boat. 6d line

Metal Tennis Racket Metal rims finished in different colours. 6d line
Style No.86. Size 18″. 1920

Tin Horn 1920

Clock Clockwork movement worked by pulling chain. Style No.15. Size 8 high 1927

Jumping Rabbit or Hare Provisional Patent No.4477. Style No.33. Size 5¾″ 1931

Automatic Pistol firing pellets. 6d line
Style No.24. Size 4¾″. 1931

Aeroplane de Luxe with RAF markings
Style No.30. Size 9½″ long. 1930

Perambulator Style No.32. Size 5½″ 1931

GAMES

Humpty-Dumpty Shooting Game with two pistols and refill pellets. Style No.36 1931

Balloon Girl Shooting game with celluloid balls and two pistols
Style No.37. 1931

Shooting Skittles with 2 pistols
Style No.39. 1932

Auto Gee, Race Game Patent No.31128. 1930

Greyhound Race Game Size 8″ dia.
Style No.18. 1928

Bob-about Game with 2 pistols
Style No.38. 1932

The following pages are a complete reproduction of the **A Wells & Co.** 1931 catalogue

No. 5/1.

ENGINE TENDER AND PASSENGER COACH

Box, $3\frac{1}{4}''$ x $11\frac{1}{2}''$ x $2\frac{3}{4}''$.

No. 5/2.

ENGINE TENDER AND GOODS TRUCK

Box, $3\frac{1}{4}''$ x $11\frac{1}{2}''$ x $2\frac{3}{4}''$.

No. 5/3.

ENGINE TENDER AND PETROL TANK

Box, $3\frac{1}{4}''$ x $11\frac{1}{2}''$ x $2\frac{3}{4}''$.

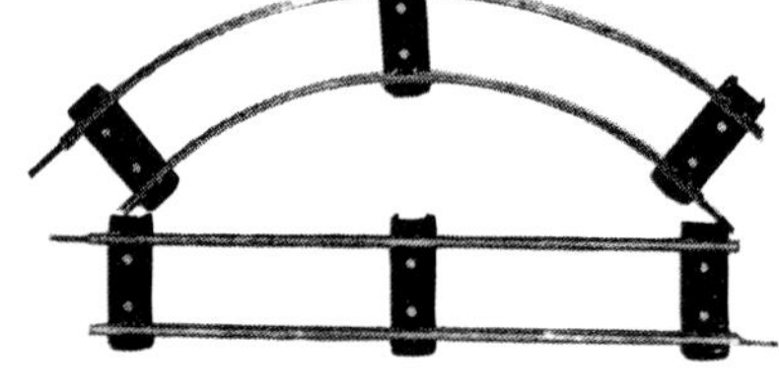

No. 1/3. No. 1/4.

No. 1/3 piece 16″ Circle Track.

No. 1/4 piece $10\frac{1}{4}''$ Straight Length.

Style No. 5.

CLOCKWORK LOCOMOTIVE

Solid gears, lead wheels to fit O gauge Train Track.
Colour: Red, Black and Gold.
Packed ½ dozen in box. 5″ long, 2″ wide, 3″ high.

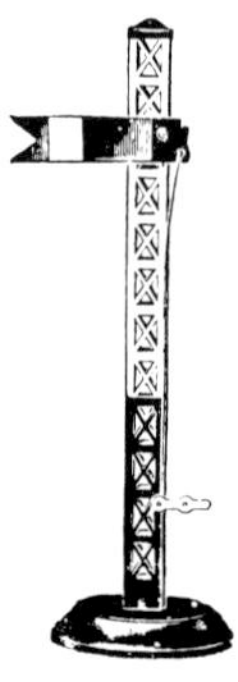

Style No. 8.

RAILWAY SIGNAL

Colour: Red, Black and White.
$9\frac{1}{2}''$ high, 3″ base.
Packed ½ dozen in box.

Style No. 12.

CLOCKWORK MODEL FIRE ENGINE

Improved clockwork with solid brass cut pinion gear.
Colour: Red, White, Black and Gilt.
Packed $\frac{1}{2}$ dozen in box.
Size: 6″ long, $2\frac{1}{2}$″ wide, $3\frac{1}{2}$″ high.

Style No. 10.

CLOCKWORK MODEL RACING CAR

(NUMBERED 1 to 10.)

Improved clockwork with solid brass cut pinion gear.
Colours: Yellow and Black, and Blue and Black.
Packed $\frac{1}{2}$ dozen in box.
Size: $6\frac{1}{2}$″ long, $2\frac{1}{2}$″ wide, 3″ high.

Style No. 7.

MODEL CRANE

Ratchet wind. Made to fit O gauge Train Tracks.
Colour: Red, Black and White.
Packed $\frac{1}{2}$ dozen in box.
Size: $6\frac{1}{2}$″ long, 2″ wide, $5\frac{1}{2}$″ high.

Style No. 9.

CLOCKWORK MODEL FIRE ESCAPE

Improved clockwork with solid brass cut pinion gear, and extending ladder.
Colour: Red, White and Black.
Packed $\frac{1}{2}$ dozen in box.
Size: 6″ long, $2\frac{1}{2}$″ wide, $3\frac{1}{2}$″ high.

Style No. 4.

MODEL "ROYAL MAIL" MOTOR CAR

Solid gears.
Colour: Red, Black and Gold.
Packed $\frac{1}{2}$ dozen in box.
Size: 5″ long, $2\frac{1}{2}$″ wide, $3\frac{1}{4}$″ high.

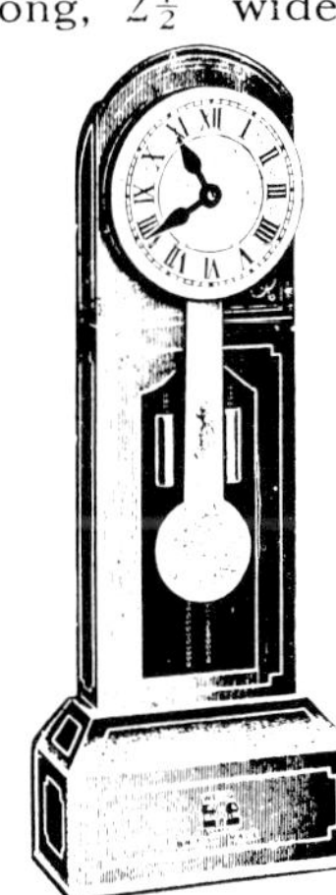

No. 15.

GRANDFATHER CLOCK

Clockwork Movement.
Height 8″.
Packed $\frac{1}{2}$ dozen in box.

Style No. 14.

CLOCKWORK MODEL SALOON CAR

Colours: Yellow and Black.
Red ,,
Blue ,,

Size: 6″ long, $2\frac{1}{2}$″ wide, 3″ high.
Packed $\frac{1}{2}$ dozen in box.

Style No. 17.

CLOCKWORK MODEL DELIVERY VAN

Solid Gears.
Colours: Green, Black, Red and Yellow.
Size: 5″ long, $2\frac{1}{2}$″ wide, $3\frac{1}{4}$″ high.
Packed $\frac{1}{2}$ dozen in box.

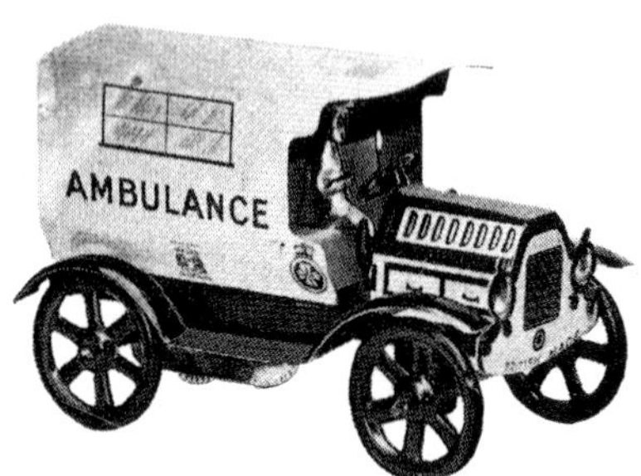

Style No. 13.

CLOCKWORK AMBULANCE VAN

Colour: White, Black and Red.
Size: 5″ long, $2\frac{1}{2}$″ wide, $3\frac{1}{4}$″ high.
Packed $\frac{1}{2}$ dozen in box.

Style No. 16.

CLOCKWORK MODEL OF ICE CREAM CARRIER

Colour: Red, Black, White and Silver.
Size: $4\frac{1}{2}$″ long, $2\frac{1}{2}$″ wide, 3″ high.
Packed $\frac{1}{2}$ dozen in box.

Style No. 19.

CLOCKWORK MODEL PETROL LORRY

Colour: Green and Yellow.
Size: 5″ long, $2\frac{1}{2}$″ wide, $3\frac{1}{4}$″ high.
Packed $\frac{1}{2}$ dozen in box.

Style No. 6.

CLOCKWORK MOTOR DELIVERY LORRY

Solid Gears.
Colour: Red, Black and White.
Size: $4\frac{3}{4}$″ long, $2\frac{1}{2}$″ wide, 3″ high.
Packed $\frac{1}{2}$ dozen in box.

No. 20.

CLOCKWORK
MOTOR AMBULANCE

Each in Box: 7″ x $3\frac{3}{4}$″ x $4\frac{1}{4}$″.

No. 21.

CLOCKWORK
ROYAL MAIL

Each in Box: 7″ x $3\frac{3}{4}$″ x $4\frac{1}{4}$″.

No. 22.

CLOCKWORK
DELIVERY VAN

Each in Box: 7″ x $3\frac{3}{4}$″ x $4\frac{1}{4}$″.

Style No. 18

GREYHOUND RACE GAME
Printed in Colour.

Size 8″ diameter. Boxed $\frac{1}{2}$-dozens.

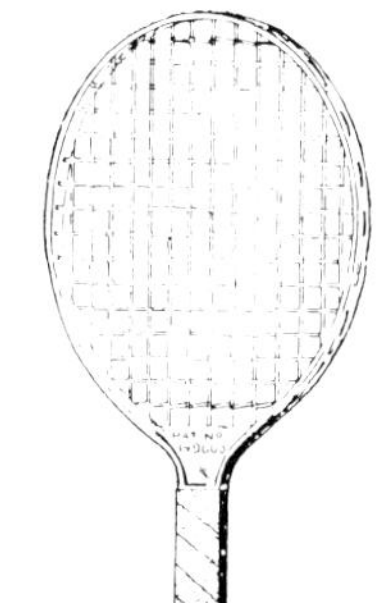

Style No. 86.

METAL FRAME RACQUET

Packed 2 dozen in box.
18″ long, $6\frac{3}{4}$″ wide.

No. 24.

CATTLE TRUCK

Highly decorated.
Size: 4″ long, 1¾″ wide, 3″ high.
Packed 1 dozen in box.

No. 23.

RAILWAY CARRIAGE

Highly decorated.
Size: 4″ long, 1¾″ wide, 3″ high.
Packed 1 dozen in box.

No. 26.

PULLMAN COACH

Highly Decorated.
Size: 4″ long, 1¾″ wide, 3″ high.
Packed 1 dozen in box.

No. 25

B.P. PETROL TANK

Colour: Green and Yellow.
Size: 4″ long, 1¾″ wide, 3″ high.
Packed 1 dozen in box.

TRAIN SETS

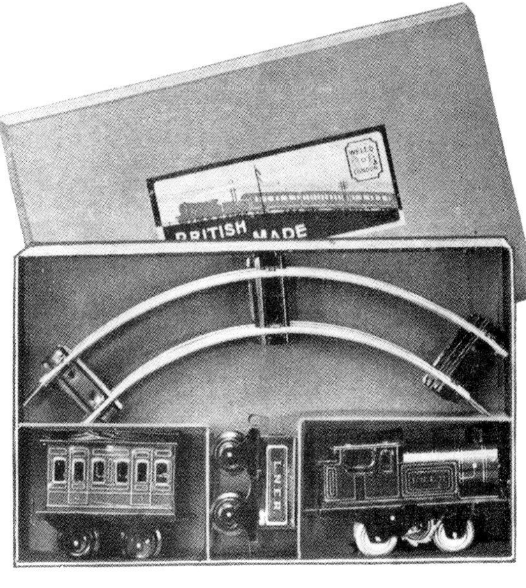

No. L/1.
Engine Tender and One Carriage
with Circle Track.
Box Size: 12" x $7\frac{1}{4}$" x $2\frac{3}{4}$".

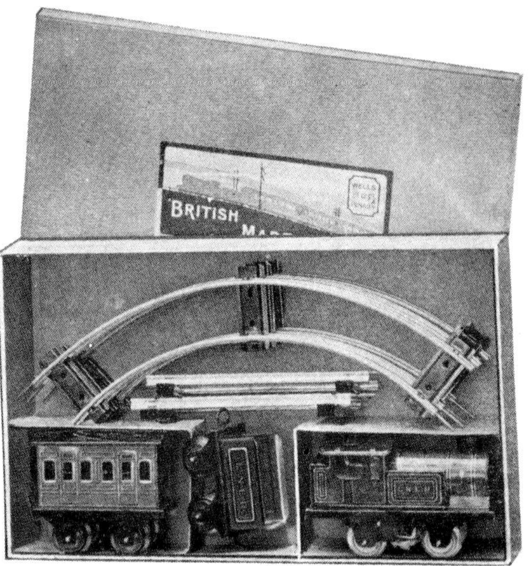

No. L/2.
Engine Tender and One Carriage
with Oval Track.
Box Size: 12" x 8" x $2\frac{3}{4}$".

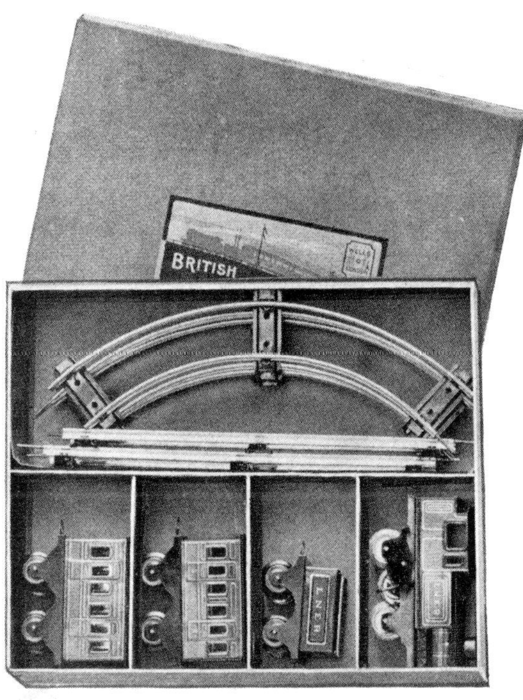

No. L/3.
Engine Tender and Two Carriages
with large Oblong Track.
Box Size: 12" x 10" x $2\frac{3}{4}$".

SOLID WELDED TRAIN TRACK

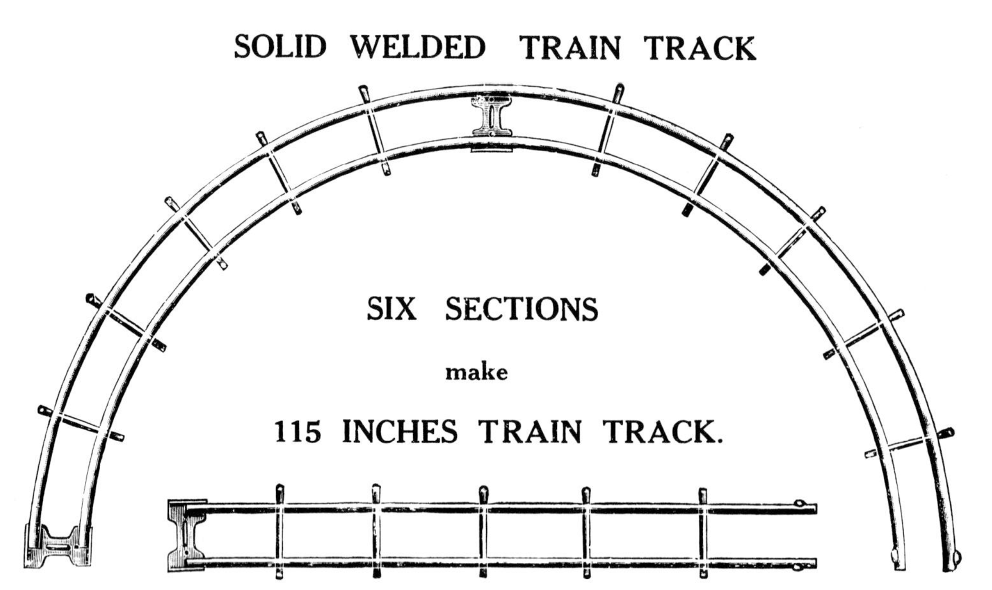

SIX SECTIONS

make

115 INCHES TRAIN TRACK.

No. 11.

JUNCTIONS

4 Circle sections make a circle railway track of 76 inches, 4 circles and 2 straight sections make 115 inch oblong railway track. 6 circles, 4 straight and 1 junction piece make a figure eight railway track of 160 inches.

Instructions for Assembling Figure Eight Railway Track.

The mitred end of straight rail to be slightly pressed and slipped into junction piece, the two bridge ends to be opposite each other as sketch. Then assemble the remaining circles.

No. 1.

Straight Sections

18″ long.

Packed 1 doz in box

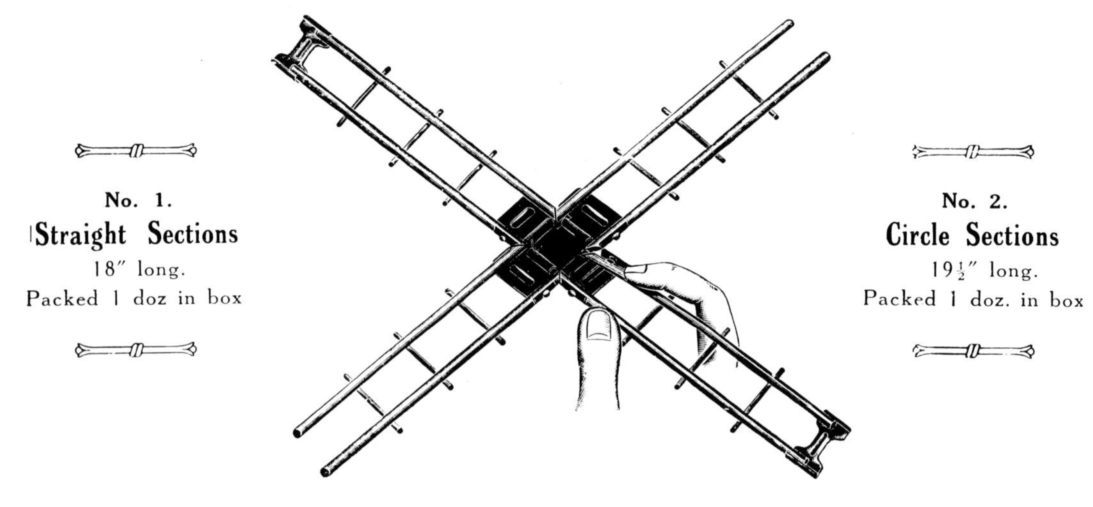

No. 2.

Circle Sections

19½″ long.

Packed 1 doz. in box

Style No. 30.

CLOCKWORK
MODEL "AEROPLANE DE LUXE."

Highly decorated.

Size: $9\frac{1}{2}''$ long, $2''$ high, $8''$ across wings.
Packed $\frac{1}{2}$-dozen in box ($11'' \times 10'' \times 2\frac{3}{8}''$).

Style No. 31.

CLOCKWORK
MODEL "EXPRESS" DELIVERY VAN.

Solid gears.

Colour: Yellow and Black.
Packed $\frac{1}{2}$-dozen in box.
Size: $5''$ long, $2\frac{1}{2}''$ wide, $3\frac{1}{4}''$ high.

Style No. 36.

"HUMPTY-DUMPTY" SHOOTING GAME.

Size: $21\frac{1}{4}''$ x $11\frac{1}{2}''$ x $1\frac{1}{4}''$.

This is an entirely new line and makes a fascinating game for two or more players.

"Humpty-Dumpty" is made up sitting on the wall, ready for our young sharp-shooters to give him his "great fall."

Two repeating Pistols and two Boxes of Refills are supplied in each game.

Each player can have 5 or 10 shots as arranged. The Winner is the one to score the most points according to the numbers shown, when "Humpty-Dumpty" is knocked off the wall.

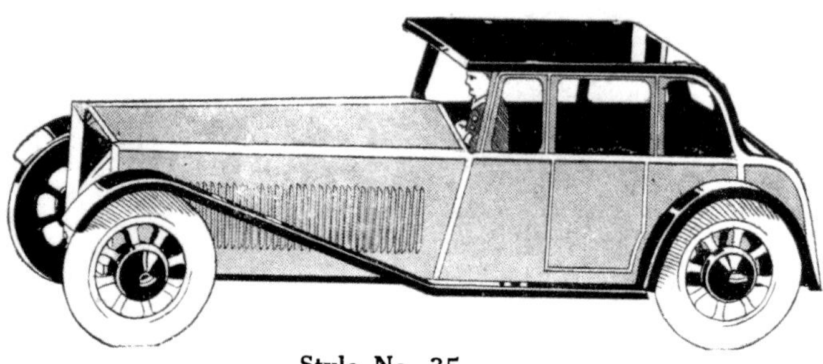

Style No. 35.

CLOCKWORK COUPE CAR.

Packed each in a Box.

Size: $7\frac{1}{4}''$ x $3\frac{1}{4}''$ x $2\frac{5}{8}''$.

Style No. 37.

"BALLOON GIRL" SHOOTING GAME.

Size: $21\frac{1}{4}''$ x $11\frac{1}{2}''$ x $1\frac{1}{2}''$.

This is another entirely new line.

Five Dancing Girls with their balloons make the Target. Celluloid Balls are used for the Balloons, and are held in position as shown in the illustration.

This game calls for a little more skill than is required for "Humpty-Dumpty," as the Bullets must strike the Balls in the centre to dislodge them.

Each player may have 5 or 10 shots as agreed upon. The Winner being the player who shoots out the 5 Balls with the least quantity of shots.

This is a most fascinating game which will appeal to both young and old.

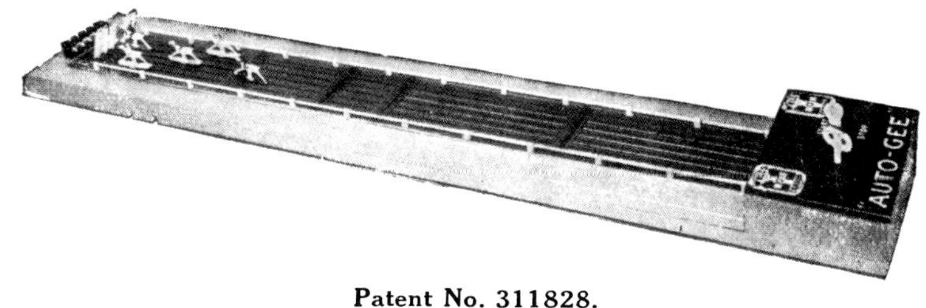

Patent No. 311828.
Foreign Patents granted.

"AUTO-GEE" RACE GAME.

(Small Model.)

Length 29″, Width 5″, Depth $2\frac{1}{2}''$.

Nett Weight $2\frac{3}{4}$ lbs.

Retail Price **10/6** each.

Beautifully boxed with full instructions attached.
Complete with Betting Board and Chalk.

Style No. 6

CLOCKWORK MODEL DELIVERY LORRY.

Highly decorated

Size : 6¼" long, 3¼" high, 2½" wide.
Packed ½-dozen in box.

Style No. 32

MODEL PERAMBULATOR.

Size : 5½" long, 4" high, 2¾" wide.
Packed ½-dozen in box.

Style No. 34

AUTOMATIC PISTOL

Packed each in a box.

Size : $4\frac{3}{4}''$ long, $3\frac{7}{8}''$ wide, $\frac{3}{4}''$ deep.

Refills : Boxes containing 12 pellets.

Style No. 33

JUMPING RABBIT

Packed each in a Box.

Size : $5\frac{3}{4}''$ long, $5''$ deep, $2\frac{5}{8}''$ wide.

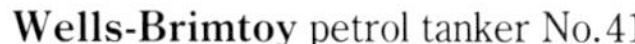

Wells-Brimtoy petrol tanker No.41

Wells-Brimtoy steam roller No.64

Wells-Brimtoy tip truck No.61

Wells-Brimtoy Ltd 1932–39

Factories: Riverside Works, Highbury (Brimtoy)
Somers Road, Walthamstow (A Wells)
Stirling Road, Walthamstow (A Wells)
Sales Office: 1936, White Street
Trademarks: Nelson's Column. Wells o' London

After the amalgamation of the firms Brimtoy Ltd and A Wells & Co., the Brimtoy factory in north London continued the production of its former main lines. The A Wells & Co. factories in Walthamstow, added new lines to its former 3d and 6d and 1s lines by adding larger and more expensive versions of its old lines and adding new items, such as in 1938, wooden toys and nursery furniture. By 1937/38 the standard cars, vans (Royal Mail Express, Carter Peterson and Ambulance) were built with a lower chassis.

CARS AND OTHER VEHICLES

Riley Sports Car Clockwork
Catalogue No.92. Size 9$\frac{1}{4}$". 1934

Coupé Clockwork. Catalogue No.63
Size 8$\frac{1}{2}$". 1934

Limousine with chauffeur and 3 windows. Red, blue and black. Clockwork
Catalogue No.62. Size 8". 1936

Bluebird Racing Car Blue and cream
Union Jacks on tail. Clockwork
Catalogue No.77. Size 11$\frac{1}{4}$". 1936

Racing Car Clockwork
Catalogue No.101. Size 9". 1934

Limousine with chauffeur and 2 windows. Red, green and cream
Clockwork. Catalogue No.141. Size 8"
1934

Limousine with sliding roof. Red, black and blue. Clockwork. Catalogue No.142
Size 14$\frac{1}{2}$". 1934

Limousine with sliding roof and 2 lights
Clockwork. Catalogue No.143. Size 14$\frac{1}{2}$"
1934

Shell Petrol Lorry Clockwork
Catalogue No.41. Size 6$\frac{1}{2}$". 1934 **p. 142*

Royal Mail Van Clockwork
Catalogue No.68. Size 7". 1934
Catalogue No.21. Size 8$\frac{1}{2}$". 1934

Carter Paterson Van with 2 doors
Clockwork. Catalogue No.22. Size 8$\frac{1}{2}$"
1934

Bedford Van with tailboard. Clockwork
Catalogue No.42. Size 8$\frac{1}{2}$". 1934

Ambulance with 2 doors. Clockwork
Catalogue No.20. Size 8$\frac{1}{2}$". 1934 **p. 134*

Delivery Van Assorted colours
Clockwork. Catalogue Nos. 67 & 68
Size 7". 1934

Police Van Number Plate W417
Catalogue No. 20. Size 7". 1937 **p. 134*

Police Patrol Car Loud speaker on roof, gong rings as car moves. Clockwork
Catalogue No. 159. Price 36s per dozen
1940

Tractor Red and yellow. Clockwork
Catalogue No. 66. Size 5$\frac{3}{4}$". 1934

Steam Roller Red and green
Clockwork. Catalogue No. 64. Size 7$\frac{1}{2}$"
1936

Breakdown Lorry Green and yellow
Clockwork. Catalogue No. 76. Size 9$\frac{3}{4}$"
1936 **p. 135*

Omnibus Clockwork. Catalogue No. 74
Size 7". 1936

Char-à-banc Brown and blue
Clockwork. Passengers and driver in windows. Catalogue No. 69. Size 8$\frac{3}{4}$"
1936

Trolley Bus Clockwork. Size 8$\frac{1}{4}$"
Catalogue No. 131. Price 12s per dozen

Tip Truck with lever Red, black and yellow. Clockwork. Catalogue No. 61
Size 10". 1936

Fire Escape with detachable ladder
Clockwork. Catalogue No. 12N. Size 8"
1936 **p. 135*

Fire Engine Clockwork
Catalogue No. 75. Size 8"

Wells-Brimtoy miniature paddle boat No.70

Wells-Brimtoy Silver Streak locomotive No.73

MINIATURE TOYS
Clockwork Slow Motion

Omnibus LPTB Red, cream and blue Clockwork. Catalogue No. 153. Size 4″ 1934

Chrysler Car Orange and cream Clockwork. Catalogue No. 150. Size 4″ 1934

Rolls Royce Silver and grey. Clockwork Catalogue No. 151. Size 4″. 1934

Road Roller Green, black and red Clockwork. Catalogue No. 152. Size 4″ 1934

Crocodile Green and black Catalogue No. 161. Size 7½″. 1934

Snail Clockwork. Catalogue No. 160 Size 4½″. 1934

Paddle Boat Red, yellow and blue Clockwork. Catalogue No. 70. Size 11″ 1936

MICKEY MOUSE TOYS

Mickey Mouse Pram Minnie Mouse pushing pram and two baby mice Clockwork. Catalogue No. 146. Size 7½″ 1936

Mickey Mouse Humming Top Catalogue No. 145. Size dia. of top 3½″ 1935

Mickey Mouse Handcar with house and station. 80″ of track. Catalogue No. 300 Size of handcar 7½″. 1936

Mickey Mouse Circus Train The Handcar and the Circus Train were first produced by the Lionel Corporation in the USA in 1934 with Walt Disney's co-operation. Manufacturers' rights in Great Britain granted to A Wells & Co.

RAILWAYS

Locomotive No. 7173 Clockwork, 0 gauge. Red, black and yellow Catalogue No. 73. Size 6½″. 1936

Streamlined Locomotive No. 2509 Clockwork, to fit 0 gauge Grey with red and black lining Catalogue No. 73/1. Size 6½″. 1936

Locomotive No. 4067 Sparking, clockwork. Catalogue No. 40. Size 9½″ 1933. Without sparks Catalogue No. 37. Size 9½″. 1933

Wells-Brimtoy Mickey Mouse Handcar No.300

Golden Eagle Streamlined, clockwork 1937

Silver Streak Clockwork. 1936–38 Catalogue No.73

AEROPLANES

Double Wing Clockwork Catalogue No. 301. Size 8″ wing span 1933

Double Wing 9A AXF on wing Clockwork. Catalogue No. 302. Size 13½″ wing span. 1934

Single Wing 301 on wing Catalogue No. 71. Size 14½″ wing span 1933

Single Wing with pilot. Clockwork Catalogue No. 90. Size 13½″ wing span 1936

Gyroplane Aeroplane on stand with gyro top. Pat. No. 32611. Retail price 5s Catalogue No. 303. Size 12″. 1934

Wells-Brimtoy single wing plane No.71 (right)

MISCELLANEOUS

Telephone with bell Catalogue No. 78 Size 6¾″. 1936

Repeater Cap Guns Catalogue No. 43 Size 8″. 1934
Catalogue No. 49. Size 4½″. 1934

Carpet Sweepers 'Well swept' Catalogue Nos. 28/1, 28/3 and 28/5 Sizes 6½″, 4¼″ and 7″

Carpet Sweeper mop and broom Catalogue No.90/2

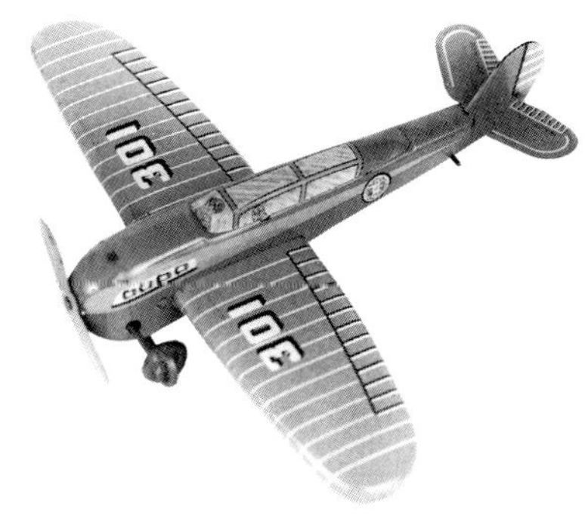

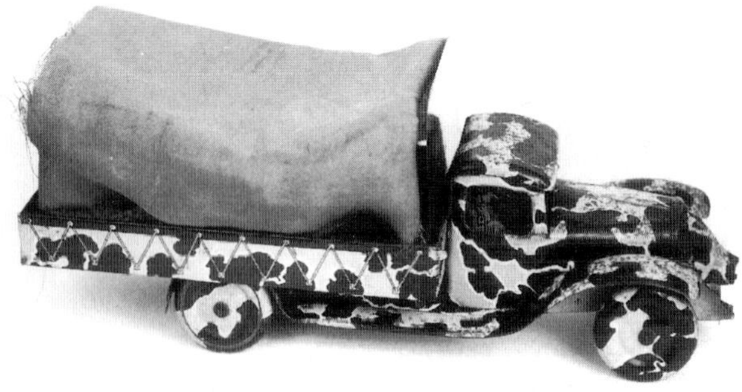

Wells-Brimtoy camouflaged army lorry No. 138

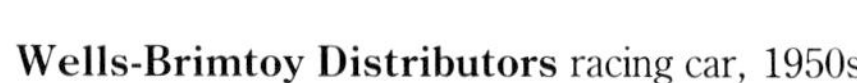

Wells-Brimtoy Distributors racing car, 1950s

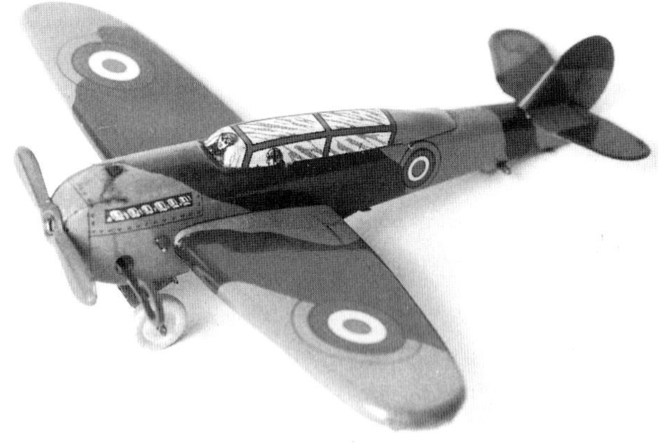

Wells-Brimtoy camouflaged aeroplane, 1940

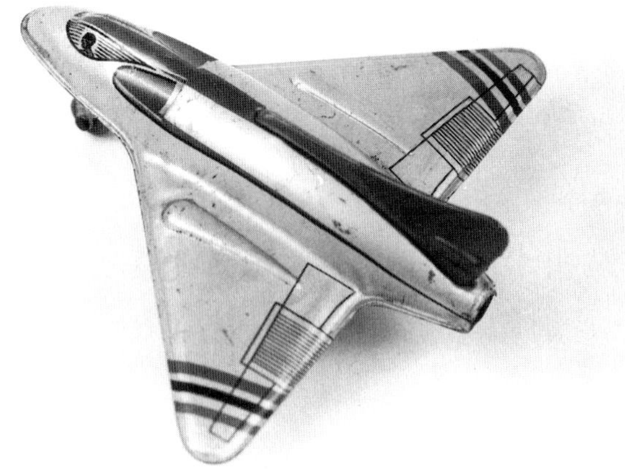

Wells-Brimtoy Distributors Wonderjet aeroplane No. 192

Wells-Brimtoy Ltd
The War Years 1939–1944

By 1940, 99% of Wells-Brimtoy's production was for the Ministry of Aircraft production. They made gas masks, limpet mines, anti-vibration devices, sten gun magazines.

The London factories and sales office were damaged during the blitz. New factories were opened in Holyhead, North Wales and a subsidiary firm, the Welnut Engineering Company, in Barnet under the direction of A Wells' daughter, Mrs Hilda Kirby. In 1940, however, a few toys were still being made for export – mainly military vehicles.

MILITARY VEHICLES

Tank Clockwork, camouflaged. 1934 Catalogue No. 65. Size 6″

Large Army Lorry Clockwork with searchlight. Catalogue No. 137. Size 9″ Price 34s/6d per dozen. 1940 **p. 138*

Large Army Lorry Clockwork with anti-aircraft gun. 1946. Catalogue No. 138 Size 9″. Price 34s/6d per dozen **p. 138*

Large Covered Army Waggons Clockwork. Catalogue No. 138. Size 9″ 1940. Price 30s/5d per dozen **p. 138*

ARP Lorry Clockwork. 1940 Catalogue No. 18. Size 9″ Price 8s per dozen

OTHER VEHICLES

Green Line Bus Clockwork with 'Glasgow to Exeter' on its side Catalogue No. 122. Price 8s per dozen, retail 1s each

Breakdown Lorry Clockwork Size 7″. 1944 **p. 135*

Wells-Brimtoy Distributors Ltd
1945–1965

Progress Works, Stirling Road, Walthamstow, and Beachyard Works, Holyhead, Wales

Private Co. Registered 24 January 1949

Object of new company to carry on the business of metal printers and stampers, manufacturers and importers of and wholesale and retail dealers in toys, games, puzzles, novelties, amusements and sports goods etc.

Directors: Alfred C Wells, Mrs Hilda Kirby, Alfred W J Wells. Directors of A Wells and Co. Ltd and Welnut Engineering Co. Ltd

Immediately after the War, the North Wales factory was switched to the mass production of the 'Weltime' alarm clock for another subsidiary, the Anglesey Instrument and Clock Company.

The Welnut Engineering Co. which had also moved to Holyhead changed to the production of tin whistles and noise makers for the 'toy filling trade' and the Walthamstow factory in Stirling Road resumed the production of lithographed toys and games.

In 1952, an injection moulding plant was installed mainly for the manufacture of plastic household goods, but shortly hybrid toys start to appear with moulded plastic parts. By 1955, when the new trademark 'Welsotoys' was adopted, the number of plastic and wood toys continued to grow.

MECHANICAL POCKETOY SERIES

Steam Roller 1945. Catalogue No. 501 Size 4″

Omnibus 1945. Catalogue No. 503 Size $4\frac{1}{8}$″

Regent Petrol Lorry 1955 Catalogue No. 506. Size $4\frac{3}{8}$″.

Green Line Bus 1945 **p. 139* Catalogue No. 507. Size $4\frac{1}{2}$″

Removal Van Opening rear doors Catalogue No. 508. Size $4\frac{1}{4}$″. 1945

Long Wheel-Base Truck 1945 Catalogue No. 510. Size $5\frac{1}{2}$″

Long Wheel-Base Covered Van 1945 Removable Luton type body Catalogue No. 511. Size $5\frac{1}{4}$″

Tip Truck Realistic tipping action Catalogue No. 512. Size $3\frac{5}{8}$″. 1945

Short Wheel-Base Lorry and Trailer Detachable trailer Catalogue No. 513. Size $6\frac{1}{2}$″. 1945

Novelty Stop-Go Trolley **p. 139* Bus Catalogue No. 516. Size $4\frac{1}{4}$″. 1955

Short Wheel-Base Breakdown Lorry with working crane Catalogue No. 514. Size 4″. 1945

Articulated Pantechnicon Detachable trailer, opening rear door and removable body. Catalogue No. 520. Size $6\frac{1}{2}$″. 1945

Refuse Truck with sliding side covers Catalogue No. 527. 1945

Wells-Brimtoy Distributors Esso petrol tanker No.761

VEHICLES

Road Coach 1944+. Catalogue No.121
Size 11⅛″.

ERA Racer 1945+. Catalogue No.98
Size 8″

Trolley Bus 1945+. Catalogue No.105
Size 6¾″

Diesel Road Roller with reversible action. Catalogue No.176. Size 8″. 1940+

Tip Truck 1940+. Catalogue No.127
Size 7″

Tip Truck with trailer. 1945+
Catalogue No.128. Size 10½″

Breakdown Lorry with working crane
Catalogue No.129. Size 11″. 1945+

Regent Petrol Lorry 1945+
Catalogue No.174. Size 10″

Road Roller reversible. 1945+
Catalogue No.123. Size 6½″

MECHANICAL WALKING FIGURES

Father Christmas 1945
Catalogue No.147. Size 4¾″

Penguin 1945. Catalogue No.151
Size 4¾″

Inverted Clown 1945
Catalogue No.152. Size 4¾″

Brown Bear 1945. Catalogue No.153
Size 4¾″

Jumping Kangaroo 1945. Proven Patent No.4477. Catalogue No.93
Size 5¼″

Clown 1945. Catalogue No.148. Size 4¾″

Walking Pig 1945. Catalogue No.149
Size 3¾″

Mother Goose Catalogue No.156
Size 4¾″

Drummer Boy Proven Patent No.3872
Catalogue No.66. Size 5¾″. 1945+

Clucking Chicken push-along. 1945+
Proven Patent No.23710
Catalogue No.134. Size 7½″

Wells-Brimtoy Distributors mechanical 'Drummer Boy' No.66

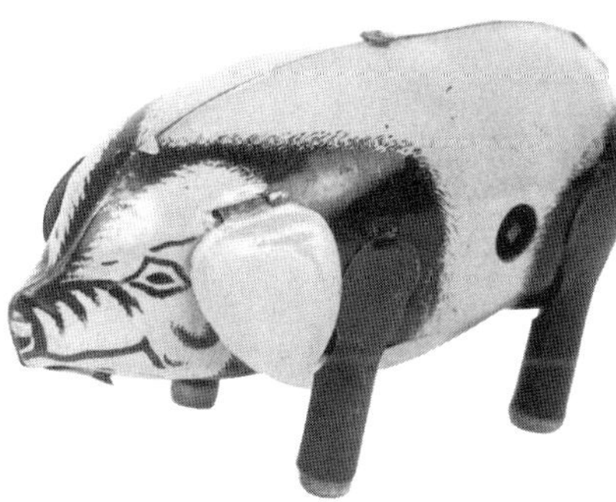

Wells-Brimtoy Distributors mechanical 'Walking Pig' No.149

PLANES

Wonderjet Plane 1953
Gyroscopic movement, siren sound
Patent No.30096/50. Catalogue No.192

DOMESTIC TOYS

Gas Stove with 4 plates, frying pan, saucepan and lid. Catalogue No.169
Size 10″. 1945

Carpet Sweeper 1945+
Catalogue No.106 and 116. Size 5″ and 7″

Sweeper Set 1945+. Catalogue Nos 117, 118, 119, 120. Size of card 23″, 29″, 20″ and 28″

Brush and Pan Set 1945+
Catalogue No.112. Size of card 10″

MISCELLANEOUS

Bell Roller Chimes No.1 and 2. 1945+
Catalogue No.216/217. Size 20″ and 26″

Bell Roller Chimes No.3 with coloured wooden spinners. Catalogue No.218
Size 26″. 1945+

Double Bell Chimes with wooden spinners on metal base
Catalogue No.219. 1945+

Swimming Fish 1945
Catalogue No.9/150. Size 11½″

TRAINS

Diesel Train Golden Streak 1945+
Catalogue No.97. Size 9″

Floor Loco 1945+. Catalogue No.36
Size 9″

Train Sets 1945+
Catalogue Nos. 366G, 367, 357, 362, 352, 354, 355, 356, 353, 360, 335, 337

Train Set Accessories 1945+
Catalogue Nos. 8, 29, 723, 33, 48, 554, 236, 237, 44, 45

0 Gauge Rails No.660, 114, 191, 190
1945+

Passenger and Goods Rolling Stock Catalogue Nos. 8050, 158, 700, 58, 52, 801, 805, 802, 806, 803, 55, 8055, 57. 1945+

Advertisements from *Games and Toys* (left to right from top) 1953, 1954, 1953, 1957

Welsotoys 1955–72

Saloon Car Lithographed metal Catalogue No. 908. Size 3½″. 1955–65

Fire Chief Car Lithographed metal car with siren. Catalogue No. 222. Size 4″ 1955–65

Open Truck chassis with printed metal back. Catalogue No. 906. Size 4¼″ 1955–65

GYRO TOYS

Jeep Strongly constructed metal toy, brightly lithographed with polythene wheels, friction drive motor Catalogue No. 95. Size 6″. 1955

Fire Engine Lithographed metal with adjustable escape ladder, plastic wheels, friction drive motor. Catalogue No. 146 Size 6¼″. 1955

Pelican Removal Van Lithographed metal, plastic wheels, opening rear door, friction drive motor. Catalogue No. 30 Size 6¼″. 1955

Trolley Bus Lithographed metal, plastic wheels, friction drive motor Catalogue No. 111. Size 6″. 1955

Long Distance Coach Lithographed metal, plastic wheels, friction drive motor Catalogue No. 136. Size 7″. 1955

Esso Petrol Tanker Lithographed metal, plastic wheels, friction drive motor Catalogue No. 761. Size 6¾″. 1955

Regent Petrol Lorry 1955 Catalogue No. 506. Size 4⅜″

Gyro Drive Petrol Bus Lithographed metal plate in authentic transport colours, plastic wheels. Catalogue No. 517 Size 4¼″. 1955

Routemaster 'Esso' Bus 1955 Catalogue No. 23. Size 6″

Greenline Bus 1955 Lithographed metal with plastic wheels, friction drive motor. Size 7¼″ *p. 139*

GIANT GYRO SERIES

Gyro Tank Moveable plastic turret, lithographed metal, friction drive motor with clicker mechanism imitating gunfire Catalogue No. 160. Size 7½″. 1955

Highway Patrol Car with siren, lithographed metal in the authentic Highway Patrol colours of dark blue and white with coloured emblems of the Highway Patrol shown on the white panel on the side of the car. Friction drive motor. Catalogue No. 145. Size 11¼″. 1955

Touring Car Lithographed metal plate in brilliant colours, friction drive motor Catalogue No. 144. Size 11″. 1955

PLANES

Jirojex Monoplane 1955. Lithographed friction drive motor. Catalogue No. 267 Size 7″

Gyro Aeroplane Lithographed plate Catalogue No. 562. Size 4″. 1955

TRAINS

Royal Scot Locomotive Lithographed metal, plastic wheels, friction drive motor Catalogue No. 731. Size 6″. 1955

Tank Locomotive Lithographed metal, plastic wheels, friction drive motor Catalogue No. 74. Size 5″. 1955

Clockwork Train Sets 1955 Catalogue Nos. 304, 352, 305, 306, 811, 815, 812, 816, 813, 814, 817, 818, 819, 820, 821, 822, 823, 323, 824, 825, 826, 827

Train Set Accessories 1955 Catalogue Nos. 6–8, 414, 415, 48, 417, 418

DOMESTIC WARE

Carpet Sweepers 1955 Catalogue Nos. 115, 116. Size 18″ and 25″

Hoover Toy Vacuum Cleaner The word 'Hoover' is the registered trademark of Hoover Ltd, and is used by A Wells & Co. on this cleaner by permission of Hoover Ltd. Catalogue No. 260. Size 24″ 1955

Carded Wells-Brimtoy Dustpan Set Dustpan brush and mop. Catalogue No. 112. Size 10″. 1955

Broom Cupboard 1955 Catalogue No. 286. Size 1½″

Miniature Dresser 1955 Catalogue No. 282. Size 1½″

Miniature Refrigerator 1955 Catalogue No. 285. Size 1″

Miniature Sink Unit 1955 Catalogue No. 281. Size 1″

Miniature Washing Machine with moving agitator and working wringer Catalogue No. 284. Size 1″. 1955

Washing Machine Plastic water container, hand-operated agitator fitted with drain plug. Catalogue No. 206 Size 6″. 1955

Electric Type Range Lithographed metal with large selection of plastic utensils. Catalogue No. 298. Size 6″. 1955

Refrigerator Enamel plate, lithographed interior, plastic ice trays and jelly moulds Catalogue No. 207. Size 6″. 1955

Kitchen Cabinet Opening doors and drawers and utensils. Catalogue No. 290 Size 5″. 1955

Kitchen Dresser Enamel plate, opening doors and drawers, various utensils Catalogue No. 289. Size 11″. 1955

Table and Chair Set 1955 Lithographed plate, detachable legs Catalogue No. 291. Size 3″

Brush and Broom Cupboard Enamel plate, plastic utensils. Catalogue No. 293 Size 9″. 1955

Combination Kitchen Set Sink unit, washing machine, tap unit with reservoir tank attached to the back of the toy, working taps, sink with drip tray Lithographed details include draining board, plate racks, washing machine fitted with draining tube. Catalogue No. 204 Size 20″. 1955

Electric Type Stove Lithographed metal, transparent opening doors, plastic utensils. Catalogue No. 214. Size 8″. 1955

Sink Unit Fitted washing machine, tap unit with reservoir tank at back, working taps, sink with drip tray, lithographed details. Catalogue No. 205. Size 13″. 1955

Automatic Electric Range Lithographed plate, transparent door and movable cooking grills, on and off switch operates battery lamp. Catalogue No. 213 Size 6″. 1955

MISCELLANEOUS

Seaside Spades Metal with wooden handles. 1955. Catalogue Nos. 251, 252, 253. Size 10″, 21″, 27″

Submarine Chaser Lithographed metal deck and hull, clockwork motor with key, 2 plastic guns mounted fore and aft Catalogue No. 189. Size 10″. 1955

Speed-Y-Launch Lithographed metal hull and deck, clockwork motor with key Catalogue No. 185. Size 10″. 1955

12 Note Xylophone Press metal base, coloured notes with tune chart Catalogue No. 225. Size 12″. 1955

8 Note Xylophone Press metal base, coloured notes with tune chart Catalogue No. 229. Size 8″. 1955

Hobby Horse Push-along Coloured spinners and tinkle chime Catalogue No. 234. Size 36″. 1955

'Sooty' Push-along Drummer, Sooty beats drum. Catalogue No. 259. Size 10″ 1955

Mickey Mouse Drawing Tutor No. 99, 1955

Friction Drive Pocketoys

No. 527 Refuse Lorry. Plastic Chassis. Metal body with tipping action, and sliding covers. Size 3½" x 1⅝" x 1¼". Packed one dozen per box, six dozen per outer.

No. 902 Ice Cream Lorry. Plastic Chassis. Printed metal body, with opening rear door and side service counter. Size 4" x 1½" x 1½". Packed one dozen per box, six dozen per outer.

No. 540 Road Cleaning Lorry. Plastic Chassis. Printed metal body. Size 3¼" x 1¼" x 1½". Packed one dozen per box, six dozen per outer.

No. 222 Fire Chief Car. Brightly lithographed metal car with siren. Size 4" x 2" x 1". Packed two dozen per box, six dozen per outer.

No. 907 Grocer's Van. Plastic Chassis. Printed metal body with opening rear door. Size 4" x 1" x 1½". Packed one dozen per box, six dozen per outer.

No. 900 Removal Van. Plastic Chassis. Printed metal body with opening rear door. Size 4" x 1" x 1½". Packed one dozen per box, six dozen per outer.

No. 904 Tip Lorry. Plastic Chassis. Printed metal body with tipping action. Size 3½" x 1¾" x 1½". Packed one dozen per box, six dozen per outer.

No. 903 Esso Petrol Lorry. Plastic Chassis. Printed metal body. Size 3½" x 1¼" x 1½". Packed one dozen per box, six dozen per outer.

No. 906 Open Truck. Chassis with printed metal back. Size 4¼" x 1¼" x 1½". Packed one dozen per box, six dozen per outer.

No. 905 Side Tip Lorry. Plastic Cab. Metal Tipper 1 dozen a box. Size 3½" x 1¾" x 2¼". Packed 6 dozen per outer.

WELLS-BRIMTOY DISTRIBUTORS LTD.

These two pages show the final series of Pocketoys by **Welsotoys** from the 1955 catalogue

Friction Drive Pocketoys

No. 908 Saloon Car. Lithographed metal. Size 3½" x 1½" x 1". Packed two dozen per box, twelve dozen per outer.

No. 552 Sand and Gravel Lorry. Plastic Chassis. Printed metal body. Size 3½" x 1½" x 1½". Packed two dozen per box, six dozen per outer.

No. 519 Morris Minor Car. Plastic body and wheels. Size 3½" x 1¼" x 1½". Packed two dozen per box, twelve dozen per outer.

No. 514 Breakdown Lorry. Plastic Chassis Metal Crane Arm. Size 3½" x 1½" x 1½". Packed two dozen per box, six dozen per outer.

No. 512 Open Truck. Plastic Chassis. Printed metal body. Size 3¼" x 1½" x 1½". Packed two dozen per box, six dozen per outer.

No. 563 Transport Lorry. Plastic Chassis. Printed metal body. Size 3½" x 1¼" x 1½". Packed two dozen per box, six dozen per outer.

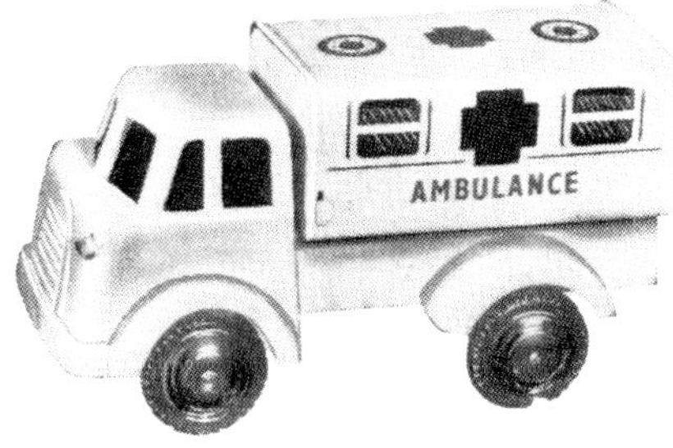

No. 553 Ambulance. Plastic Chassis. Printed metal body. Size 3¼" x 1¾" x 1½". Packed two dozen per box, six dozen per outer.

No. 559 Builder's Lorry. Plastic Chassis. Printed metal body. Size 3¼" x 1¾" x 1½". Packed two dozen per box, six dozen per outer.

WELLS-BRIMTOY DISTRIBUTORS LTD.

CMT Wells Kelo Ltd
1973–the present day

Progress Works, Kingsland, Holyhead, Gwynedd

Trainsets Clockwork. Inter-City passenger and goods. Produced in tin until 1985

Seaside Spades Produced in tin until 1986

Tubular Steel Toys

Mini Mum Toys
- Ironing boards
- Cleaning sets
- Dolly pushchairs and prams
- Toy Hoovers

Busy Bee Wheel Toys
- Trikes
- Scooters

Nursery Toys
- Baby rocker with seat
- Springing horse

Pogo Sticks

CMT Wells Kelo catalogue cover, 1984

The following 29 pages reproduce in full the 1951
Wells-Brimtoy Distributors Ltd catalogue

Foreword

Soon after the first World War in the year 1919 our Chairman, Mr. A. W. J. Wells opened a small toy manufacturing business in Dame Street, Islington, N.1. This venture proved to be the nucleus of what is now a progressive and successful organisation.

Weathering the lengthy depression which followed the first World War, Mr. Wells moved his business to larger premises in Shepherdess Walk, Islington, N.1. and then again to an even larger factory in Somers Road, Walthamstow, where the policy enacted during this time made it possible for him to erect the factory in Stirling Road, Walthamstow, which today is the home of this large organisation.

The year 1932 brought further progress with the acquisition of the toy factory of Brimtoy Ltd., which was even at that time, known throughout Britain and, indeed, in many countries overseas for competitive train sets, accessories and toy stoves. In 1949 A. Wells & Co. Ltd. and Brimtoy Ltd. formed the company of Wells-Brimtoy Distributors Ltd., which is now the Sales Organisation for both companies.

Thus it can be seen that the spirit of enterprise and progress shown by Mr. Wells has put his organisation in the forefront of toy manufacturers. It may also be interesting to note that our subsidiary Company—The Anglesey Instrument & Clock Co.—are manufacturers of various mechanisms and Timepieces.

The Company enjoys renowned reputation for its products, particularly for the reliability of the clockworks. The brightly coloured coachwork of the toys has proved immensely popular, and it is with pride that we offer the merchandise shown in the following pages, knowing them to be, as a direct result of many years of experience in production and ingenuity of design, unsurpassed both for quality and price.

MECHANICAL TOYS
ROLLER CHIMES
216 BELL ROLLER CHIMES, No. 1
4in. diameter wheels. Overall length: 20½in.
217 BELL ROLLER CHIMES, No. 2
5¼in. diameter wheels. Overall length: 26½in.
218 BELL ROLLER CHIMES, No. 3
With coloured wooden spinners. 5¼in. diameter wheels. Overall length: 26¾in.
No. 216
Bell Roller Chimes, No. 1
No. 218
Bell Roller Chimes, No. 3
No. 217
Bell Roller Chimes, No. 2
219 DOUBLE BELL CHIMES
With wooden spinners on metal base.
No. 219
Double Bell Chimes
BRIMTOY BRAND
BRITISH MAKE
WELLS-BRIMTOY DISTRIBUTORS LTD.

MECHANIC
Mechanical
POCKETOY SERIES
LONDON
GUILDFORD VICTORIA HERTFORD
GREENLINE
No. 507
Green Line Bus
No. 501
Steamroller
Brimtoy POCKETOY Series
TRANSPORT
No. 503
Omnibus
REGENT
No. 506
Regent Petrol Lorry
501 STEAM ROLLER
Size - 4in. x 2in. x 1⅞in.
503 OMNIBUS
Size - 4½in. x 1¼in. x 1⅞in.
506 REGENT PETROL LORRY
Size - 4⅜in. x 1⅝in. x 1⅞in.
507 GREEN LINE BUS
(Sliding Door)
Size - 4⅞in. x 1⅞in. x 1⅞in.
ALL TOYS ILLUSTRATED ON THIS PAGE ARE BOXED INDIVIDUALLY
REGISTERED
WELLS
LONDON
TRADE MARK
A. WELLS & CO. LTD. & BRIMTOY LTD.

AL TOYS
Mechanical
POCKETOY SERIES
No. 512
Tip Truck
POCKETOY
REMOVAL VAN
No. 508
Removal Van
No. 510
Long Wheel-base Truck
POCKETOY TRANSPORT
508 REMOVAL VAN
Opening rear doors.
Size - - $4\frac{3}{8}$in. x $1\frac{5}{8}$in. x $1\frac{7}{8}$in.
510 LONG WHEEL-BASE TRUCK
Size - - $5\frac{1}{4}$in. x $1\frac{5}{8}$in. x $1\frac{3}{4}$in.
511 LONG WHEEL-BASE COVERED VAN
Removable Luton type body.
Size - - $5\frac{1}{4}$in. x $1\frac{5}{8}$in. x $2\frac{5}{8}$in.
512 TIP TRUCK
Realistic Tipping action.
Size - - $3\frac{5}{8}$in. x $1\frac{1}{2}$in. x $1\frac{5}{8}$in.
No. 511
Long Wheel-base
Covered Van
ALL TOYS ILLUSTRATED ON THIS PAGE ARE BOXED INDIVIDUALLY.
BRIMTOY BRAND
BRITISH MAKE
WELLS-BRIMTOY DISTRIBUTORS LTD.

MECHANIC
Mechanical
POCKETOY SERIES
No. 513
Short Wheel-Base Lorry and Trailer
No. 519
Morris (Plastic Body)
513 SHORT WHEEL-BASE LORRY AND TRAILER
(Detachable Trailer)
Size - - 6¼in. x 1⅝in. x 1¾in.
516 NOVELTY STOP-GO TROLLEY BUS
Size - - 4¼in. x 2in. x 1¼in.
519 MORRIS (Plastic Body)
(Assorted Colours)
Size - - 3½in. x 1¼in. x 1½in.
WELLS · BRIMTOY DISTRIBUTORS LTD
TRANSPORT
STOP
AND
GO
No. 516
Novelty Stop-Go Trolley Bus
Trolley Bus
REGISTERED
WELLS
O'
LONDON
TRADE MARK
ALL TOYS ILLUSTRATED ON THIS PAGE ARE BOXED INDIVIDUALLY
A. WELLS & CO. LTD. & BRIMTOY LTD.

A L T O Y S
Mechanical
POCKETOY
SERIES
No. 527
Refuse Truck
No. 514
Short Wheel-base
Breakdown Lorry
No. 524
Morris Car (Plastic Body)
and Trailer
514 SHORT WHEEL - BASE BREAKDOWN LORRY
With working Crane.
Size - 4in. x 1⅝in. x 1¾in.
520 ARTICULATED PANTECHNICON
(Detachable Trailer)
Opening rear door and removable body.
Size - 6½in. x 1⅝in. x 2¼in.
524 MORRIS CAR (Plastic Body) and TRAILER
(Assorted Colours)
Size - 5¾in. x 1¼in. x 1½in.
527 REFUSE TRUCK
Sliding side covers.
ALL TOYS ILLUSTRATED ON THIS PAGE ARE BOXED INDIVIDUALLY
TRANSPORT
LONDON BIRMINGHAM GLASGOW
No. 520
Articulated Pantechnicon
BRIMTOY BRAND
BRITISH MAKE
WELLS-BRIMTOY DISTRIBUTORS LTD.

M E C H A N I C
Mechanical
WALKING
FIGURES
147 FATHER CHRISTMAS
Height - - 4¾in.
151 PENGUIN
Height - - 4in.
152 INVERTED CLOWN
Height - - 4¾in.
153 BROWN BEAR
Height - - 4¾in.
No. 153
Brown Bear
No. 151
Penguin
No. 152
Inverted Clown
REGISTERED
WELLS
LONDON
TRADE MARK
ALL TOYS ILLUSTRATED ON THIS PAGE ARE BOXED INDIVIDUALLY
A. WELLS & CO. LTD. & BRIMTOY LTD.

A L T O Y S
Mechanical WALKING FIGURES
No. 148
Clown
No. 149
Walking Pig
No. 156
Mother Goose
No. 60. Rabbit
Size : 6in. x 4¾in.
No. 93. Jumping Kangaroo
Size : 6¼in. x 5½in.
No. 148. Clown
Size : 4¾in.
No. 149. Walking Pig
Size : 4½in. x 2½in.
No. 156. Mother Goose
Size : 4¾in.
No. 60
Jumping Rabbit
Prov. Pat. No. 4477
No. 93
Jumping Kangaroo
Prov. Pat. No. 4477.
ALL TOYS ILLUSTRATED ON THIS PAGE ARE BOXED INDIVIDUALLY
WELLS-BRIMTOY DISTRIBUTORS LTD.
BRIMTOY BRAND
BRITISH MAKE

M E C H A N I C
Mechanical TOYS
No. 9/150
Swimming Fish
No. 123
Road Roller
(Reversible)
No. 66. DRUMMER BOY
Size: 5¼in. x 4½in. x 1¾in. Each in box.
No. 123. ROAD ROLLER
Size: 6½in. x 3¼in. x 3in. ½ dozen in box.
No. 134. CLUCKING CHICKEN
Size 7½in. x 6in. x 5½in. Each in box.
No. 9/150. SWIMMING FISH
Size: 11½in. x 3in. x 2½in. Each in box.
No. 134
Clucking Chicken
(Push-along)
Prov. Pat. No. 23710.
No. 66
Drummer Boy
Prov. Pat. No. 3873.
REGISTERED
WELLS
O'
LONDON
TRADE MARK
A. WELLS & CO. LTD. & BRIMTOY LTD.

A L T O Y S
Mechanical
TOYS
GOLDEN EAGLE
2509
No. 94
Golden Eagle
Locomotive
PRIVATE
No. 121
Road Coach
EXPRESS TRANSPORT
No. 68
Express Transport
68 EXPRESS TRANSPORT
Size - 7in. x 3⅝in. x 3¼in.
77 RACING CAR
Size - 11⅛in. x 3½in. x 3in.
94 GOLDEN EAGLE
LOCOMOTIVE
To fit "O" Gauge Rails.
Size - 6½in. x 2¼in. x 2¾in.
97 DIESEL TRAIN
"Golden Streak"
Size - 9¼in. x 1¾in. x 2¼in.
121 ROAD COACH
Size - 7¼in. x 3½in. x 3in.
No. 77
Racing Car
GOLDEN STREAK
No. 97
Diesel Train "Golden Streak"
ALL TOYS ILLUSTRATED ON THIS PAGE ARE PACKED ½-DOZEN IN A BOX
WELLS-BRIMTOY DISTRIBUTORS LTD.
BRIMTOY BRAND
BRITISH MAKE

M E C H A N I C
Mechanical
TOYS
98 E.R.A. RACER
Size - 8¾in. x 3¼in. x 2¾in.
(½ dozen in a box.)
105 TROLLEY BUS
Size - 6¾in. x 4in. x 2½in.
(½ dozen in a box.)
BUY BRITISH
TRANSPORT BUS
804
No. 105
Trolley Bus
No. 98
E.R.A. Racer
No. 70
Paddle Boat
GREEN LINE
No. 122
Green Line Bus
70 PADDLE BOAT
Size - 11in. x 4in. x 3½in.
(Individually boxed.)
73 LOCOMOTIVE (Royal Scot), with Brake.
To fit "O" Gauge rails.
Size - 6¼in. x 2½in. x 2¾in.
(½ dozen in a box.)
122 GREEN LINE BUS
Size - 7¼in. x 2¾in. x 2¾in.
(½ dozen in a box.)
ROYAL SCOT
7171
No. 73
Royal Scot Locomotive
REGISTERED
WELLS
LONDON
TRADE MARK
A. WELLS & CO. LTD. & BRIMTOY LTD.

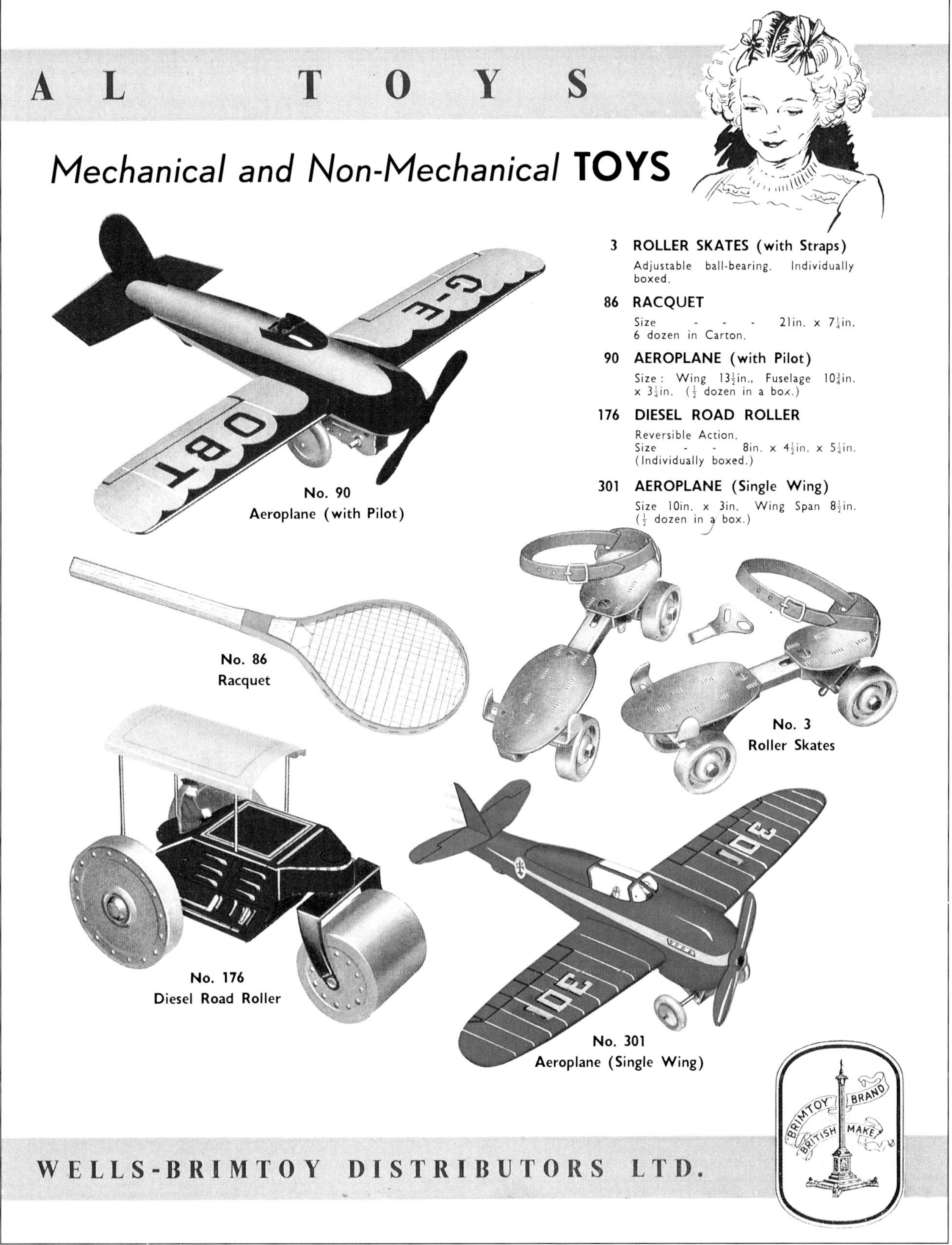
A L T O Y S
Mechanical and Non-Mechanical TOYS
3 ROLLER SKATES (with Straps)
Adjustable ball-bearing. Individually boxed.
86 RACQUET
Size - - - 21in. x 7¼in.
6 dozen in Carton.
90 AEROPLANE (with Pilot)
Size: Wing 13½in., Fuselage 10¾in. x 3¼in. (½ dozen in a box.)
176 DIESEL ROAD ROLLER
Reversible Action.
Size - - 8in. x 4½in. x 5¼in.
(Individually boxed.)
301 AEROPLANE (Single Wing)
Size 10in. x 3in. Wing Span 8½in.
(½ dozen in a box.)
G-E
OBT
No. 90
Aeroplane (with Pilot)
No. 86
Racquet
No. 3
Roller Skates
No. 176
Diesel Road Roller
301
No. 301
Aeroplane (Single Wing)
BRIMTOY BRAND
BRITISH MAKE
WELLS-BRIMTOY DISTRIBUTORS LTD.

M E C H A N I C
Mechanical TOYS
No. 127. Tip Truck only.
No. 128. Tip Truck with Trailer.
127 TIP TRUCK
128 TIP TRUCK with TRAILER
Truck size 10½in. x 3¾in. x 3½in.
Trailer size 7in. x 3¾in. x 3½in.
129 BREAKDOWN LORRY
With Working Crane.
Size 11¾in. x 3¾in. x 4in.
131 TROLLEY BUS
Size 8¼in. x 2¾in. x 5in.
133 FIRE ESCAPE
Extending Ladder and Turntable.
Size 9½in. x 4¾in. x 5in.
BUY BRITISH
657
TRANSPORT BUS
No. 131
Trolley Bus
FIRE ENGINE
No. 133
Fire Escape
BREAKDOWN SERVICE
No. 129
Breakdown Lorry
REGISTERED
WELLS
LONDON
TRADE MARK
ALL TOYS ILLUSTRATED ON THIS PAGE ARE BOXED INDIVIDUALLY
A. WELLS & CO. LTD. & BRIMTOY LTD.

A L T O Y S
Mechanical
TOYS
36 FLOOR LOCO
Size - 9$\frac{1}{2}$in. x 2$\frac{1}{4}$in. x 3$\frac{3}{4}$in.
(Boxed individually)
61 TIP TRUCK
(With Lever)
Size - 10in. x 4in. x 3$\frac{1}{4}$in.
($\frac{1}{2}$ dozen in a box)
4 3 6 7
No. 36
Floor Loco
130 PETROL BUS
Size - 8$\frac{1}{4}$in. x 2$\frac{3}{4}$in. x 4$\frac{1}{4}$in.
(Boxed individually)
174 REGENT PETROL LORRY
Size - 10in. x 4in. x 3$\frac{1}{2}$in.
(Boxed individually)
No. 61
Tip Truck
REGENT
BUY BRITISH
TRANSPORT BUS
MADE IN ENGLAND
No. 174
Regent Petrol Lorry
No. 130
Petrol Bus
BRIMTOY BRAND
BRITISH MAKE
WELLS-BRIMTOY DISTRIBUTORS LTD.

M E C H A N I C
New Range of
TOY STOVES
No. 82
Kitchen Range
No. 72
Chimney Stove
72 CHIMNEY STOVE
Comprising 1 Saucepan, 2 Stewpans. Size 6in. x 6¼in. x 4in.
82 KITCHEN RANGE
With fitted Plate Rack, 1 Grater, 1 Round Dish, 1 Square Dish, 1 Saucepan, 1 Stewpan. Size 6in. x 5¼in. x 3¾in.
211 ELECTRIC LIGHT STOVE
With electric light fittings for battery use. 2 Doors (open), Fire and Ash Pan, Flue. Utensils comprising: 3 Plates, 1 Square Dish, 2 Round Dishes, 1 Grater, 1 Frying Pan, 1 Large Stewpan, 1 Kettle, 2 Saucepans with lids. Size 8¼in. x 8¼in. x 4¾in.
No. 211
Electric Light Stove
STOVE No. 211 PACKED INDIVIDUALLY. No. 72 and No. 82 PACKED ½-DOZ. IN A BOX.
REGISTERED
WELLS
O'
LONDON
TRADE MARK
A. WELLS & CO. LTD. & BRIMTOY LTD.

A L T O Y S

New Range of

TOY STOVES

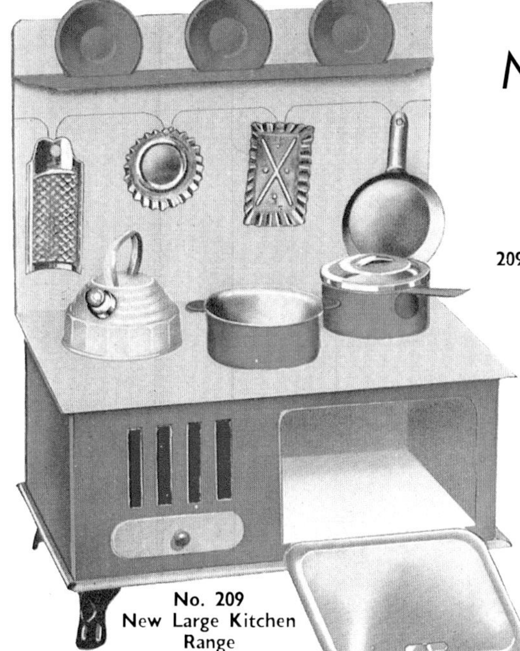

No. 209
New Large Kitchen Range

209 NEW LARGE KITCHEN RANGE

With a Drop Door, Fire and Ash Pan. Utensils: 3 Plates, 1 Grater, 1 Frying Pan, 1 Round Dish, 1 Square Dish, 1 Kettle, 1 Large Stewpan, 1 Saucepan and Lid. Size 6½in. x 4½in. x 8in.

Individually Boxed.

No. 169
Gas Stove

169 GAS STOVE

4 Plates, 1 Frying Pan, 1 Saucepan and Lid.
Size - 10in. x 4½in. x 3½in.
Packed ½ dozen in box.

No. 79
Child's Kitchen Range

79 CHILD'S KITCHEN RANGE

Size 6in. x 4in. x 6in. With 4 plates, 1 Stewpan, 1 Saucepan and Lid. Packed ½ dozen in box.

No. 9/19
Cinderella and Prince Charming

No. 99
Mickey Mouse
Handcar

A L T O Y S

Walt Disney

CINDERELLA SWEEPER SETS

No. 119

No. 112

No. 116

No. 106

No. 120

No. 106. CARPET SWEEPER
Size : $5\frac{1}{4}$in. x $3\frac{1}{4}$in. x $1\frac{3}{4}$in. 6 in box.
No. 112. BRUSH & PAN SET
Size of Card : 10in. x 10in.
No. 116. CARPET SWEEPER
Size : 7in. x $4\frac{1}{4}$in. x 2in. 3 in box.
No. 117. SWEEPER SET
Size of Card : $23\frac{1}{2}$in. x $7\frac{1}{2}$in.
No. 118. SWEEPER SET
Size of Card : 29in. x $9\frac{1}{2}$in.
No. 119. SWEEPER SET
Size of Card : $20\frac{1}{4}$in. x 11in.
No. 120. SWEEPER SET
Size of Card : $28\frac{1}{2}$in. x $14\frac{1}{2}$in.

No. 117

No. 118

WELLS-BRIMTOY DISTRIBUTORS LTD.

BRIMTOY BRAND BRITISH MAKE

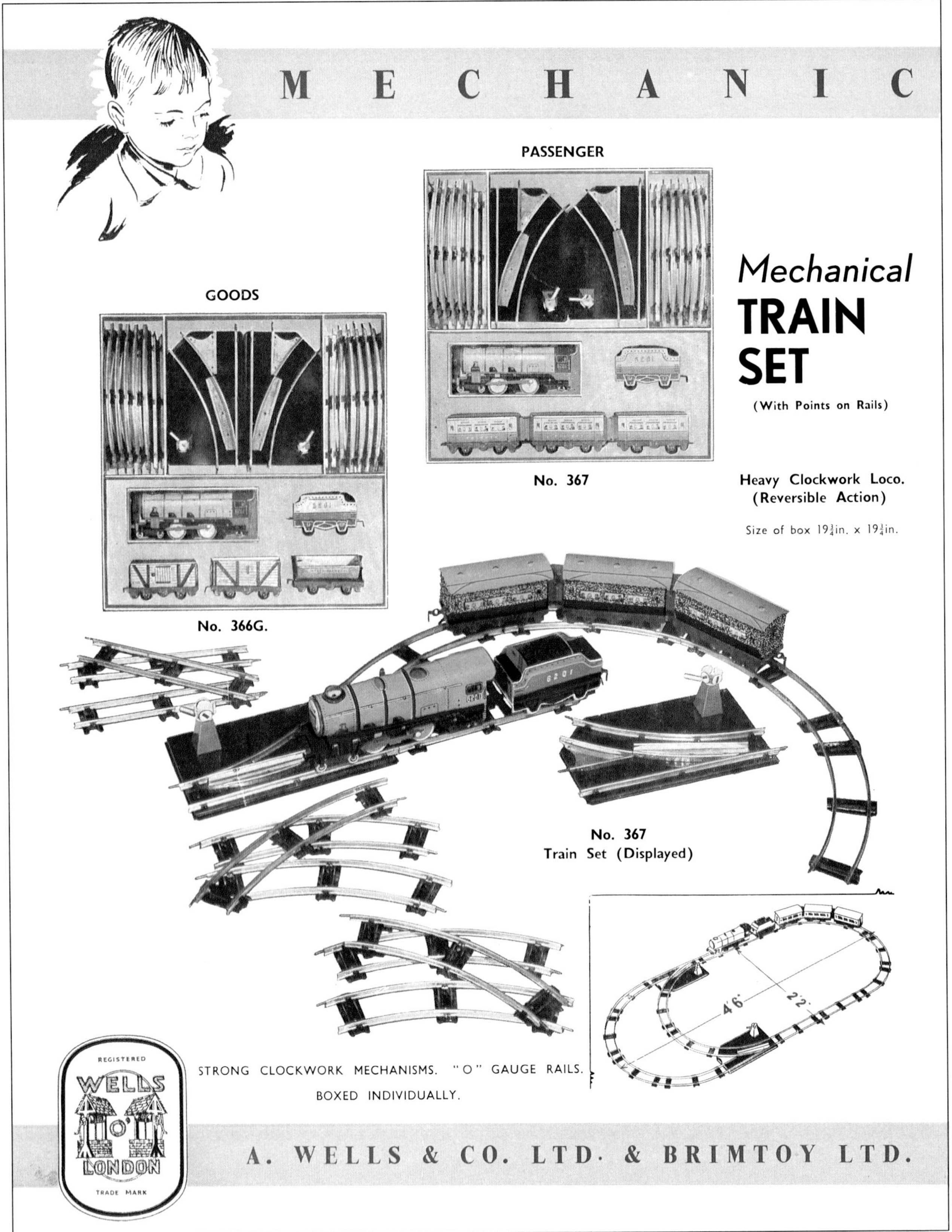
M E C H A N I C
PASSENGER
GOODS
Mechanical
TRAIN
SET
(With Points on Rails)
No. 367
No. 366G.
Heavy Clockwork Loco.
(Reversible Action)
Size of box 19¾in. x 19¾in.
No. 367
Train Set (Displayed)
4'6"
2'2"
REGISTERED
WELLS
'O'
LONDON
TRADE MARK
STRONG CLOCKWORK MECHANISMS. "O" GAUGE RAILS.
BOXED INDIVIDUALLY.
A. WELLS & CO. LTD. & BRIMTOY LTD.

A L T O Y S

Mechanical
TRAIN SETS

357 TRAIN SET
Engine and Tender, 2 Trucks, 1 Small Signal, 1 Small Telegraph Pole, 4 Curved Rails, Cut-out Box, attractive Train Label.
Size of box: 12½in. x 13½in. x 2¾in.

No. 357. Train Set.

No. 362. Train Set.

No. 362
Train Set (Displayed)
Engine and Tender, 2 Passenger Coaches, Station, Signal and Box. 6 Curved Rails. Cut-out Box, attractive Train Label.
Size of Box: 14¾in. x 14¼in. x 2¾in.

ALL STRONG CLOCKWORK MECHANISMS. "O" GAUGE RAILS.

WELLS-BRIMTOY DISTRIBUTORS LTD.

"BRIMTOY" BRAND
BRITISH MAKE

M E C H A N I C

Mechanical

TRAIN SETS

ALL STRONG CLOCKWORK MECHANISMS.
"O" GAUGE RAILS.

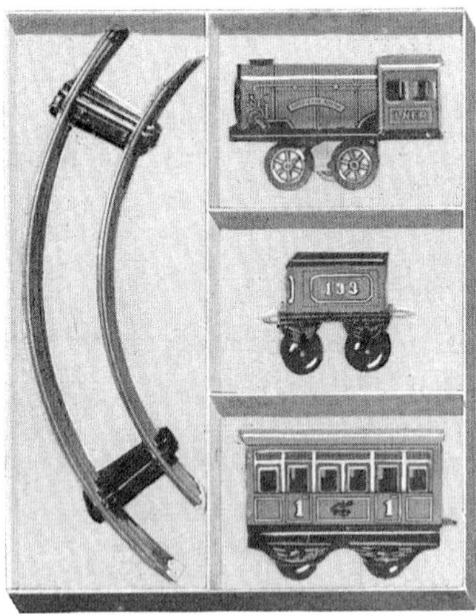

No. 352. Train Set.

Small Engine and Tender, Coach, 4 small Curved Rails. Coloured Box. Size of Box: 8½in. x 10½in. x 2¼in.

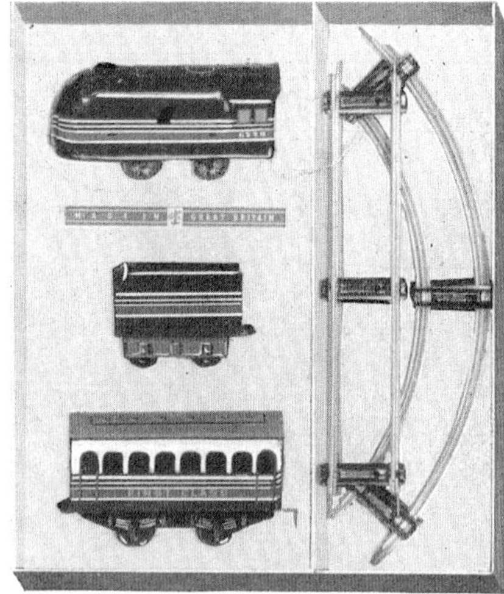

No. 354. Train Set.

Coronation Engine and Tender, Coach, 4 Curved Rails, 2 Straight Rails. Cut-out Display. Coloured Box. Size of Box: 10in. x 12in. x 2½in.

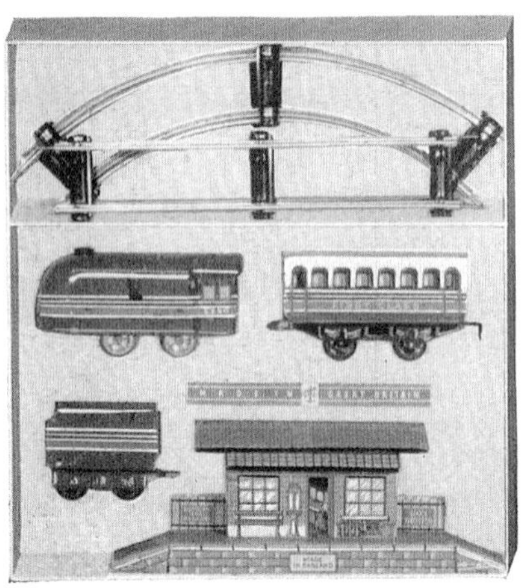

No. 355. Train Set.

Coronation Engine and Tender, Coach, Station, 4 Curved Rails, 2 Straight Rails. Cut-out Display. Coloured Box. Size of Box: 12½in. x 12½in. x 2¾in.

No. 356. Train Set.

Coronation Engine and Tender, 2 Coaches, Station, 4 Curved Rails, 2 Straight Rails. Cut-out Display. Coloured Box. Size of Box: 15in. x 12⅜in. x 2¾in.

A. WELLS & CO. LTD. & BRIMTOY LTD.

A L T O Y S

Mechanical

TRAIN SETS

No. 353. Train Set.

Engine and Tender, Goods Van, Small Signal, 4 Curved Rails, 2 Small Straight Rails. Cut-out Display, Coloured Box. Size of Box: 16in. x 10¼in. x 2in.

No. 353. Train Set.

No. 360. Train Set.

Engine and Tender, Truck, Side-tip Truck, B.P. Truck, Signal Box and Signal, Tunnel, 6 Heavy Curved Rails, 2 Heavy Straight Rails. Box Type Lid. Coloured Box. Attractive Train Label. Size of Box: 15¼in. x 16in. x 2¾in.

No. 360
Train Set (Displayed)

ALL STRONG CLOCKWORK MECHANISMS. "O" GAUGE RAILS.

WELLS-BRIMTOY DISTRIBUTORS LTD.

BRIMTOY BRAND
BRITISH MAKE

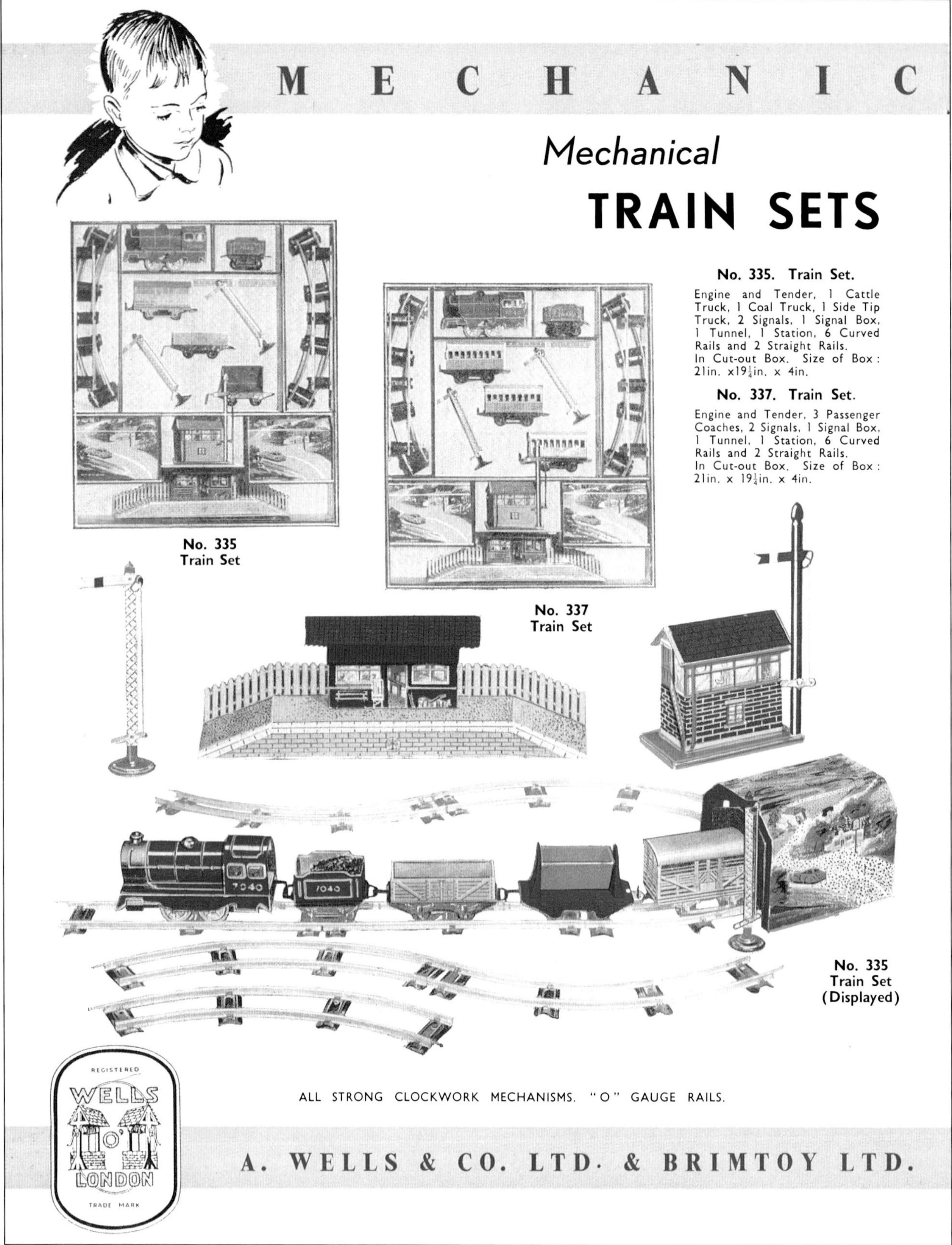
M E C H A N I C
Mechanical
TRAIN SETS
No. 335. Train Set.
Engine and Tender, 1 Cattle Truck, 1 Coal Truck, 1 Side Tip Truck, 2 Signals, 1 Signal Box, 1 Tunnel, 1 Station, 6 Curved Rails and 2 Straight Rails.
In Cut-out Box. Size of Box: 21in. x19¾in. x 4in.
No. 337. Train Set.
Engine and Tender, 3 Passenger Coaches, 2 Signals, 1 Signal Box, 1 Tunnel, 1 Station, 6 Curved Rails and 2 Straight Rails.
In Cut-out Box. Size of Box: 21in. x 19¾in. x 4in.
No. 335
Train Set
No. 337
Train Set
No. 335
Train Set
(Displayed)
REGISTERED
WELLS
LONDON
TRADE MARK
ALL STRONG CLOCKWORK MECHANISMS. "O" GAUGE RAILS.
A. WELLS & CO. LTD. & BRIMTOY LTD.

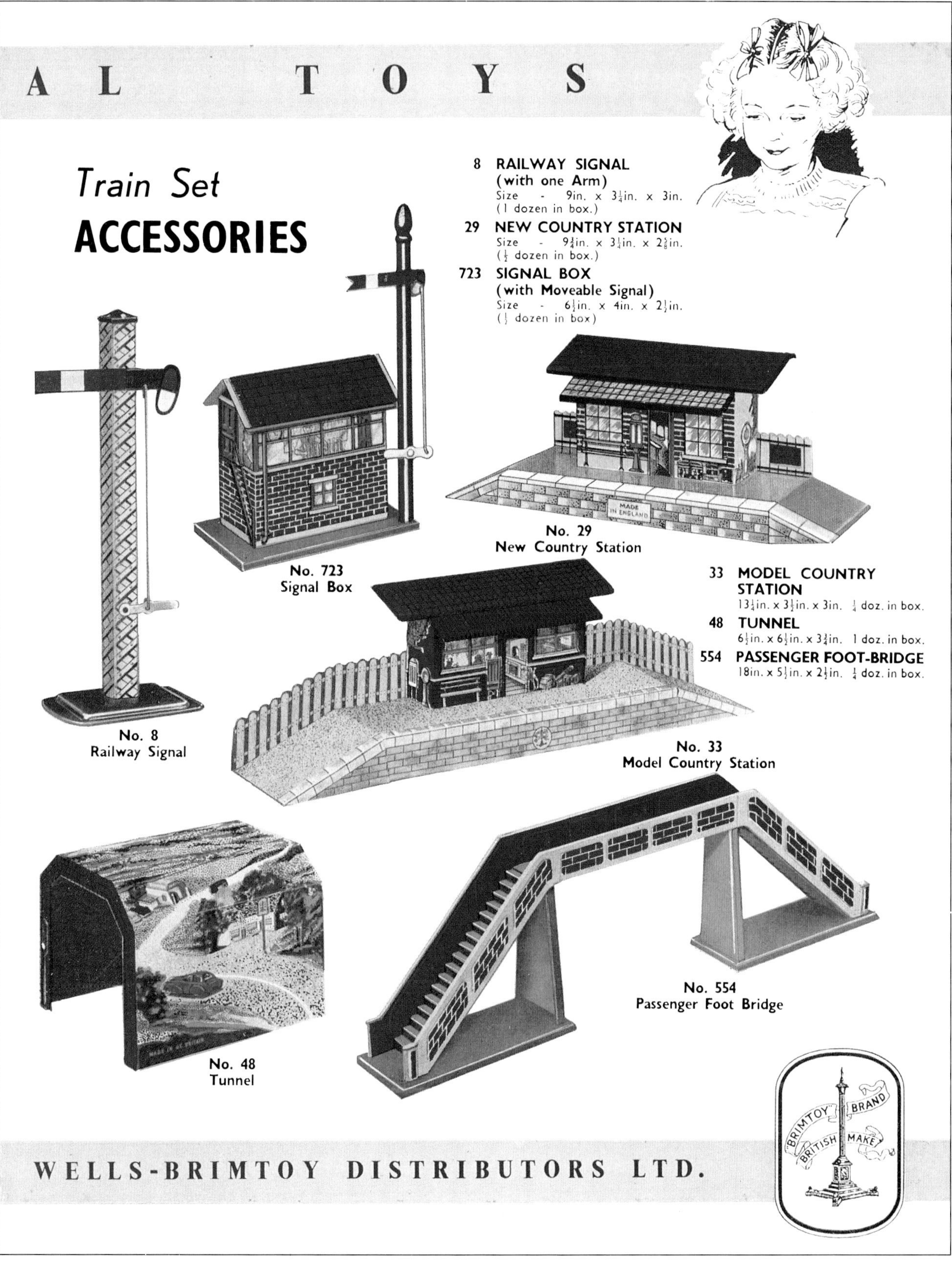
A L T O Y S
Train Set
ACCESSORIES
8 RAILWAY SIGNAL
(with one Arm)
Size - 9in. x 3¼in. x 3in.
(1 dozen in box.)
29 NEW COUNTRY STATION
Size - 9¾in. x 3¼in. x 2⅝in.
(½ dozen in box.)
723 SIGNAL BOX
(with Moveable Signal)
Size - 6½in. x 4in. x 2½in.
(½ dozen in box)
No. 723
Signal Box
No. 29
New Country Station
33 MODEL COUNTRY STATION
13¼in. x 3½in. x 3in. ¼ doz. in box.
48 TUNNEL
6½in. x 6½in. x 3¾in. 1 doz. in box.
554 PASSENGER FOOT-BRIDGE
18in. x 5½in. x 2½in. ¼ doz. in box.
No. 8
Railway Signal
No. 33
Model Country Station
No. 48
Tunnel
No. 554
Passenger Foot Bridge
BRIMTOY BRAND
BRITISH MAKE
WELLS-BRIMTOY DISTRIBUTORS LTD.

MECHANICAL TOYS
Mechanical and Non-Mechanical
TOYS
MADE IN ENGLAND
No. 102
Telephone
102 TELEPHONE
With realistic dialling movement and ringing bell.
166 SPEED BOAT (Mechanical)
Plastic hull and deck.
167 SPEED BOAT (Mechanical)
Plastic hull and deck.
236 RAILWAY TUNNEL
Made of strong lightweight composition.
237 RAILWAY TUNNEL
(with embankments)
Made of strong lightweight composition
No. 237
Composition Railway Tunnel with Embankments
No. 236
Composition Railway Tunnel
No. 166
Model Speed Boat (Mechanical)
These Speed Boats are fitted with strong long-running clockwork mechanisms.
No. 167
Model Speed Boat (Mechanical)
REGISTERED
WELLS
LONDON
TRADE MARK
A. WELLS & CO. LTD. & BRIMTOY LTD.

MECHANICAL TOYS

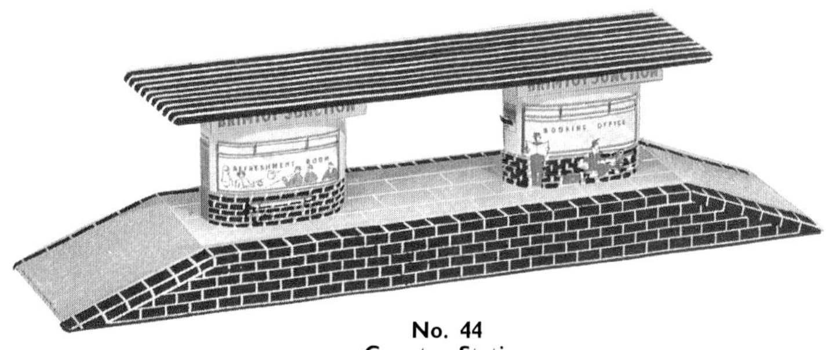

No. 44
Country Station
(Island Type Platform)

Train Set

ACCESSORIES

"0" GAUGE RAILS

ALL RAILS PACKED
THREE DOZEN IN A BOX

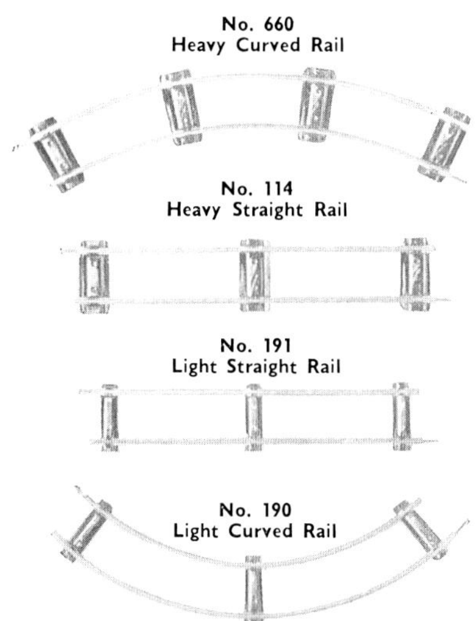

No. 660
Heavy Curved Rail

No. 114
Heavy Straight Rail

No. 191
Light Straight Rail

No. 190
Light Curved Rail

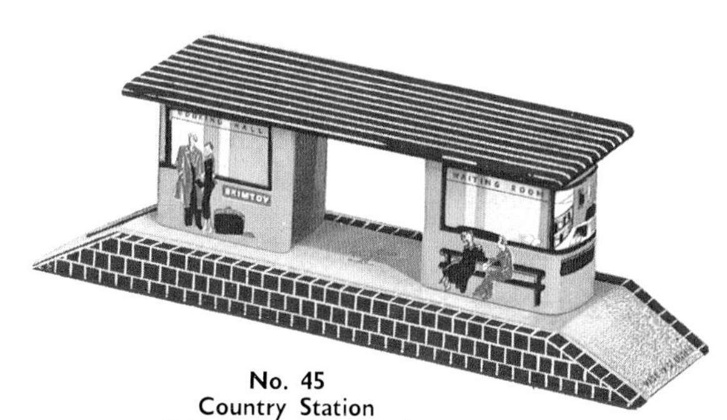

No. 45
Country Station
(Island Type Platform)

44 COUNTRY STATION
Island Type Platform with Booking Office and Refreshment Room.
Size 12½in. x 3in. x 3in. Packed ¼ dozen in a box.

45 COUNTRY STATION
Island Type Platform with Booking Hall and Waiting Room.
Size 9¾in. x 2⅛in. x 3in. Packed ½ dozen in a box.

WELLS-BRIMTOY DISTRIBUTORS LTD.

TRAIN SET ACCESSORIES

No. 8050. Coach
Size $5\frac{1}{4}$in. x $2\frac{1}{4}$in. x $2\frac{3}{4}$in.

No. 801. Bogey Wheel Pullman Coach
Size $7\frac{7}{8}$in. x $2\frac{1}{4}$in. x $2\frac{5}{8}$in.

No. 55. Shell Tanker
Size $5\frac{1}{4}$in. x $2\frac{1}{4}$in. x $2\frac{3}{4}$in.

No. 158. Coach
Size $5\frac{1}{4}$in. x $2\frac{1}{4}$in. x $2\frac{3}{4}$in.

No. 8055. Goods Truck
Size $5\frac{1}{2}$in. x $2\frac{1}{4}$in. x $2\frac{3}{4}$in.

No. 700. Coach
Size $5\frac{1}{2}$in. x $2\frac{1}{4}$in. x $2\frac{3}{4}$in.

No. 8055. Goods Truck
Size $5\frac{1}{2}$in. x $2\frac{1}{4}$in. x $2\frac{3}{4}$in.

No. 58. Refrigeration Van
Size $5\frac{1}{4}$in. x $1\frac{3}{4}$in. x 3in.

No. 52. Open Truck
Size $5\frac{1}{4}$in. x $2\frac{1}{4}$in. x $1\frac{3}{4}$in.

No. 57. Tip Truck.
Size $5\frac{1}{4}$in. x $1\frac{3}{4}$in. x $2\frac{1}{2}$in.

No. 803. Bogey Wheel Open Truck
Size $7\frac{3}{4}$in. x $2\frac{1}{4}$in. x $2\frac{1}{8}$in.

Passenger and Goods Rolling Stock.

To fit "O" gauge rails. All coachwork brightly coloured.

Nos. 801/805/802/806/803/58 packed 6 in a box.
Nos. 8050/158/700/52/55/8055/57 packed 12 in a box.

WELLS-BRIMTOY DISTRIBUTORS LTD.
2509
FIRST CLASS
Train sets & Pocketoys
657
BREAKDOWN SERVICE
REGISTERED
WELLS
O'
LONDON
TRADE MARK
BRIMTOY
BRAND
BRITISH MAKE
PROGRESS WORKS, STIRLING ROAD, WALTHAMSTOW, LONDON, E.17
TELEPHONE: LARKSWOOD 2691-4
TELEGRAMS: WELSOTOYS-WALT-LONDON

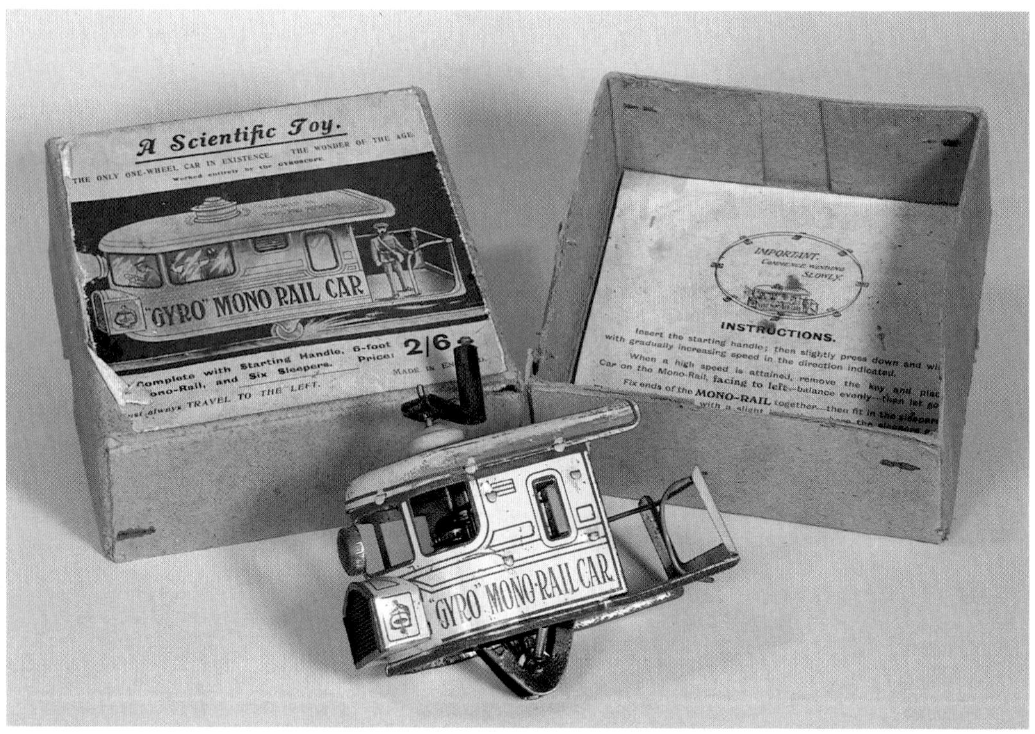

This interesting clockwork saloon may have been made for Marks & Spencer as a special line by Wells, c.1935 (top)

A fascinating clockwork gyroscopic monorail vehicle, c.1912, imprinted 'Made in England' (bottom)

APPENDIX V

Early English Catalogue

A rare and early catalogue issued by A Francois of Birmingham c.1870. This catalogue is typical of many similar publications by British model houses or 'dock-yards' as they were known. Their offerings were a mix of 'in-house' manufacture and bought-in merchandise, which in many instances were of French origin.

"Our true intent is all for your delight."—Mid. Sum. Night's Dream.

FIFTH EDITION.

PRICE LIST

OF

MODEL STEAM ENGINES,

EYE GLASSES,

Achromatic Opera & Field Glasses,

ETC., ETC.,

SUPPLIED (to letter order only)

BY

A. FRANCOIS,

SPECIALIST,

Devonshire Place, Ryland Road, BIRMINGHAM.

SHIPWAY BROS., PRINTERS, [PRICE TWOPENCE.] 39, MOOR STREET, BIRMINGHAM.

"I will content you if what pleases you contents you."—As You Like It, Act v., sc. i.

"I shall desire you of more acquaintance."—Mid. Sum. Night's Dream.

No. 93.

No. 93—Locomotive, bright brass, gun metal dome, buffers, etc. length 9 inches 27/

No. 94.

„ 94—Locomotive, bright brass, whistle, valve, steam and water taps, etc., length 9 inches 19/6

No. 96.

No. 95—Japanned Locomotive, as No. 96 .. .. 14/6

„ 96—Copper Boiler on brass frame, dome, valve, whistle, steam and water taps, etc., $9\frac{1}{2}$in. long, quite new .. 25/-

A. Francois, Specialist, Birmingham.

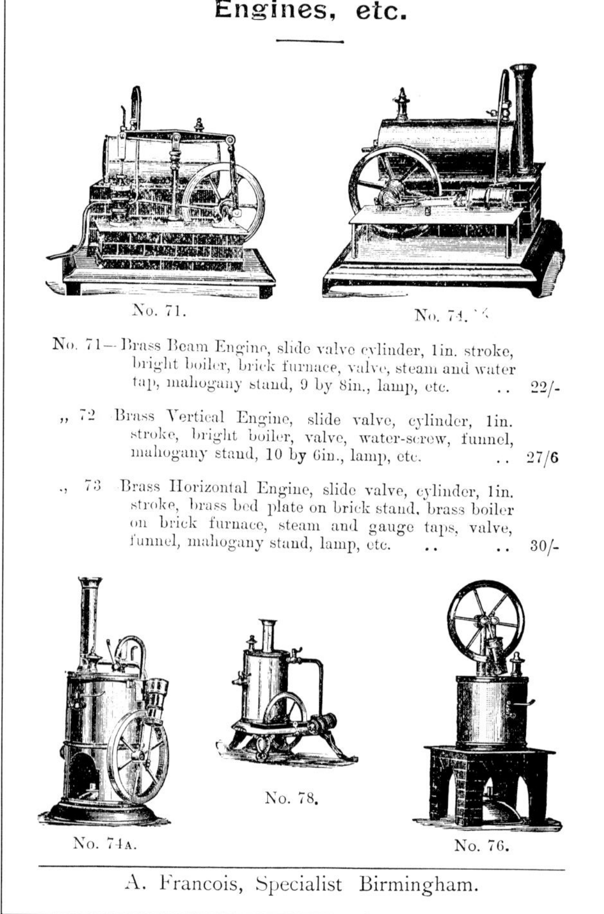

Engines, etc.

No. 71. No. 74.

No. 71—Brass Beam Engine, slide valve cylinder, 1in. stroke, bright boiler, brick furnace, valve, steam and water tap, mahogany stand, 9 by 8in., lamp, etc. .. 22/-

„ 72—Brass Vertical Engine, slide valve, cylinder, 1in. stroke, bright boiler, valve, water-screw, funnel, mahogany stand, 10 by 6in., lamp, etc. .. 27/6

„ 73—Brass Horizontal Engine, slide valve, cylinder, 1in. stroke, brass bed plate on brick stand, brass boiler on brick furnace, steam and gauge taps, valve, funnel, mahogany stand, lamp, etc. 30/-

No. 74A. No. 78. No. 76.

A. Francois, Specialist Birmingham.

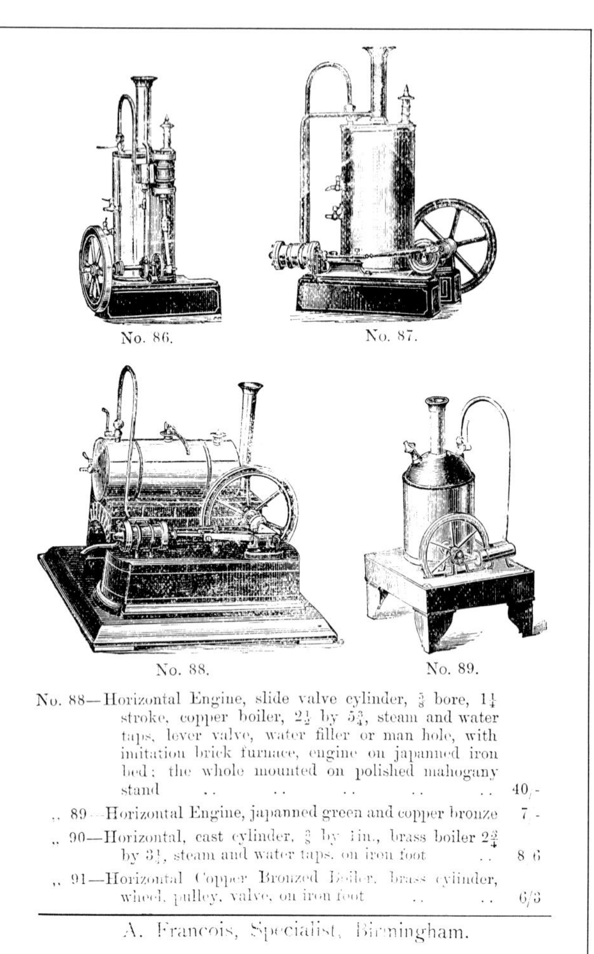

No. 86. No. 87.

No. 88. No. 89.

No. 88—Horizontal Engine, slide valve cylinder, $\frac{5}{8}$ bore, $1\frac{1}{4}$ stroke, copper boiler, $2\frac{1}{2}$ by $5\frac{3}{4}$, steam and water taps, lever valve, water filler or man hole, with imitation brick furnace, engine on japanned iron bed; the whole mounted on polished mahogany stand 40/-

„ 89—Horizontal Engine, japanned green and copper bronze 7/-

„ 90—Horizontal, cast cylinder, $\frac{3}{8}$ by 1in., brass boiler $2\frac{3}{4}$ by $3\frac{1}{4}$, steam and water taps, on iron foot .. 8/6

„ 91—Horizontal Copper Bronzed Boiler, brass cylinder, wheel, pulley, valve, on iron foot 6/3

A. Francois, Specialist, Birmingham.

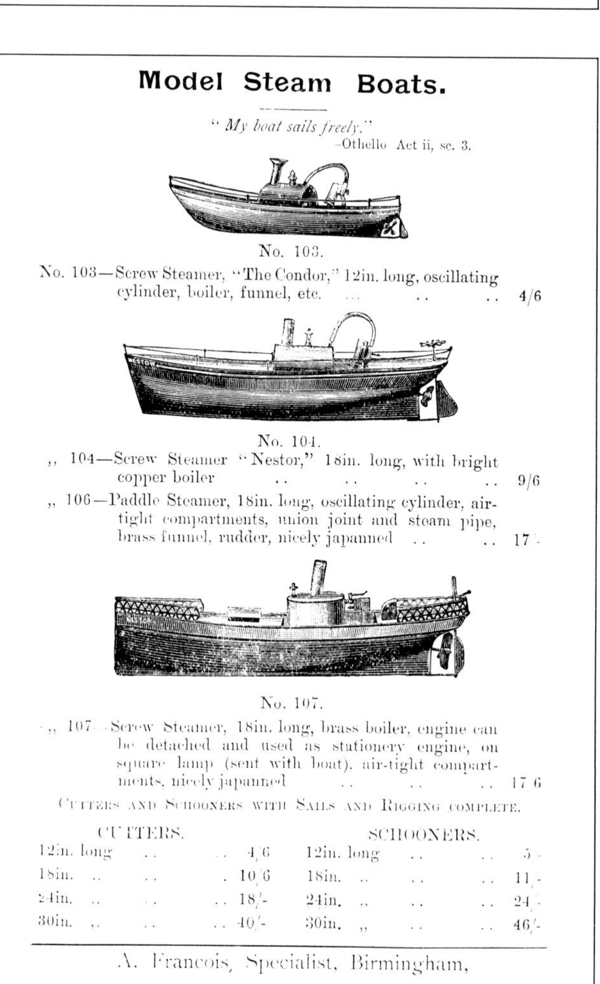

Model Steam Boats.

"My boat sails freely."
—Othello Act ii, sc. 3.

No. 103.

No. 103—Screw Steamer, "The Condor," 12in. long, oscillating cylinder, boiler, funnel, etc. 4/6

No. 104.

„ 104—Screw Steamer "Nestor," 18in. long, with bright copper boiler 9/6

„ 106—Paddle Steamer, 18in. long, oscillating cylinder, air-tight compartments, union joint and steam pipe, brass funnel, rudder, nicely japanned 17/-

No. 107.

„ 107—Screw Steamer, 18in. long, brass boiler, engine can be detached and used as stationery engine, on square lamp (sent with boat), air-tight compartments, nicely japanned 17/6

CUTTERS AND SCHOONERS WITH SAILS AND RIGGING COMPLETE.

CUTTERS.		SCHOONERS.	
12in. long	4/6	12in. long	5/-
18in.	10/6	18in.	11/-
24in.	18/-	24in. „	24/-
30in. „	40/-	30in. „	46/-

A. Francois, Specialist, Birmingham,

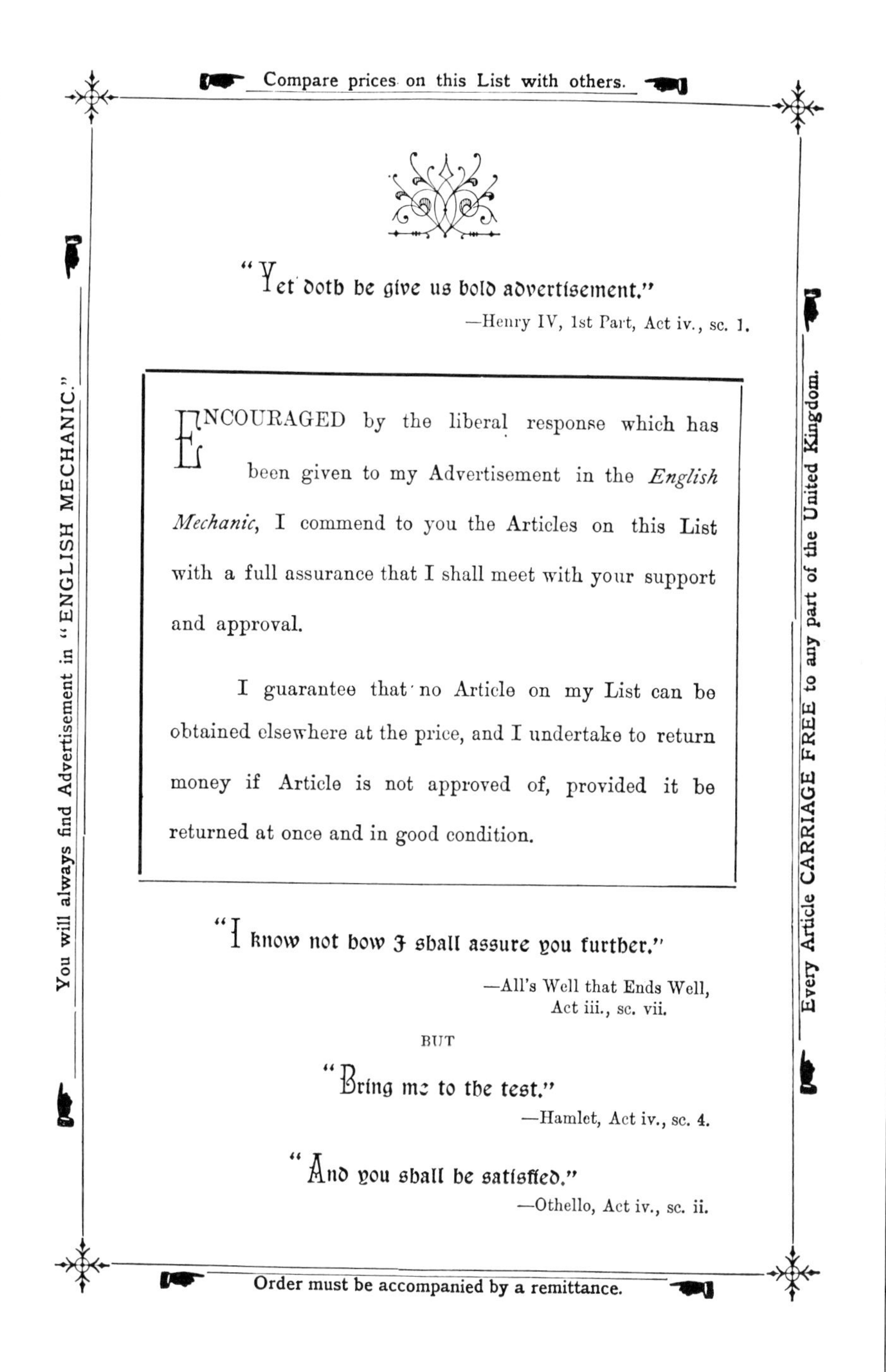

Compare prices on this List with others.

You will always find Advertisement in "ENGLISH MECHANIC."

Every Article CARRIAGE FREE to any part of the United Kingdom.

"Yet doth he give us bold advertisement."

—Henry IV, 1st Part, Act iv., sc. 1.

ENCOURAGED by the liberal response which has been given to my Advertisement in the *English Mechanic*, I commend to you the Articles on this List with a full assurance that I shall meet with your support and approval.

I guarantee that no Article on my List can be obtained elsewhere at the price, and I undertake to return money if Article is not approved of, provided it be returned at once and in good condition.

"I know not how I shall assure you further."

—All's Well that Ends Well,
Act iii., sc. vii.

BUT

"Bring me to the test."

—Hamlet, Act iv., sc. 4.

"And you shall be satisfied."

—Othello, Act iv., sc. ii.

Order must be accompanied by a remittance.

APPENDIX VI

Early Patent Application

This 1891 patent application by Desiré Thomas Piot for a steam generator particularly useful for toys boats was typical of the plethora of inventions for toys that were submitted for patenting in the late 19th century. A small put-put boat utilising this invention was marketed by J Robinson (*see page 30*).

N° 20,081  **A.D. 1891**

Date of Application, 19th Nov., 1891
Complete Specification Left, 18th Aug., 1892—Accepted, 15th Oct., 1892

PROVISIONAL SPECIFICATION.

Improvements in Steam Generators.

I, Desire Thomas Piot, of No. 71, Bolsover Street, Euston Road, in the County of Middlesex Electrician do hereby declare the nature of this invention to be as follows :—

The object of my invention is to produce a steam generator in which the operation of feeding with water is continuous and depends upon the vaporization of the water in the heating chamber.

In carrying my invention into effect I use two or more tubes, opening into a common chamber so that the orifices thereof, and the ports or slots formed in the sides or circumference may be close to the sides of said chamber. I prefer to charge the tubes and chamber with water, and to generate steam by heating said chamber. The exit of the steam under pressure and consequent condensation by contact with the atmosphere or other surrounding medium causes a reverse current by which the water of condensation or other water may be drawn into the generator.

The chief feature of my said invention is to place a small volume of fluid in direct contact with a source of heat, and to utilise the pressure for producing mechanical work, the volume of liquid under action being always supplied by its own condensation either by using the water thereof or utilising the attenuated pressure to draw in water from other sources and produce a continuous action.

My said invention is especially useful in the case of toy boats, where the propulsion depends upon the pressure of steam acting directly upon the water, and the consequent condensation serves to supply the feed by convection.

Dated this 18th day of November 1891.

FREDK. WALKER,
11, Furnival Street, Holborn, London, E.C., Agent for the Applicant.

COMPLETE SPECIFICATION.

Improvements in Steam Generators.

I Desire Thomas Piot of No 71 Bolsover Street Euston Road in the County of Middlesex, Electrician do hereby declare the nature of this invention and in what manner the same is to be performed, to be particularly described and ascertained in and by the following statement :—

The object of my invention is to produce a steam generator in which the operation of feeding with water is continuous and depends upon the vaporization of the water in the heating chamber.

In order that my invention may be the better understood I have appended the accompanying sheet of drawings in which

Figure 1 is a side elevational view of a model boat having my improved steam generator adapted thereto.

Figure 2 is a plan of the same and

Figure 3 is a transverse section of my improved generator.

In carrying my invention into effect I employ two or more tubes A A[1] one of said tubes A[1] may be slightly longer than the other, one end of the tubes opening into a chamber B common to the two so that the orifices, ports or slots which may be formed in the sides or circumference may be close to the sides of the above mentioned chamber B, I prefer to charge the tubes and chamber with water and to generate steam by heating said chamber in any suitable manner.

The exit of steam under pressure and consequent condensation by contact with

[*Price 8d.*]

When used merely as a generator the open ends of the tubes would be immersed in a tank of water.

Dated this 16th day of November 1897.

THOMAS ERNEST HALFORD,
11, Furnival Street, London, E.C., Applicant's Agent.

COMPLETE SPECIFICATION.

Improvements in Steam Generators applicable for Propelling Boats.

I, Désiré Thomas Piot, of 10, Buckingham Street, Titchfield Street, in the County of London, Engineer, do hereby declare the nature of this invention and in what manner the same is to be performed, to be particularly described and ascertained in and by the following statement:—

The object of this invention is to produce a steam generator having an automatic continuous feed the said feed being effected by the evaporation of the water in the generator.

Now according to this invention I provide a vertical vessel of any suitable size and shape but preferably elliptical in cross section and having an inclined bottom.

When applying my invention to propelling boats I provide two pipes or tubes which project beyond the stern of the boat in a horizontal direction and are also bent upwards at any suitable angle.

The upper portion of the said pipes or tubes are passed into the said vertical vessel and are secured therein by any suitable means the upper ends of the said pipes or tubes being almost in contact with the underside of the top of the vertical vessel.

The tubes enter the inclined bottom of the vertical vessel at the highest part thereof and extend diagonally to the top of the said vessel the tubes being disposed across the smaller diameter thereof.

The upper end of each tube has a narrow slot therein opposite to the side of the vertical vessel nearest to it.

The top of the vertical vessel is provided with an escape valve which may be either spring loaded or dead weighted or otherwise the said valve fitting steam tight on a suitable seating.

The heat is mainly applied to the bottom of the vertical vessel near the junction of the said vessel with the tubes.

And in order that my said invention may be fully understood I will proceed to explain the same with reference to the accompanying sheet of drawings in which

Fig. 1 represents elevation of a toy steamboat fitted with a steam generator and propelling apparatus constructed according to this invention.

Fig. 2 is section through boat and generator.

Fig. 3 is plan of boat.

Fig. 4 is section of boat shewing a modified form of generator.

Fig. 5 is cross section through generator.

The same letters denote the same parts in all the figs.

a is a boat preferably made of metal *b* is a tank or receiver for oil or spirit *c* the wick *d* the steam generator which consists of a vertical elliptical vessel having an inclined bottom *f*. The said vessel is provided with a spring loaded or other suitable escape valve *g* fitted to the top thereof *h h* are two pipes or tubes extending from near the top of the vessel *d* diagonally across the same the said tubes being placed side by side across the smaller diameter of the said vessel.

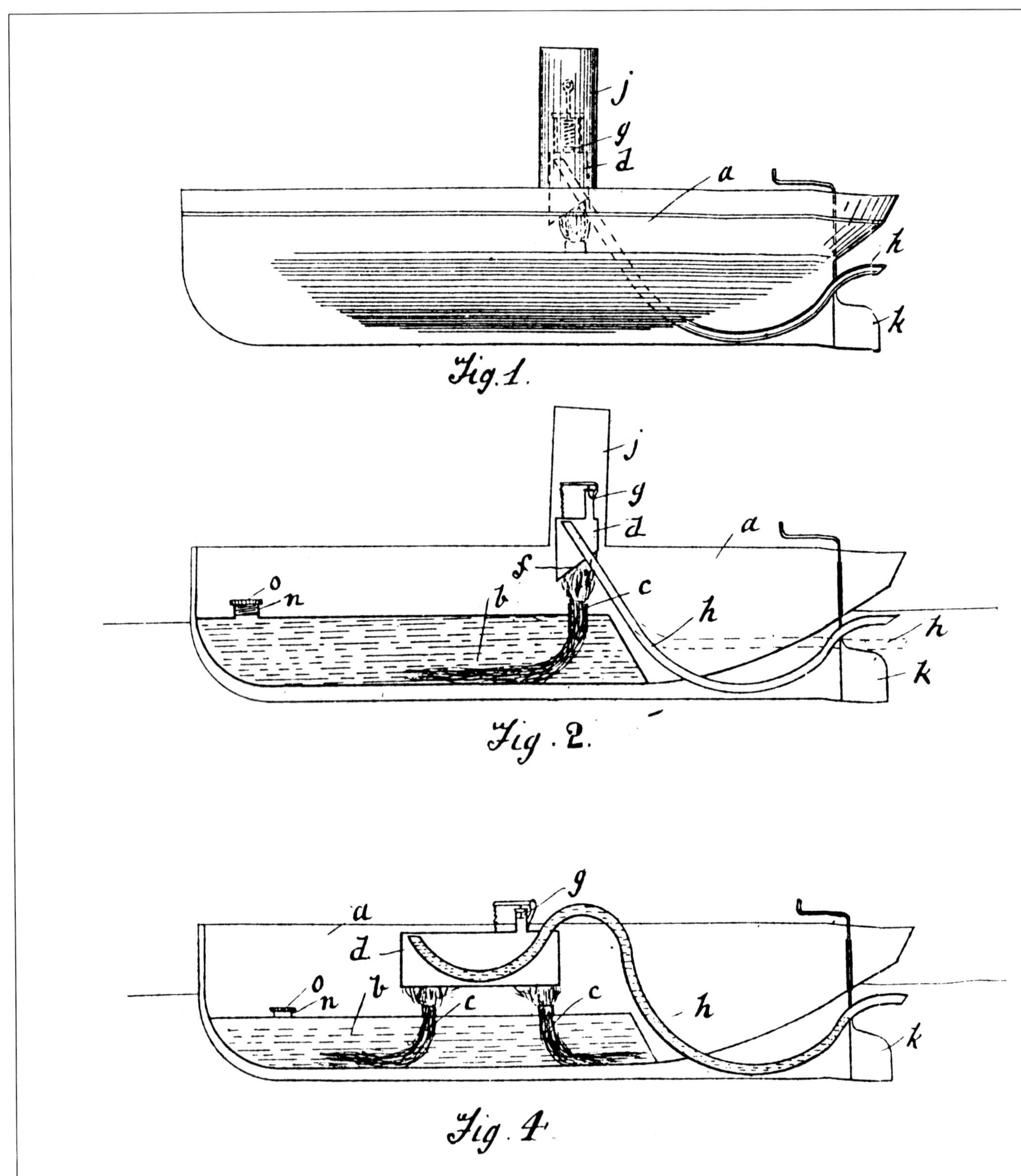

Piot's Complete Specification for the first jet-propelled 'put-put' toy boat 1891

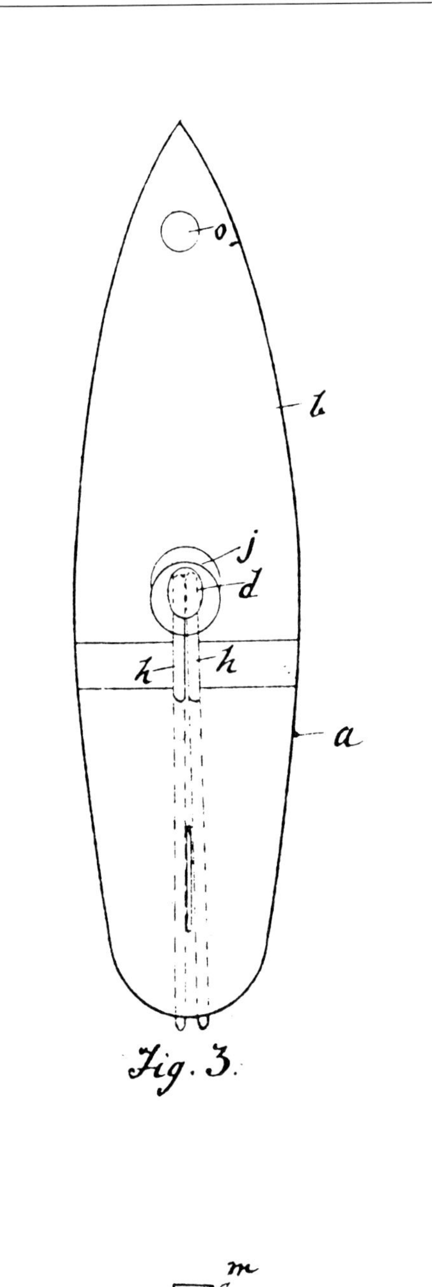

Fig. 3.

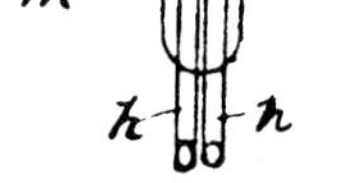

Fig 5

Fig I

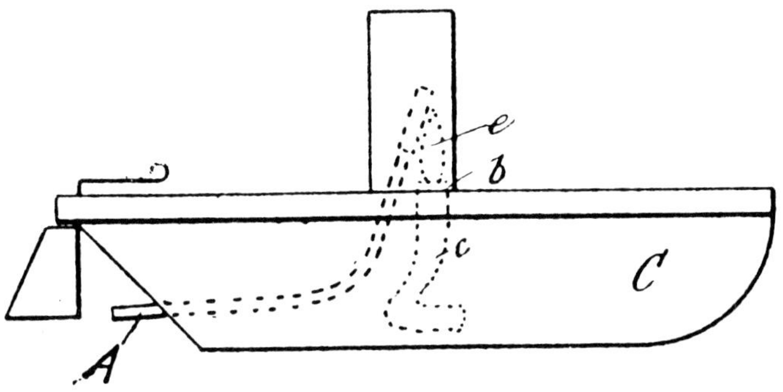

Fig II

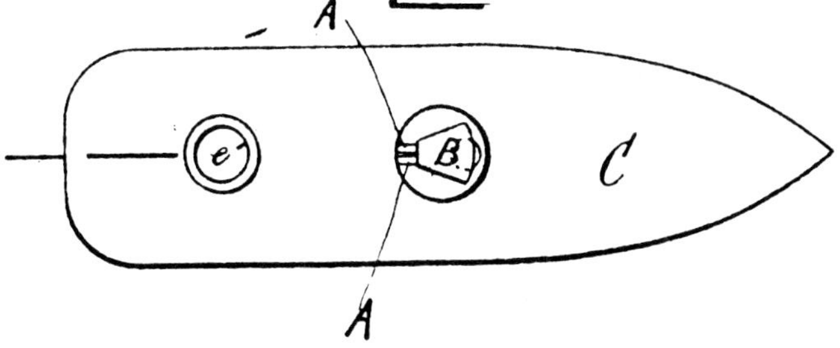

Fig III

APPENDIX VII

Lesser Known Constructional Outfit Makers

Meccano was the outstanding constructional toy in the first half of the 20th century. However, many small companies, some of whose catalogues are illustrated here, attempted to compete. Some were derivative such as Pioneer or Primus, others completely original. None really challenged Meccano and it was the Danish-made Lego system that effectively ended constructional toy manufacture in Britain.

JUNEERO

what it is and what it does

THE Juneero Patent Multi-purpose Tool is a correctly designed engineering device for making, modelling and mending in metal.

With it, special metal Strip, Angle Iron and Rod is supplied and many accessories, including Thread Cutting Die, Bolts, Nuts, Smooth and Corrugated Metal Plate, both plain and coloured, Cutting Shears, Glass Substitutes, etc.

It will cut Juneero metal Strip, Angle Iron or Rod to any desired measurement.

It will punch Juneero metal Strip and Angle Iron for bolting and riveting.

It will bend Juneero metal Strip and Rod as required.

It will hold Juneero metal Rod for thread cutting with die provided.

Instructions are supplied which enable all these operations to be done easily by the youngest novice.

Overleaf will be found illustrations of some of the models, toys and household articles that are being made with JUNEERO. For repair work the JUNEERO Tool is invaluable.

Pages from **Juneero** 1930s catalogue (above and top right)

'Prestacon' advertisement in the Economic Electric Co. late 1940s catalogue (below right)

models

toys

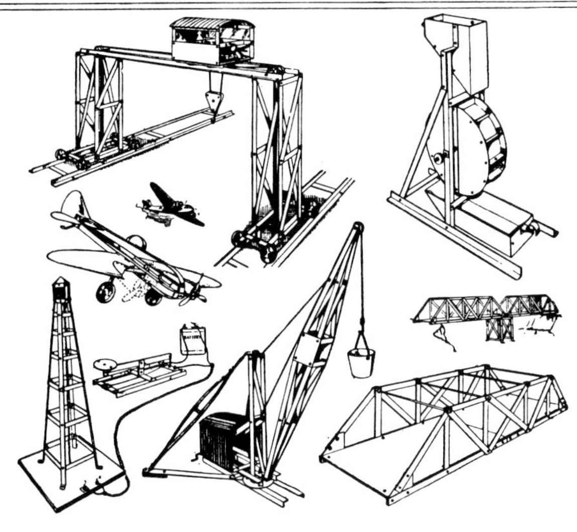

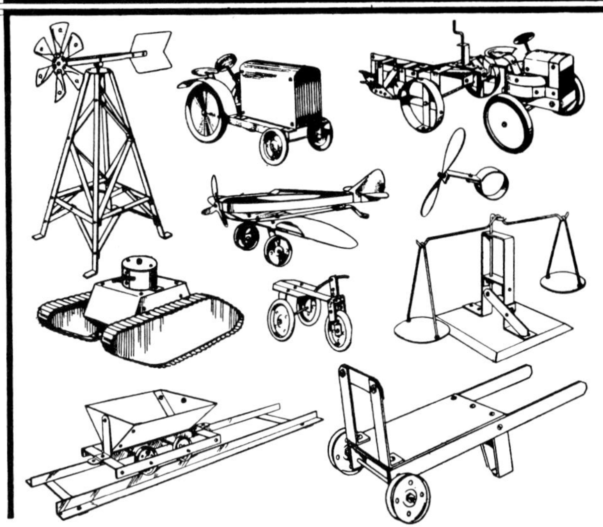

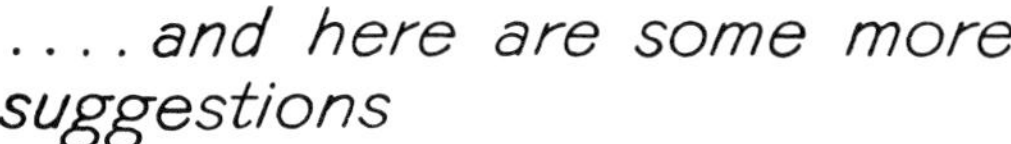

There is literally no limit to the number of models that can be made with Juneero. It is governed solely by the ingenuity of the user! For almost anything that can be made by engineers can be duplicated as a model with the help of Juneero. The following are typical examples :—

All types of Motor Cars and Aeroplanes. Model Railway Equipment. All styles of Cranes, Pylons and Bridges. Trucks and Lorries. Sheds, Hangars and Towers.

. . . . but any boy will think of plenty more . . . ***such as these***

There's no scarcity of toys for the lucky boy who has a Juneero set, for he can go on making new ones to his heart's content. For instance, even a very young boy can make such toys as :—

Farmyard Buildings	Stiles and Gates
Dolls' Furniture	Windmills
All Kinds of Mechanical Toys and Figures	
Railway Signals	Battleships
Carts and Trucks	Pin-table Games

MODEL ENGINEERING PRESTACON

An Invention that brings real engineering to the Model Maker

WHAT PRESTACON DOES

You can make models exactly as you want them because you engineer the parts yourself. No more standardised "bits and pieces," but your own precision worked parts that give a realistic look to every model. With the Prestacon Press you can work out your own ideas just as it would be done in a real engineering workshop—and there's no limit to the scope Prestacon gives you. If you are a handyman as well as a model maker, you'll find the Prestacon Press indispensable on hundreds of jobs where sheet metal is used.

No. 1

Comprising the Prestacon Press and all necessary tools together with a working quantity of metal parts, nuts, bolts, etc. Price 55/–

Accurately positioned Self-Locating, no marking out Prestacon does it all for you.

The Prestacon Press pierces round and square holes, cuts straight or curved slots and rectangular and circular holes and bends metal plates up to 3″ wide to angles up to 45°. All these operations can be carried out at any position on a metal plate and each operation can be reproduced on any number of plates with complete accuracy. This is due to an ingenious arrangement of indexed holes into which the "location" or "guide" bars fit at right angles to each other. These guide bars form set edges against which the metal for working is placed. No measurements have to be made by the operator and it takes only a few seconds to change the position of the metal or the operation of the press. The guide bars also provide for a "minus" working which allows for metal thickness when bending or when piercing holes to match inside an angle.

The Prestacon Press, complementary tools and unworked metal parts are available in several outfits, details of which are given overleaf.

No. 10

A complete construction outfit including the Prestacon Press, all necessary tools and a very comprehensive selection of metal plates, strips, axles, angles, gear and pulley wheels, nuts, bolts, etc., sufficient to make the models shown in the instruction leaflet accompanying the outfit. Price 84/–

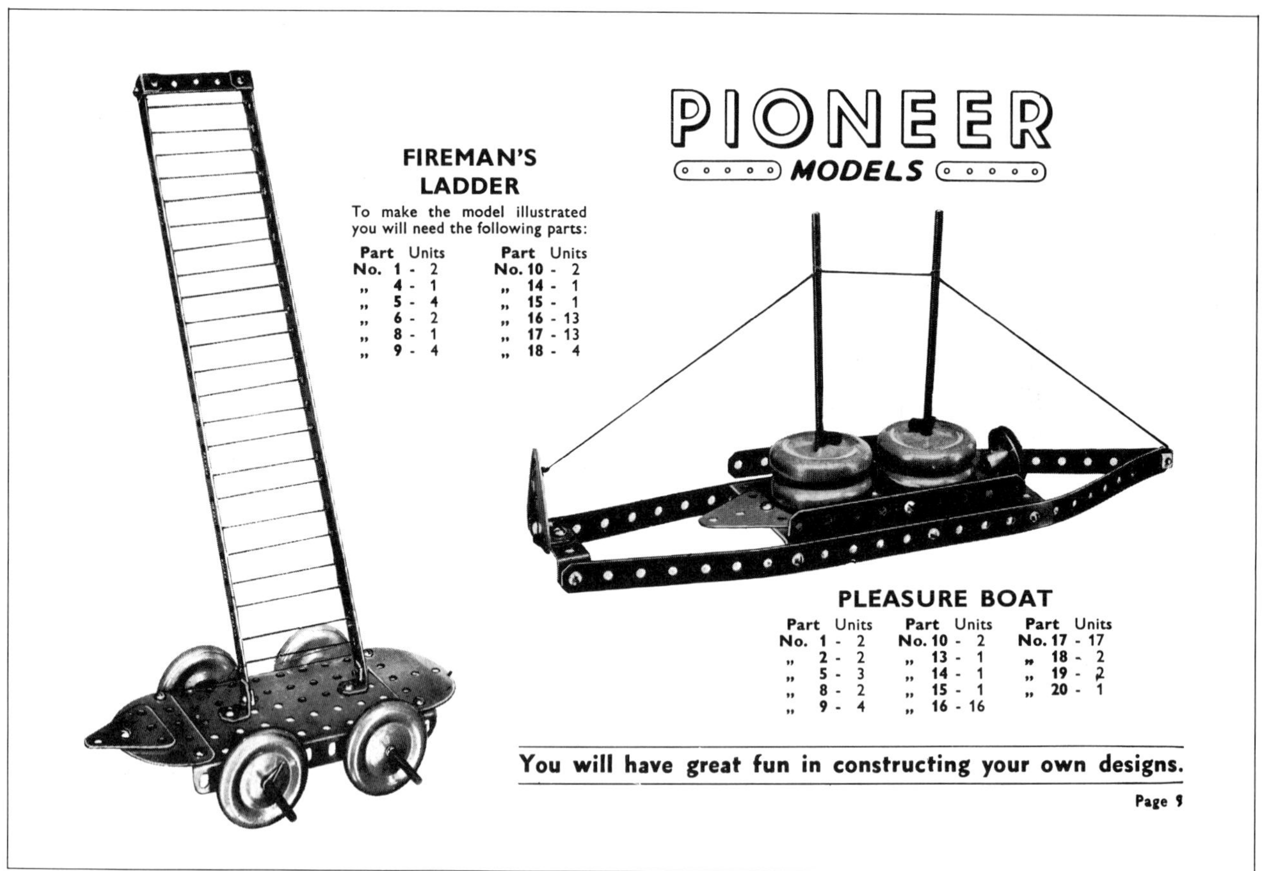

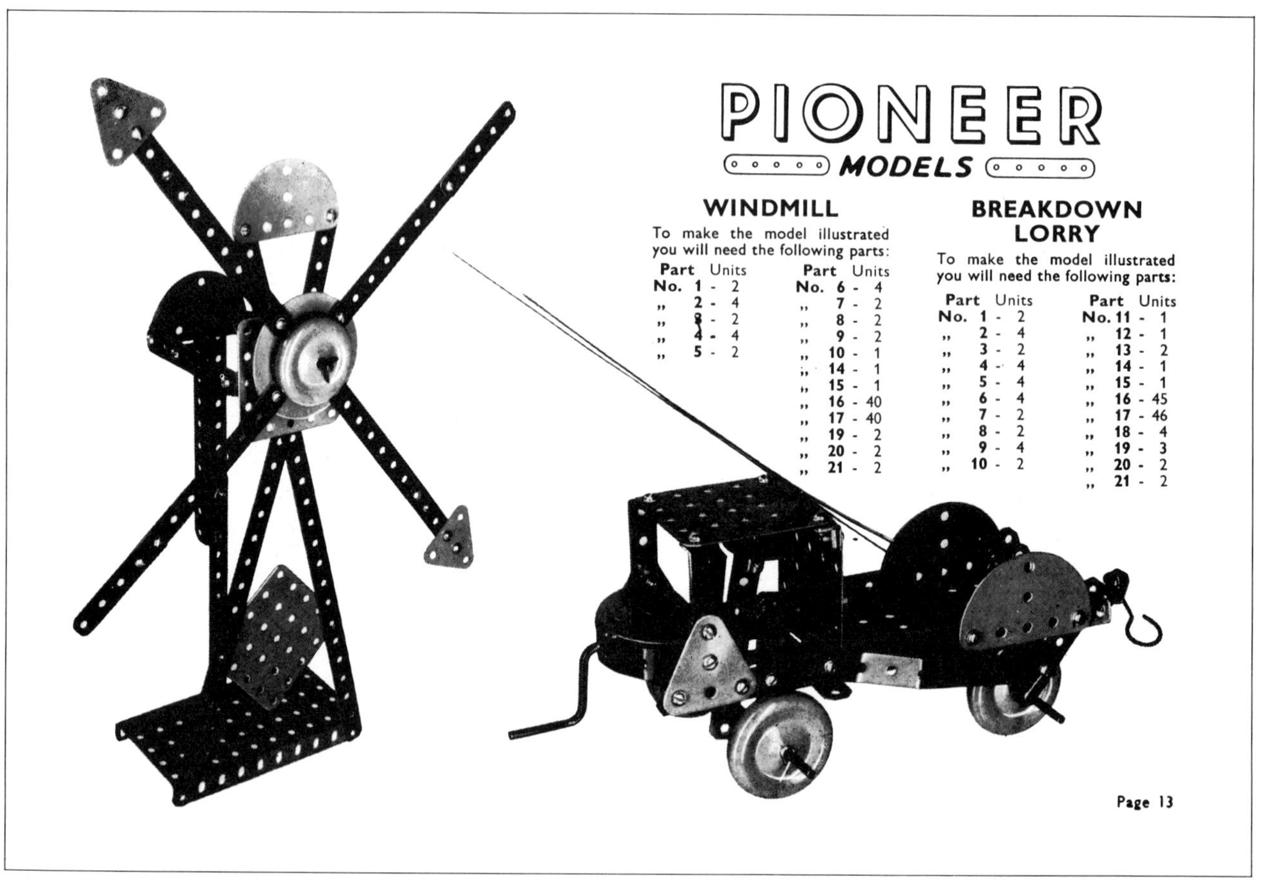

The trade name 'Pioneer' was registered in 1926 by F A Davis Ltd, but had been used in 1924 as the name of a metal car sold by Alfred Davies Toy Co. of Holloway, London N7. The construction set is illustrated in a 1950s Lines Bros catalogue with the 'Frog' trademark of the International Model Aircraft company a subsidiary of Lines Bros.

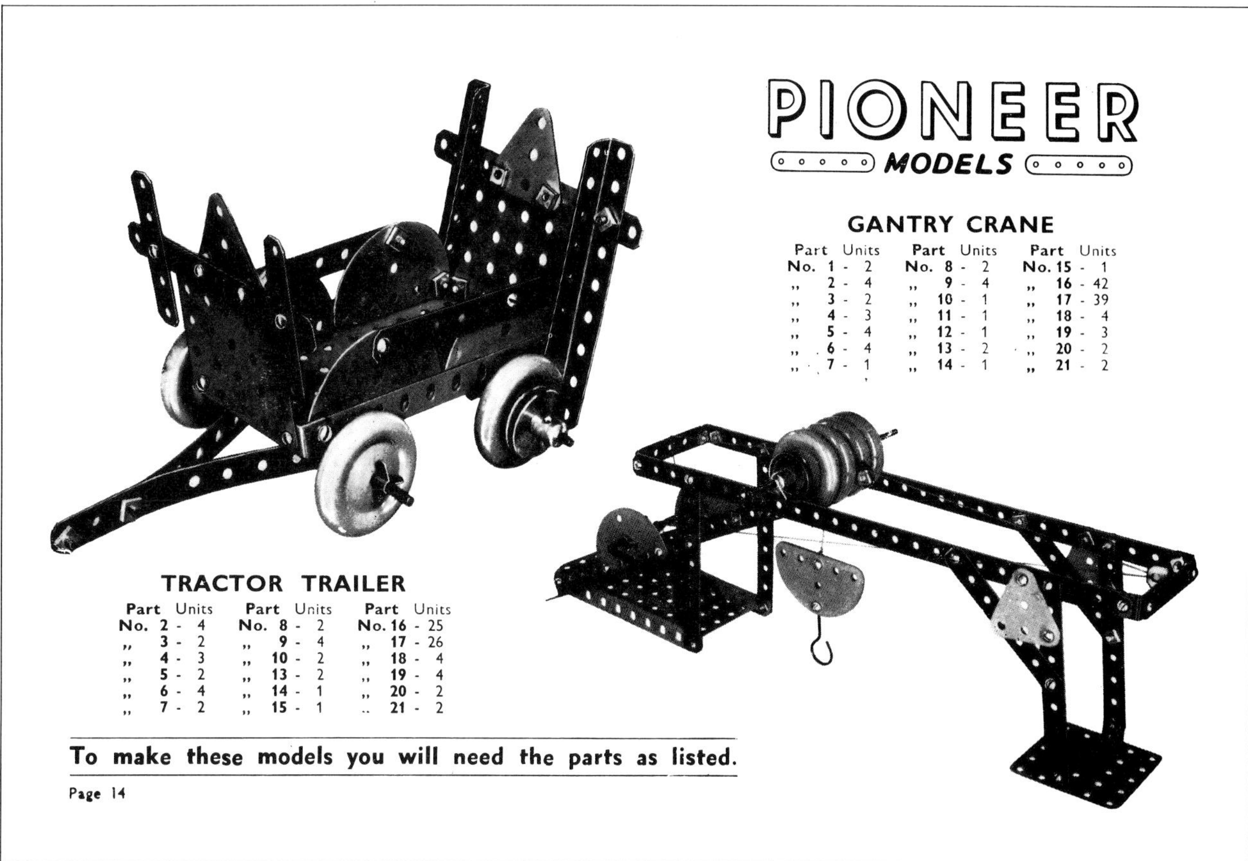

PIONEER

MODELS

GANTRY CRANE

Part No.	Units	Part No.	Units	Part No.	Units
1	2	8	2	15	1
2	4	9	4	16	42
3	2	10	1	17	39
4	3	11	1	18	4
5	4	12	1	19	3
6	4	13	2	20	2
7	1	14	1	21	2

TRACTOR TRAILER

Part No.	Units	Part No.	Units	Part No.	Units
2	4	8	2	16	25
3	2	9	4	17	26
4	3	10	2	18	4
5	2	13	2	19	4
6	4	14	1	20	2
7	2	15	1	21	2

To make these models you will need the parts as listed.

Page 14

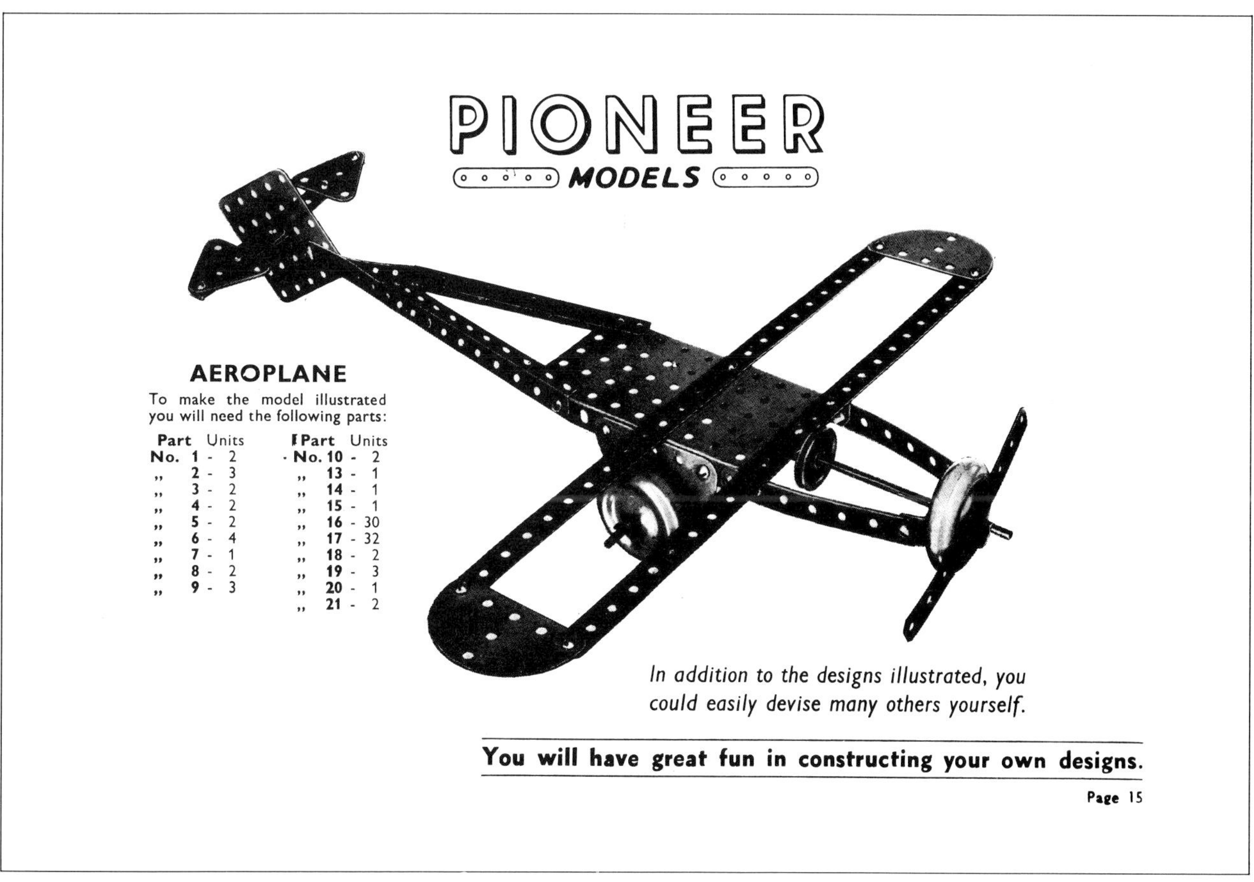

PIONEER

MODELS

AEROPLANE

To make the model illustrated you will need the following parts:

Part No.	Units	Part No.	Units
1	2	10	2
2	3	13	1
3	2	14	1
4	2	15	1
5	2	16	30
6	4	17	32
7	1	18	2
8	2	19	3
9	3	20	1
		21	2

In addition to the designs illustrated, you could easily devise many others yourself.

You will have great fun in constructing your own designs.

Page 15

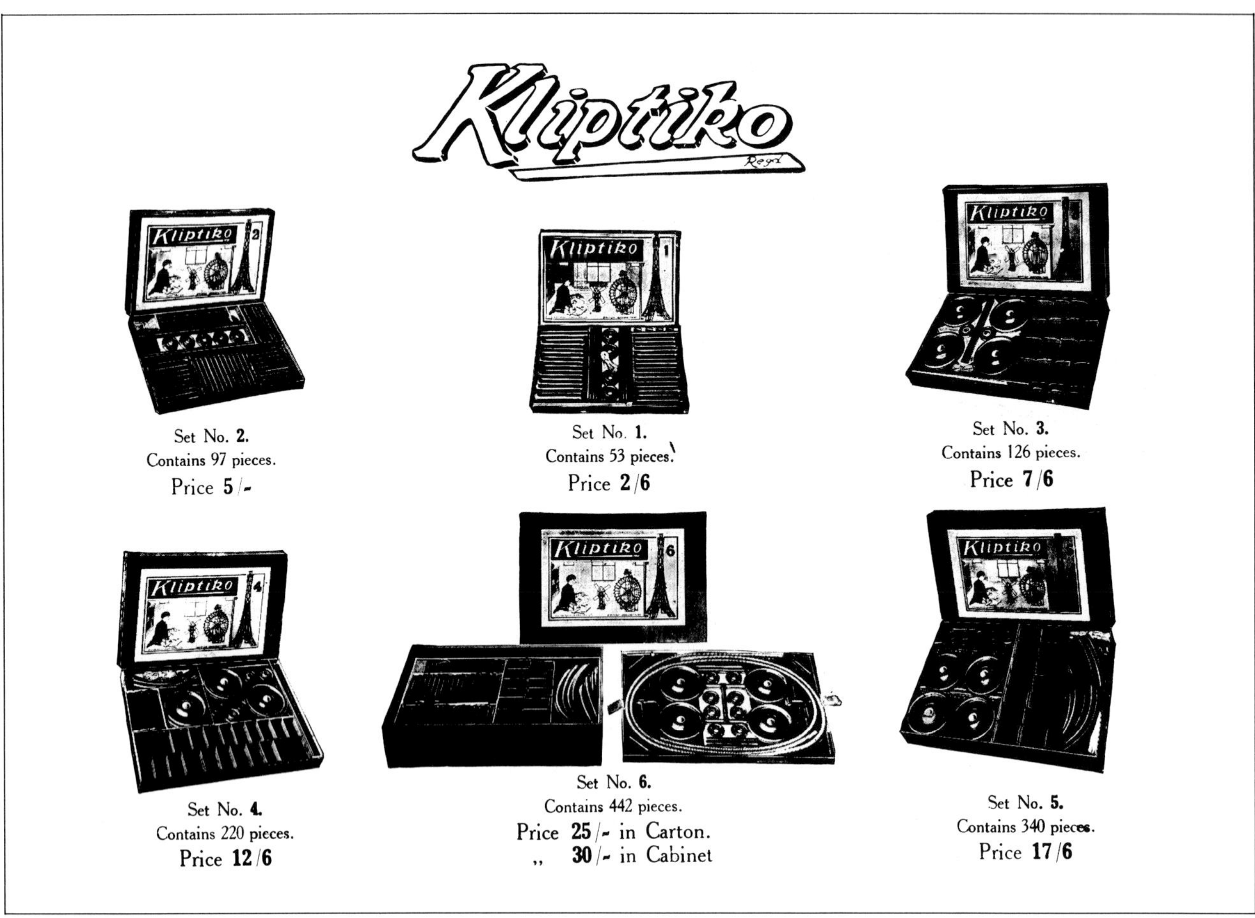

Kliptiko
Regd.

Parts Required.

183	..	4	in. Clips.
6	..		Half Clips.
21	..	10	in. Tubes.
14	..	6$\frac{5}{8}$	in. Tubes.
18	..	4	in. Tubes.
10	..	2	in. Tubes.
4	..	6	in. Bent Tubes.
2	..	1$\frac{1}{2}$	in. Wheels.
4	..	3$\frac{3}{4}$	in. Wheels.
19	..		Buckets.
24	..		Hub Caps.

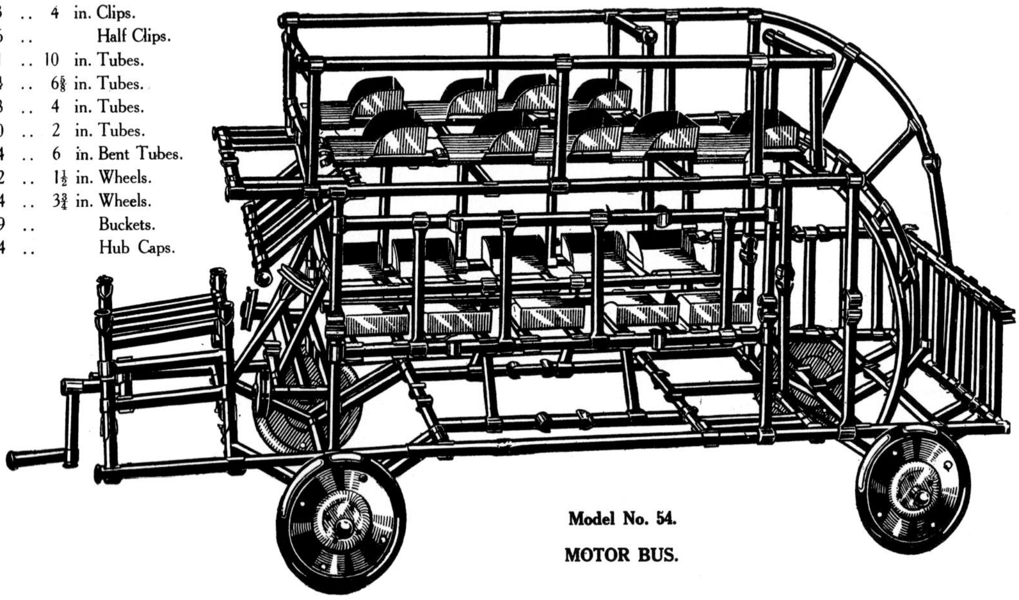

Model No. 54.

MOTOR BUS.

See illustration on next page for frame of the above model.

Pages from **William Bailey's** 1920 'Kliptiko' catalogue

KLIPTIKO PARTS

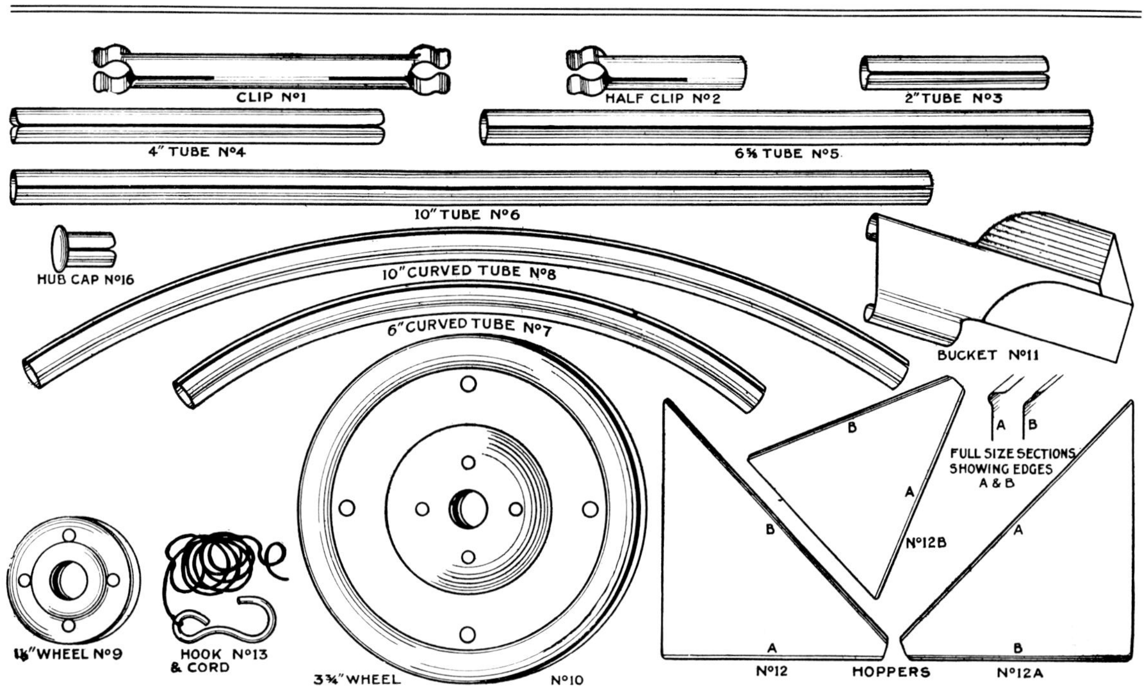

FOLLOW INSTRUCTIONS AS ILLUSTRATED ON OPPOSITE PAGE.

INSTRUCTIONS.

The tubular pieces with spring-jaws shown in the following illustrations are called Clips, and those without are called Tubes.

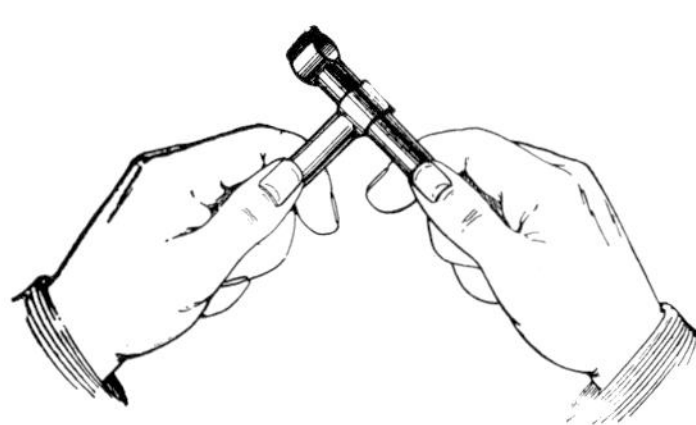

Fig. 1.

In this illustration you will see how the Clips fix on one another, simply by pushing the spring-jaws over the plain part until they snap on.

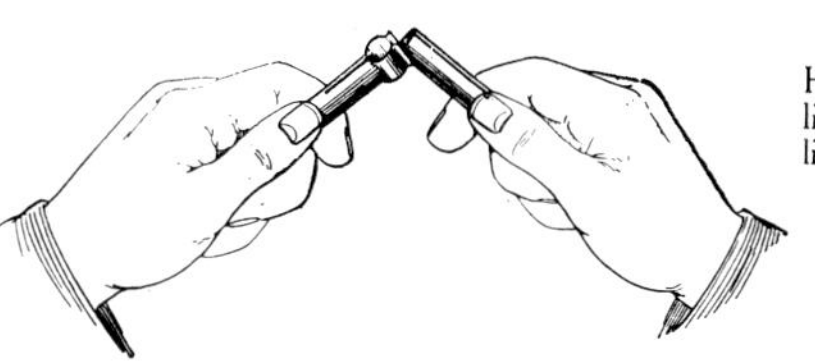

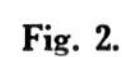

Fig. 2.

This will show how to hold a Tube to fix it into a Clip. Just hold the Clip firmly and place the end of the Tube near the middle of the jaws, then press the Tube into the Clip, at the same time bring the Tube in a straight line with the Clip by raising the right hand a little.

Fig. 3.

Having brought the Tube in a straight line with the Clip, push the Tube in a little to make it firm.

Fig. 4.

Having shown how to use the Clips, we will now illustrate how to fix the Tubes together: Get two Tubes as illustrated in Fig. 4, place them end to end so that the end of each will enter the gap of the other, then slide them into one another the required distance, as shown in Fig. 5.

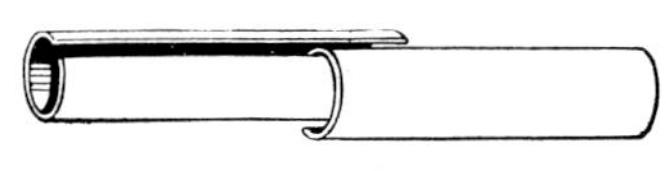

Fig. 5.

Hold one firmly and twist the other, as shown in Fig. 6.

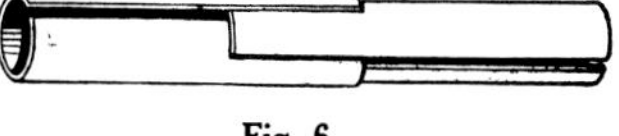

Fig. 6.

Twist the Tube right round and you will find that the one Tube will enter the other quite easily and remain firm, as in Fig. 7.

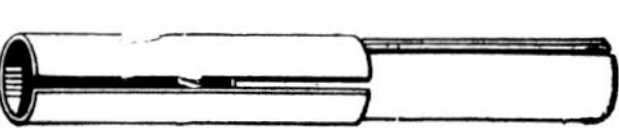

Fig. 7.

Quite a firm joint will result if you follow out the simple instructions.

REMEMBER, you may become the proud possessor of a big set by adding from time to time Accessory sets which are on sale to convert whichever set you have to the set larger. See page 38.

Bibliography

Alford, B W E, *W D & H O Wills*, Methuen, 1973

Bartholomew, Charles, *Mechanical Toys*, Hamlyn, 1979

Bartok, Peter, *The Minic Book*, New Cavendish Books, 1987

Bapst, G, *Les Metaux dans l'Antiquité et au Moyen Age*, Masson, Paris, 1884

Beardsley, Roger, *The Hornby Companion*, Hornby Companion Series Vol. 8, New Cavendish Books

Booth, Charles, *Life & Labour of the People in London*. Second Series, Macmillan, 1903

Bouusse, H, *Gyroscopes et Projectiles*, Delagrave, Paris, 1923

Buhler, *Tin Toys 1945–1975*, Bergström & Boyle, 1978

Cadbury, Betty, *Playthings Past*, David & Charles, 1976

Cerarn, C W, *Archaeology of the Cinema*, Thames & Hudson, 1965

Cieslik, Jurgen & Marianne, *Lehmann Toys*, New Cavendish Books, 1983

Clark, Hyla M, *The Tin Can Book*, New American Library, New York, 1977

Coghlan, H H, *Notes on Prehistoric Metallurgy of Copper and Bronze in the Old World*, Pitt Rivers Museum

Cook, Olive, *Movement in Two Dimensions*, Hutchinson, 1963

Corley, T A B, *Quaker Enterprise in Biscuits, Huntley & Palmers of Reading 1882–1972*

Historical Society, *Some Notes on the History of Huntley, Boorne & Stevens*

Crofts, William Francis, *Croft's London, What to See*, 1859

Culff, Robert, *The World of Toys*, Hamlyn, 1969

Daiken, Leslie, *Children's Toys Through the Ages*, Batsford, 1952

Davis, Alex, 'Printers on their Metal Artidesin', *British Printer*, 1970
Toward a History of Tin Printing, 1972

Dove, P, *Account of Andrew Farranton – The Founder of English Political Economy*, Johnstone & Hunter, 1676–1677

Dunham, Leonard W, *Money-boxes*, Chubb & Sons Lock & Safe Co. Ltd, 1972

Ellis, Alan F, *Hornby Dublo Compendium*, Hornby Companion Series Vol. 3A, New Cavendish Books, 1986

Ellis, Hamilton, *Model Railways 1838–1939*, Allen & Unwin, 1962

Fawdry, Kenneth & Marguerite, *Pollock's History of English Dolls & Toys*, Ernest Benn, 1979

Flick, Pauline, *Discovering Toys & Toy Museums*, Shire Publications, 1971

Flower, Philip William, *A History of the Trade in Tin*, George Bell & Sons, 1880

Foster, Michael, *Hornby Dublo Trains*, Hornby Companion Series Vol. 3, New Cavendish Books, 1980

Franklin, Michael, *British Biscuit Tins, 1868–1939*, New Cavendish Books, 1979

Fraser, Antonia, *A History of Toys*, 1966

Fritz, Helmut & Maximilian, *Blechspielzeug*, Harenberg Kommunikation, Dortmund, Germany, 1981

Fuller, Roland, *The Bassett-Lowke Story* New Cavendish Books, 1984

Gamble, Jim, *The Meccano System Compendium*, The Hornby Companion Series Vol. 6, New Cavendish Books, 1988
The Meccano System and the Special Purpose Meccano Sets, New Cavendish Books, 1986

Garratt, John S., *Encyclopaedia of Model Soldiers*, Frederick Müller, 1981

Gibbs, Frederick William, *Rise of the Tinplate Industry*, Annal of Science

Gordon, Bob, *Toy Steam Engines*, Shire Publications, 1985

Gould, D W, *The Top*, Bailey Brothers & Swinfen, 1975

Gould, M P, *Frank Hornby* (Reprint of 1915 edition) New Cavendish Books

Gowland, W, *Copper and its Alloys in Early Times*

Graebe, Chris & Julie, *Gauge 0 Compendium*, Hornby Companion Series Vol. 5A, New Cavendish Books, 1989
The Hornby Gauge 0 System, Hornby Companion Series Vol. 5, New Cavendish Books, 1984

Greilsamer, Jacques & Azema, Bertrand, *Catalogue of Model of the World*, Stephens, Stephens, 1967

Griffiths, David, *The Golden Age of Printed Tin Packaging*, Studio Vista

Hare, W E & Hedges, E S, *Tinplate*, Edward Arnold, 1945

Harley, Basil, *Toy Boats*, Shire Publications, 1987

Hedges, E S, *Tin in Social and Economic History*, Edward Arnold, 1964
Tin and its Alloys, Edward Arnold, 1960

Herbert, W, *History of the Twelve Great Livery Companies of London*, 1836

Hillier, Mary, *Automata and Mechanical Toys*, Jupiter Books, 1976

Hoare, W E, *The Technology of Tinplate*, Edward Arnold, 1965
Development of the Tinplate Industry in Great Britian

Hornby, Frank, *Life Story of Meccano*, New Cavendish Books, 1979

Huntington, Bernard, *Along Hornby Lines*, Oxford Publishing Co., 1976

Kemp, *Directory of Manufacturers, Merchants & Shippers*, 1915/16

King, Constance Eileen, *The Encyclopaedia of Toys*, Hale, 1978

Kurtz, Henry & Burtt Ehrlich, *The Art of the Toy Soldier*, New Cavendish Books, 1987

Levy, Allen, *A Century of Model Trains*, New Cavendish Books, 1978
Toys at the London Toy & Model Museum, 1988

Lines, Richard, *The Art of Hornby*, Kaye & Ward, 1983
Tri-ang Toys 1937/38 Golden Era Catalogue, New Cavendish Books, 1988
FROG Model Aircraft 1932–1976, New Cavendish Books, 1989

Manduca, Joseph, *The Meccano Magazine 1916–1981*, New Cavendish Books, 1987

Michinton, W C, *The British Tinplate Industry*, Oxford University Press, 1957

Minns, J, *Railways – Model Railways Engines*, 1970

Montell, C L, *Tin*, (Published in New York), 1949

Moses, Hannah, *A Short History of the Hudson Scott Branch of the Metal Box Co.*, 1962

Moor, C J, *Tin Mining*, 1928

Murray, Patrick, *Toys*, Studio Vista, 1968

Nodin, P, *First Fifty Years and my Adventures into Commerce* (Life Story of Sir James Wallace Paton)

Opie, James, *Toy Soldiers*, Shire Publications, 1983

Pennell, Paul, *Children's Cars*, Shire Publications, 1986

Pressland, David, *The Art of the Tin Toy*, New Cavendish Books, 1976

Randall, Peter, *The Products of Binn's Road: A General Survey*, The Hornby Companion Series Vol. 1, New Cavendish Books, 1977

Reader, W J, *Metal Box – A History*, Heineman Ltd, 1976

Reder, Gustav, *Clockwork, Steam, Electric: A History of Model Railways*, Ian Allan, 1972

Richard, L W, *Old British Model Soldiers*, Tricorn Press, New York, 1970

Richardson, Mike & Sue, *Dinky Toys & Modelled Miniatures, 1931–1979*, Hornby Companion Series Vol. 4, New Cavendish Books, 1981

Ritchie, Carson I A, *Making Scientific Toys*, Lutterworth Press, 1975

Ruddell, J R, *The Britains' Collectors Check List*, Vols. 1, 2 & 3, privately published, 1980

Smith, G, *The Cassiterides* (Tin Islands), Longman, 1863

Tempest, Jack, *Collecting Tin Toys*, William Collins Sons & Co. Ltd, 1987

Trench, Patrick, *Dinky Toy Compendium*, The Hornby Companion Series Vol. 4A, New Cavendish Books, 1986

Thompson, Frank, *The Match Box Toy Price Guide 1953–1983*, Ernest Benn, 1983
The Dinky Toy Price Guide, Ernest Benn, 1982

Van Cleemput, Marcel, *The Great Book of Corgi*, New Cavendish Books, 1989

Vogel, O, *The Tinning of Metal Objects in Ancient and Modern Times*

Welton, Arno, *Mechanical Tin Toys in Colour*, Blandford Press, 1977

Wright, G, *Meccano Super Models*, Hornby Companion Series Vol. 2, New Cavendish Books, 1978

Magazines

Games and Toys, 1914–1970

Layne, Ian, Articles in *Hornby Railway Collectors' Association Journals*

Mayhew, Henry, Articles in the *Morning Chronicle*, 1851

'Pollocks World of Toys', *Pollocks Toy Museum Catalogue*, 1970

Rhodes, Joseph & Sons, Catalogues 1915–1924

Strand Magazine, Vol. 10, 1895, Article on 'Penny Toys'

Smith, Antony, 'A History of Tin Plate'. Article in a trade journal, *Tin International*, 1977

Toy Trader & Fancy Goods Trader, 1906–1930

Toy Trader, 1930–1980

Index & Sources

Collections of British tin and metal toys

Small collections of British toys may be found in many museums throughout Britain. Significant collections may be seen at the following museums:

The Bethnal Green Museum of Childhood, London E1
The Edinburgh Toy Museum, Edinburgh
The London Toy & Model Museum, London W2
Pollock's Toy Museum, 1 Scala Street, London W1

Additional Pollock's toy collections may be seen at:
Lympne Castle, Canterbury, Kent
Thirlestane Castle, Lauder, near Edinburgh

Manderston House, near Duns, Berwickshire, houses a large collection of Huntley & Palmers' biscuit tins.

The King collection in the Museum of London includes a good selection of Penny Toys.

British tin toys may be purchased at various swapmeets and toy auctions held in various locations or from the following specialist outlets:

Mint & Boxed, Edgware, Middlesex
Pete McAskie, Grays Mews, London W1
Colin Baddiell, Grays Mews, London W1

Picture credits

The majority of the photographs in this book come from the Pollock's Toy Museum collection and the New Cavendish Archive. In addition, the publishers gratefully acknowledge assistance from the following sources:

Chris Graebe
Ian Layne
Jeffrey Levitt of Mint & Boxed
Pete McAskie
Colin Baddiell
David Pressland
Sotheby's

Founders' Day outing on a Whitanco coach.
The author (founder of Pollock's Toy Museum) and the Publishers
(founders of the London Toy and Model Museum).

BRITISH AND BEST!